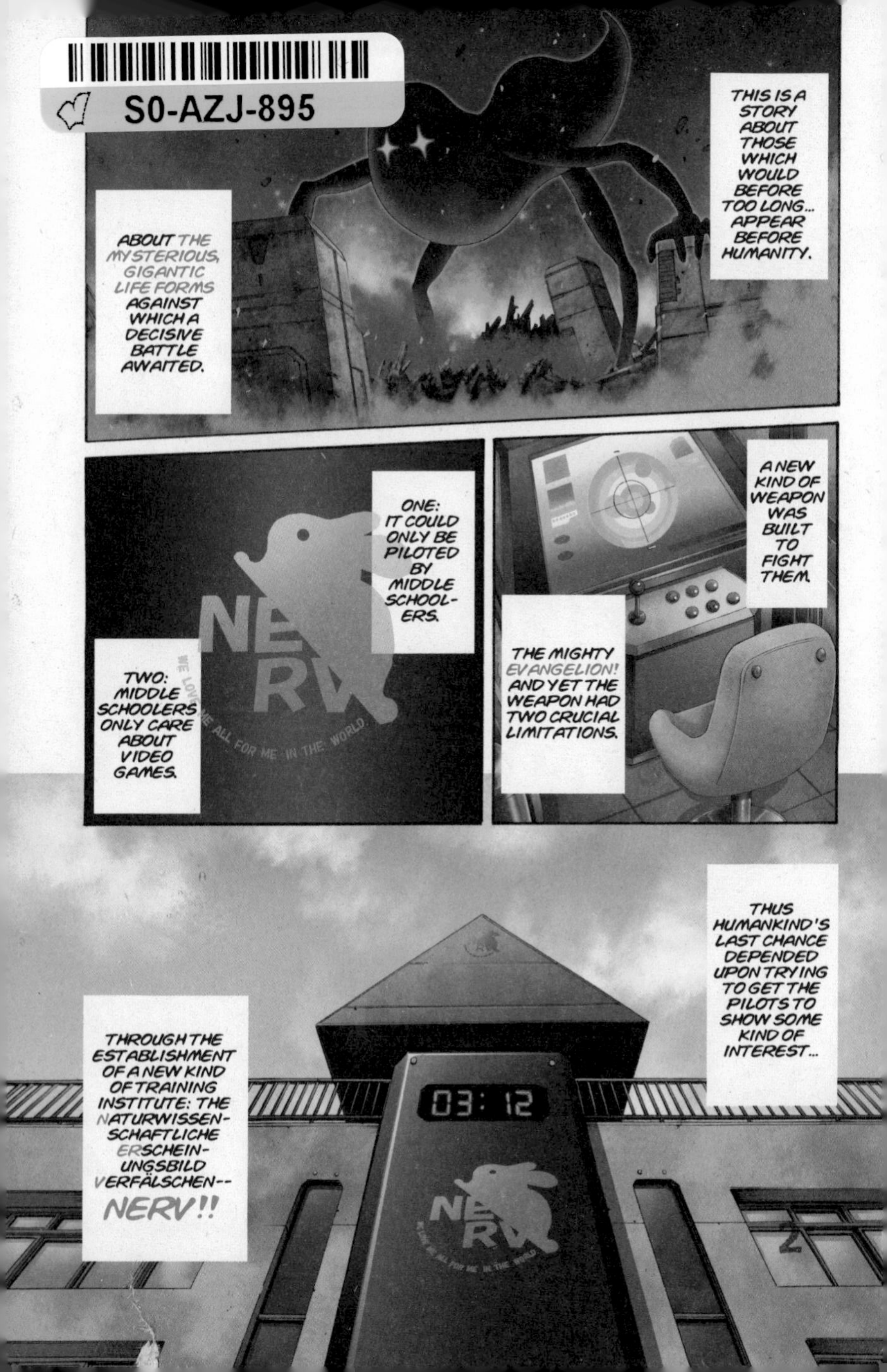
THIS IS A STORY ABOUT THOSE WHICH WOULD BEFORE TOO LONG... APPEAR BEFORE HUMANITY.
ABOUT THE MYSTERIOUS, GIGANTIC LIFE FORMS AGAINST WHICH A DECISIVE BATTLE AWAITED.
A NEW KIND OF WEAPON WAS BUILT TO FIGHT THEM.
THE MIGHTY EVANGELION! AND YET THE WEAPON HAD TWO CRUCIAL LIMITATIONS.
ONE: IT COULD ONLY BE PILOTED BY MIDDLE SCHOOL-ERS.
TWO: MIDDLE SCHOOLERS ONLY CARE ABOUT VIDEO GAMES.
THUS HUMANKIND'S LAST CHANCE DEPENDED UPON TRYING TO GET THE PILOTS TO SHOW SOME KIND OF INTEREST...
03:12
THROUGH THE ESTABLISHMENT OF A NEW KIND OF TRAINING INSTITUTE: THE NATURWISSEN-SCHAFTLICHE ERSCHEIN-UNGSBILD VERFÄLSCHEN-- NERV!!

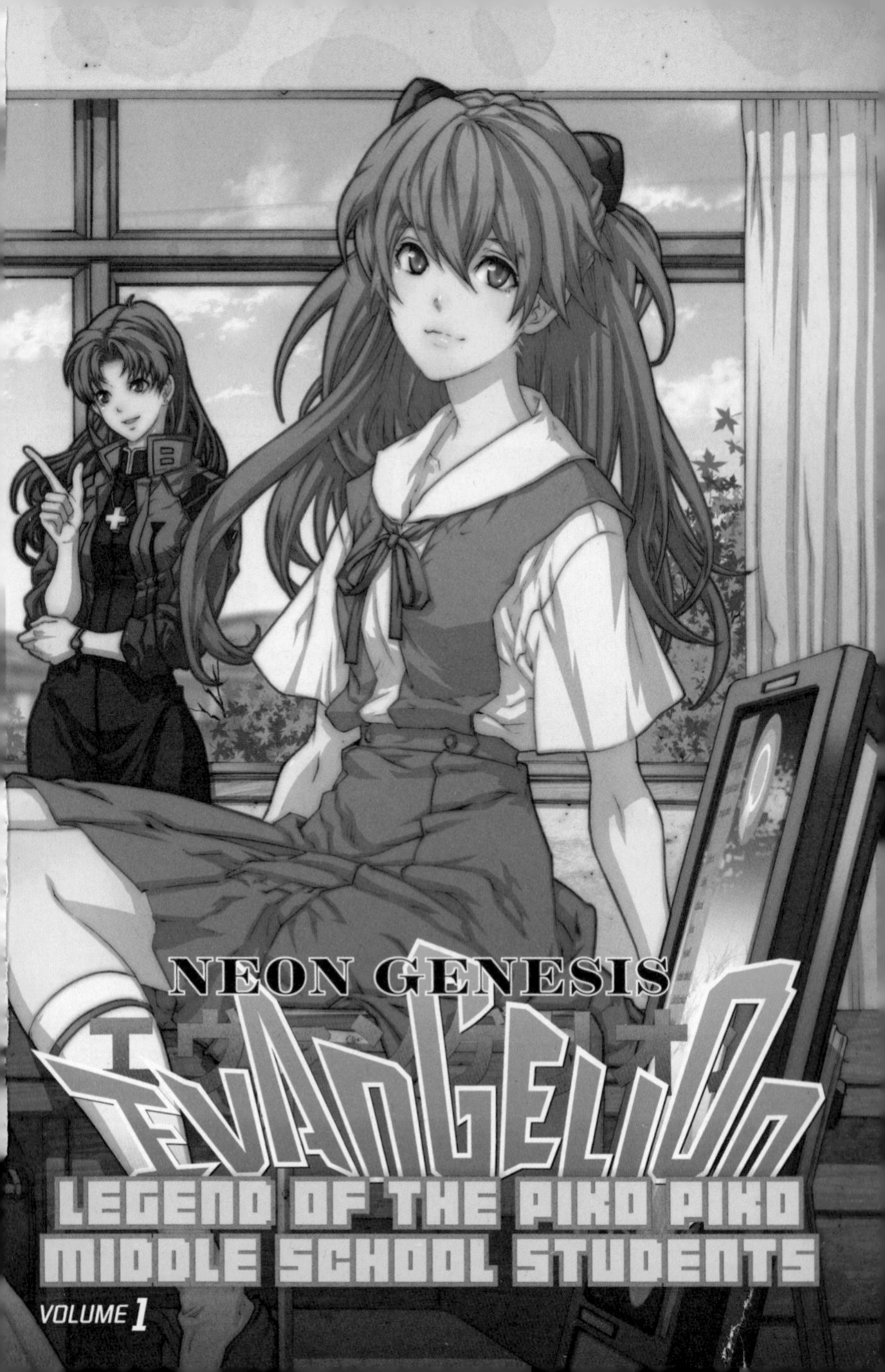
NEON GENESIS
EVANGELION
LEGEND OF THE PIKO PIKO
MIDDLE SCHOOL STUDENTS
VOLUME 1

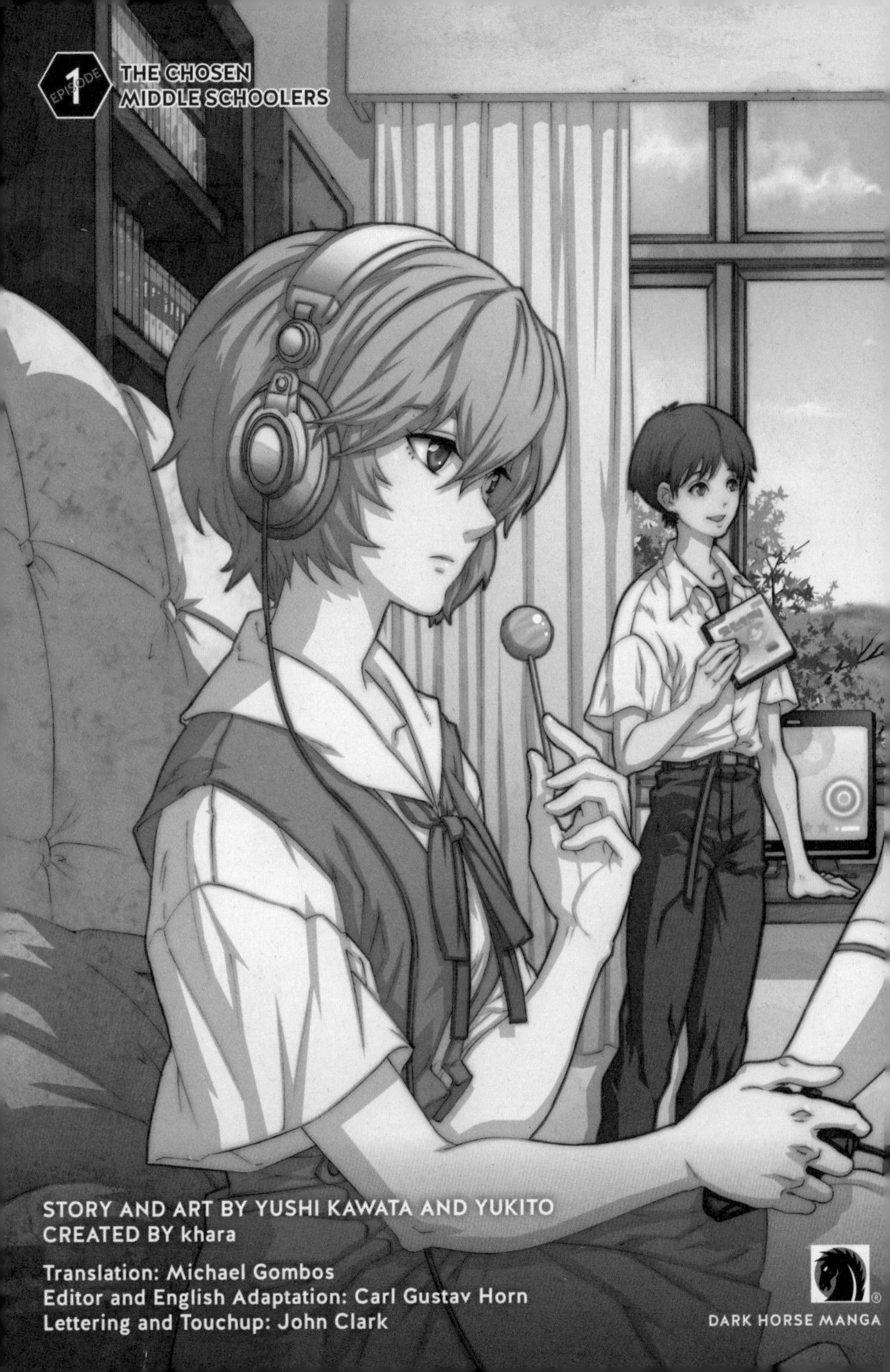

EPISODE 1

THE CHOSEN MIDDLE SCHOOLERS

STORY AND ART BY YUSHI KAWATA AND YUKITO
CREATED BY khara

Translation: Michael Gombos
Editor and English Adaptation: Carl Gustav Horn
Lettering and Touchup: John Clark

DARK HORSE MANGA

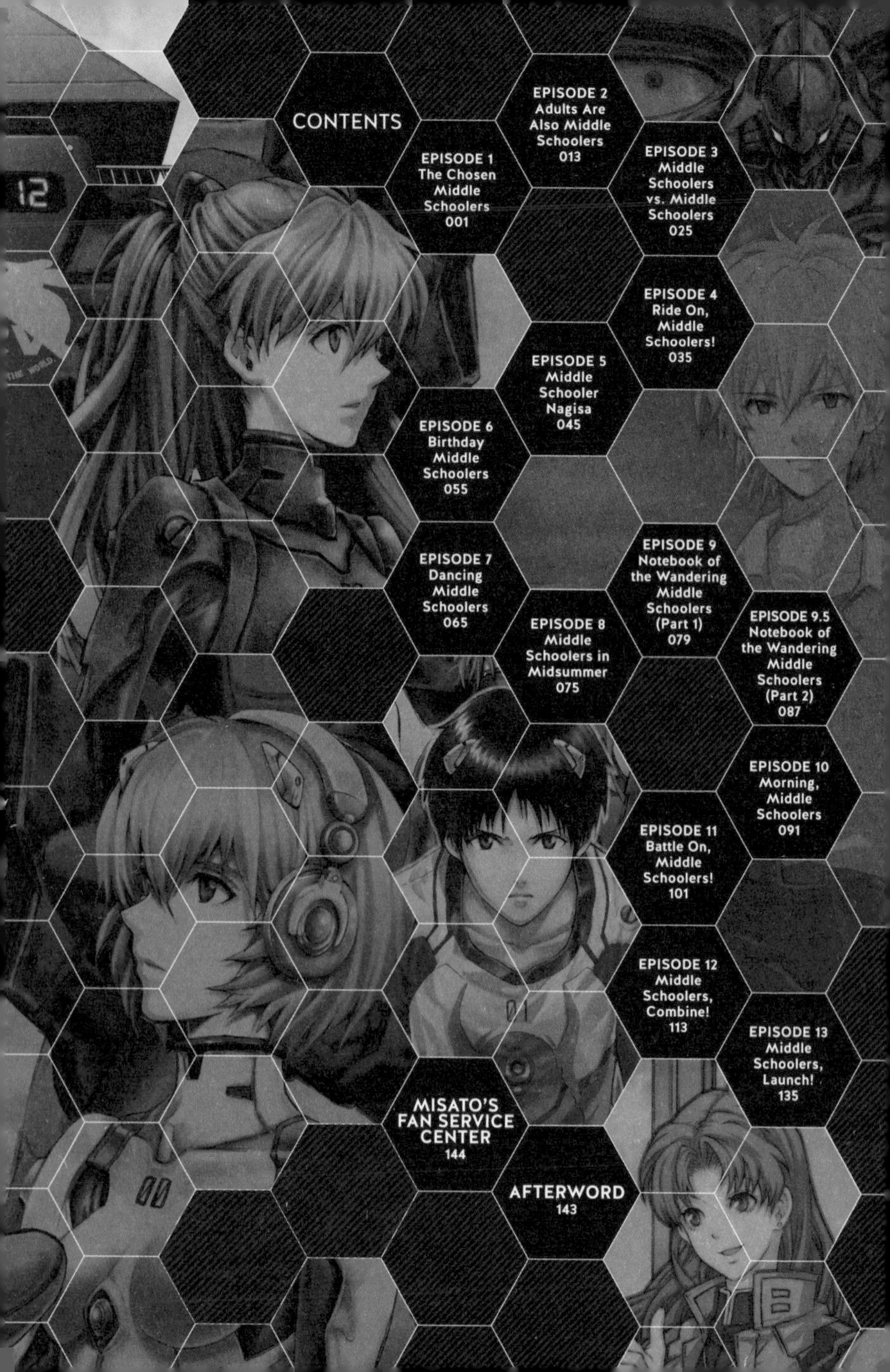

CONTENTS

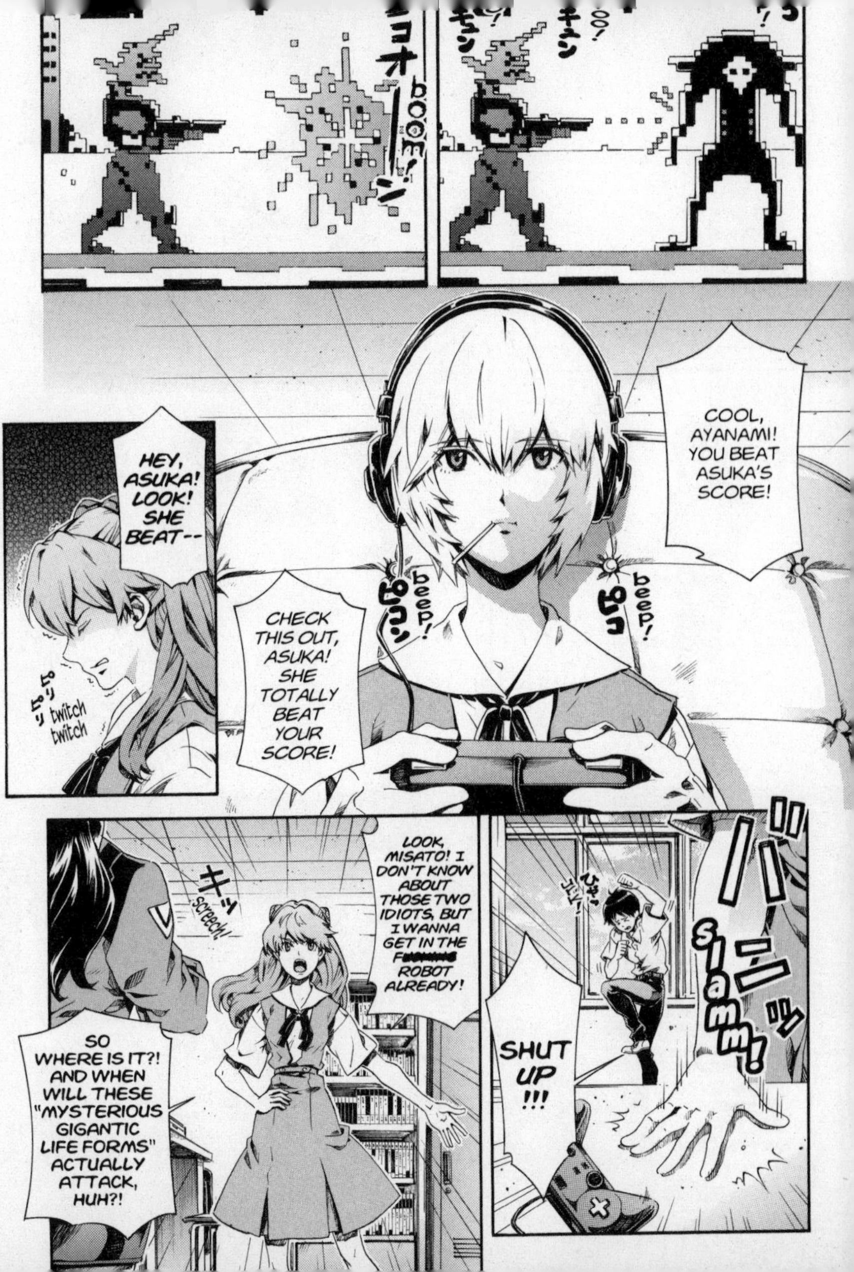
boom!
COOL, AYANAMI! YOU BEAT ASUKA'S SCORE!
beep!
beep!
CHECK THIS OUT, ASUKA! SHE TOTALLY BEAT YOUR SCORE!
HEY, ASUKA! LOOK! SHE BEAT--
twitch twitch
slamm!
SHUT UP!!!
LOOK, MISATO! I DON'T KNOW ABOUT THOSE TWO IDIOTS, BUT I WANNA GET IN THE F[redacted] ROBOT ALREADY!
screech!
SO WHERE IS IT?! AND WHEN WILL THESE "MYSTERIOUS GIGANTIC LIFE FORMS" ACTUALLY ATTACK, HUH?!

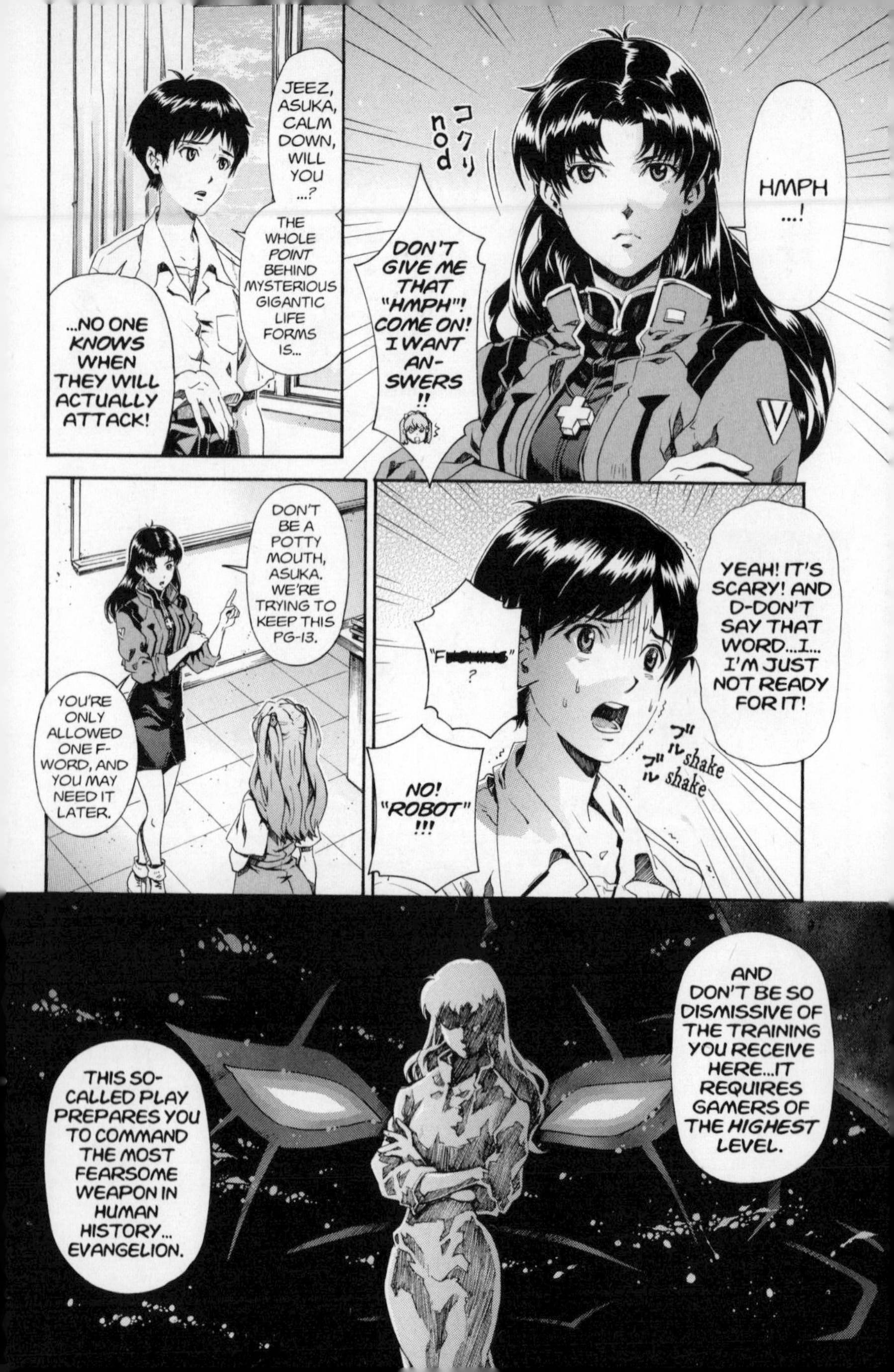
HMPH ...!
コクリ nod
JEEZ, ASUKA, CALM DOWN, WILL YOU ...?
DON'T GIVE ME THAT "HMPH"! COME ON! I WANT AN-SWERS!!
THE WHOLE POINT BEHIND MYSTERIOUS GIGANTIC LIFE FORMS IS...
...NO ONE KNOWS WHEN THEY WILL ACTUALLY ATTACK!
YEAH! IT'S SCARY! AND D-DON'T SAY THAT WORD...I... I'M JUST NOT READY FOR IT!
"F[redacted]" ?
ブル shake
ブル shake
NO! "ROBOT" !!!
DON'T BE A POTTY MOUTH, ASUKA. WE'RE TRYING TO KEEP THIS PG-13.
YOU'RE ONLY ALLOWED ONE F-WORD, AND YOU MAY NEED IT LATER.
AND DON'T BE SO DISMISSIVE OF THE TRAINING YOU RECEIVE HERE...IT REQUIRES GAMERS OF THE HIGHEST LEVEL.
THIS SO-CALLED PLAY PREPARES YOU TO COMMAND THE MOST FEARSOME WEAPON IN HUMAN HISTORY... EVANGELION.

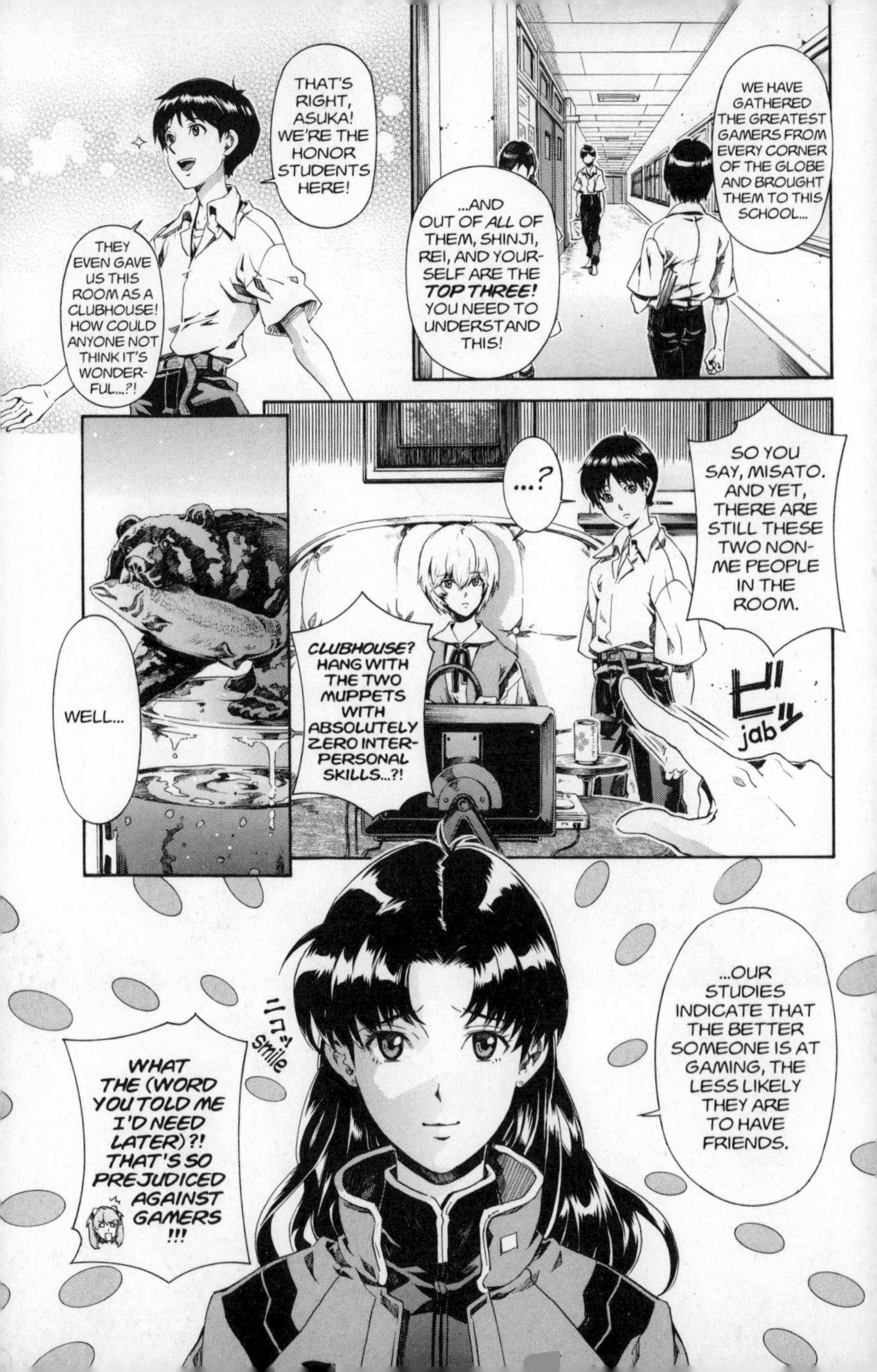
WE HAVE GATHERED THE GREATEST GAMERS FROM EVERY CORNER OF THE GLOBE AND BROUGHT THEM TO THIS SCHOOL...
...AND OUT OF *ALL* OF THEM, SHINJI, REI, AND YOURSELF ARE THE ***TOP THREE!*** YOU NEED TO UNDERSTAND THIS!
THAT'S RIGHT, ASUKA! WE'RE THE HONOR STUDENTS HERE!
THEY EVEN GAVE US THIS ROOM AS A CLUBHOUSE! HOW COULD ANYONE NOT THINK IT'S WONDERFUL...?!
SO YOU SAY, MISATO. AND YET, THERE ARE STILL THESE TWO NON-ME PEOPLE IN THE ROOM.
...?
jab
CLUBHOUSE? HANG WITH THE TWO MUPPETS WITH ABSOLUTELY ZERO INTERPERSONAL SKILLS...?!
WELL...
...OUR STUDIES INDICATE THAT THE BETTER SOMEONE IS AT GAMING, THE LESS LIKELY THEY ARE TO HAVE FRIENDS.
smile
WHAT THE (WORD YOU TOLD ME I'D NEED LATER)?! THAT'S SO PREJUDICED AGAINST GAMERS!!!

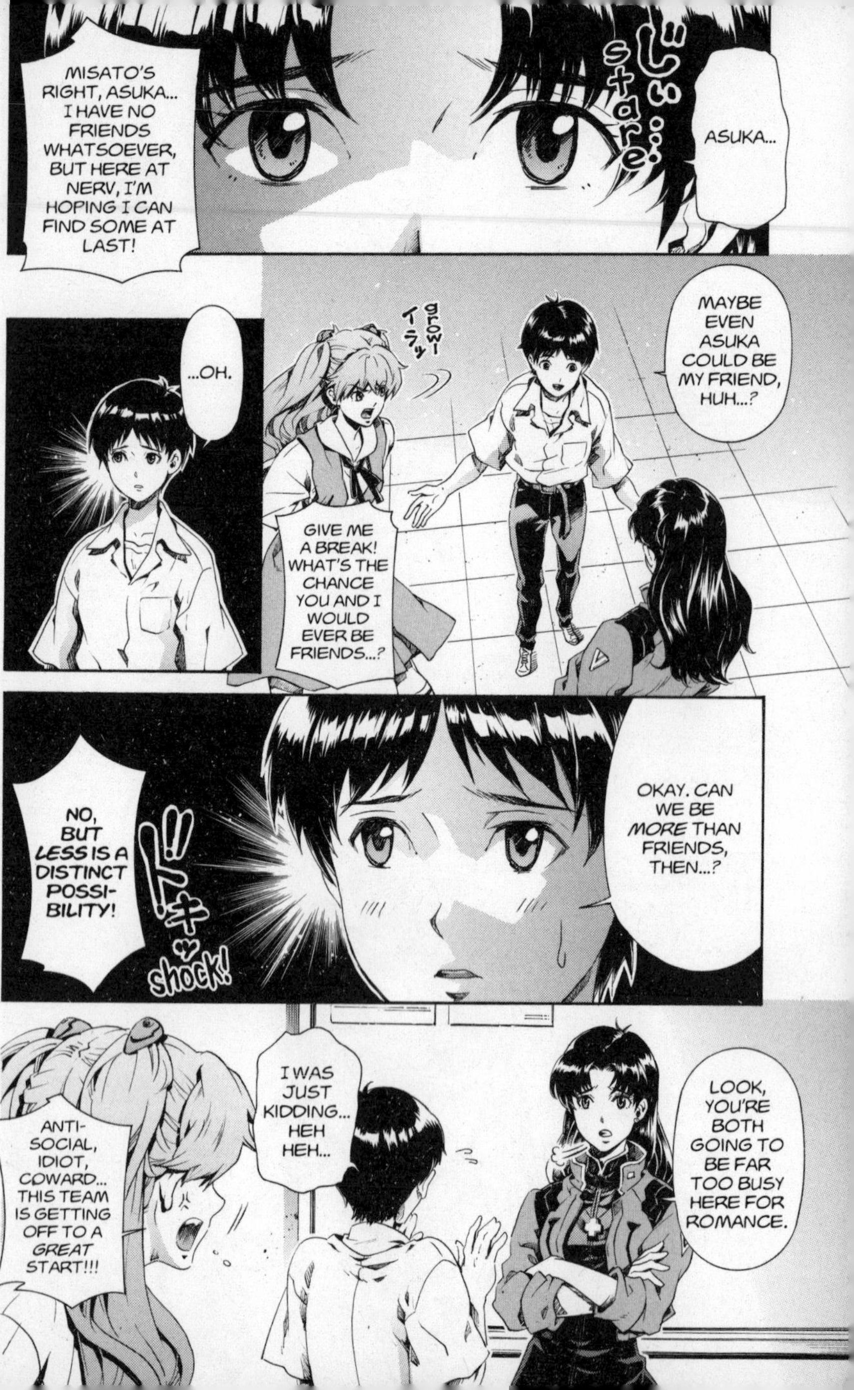
ASUKA...
じぃ... stare
MISATO'S RIGHT, ASUKA... I HAVE NO FRIENDS WHATSOEVER, BUT HERE AT NERV, I'M HOPING I CAN FIND SOME AT LAST!
MAYBE EVEN ASUKA COULD BE MY FRIEND, HUH...?
イラッ growl
GIVE ME A BREAK! WHAT'S THE CHANCE YOU AND I WOULD EVER BE FRIENDS...?
...OH.
OKAY. CAN WE BE *MORE* THAN FRIENDS, THEN...?
ドキ shock!
NO, BUT *LESS* IS A DISTINCT POSSIBILITY!
LOOK, YOU'RE BOTH GOING TO BE FAR TOO BUSY HERE FOR ROMANCE.
I WAS JUST KIDDING... HEH HEH...
ANTI-SOCIAL, IDIOT, COWARD... THIS TEAM IS GETTING OFF TO A *GREAT* START!!!

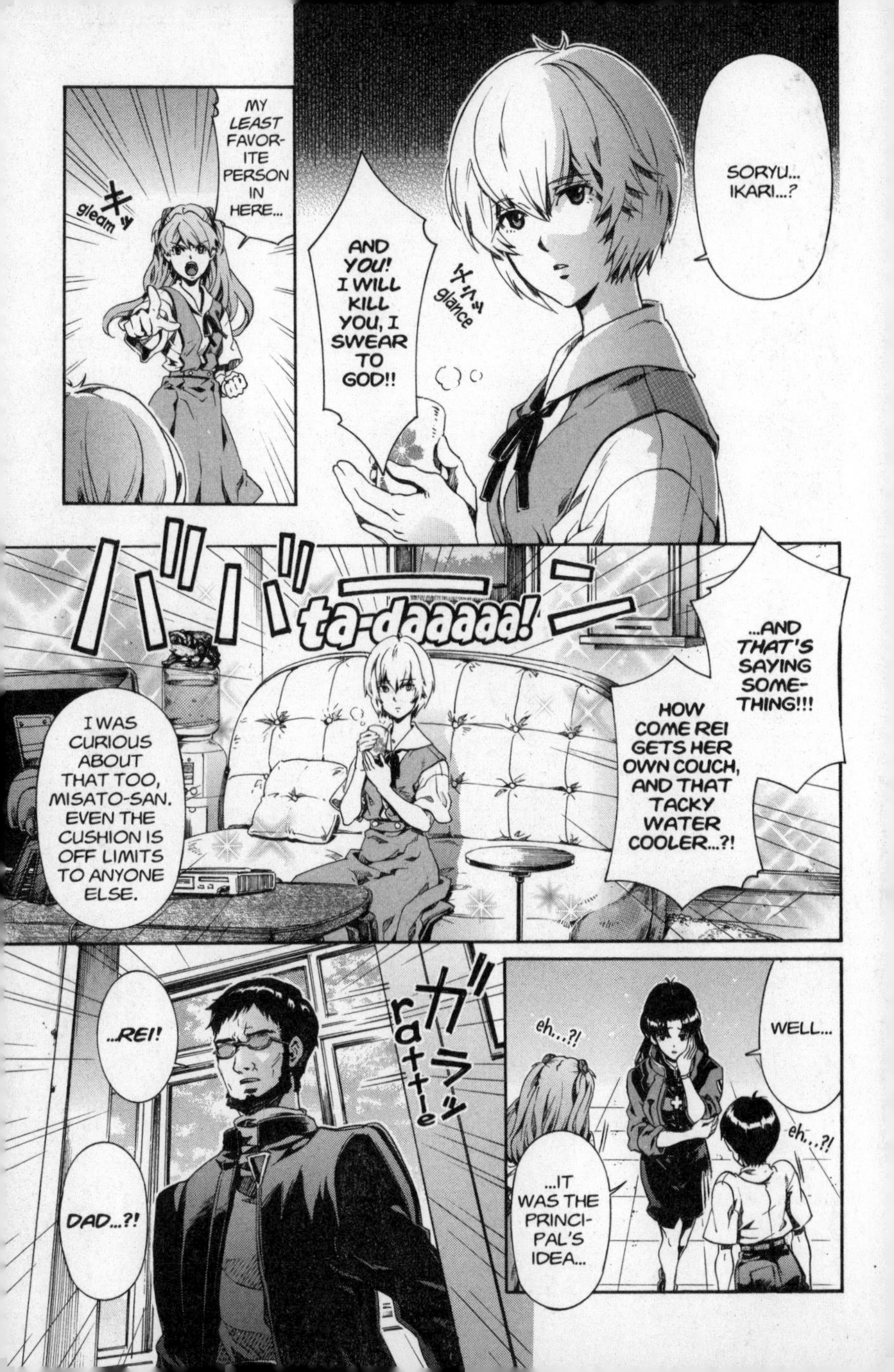
SORYU... IKARI...?
glance
AND YOU! I WILL KILL YOU, I SWEAR TO GOD!!
MY LEAST FAVOR-ITE PERSON IN HERE...
gleam
...AND THAT'S SAYING SOME-THING!!!
HOW COME REI GETS HER OWN COUCH, AND THAT TACKY WATER COOLER...?!
ta-daaaaa!
I WAS CURIOUS ABOUT THAT TOO, MISATO-SAN. EVEN THE CUSHION IS OFF LIMITS TO ANYONE ELSE.
WELL...
eh...?!
eh...?!
...IT WAS THE PRINCI-PAL'S IDEA...
rattle
...REI!
DAD...?!

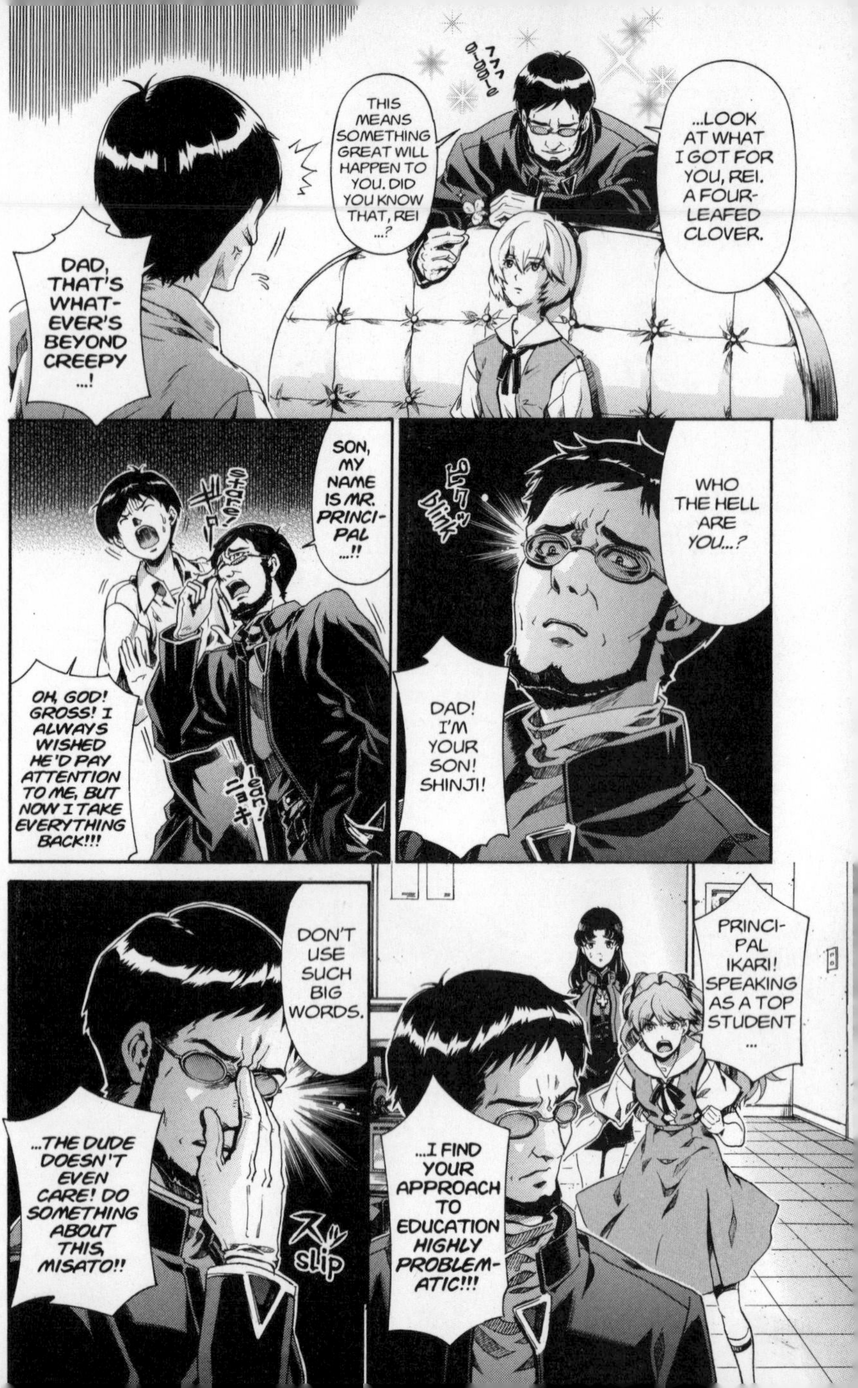
...LOOK AT WHAT I GOT FOR YOU, REI. A FOUR-LEAFED CLOVER.
フフフ giggle
THIS MEANS SOMETHING GREAT WILL HAPPEN TO YOU. DID YOU KNOW THAT, REI ...?
DAD, THAT'S WHAT-EVER'S BEYOND CREEPY ...!
WHO THE HELL ARE YOU...?
ピクッ blink
DAD! I'M YOUR SON! SHINJI!
SON, MY NAME IS MR. PRINCIPAL ...!!
stare! ギロッ
lean! ニョキ
OH, GOD! GROSS! I ALWAYS WISHED HE'D PAY ATTENTION TO ME, BUT NOW I TAKE EVERYTHING BACK!!!
PRINCI-PAL IKARI! SPEAKING AS A TOP STUDENT ...
...I FIND YOUR APPROACH TO EDUCATION HIGHLY PROBLEM-ATIC!!!
DON'T USE SUCH BIG WORDS.
スッ slip
...THE DUDE DOESN'T EVEN CARE! DO SOMETHING ABOUT THIS, MISATO!!

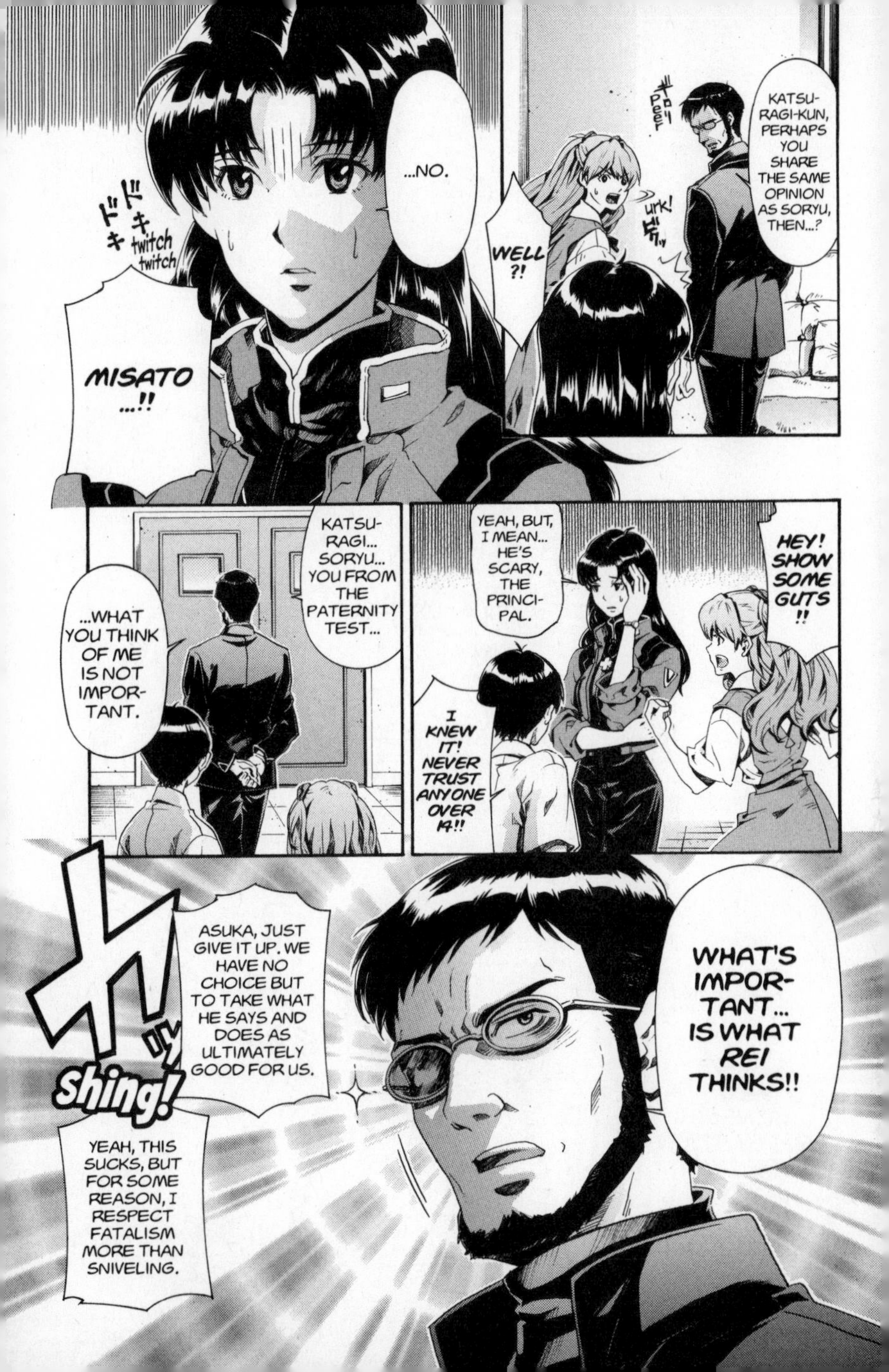

Peer
KATSU-RAGI-KUN, PERHAPS YOU SHARE THE SAME OPINION AS SORYU, THEN...?
urk!
WELL ?!
...NO.
ドキドキ twitch twitch
MISATO ...!!
HEY! SHOW SOME GUTS!!
YEAH, BUT, I MEAN... HE'S SCARY, THE PRINCIPAL.
I KNEW IT! NEVER TRUST ANYONE OVER 14!!
KATSU-RAGI... SORYU... YOU FROM THE PATERNITY TEST...
...WHAT YOU THINK OF ME IS NOT IMPOR-TANT.
WHAT'S IMPOR-TANT... IS WHAT REI THINKS!!
ASUKA, JUST GIVE IT UP. WE HAVE NO CHOICE BUT TO TAKE WHAT HE SAYS AND DOES AS ULTIMATELY GOOD FOR US.
shing!
YEAH, THIS SUCKS, BUT FOR SOME REASON, I RESPECT FATALISM MORE THAN SNIVELING.

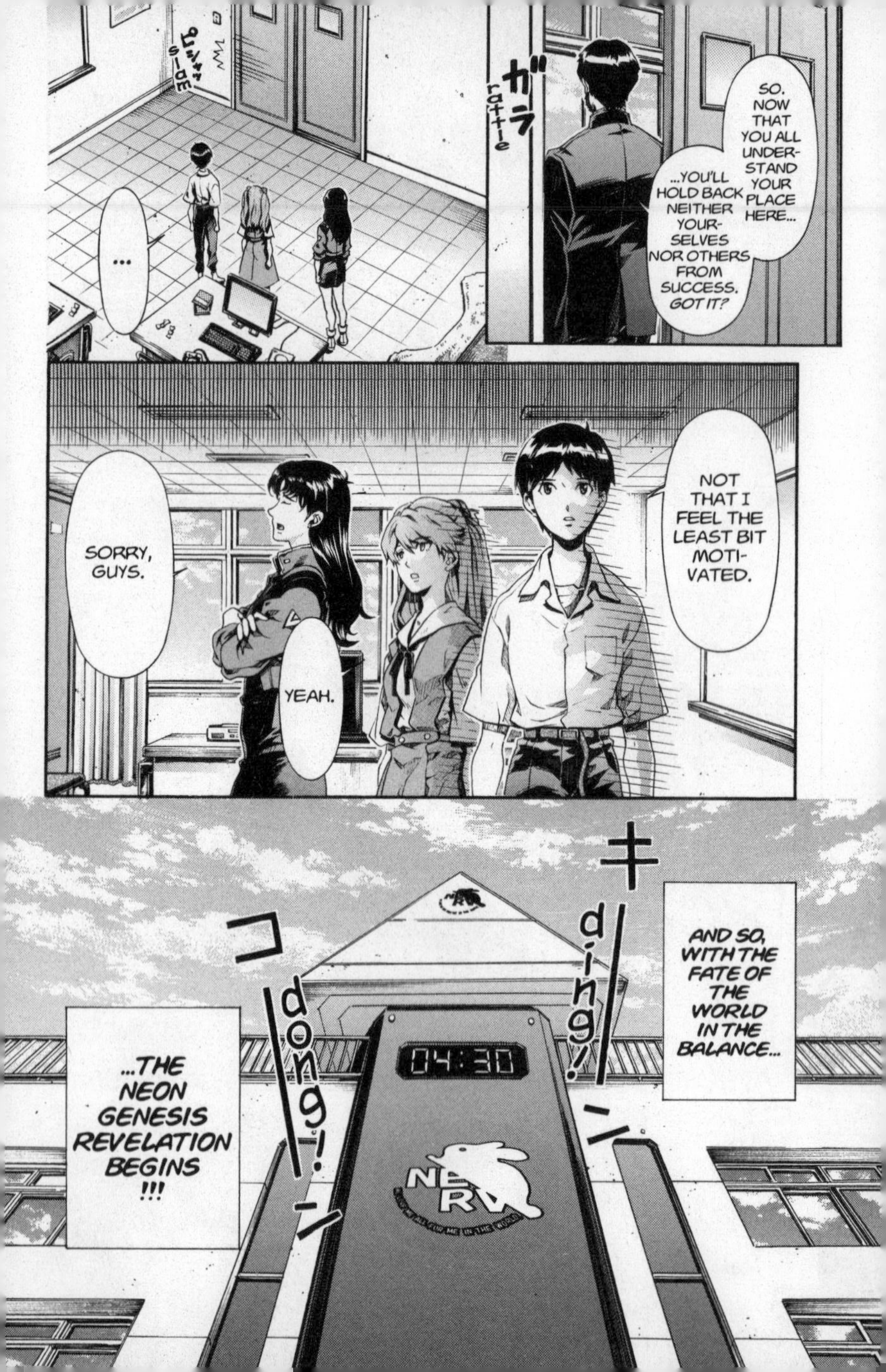

SO. NOW THAT YOU ALL UNDER-STAND YOUR PLACE HERE...
...YOU'LL HOLD BACK NEITHER YOUR-SELVES NOR OTHERS FROM SUCCESS. GOT IT?
ガラ rattle
slam
...
NOT THAT I FEEL THE LEAST BIT MOTI-VATED.
SORRY, GUYS.
YEAH.
AND SO, WITH THE FATE OF THE WORLD IN THE BALANCE...
ding!
04:30
dong!
...THE NEON GENESIS REVELATION BEGINS!!!

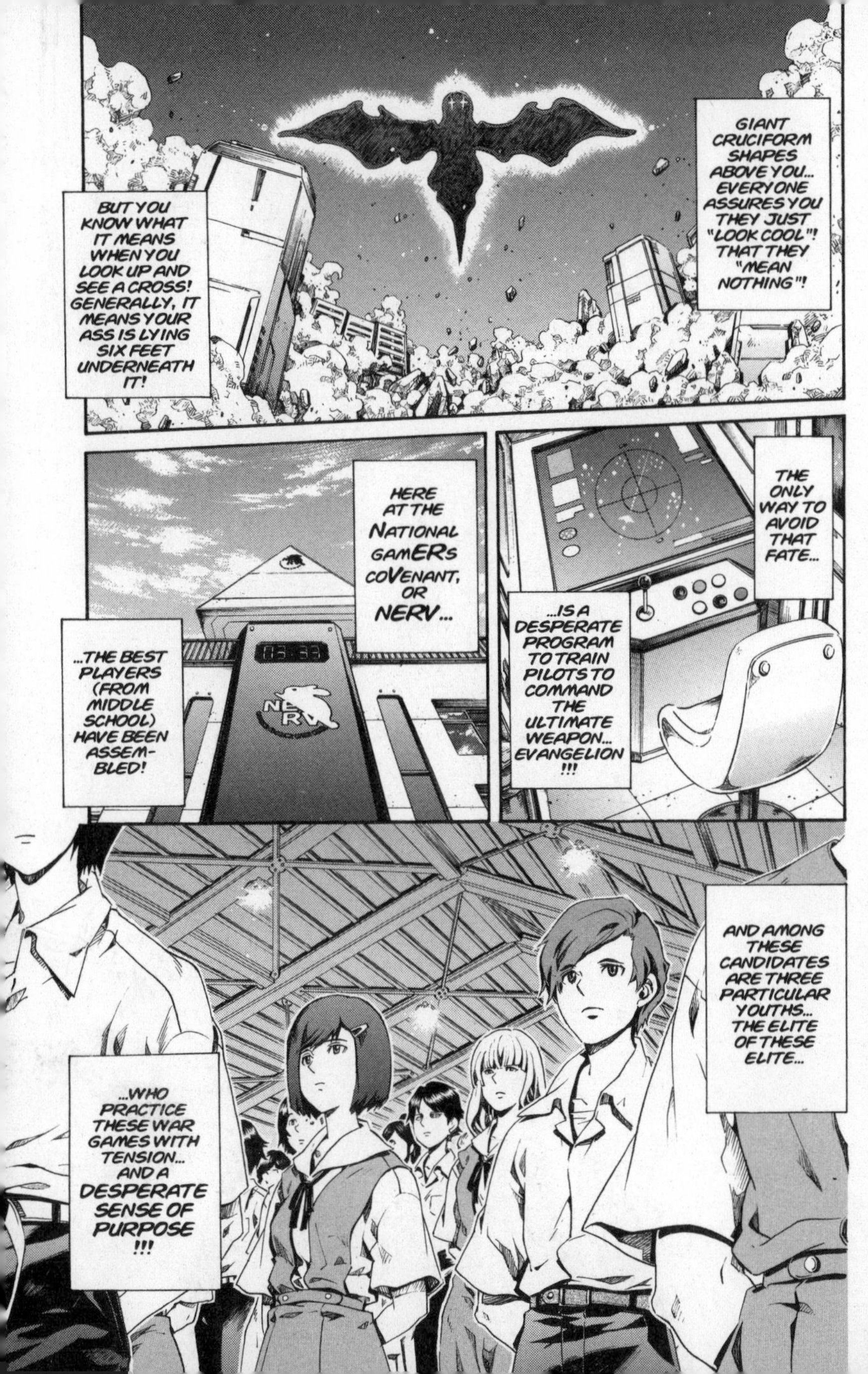
GIANT CRUCIFORM SHAPES ABOVE YOU... EVERYONE ASSURES YOU THEY JUST "LOOK COOL"! THAT THEY "MEAN NOTHING"!
BUT YOU KNOW WHAT IT MEANS WHEN YOU LOOK UP AND SEE A CROSS! GENERALLY, IT MEANS YOUR ASS IS LYING SIX FEET UNDERNEATH IT!
THE ONLY WAY TO AVOID THAT FATE...
...IS A DESPERATE PROGRAM TO TRAIN PILOTS TO COMMAND THE ULTIMATE WEAPON... EVANGELION!!!
HERE AT THE NATIONAL GAMERS COVENANT, OR NERV...
...THE BEST PLAYERS (FROM MIDDLE SCHOOL) HAVE BEEN ASSEMBLED!
AND AMONG THESE CANDIDATES ARE THREE PARTICULAR YOUTHS... THE ELITE OF THESE ELITE...
...WHO PRACTICE THESE WAR GAMES WITH TENSION... AND A DESPERATE SENSE OF PURPOSE!!!

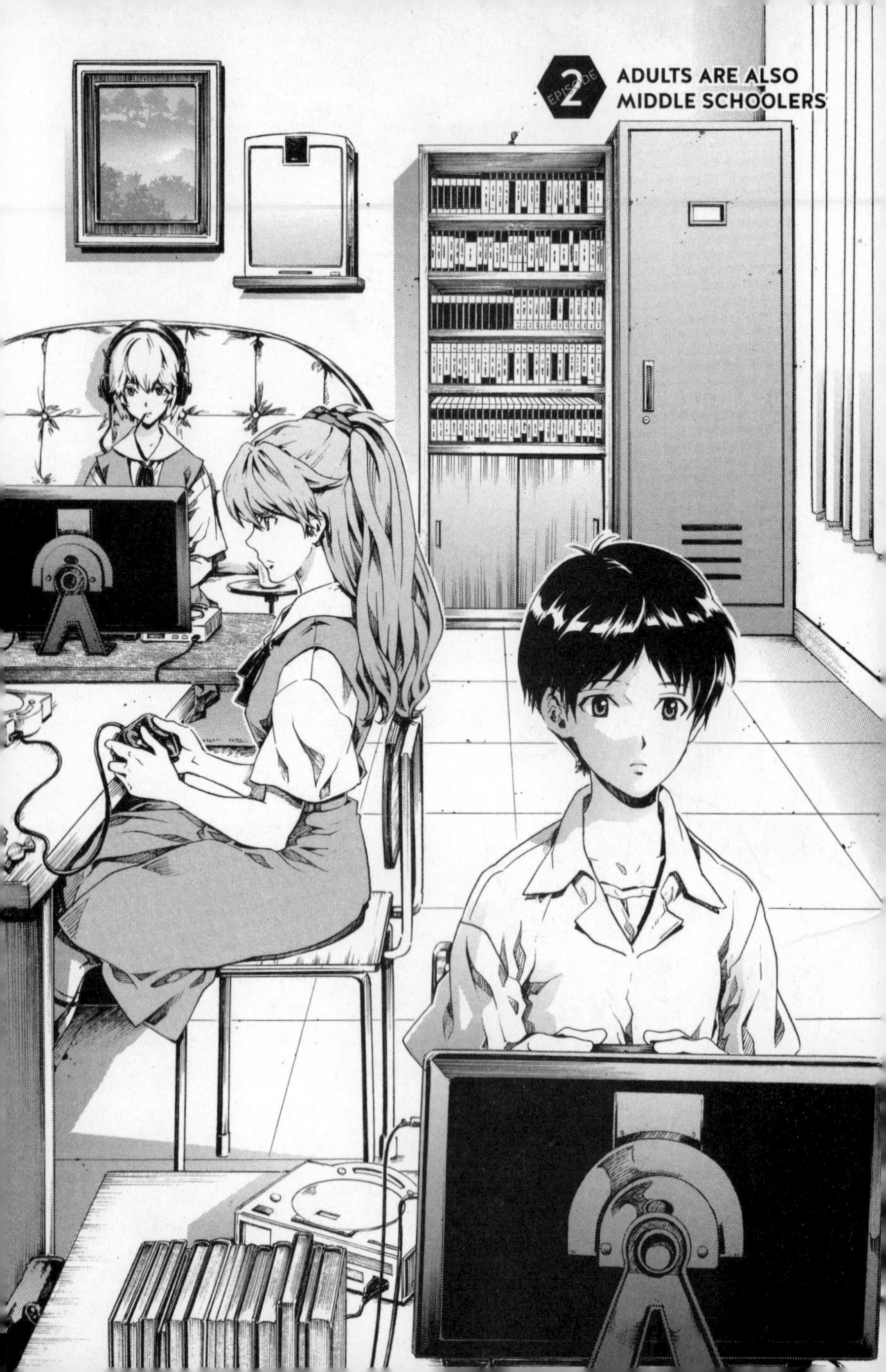
EPISODE 2
ADULTS ARE ALSO
MIDDLE SCHOOLERS

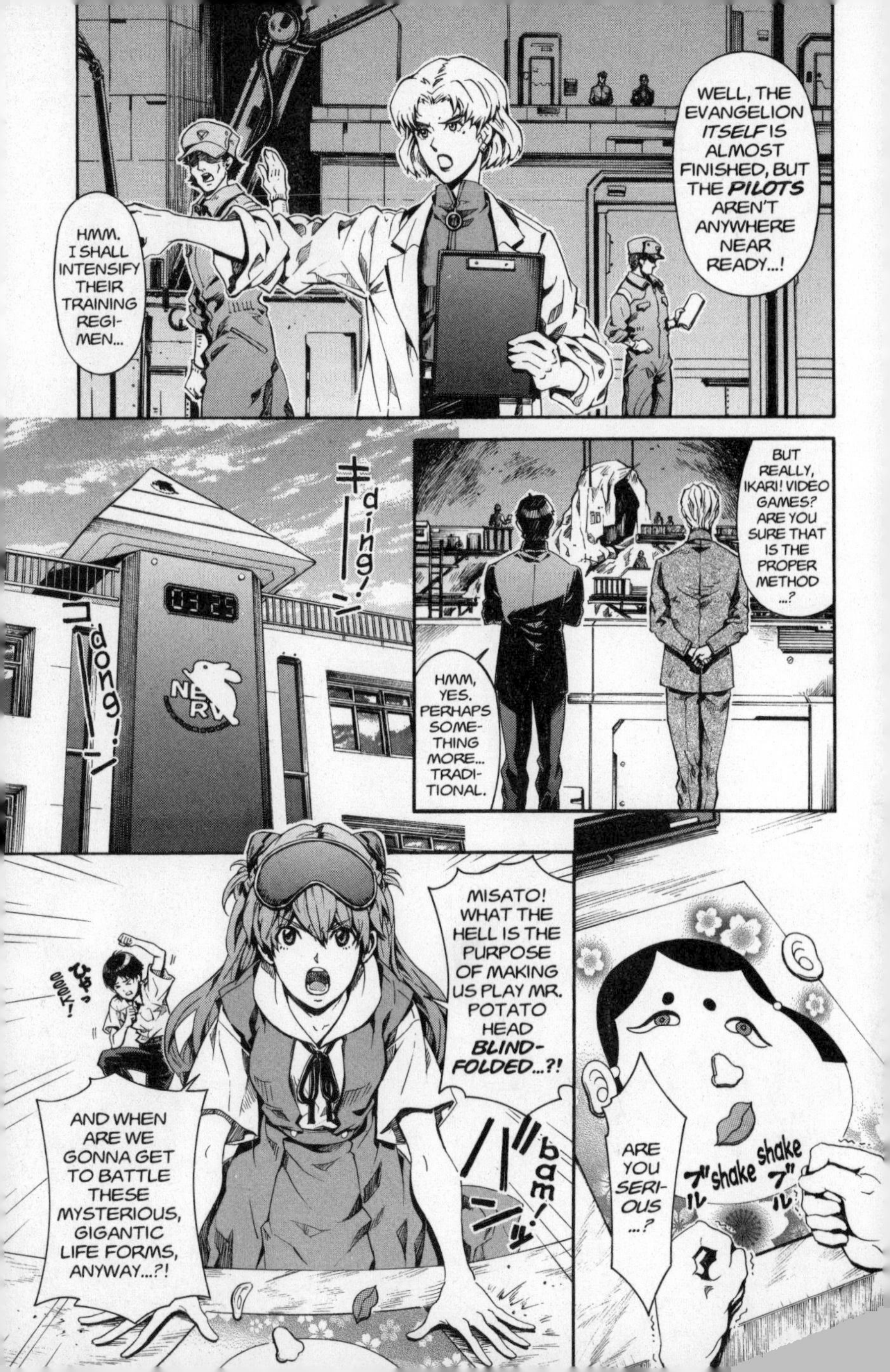
WELL, THE EVANGELION ITSELF IS ALMOST FINISHED, BUT THE PILOTS AREN'T ANYWHERE NEAR READY...!
HMM. I SHALL INTENSIFY THEIR TRAINING REGI-MEN...
BUT REALLY, IKARI! VIDEO GAMES? ARE YOU SURE THAT IS THE PROPER METHOD ...?
HMM, YES. PERHAPS SOME-THING MORE... TRADI-TIONAL.
ding!
dong!
shake
shake
ARE YOU SERI-OUS ...?
MISATO! WHAT THE HELL IS THE PURPOSE OF MAKING US PLAY MR. POTATO HEAD BLIND-FOLDED...?!
bam!
AND WHEN ARE WE GONNA GET TO BATTLE THESE MYSTERIOUS, GIGANTIC LIFE FORMS, ANYWAY...?!

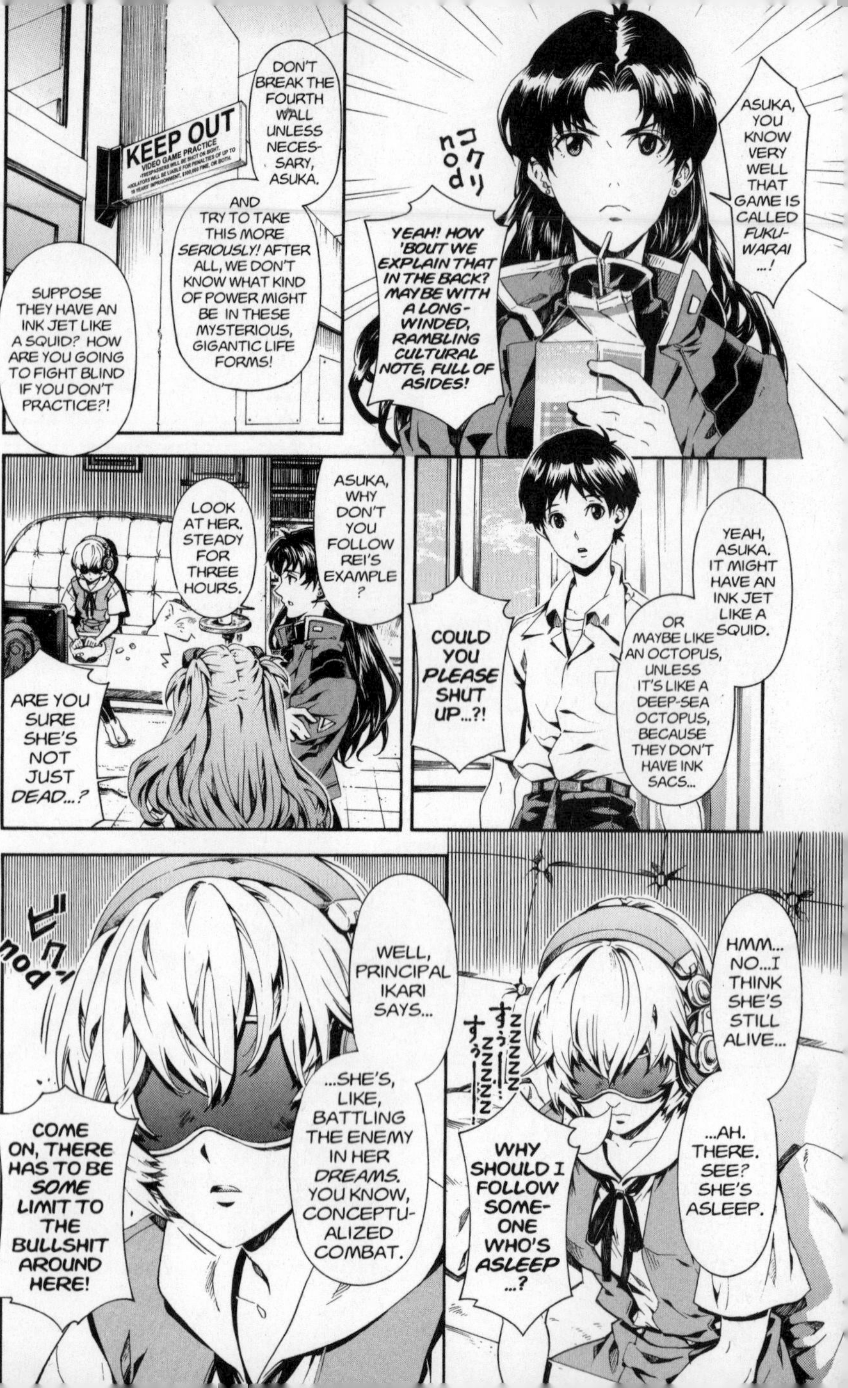
ASUKA, YOU KNOW VERY WELL THAT GAME IS CALLED *FUKU-WARAI*...!
YEAH! HOW 'BOUT WE EXPLAIN THAT IN THE BACK? MAYBE WITH A LONG-WINDED, RAMBLING CULTURAL NOTE, FULL OF ASIDES!
DON'T BREAK THE FOURTH WALL UNLESS NECES-SARY, ASUKA.
KEEP OUT
VIDEO GAME PRACTICE
AND TRY TO TAKE THIS MORE *SERIOUSLY*! AFTER ALL, WE DON'T KNOW WHAT KIND OF POWER MIGHT BE IN THESE MYSTERIOUS, GIGANTIC LIFE FORMS!
SUPPOSE THEY HAVE AN INK JET LIKE A SQUID? HOW ARE YOU GOING TO FIGHT BLIND IF YOU DON'T PRACTICE?!
YEAH, ASUKA. IT MIGHT HAVE AN INK JET LIKE A SQUID.
OR MAYBE LIKE AN OCTOPUS, UNLESS IT'S LIKE A DEEP-SEA OCTOPUS, BECAUSE THEY DON'T HAVE INK SACS...
COULD YOU *PLEASE* SHUT UP...?!
ASUKA, WHY DON'T YOU FOLLOW REI'S EXAMPLE?
LOOK AT HER. STEADY FOR THREE HOURS.
ARE YOU SURE SHE'S NOT JUST *DEAD*...?
HMM... NO...I THINK SHE'S STILL ALIVE...
...AH. THERE. SEE? SHE'S ASLEEP.
WHY SHOULD I FOLLOW SOME-ONE WHO'S *ASLEEP*...?
WELL, PRINCIPAL IKARI SAYS...
...SHE'S, LIKE, BATTLING THE ENEMY IN HER *DREAMS*. YOU KNOW, CONCEPTU-ALIZED COMBAT.
COME ON, THERE HAS TO BE *SOME* LIMIT TO THE BULLSHIT AROUND HERE!

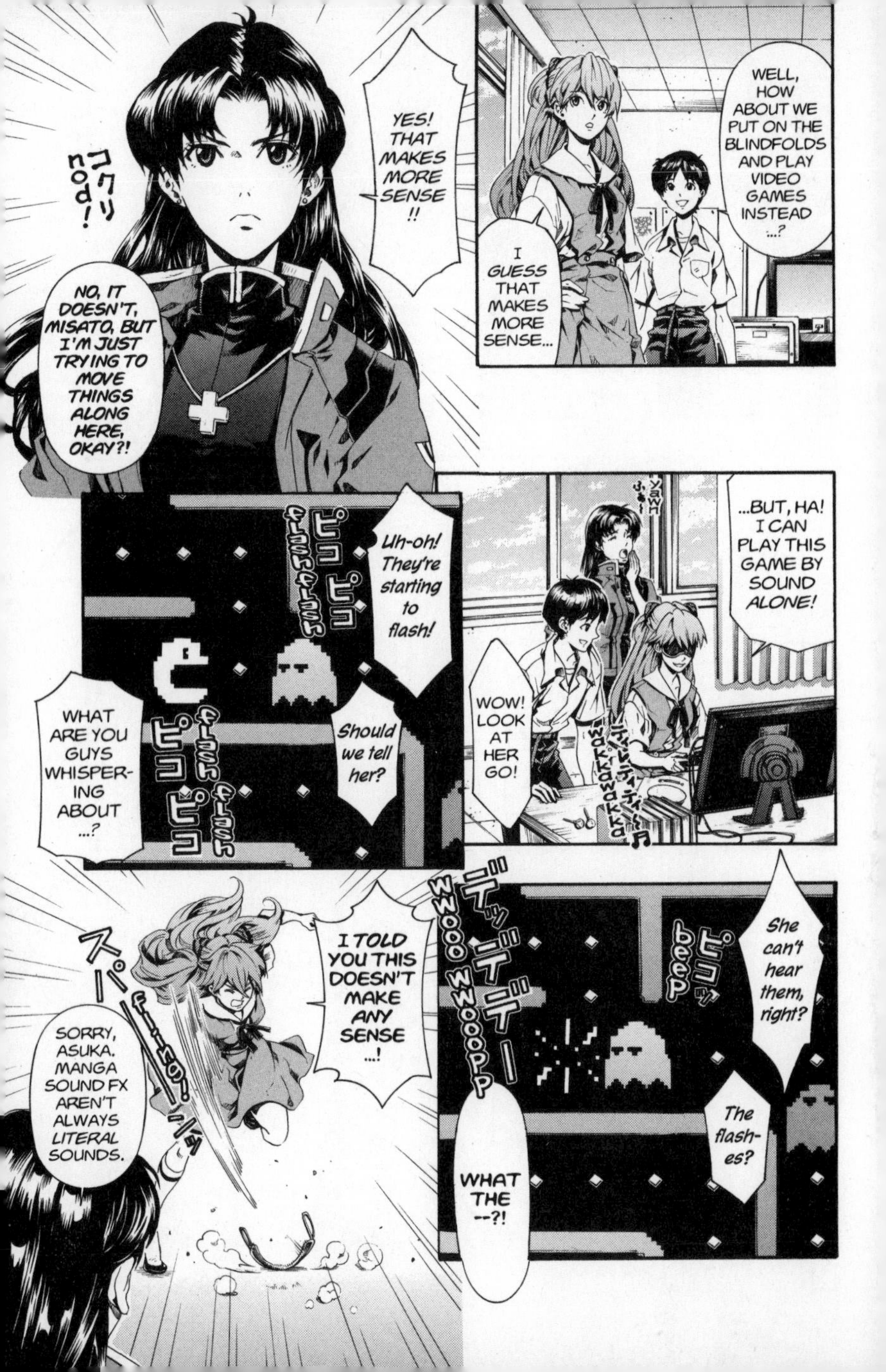
WELL, HOW ABOUT WE PUT ON THE BLINDFOLDS AND PLAY VIDEO GAMES INSTEAD ...?
I GUESS THAT MAKES MORE SENSE...
YES! THAT MAKES MORE SENSE !!
コクリ
nod!
NO, IT DOESN'T, MISATO, BUT I'M JUST TRYING TO MOVE THINGS ALONG HERE, OKAY?!
yawn
...BUT, HA! I CAN PLAY THIS GAME BY SOUND ALONE!
WOW! LOOK AT HER GO!
wakkawakka
ピコ ピコ
flash flash
Uh-oh! They're starting to flash!
Should we tell her?
ピコ ピコ
flash flash
WHAT ARE YOU GUYS WHISPERING ABOUT ...?
She can't hear them, right?
ピコッ
beep
The flashes?
WWOOO WWOOOPP
WHAT THE --?!
I TOLD YOU THIS DOESN'T MAKE ANY SENSE ...!
fling!
SORRY, ASUKA. MANGA SOUND FX AREN'T ALWAYS LITERAL SOUNDS.

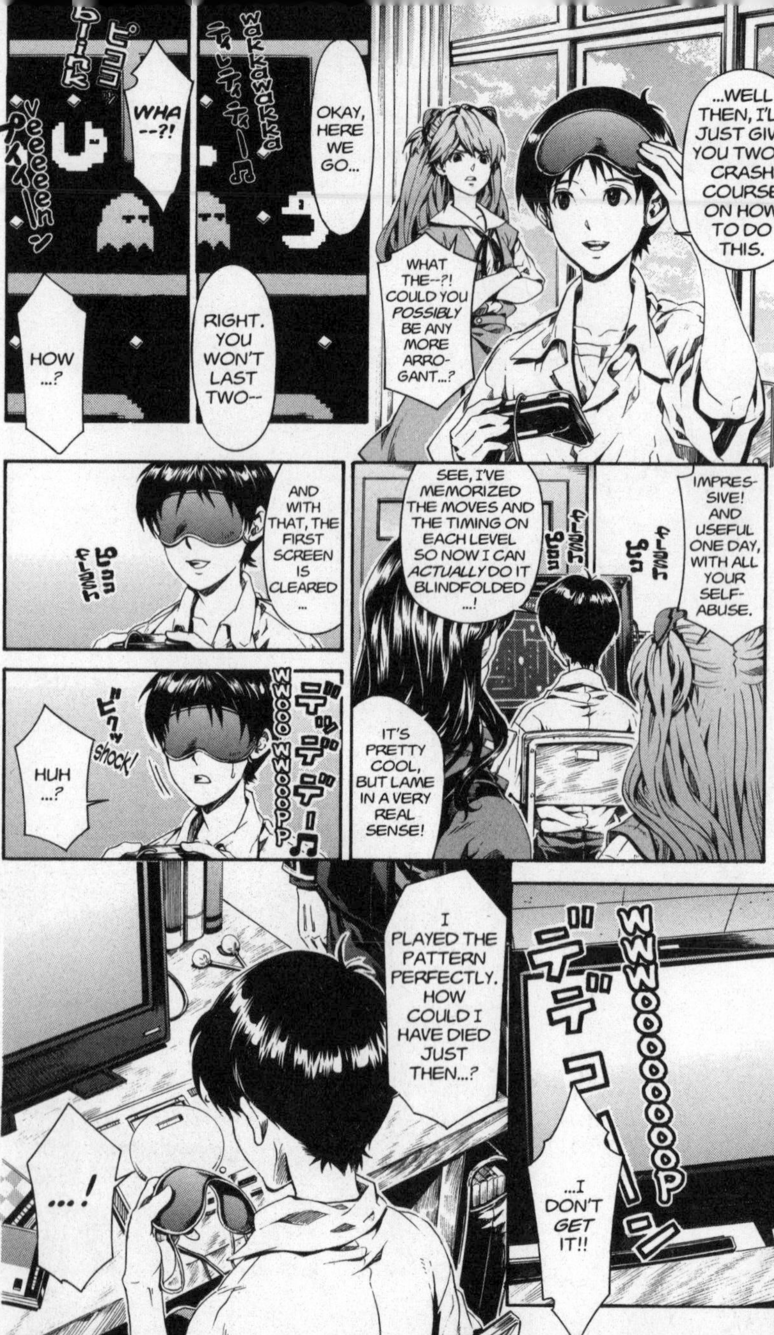
...WELL THEN, I'LL JUST GIVE YOU TWO A CRASH COURSE ON HOW TO DO THIS.
WHAT THE--?! COULD YOU *POSSIBLY* BE ANY MORE ARRO-GANT...?
OKAY, HERE WE GO...
wakkawakka
ティレティティー♫
RIGHT. YOU WON'T LAST TWO--
ピココッ
blink
WHA--?!
veeeeeen
ベイィーンッ
HOW ...?
IMPRES-SIVE! AND USEFUL ONE DAY, WITH ALL YOUR SELF-ABUSE.
SEE, I'VE MEMORIZED THE MOVES AND THE TIMING ON EACH LEVEL SO NOW I CAN *ACTUALLY* DO IT BLINDFOLDED ...!
flash
IT'S PRETTY COOL, BUT LAME IN A VERY REAL SENSE!
AND WITH THAT, THE FIRST SCREEN IS CLEARED ...
flash
WWOOO WWOOOPP
デッデデー♫
ビクッ
shock!
HUH ...?
WWWOOOOOOOOOP
デデデコーン
...I DON'T GET IT!!
I PLAYED THE PATTERN PERFECTLY. HOW COULD I HAVE DIED JUST THEN...?
...!

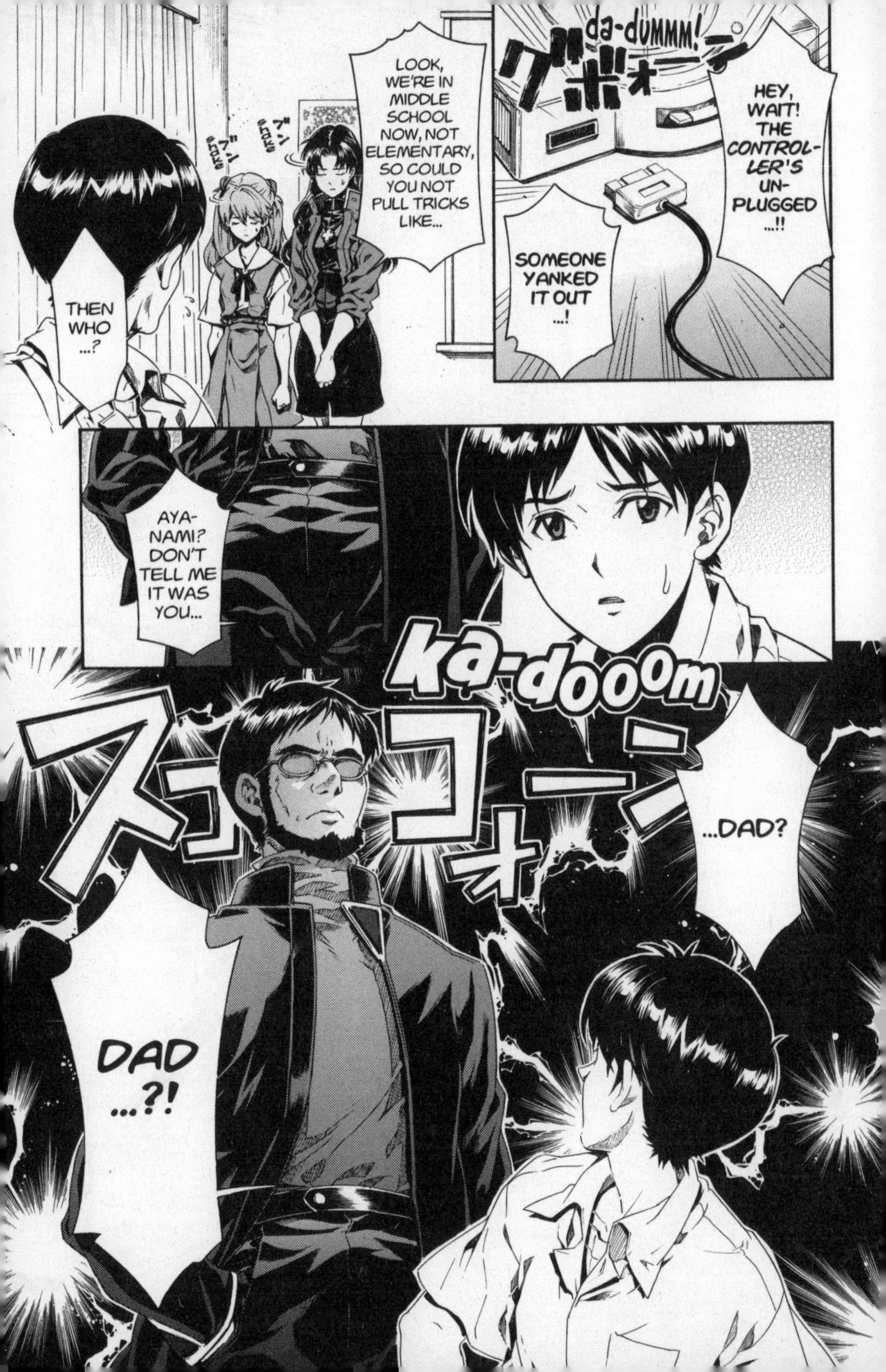
da-dummm!
HEY, WAIT! THE CONTROL-LER'S UN-PLUGGED ...!!
SOMEONE YANKED IT OUT ...!
LOOK, WE'RE IN MIDDLE SCHOOL NOW, NOT ELEMENTARY, SO COULD YOU NOT PULL TRICKS LIKE...
shake
shake
THEN WHO ...?
AYA-NAMI? DON'T TELL ME IT WAS YOU...
ka-doooom
...DAD?
DAD ...?!

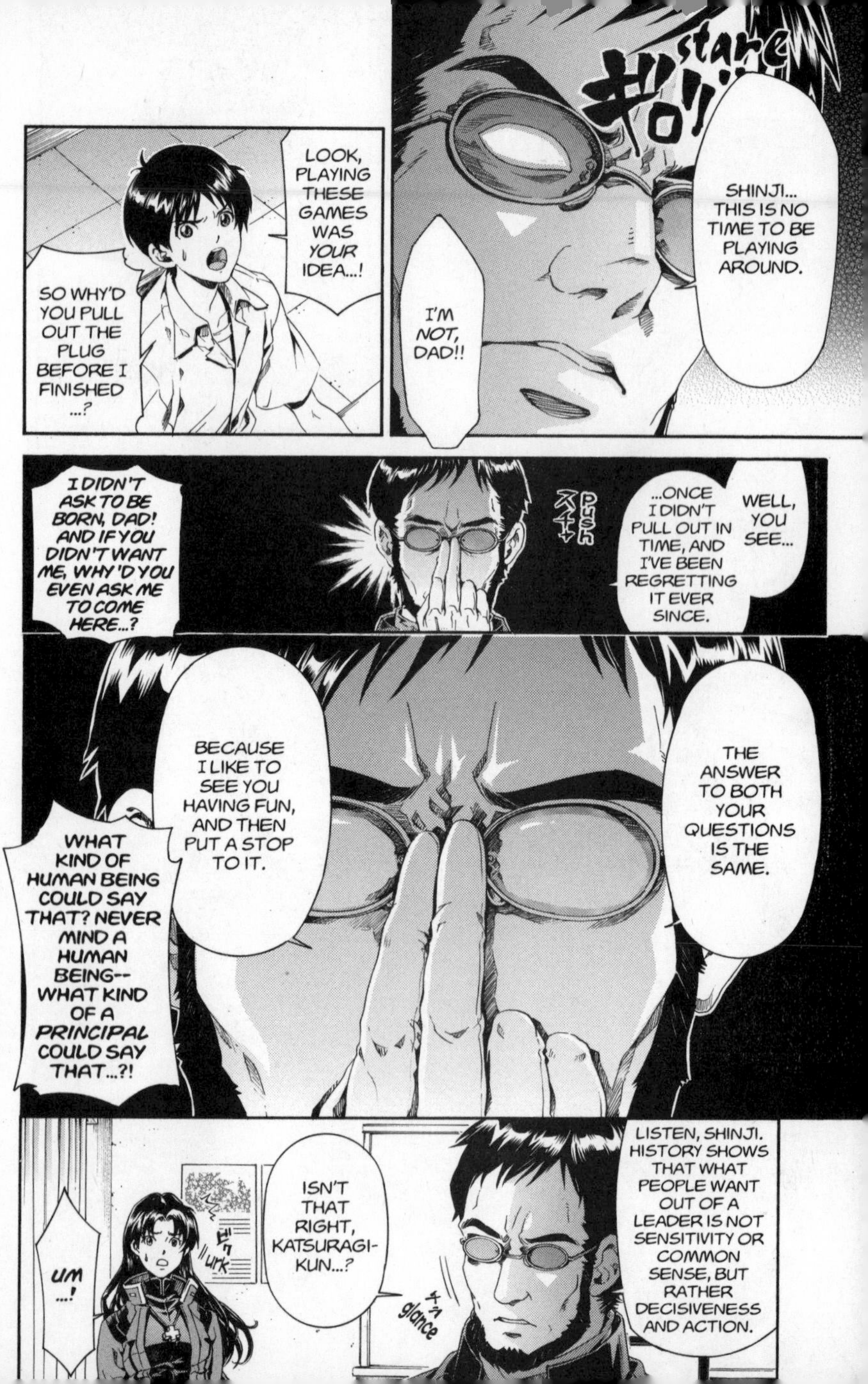
stare
SHINJI... THIS IS NO TIME TO BE PLAYING AROUND.
I'M NOT, DAD!!
LOOK, PLAYING THESE GAMES WAS YOUR IDEA...!
SO WHY'D YOU PULL OUT THE PLUG BEFORE I FINISHED...?
WELL, YOU SEE...
...ONCE I DIDN'T PULL OUT IN TIME, AND I'VE BEEN REGRETTING IT EVER SINCE.
push
I DIDN'T ASK TO BE BORN, DAD! AND IF YOU DIDN'T WANT ME, WHY'D YOU EVEN ASK ME TO COME HERE...?
THE ANSWER TO BOTH YOUR QUESTIONS IS THE SAME.
BECAUSE I LIKE TO SEE YOU HAVING FUN, AND THEN PUT A STOP TO IT.
WHAT KIND OF HUMAN BEING COULD SAY THAT? NEVER MIND A HUMAN BEING-- WHAT KIND OF A PRINCIPAL COULD SAY THAT...?!
LISTEN, SHINJI. HISTORY SHOWS THAT WHAT PEOPLE WANT OUT OF A LEADER IS NOT SENSITIVITY OR COMMON SENSE, BUT RATHER DECISIVENESS AND ACTION.
glance
ISN'T THAT RIGHT, KATSURAGI-KUN...?
urk
UM...!

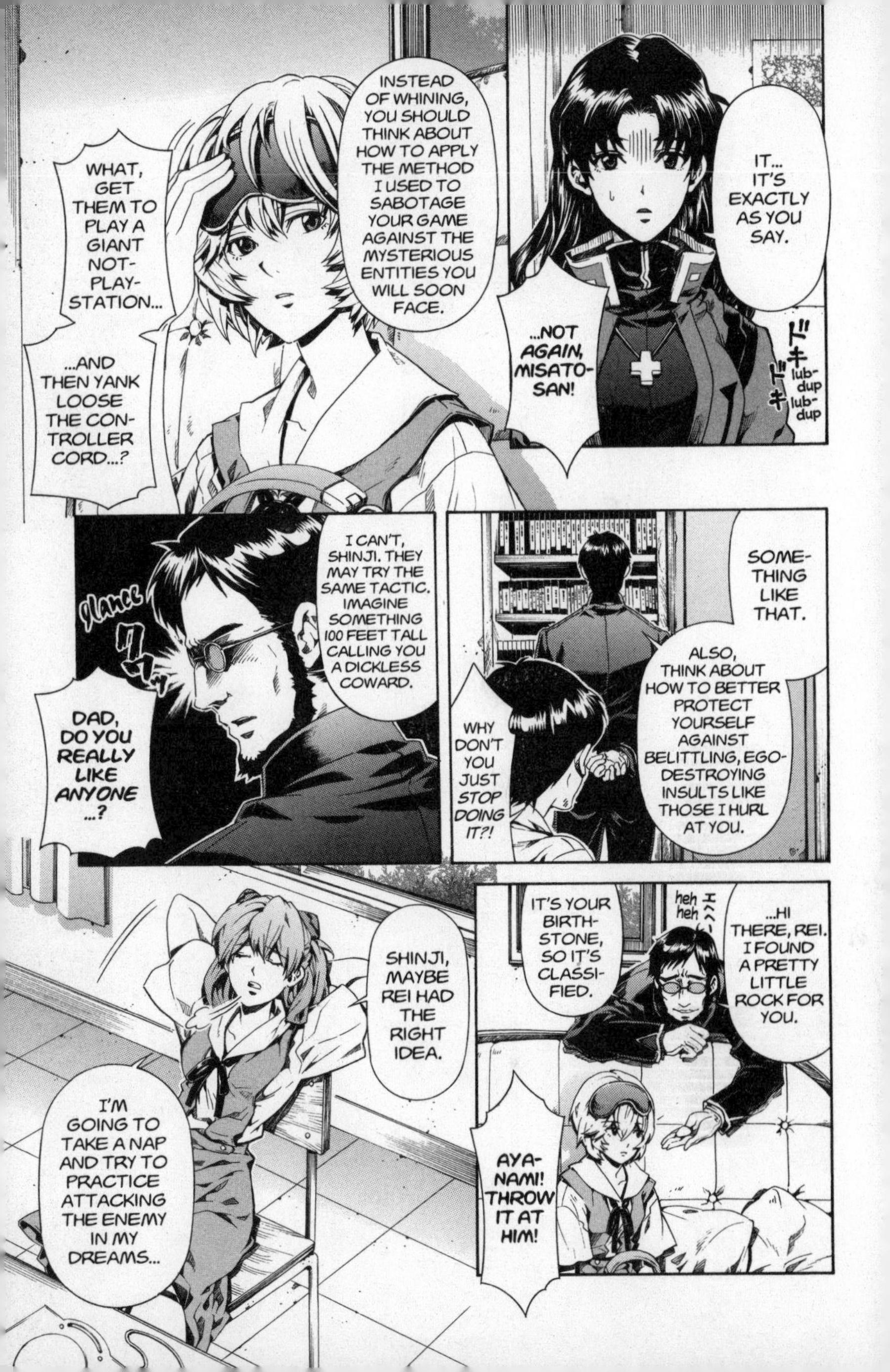
IT... IT'S EXACTLY AS YOU SAY.
ドキドキ
lub-dup lub-dup
...NOT AGAIN, MISATO-SAN!
INSTEAD OF WHINING, YOU SHOULD THINK ABOUT HOW TO APPLY THE METHOD I USED TO SABOTAGE YOUR GAME AGAINST THE MYSTERIOUS ENTITIES YOU WILL SOON FACE.
WHAT, GET THEM TO PLAY A GIANT NOT-PLAY-STATION...
...AND THEN YANK LOOSE THE CON-TROLLER CORD...?
SOME-THING LIKE THAT.
ALSO, THINK ABOUT HOW TO BETTER PROTECT YOURSELF AGAINST BELITTLING, EGO-DESTROYING INSULTS LIKE THOSE I HURL AT YOU.
WHY DON'T YOU JUST STOP DOING IT?!
I CAN'T, SHINJI. THEY MAY TRY THE SAME TACTIC. IMAGINE SOMETHING 100 FEET TALL CALLING YOU A DICKLESS COWARD.
glance
DAD, DO YOU REALLY LIKE ANYONE ...?
...HI THERE, REI. I FOUND A PRETTY LITTLE ROCK FOR YOU.
heh heh
IT'S YOUR BIRTH-STONE, SO IT'S CLASSI-FIED.
AYA-NAMI! THROW IT AT HIM!
SHINJI, MAYBE REI HAD THE RIGHT IDEA.
I'M GOING TO TAKE A NAP AND TRY TO PRACTICE ATTACKING THE ENEMY IN MY DREAMS...

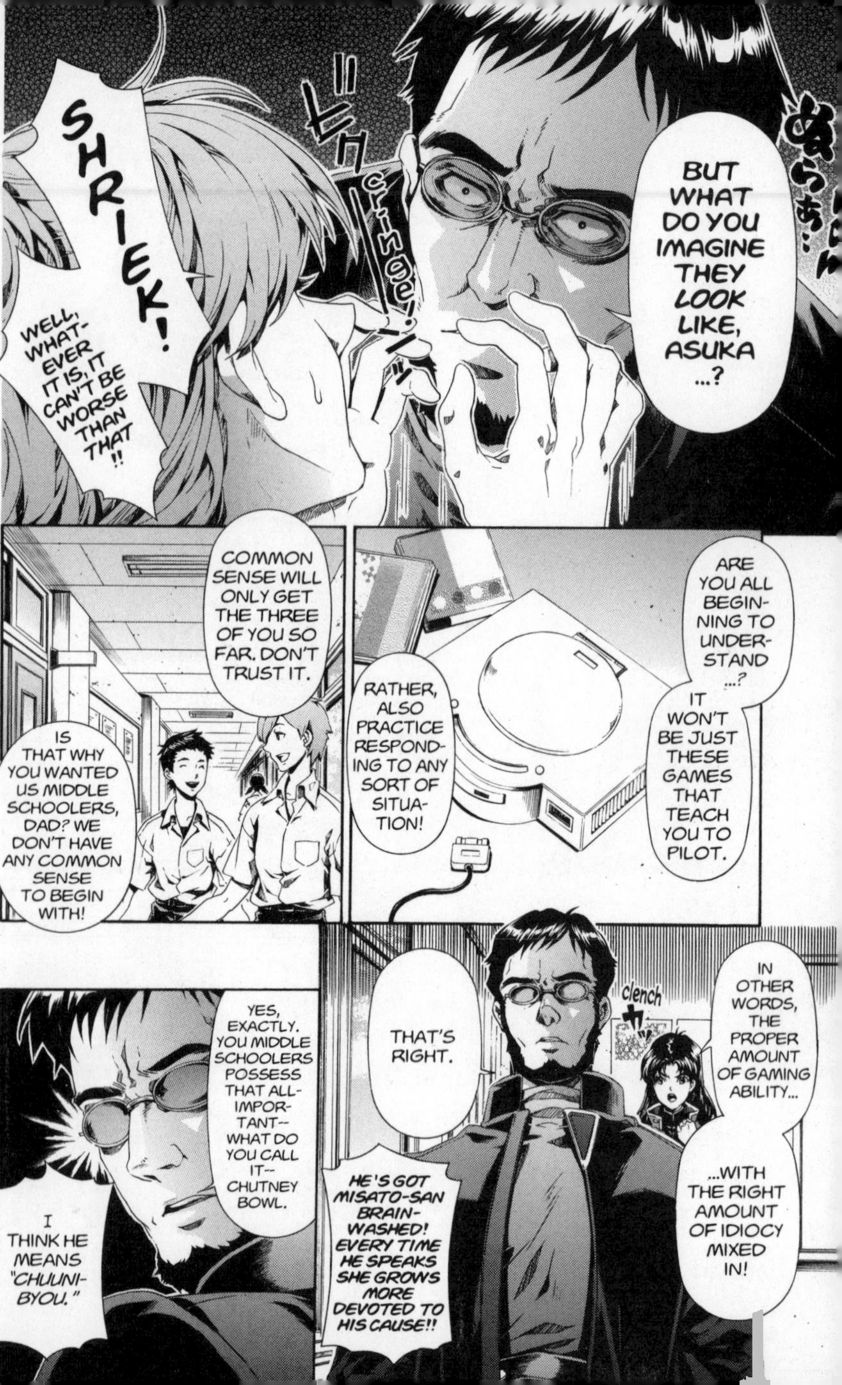
BUT WHAT DO YOU IMAGINE THEY LOOK LIKE, ASUKA ...?
cringe!
SHRIEK!
WELL, WHATEVER IT IS, IT CAN'T BE WORSE THAN THAT!!
ARE YOU ALL BEGINNING TO UNDERSTAND ...?
IT WON'T BE JUST THESE GAMES THAT TEACH YOU TO PILOT.
RATHER, ALSO PRACTICE RESPONDING TO ANY SORT OF SITUATION!
COMMON SENSE WILL ONLY GET THE THREE OF YOU SO FAR. DON'T TRUST IT.
IS THAT WHY YOU WANTED US MIDDLE SCHOOLERS, DAD? WE DON'T HAVE ANY COMMON SENSE TO BEGIN WITH!
IN OTHER WORDS, THE PROPER AMOUNT OF GAMING ABILITY...
...WITH THE RIGHT AMOUNT OF IDIOCY MIXED IN!
clench
THAT'S RIGHT.
HE'S GOT MISATO-SAN BRAINWASHED! EVERY TIME HE SPEAKS SHE GROWS MORE DEVOTED TO HIS CAUSE!!
YES, EXACTLY. YOU MIDDLE SCHOOLERS POSSESS THAT ALL-IMPORTANT--WHAT DO YOU CALL IT--CHUTNEY BOWL.
I THINK HE MEANS "CHUUNIBYOU."

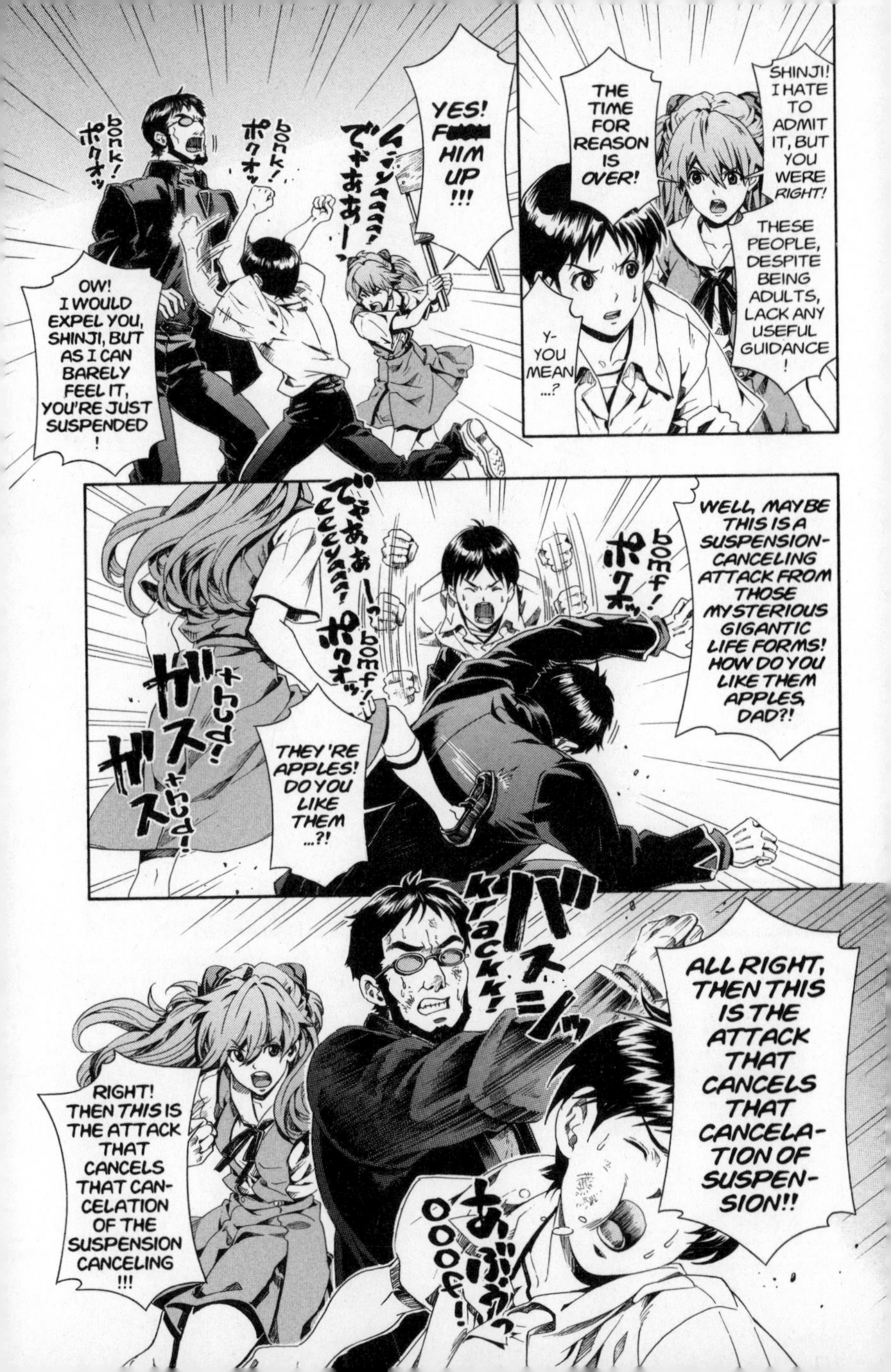
SHINJI! I HATE TO ADMIT IT, BUT YOU WERE RIGHT!
THESE PEOPLE, DESPITE BEING ADULTS, LACK ANY USEFUL GUIDANCE!
THE TIME FOR REASON IS OVER!
Y-YOU MEAN ...?
YES! F[redacted] HIM UP!!!
bonk! ポクオッ
bonk! ポクオッ
OW! I WOULD EXPEL YOU, SHINJI, BUT AS I CAN BARELY FEEL IT, YOU'RE JUST SUSPENDED!
WELL, MAYBE THIS IS A SUSPENSION-CANCELING ATTACK FROM THOSE MYSTERIOUS GIGANTIC LIFE FORMS! HOW DO YOU LIKE THEM APPLES, DAD?!
bomf! ポクオッ
eeeyaaa!
bomf!! ポクオッ
thud! ガス
thud! ガス
THEY'RE APPLES! DO YOU LIKE THEM ...?!
ALL RIGHT, THEN THIS IS THE ATTACK THAT CANCELS THAT CANCELATION OF SUSPENSION!!
krackk!
oooof!!
RIGHT! THEN THIS IS THE ATTACK THAT CANCELS THAT CANCELATION OF THE SUSPENSION CANCELING!!!

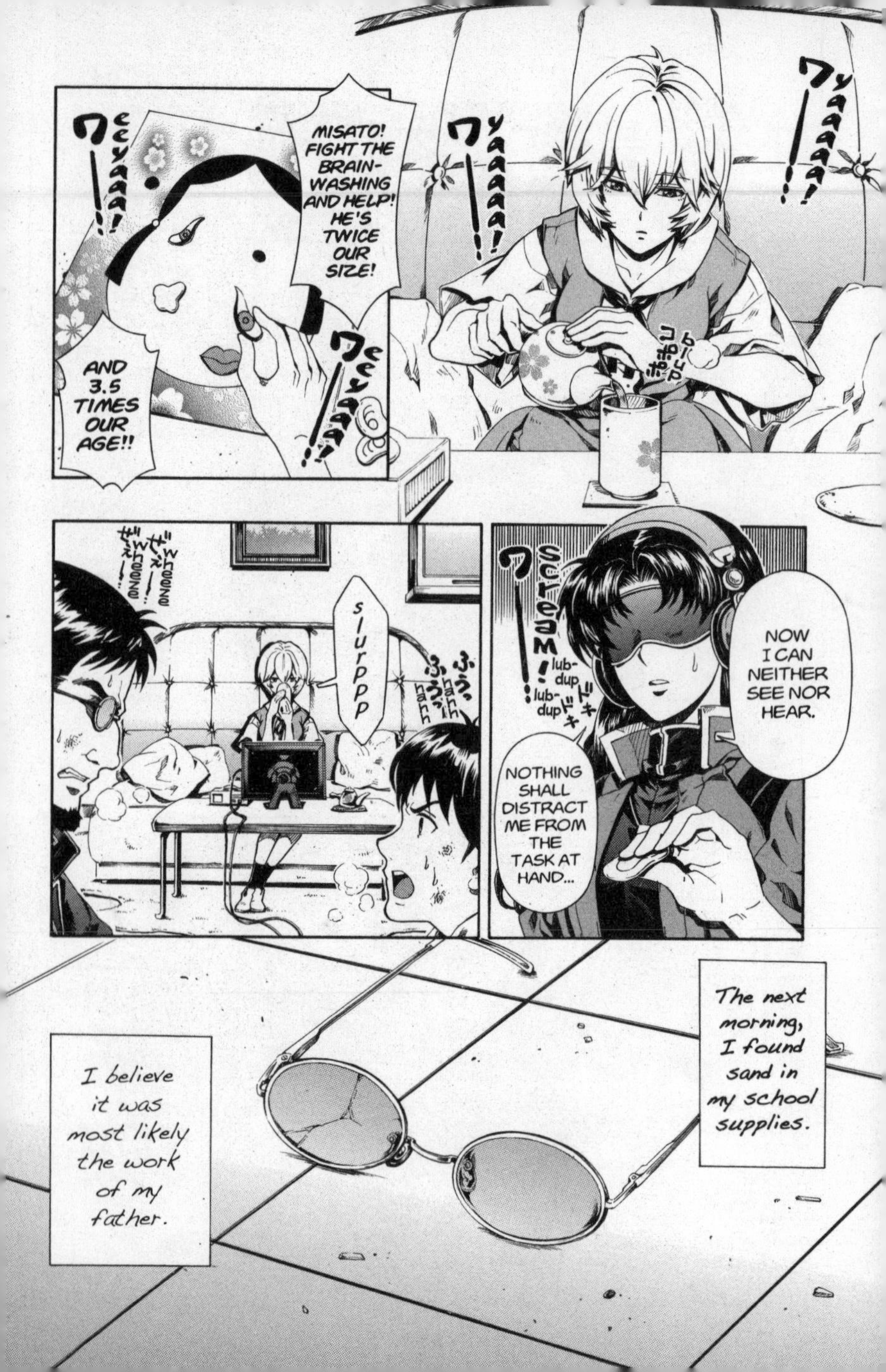
ワyaaaaa!
ワyaaaaa!!
blub-blub
MISATO! FIGHT THE BRAIN-WASHING AND HELP! HE'S TWICE OUR SIZE!
ワeeyaaa!!
ワeeyaaa!!
AND 3.5 TIMES OUR AGE!!
ワscream!!
NOW I CAN NEITHER SEE NOR HEAR.
ドキドキ lub-dup lub-dup
NOTHING SHALL DISTRACT ME FROM THE TASK AT HAND...
ふうっ ふうっ hahn hahn
slurppp
ぜぇ ぜぇ wheeze wheeze
The next morning, I found sand in my school supplies.
I believe it was most likely the work of my father.

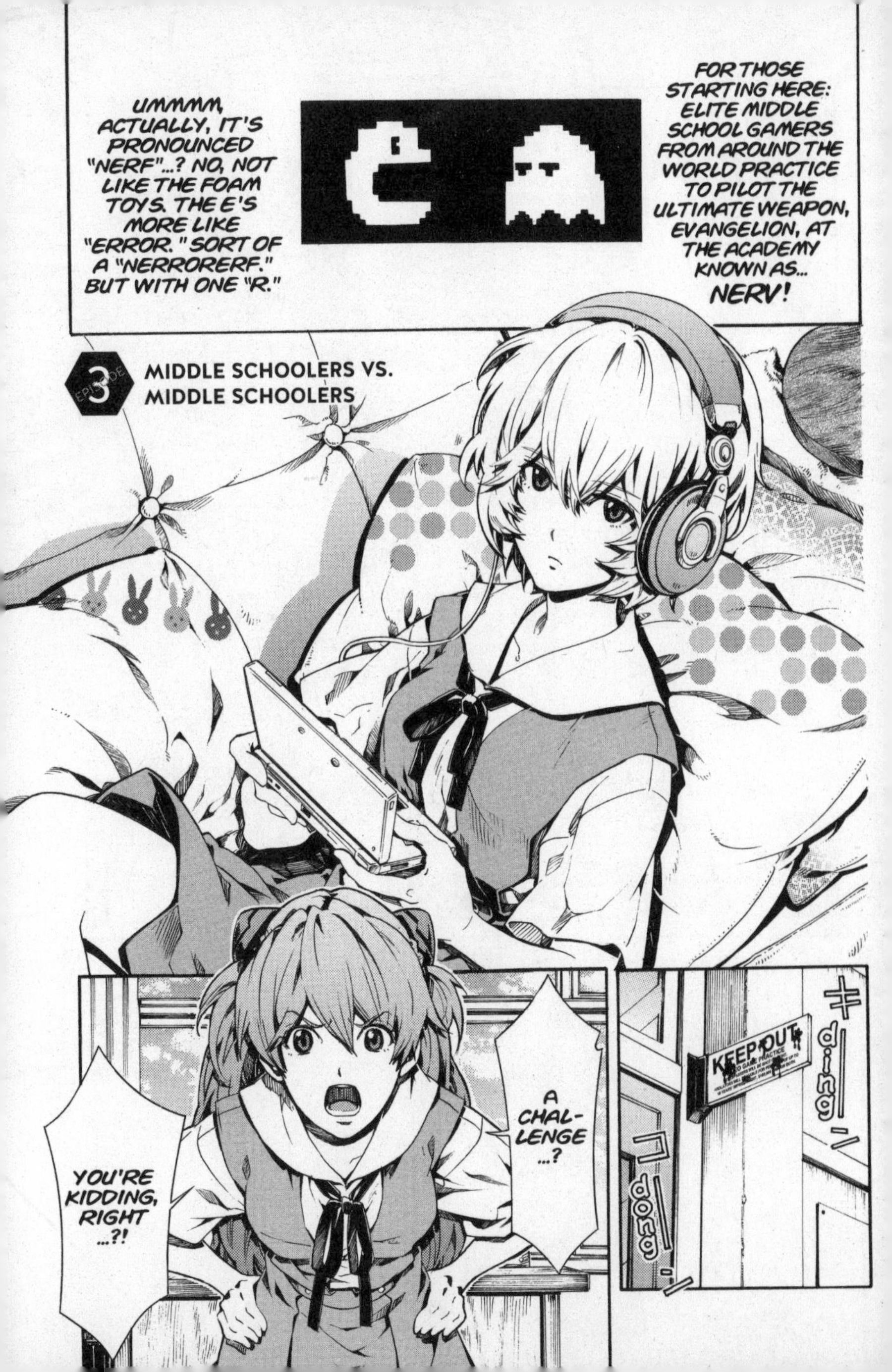
FOR THOSE STARTING HERE: ELITE MIDDLE SCHOOL GAMERS FROM AROUND THE WORLD PRACTICE TO PILOT THE ULTIMATE WEAPON, EVANGELION, AT THE ACADEMY KNOWN AS... NERV!
UMMMM, ACTUALLY, IT'S PRONOUNCED "NERF"...? NO, NOT LIKE THE FOAM TOYS. THE E'S MORE LIKE "ERROR." SORT OF A "NERRORERF." BUT WITH ONE "R."
EPISODE 3
MIDDLE SCHOOLERS VS. MIDDLE SCHOOLERS
KEEP OUT
VIDEO GAME PRACTICE
ding—!
dong—!
A CHAL-LENGE ...?
YOU'RE KIDDING, RIGHT ...?!

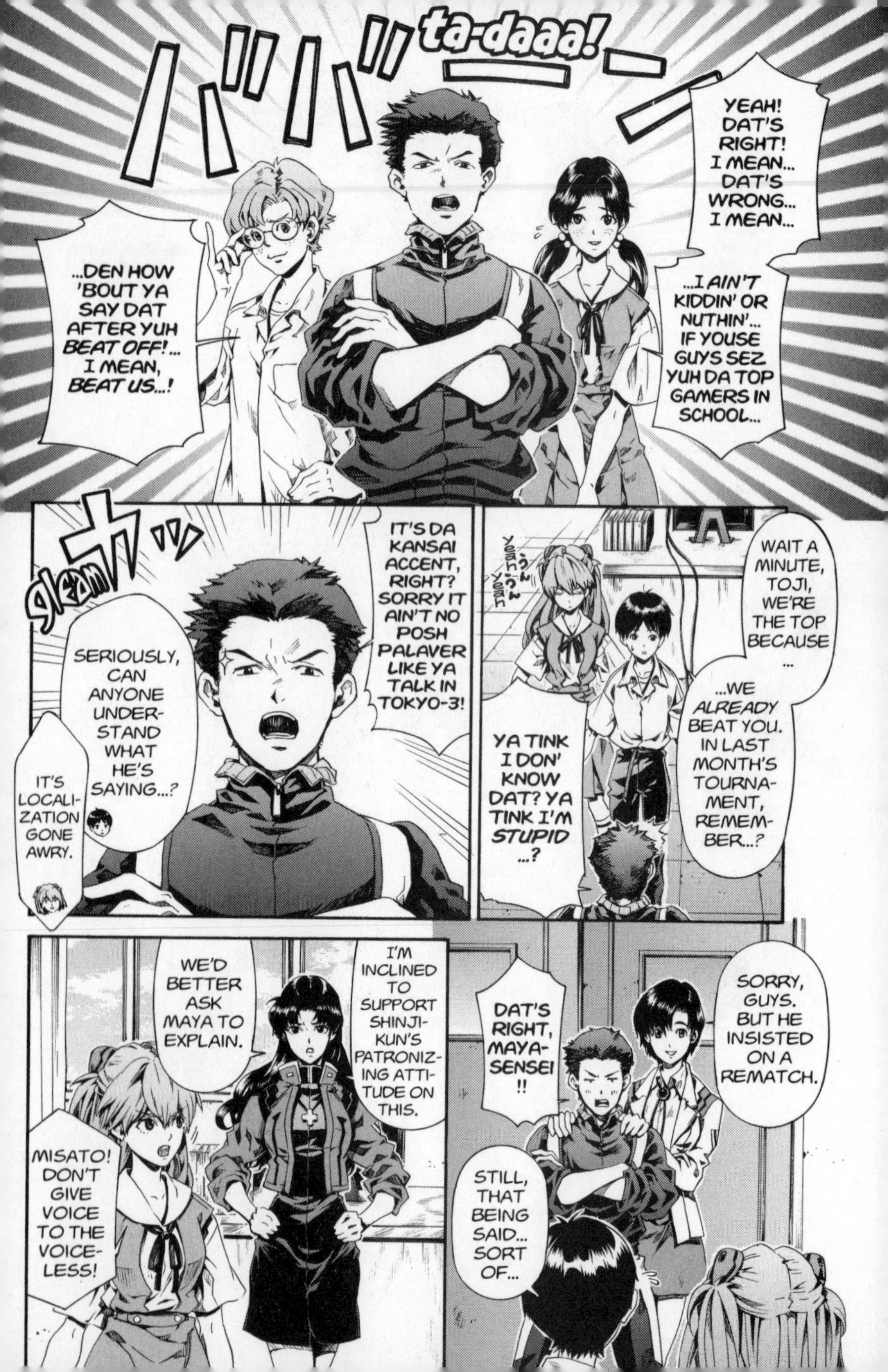
ta-daaa!
YEAH! DAT'S RIGHT! I MEAN... DAT'S WRONG... I MEAN...
...I AIN'T KIDDIN' OR NUTHIN'... IF YOUSE GUYS SEZ YUH DA TOP GAMERS IN SCHOOL...
...DEN HOW 'BOUT YA SAY DAT AFTER YUH BEAT OFF!... I MEAN, BEAT US...!
WAIT A MINUTE, TOJI, WE'RE THE TOP BECAUSE ...
yeah yeah
...WE ALREADY BEAT YOU. IN LAST MONTH'S TOURNAMENT, REMEMBER...?
YA TINK I DON' KNOW DAT? YA TINK I'M STUPID ...?
IT'S DA KANSAI ACCENT, RIGHT? SORRY IT AIN'T NO POSH PALAVER LIKE YA TALK IN TOKYO-3!
gleam
SERIOUSLY, CAN ANYONE UNDERSTAND WHAT HE'S SAYING...?
IT'S LOCALIZATION GONE AWRY.
SORRY, GUYS. BUT HE INSISTED ON A REMATCH.
DAT'S RIGHT, MAYA-SENSEI!!
STILL, THAT BEING SAID... SORT OF...
I'M INCLINED TO SUPPORT SHINJI-KUN'S PATRONIZING ATTITUDE ON THIS.
WE'D BETTER ASK MAYA TO EXPLAIN.
MISATO! DON'T GIVE VOICE TO THE VOICELESS!

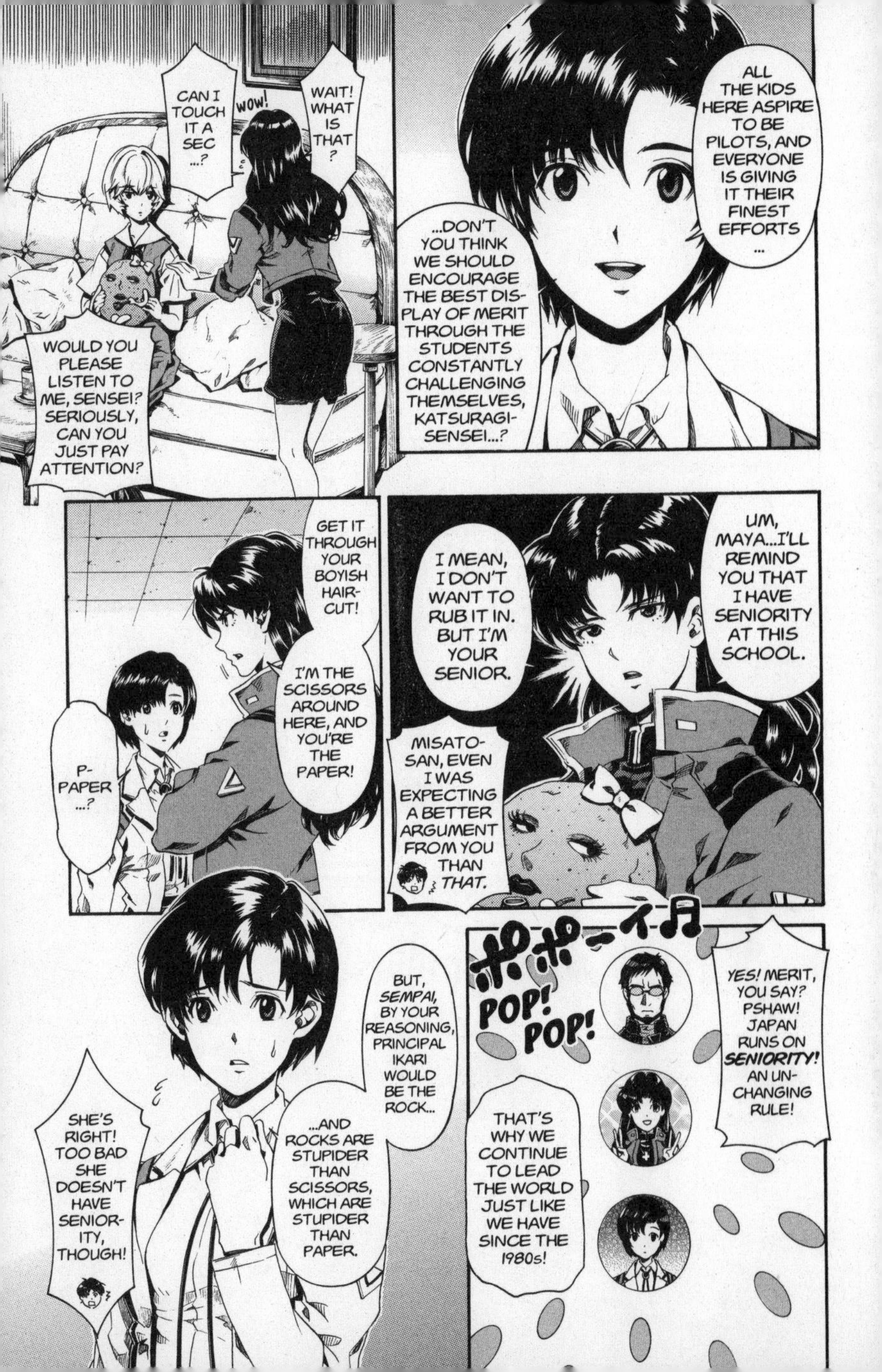
ALL THE KIDS HERE ASPIRE TO BE PILOTS, AND EVERYONE IS GIVING IT THEIR FINEST EFFORTS ...
...DON'T YOU THINK WE SHOULD ENCOURAGE THE BEST DISPLAY OF MERIT THROUGH THE STUDENTS CONSTANTLY CHALLENGING THEMSELVES, KATSURAGI-SENSEI...?
WAIT! WHAT IS THAT?
WOW!
CAN I TOUCH IT A SEC ...?
WOULD YOU PLEASE LISTEN TO ME, SENSEI? SERIOUSLY, CAN YOU JUST PAY ATTENTION?
UM, MAYA...I'LL REMIND YOU THAT I HAVE SENIORITY AT THIS SCHOOL.
I MEAN, I DON'T WANT TO RUB IT IN. BUT I'M YOUR SENIOR.
MISATO-SAN, EVEN I WAS EXPECTING A BETTER ARGUMENT FROM YOU THAN *THAT*.
GET IT THROUGH YOUR BOYISH HAIR-CUT!
I'M THE SCISSORS AROUND HERE, AND YOU'RE THE PAPER!
P-PAPER ...?
ポポーイ♫
POP! POP!
YES! MERIT, YOU SAY? PSHAW! JAPAN RUNS ON ***SENIORITY!*** *AN UN-CHANGING RULE!*
THAT'S WHY WE CONTINUE TO LEAD THE WORLD JUST LIKE WE HAVE SINCE THE 1980s!
BUT, *SEMPAI*, BY YOUR REASONING, PRINCIPAL IKARI WOULD BE THE ROCK...
...AND ROCKS ARE STUPIDER THAN SCISSORS, WHICH ARE STUPIDER THAN PAPER.
SHE'S RIGHT! TOO BAD SHE DOESN'T HAVE SENIOR-ITY, THOUGH!

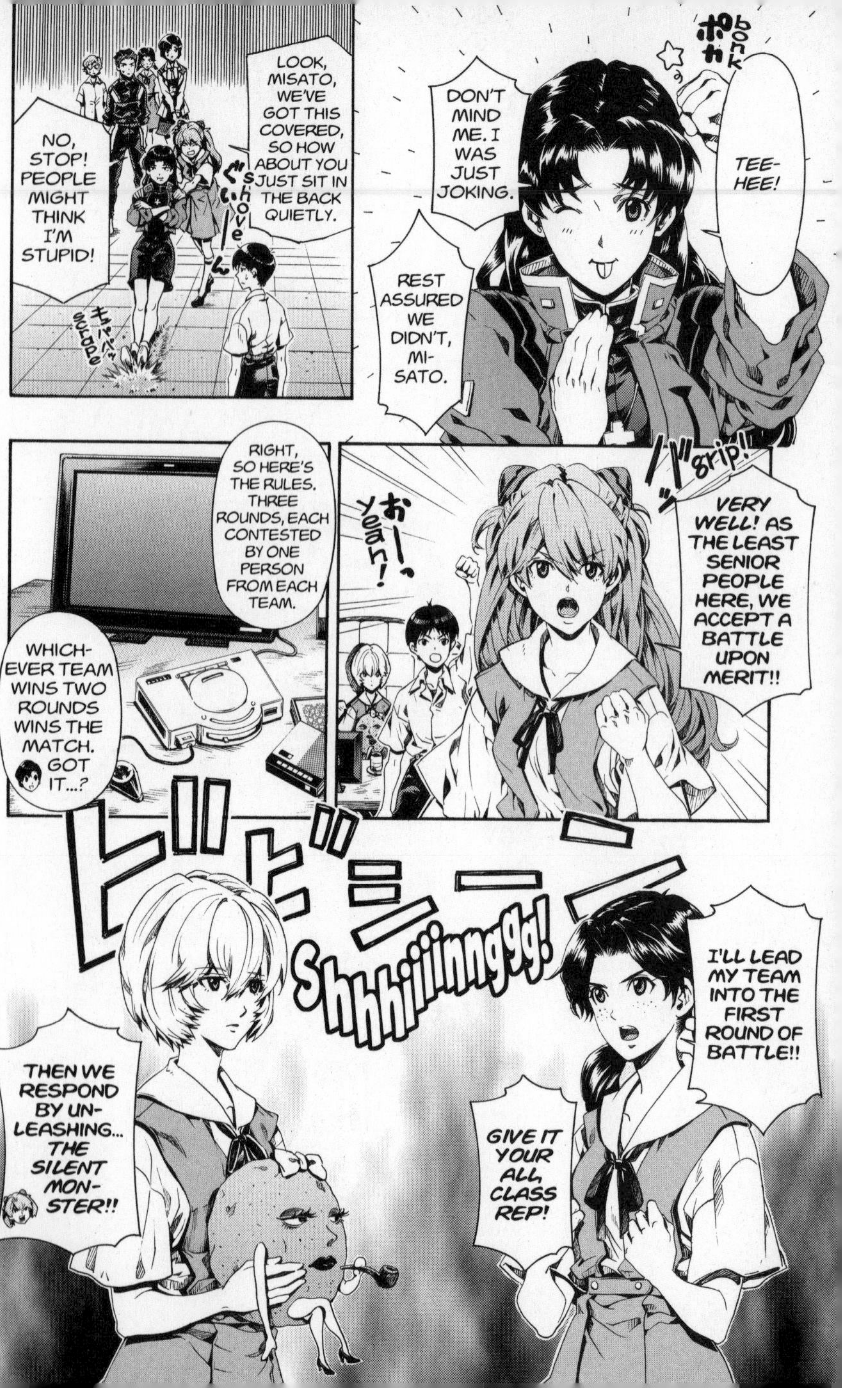
bonk
TEE-HEE!
DON'T MIND ME. I WAS JUST JOKING.
REST ASSURED WE DIDN'T, MISATO.
LOOK, MISATO, WE'VE GOT THIS COVERED, SO HOW ABOUT YOU JUST SIT IN THE BACK QUIETLY.
shove
NO, STOP! PEOPLE MIGHT THINK I'M STUPID!
scrape
grip!!
VERY WELL! AS THE LEAST SENIOR PEOPLE HERE, WE ACCEPT A BATTLE UPON MERIT!!
yeah!
RIGHT, SO HERE'S THE RULES. THREE ROUNDS, EACH CONTESTED BY ONE PERSON FROM EACH TEAM.
WHICHEVER TEAM WINS TWO ROUNDS WINS THE MATCH. GOT IT...?
Shhhiiinnggg!
I'LL LEAD MY TEAM INTO THE FIRST ROUND OF BATTLE!!
GIVE IT YOUR ALL, CLASS REP!
THEN WE RESPOND BY UNLEASHING... THE SILENT MONSTER!!

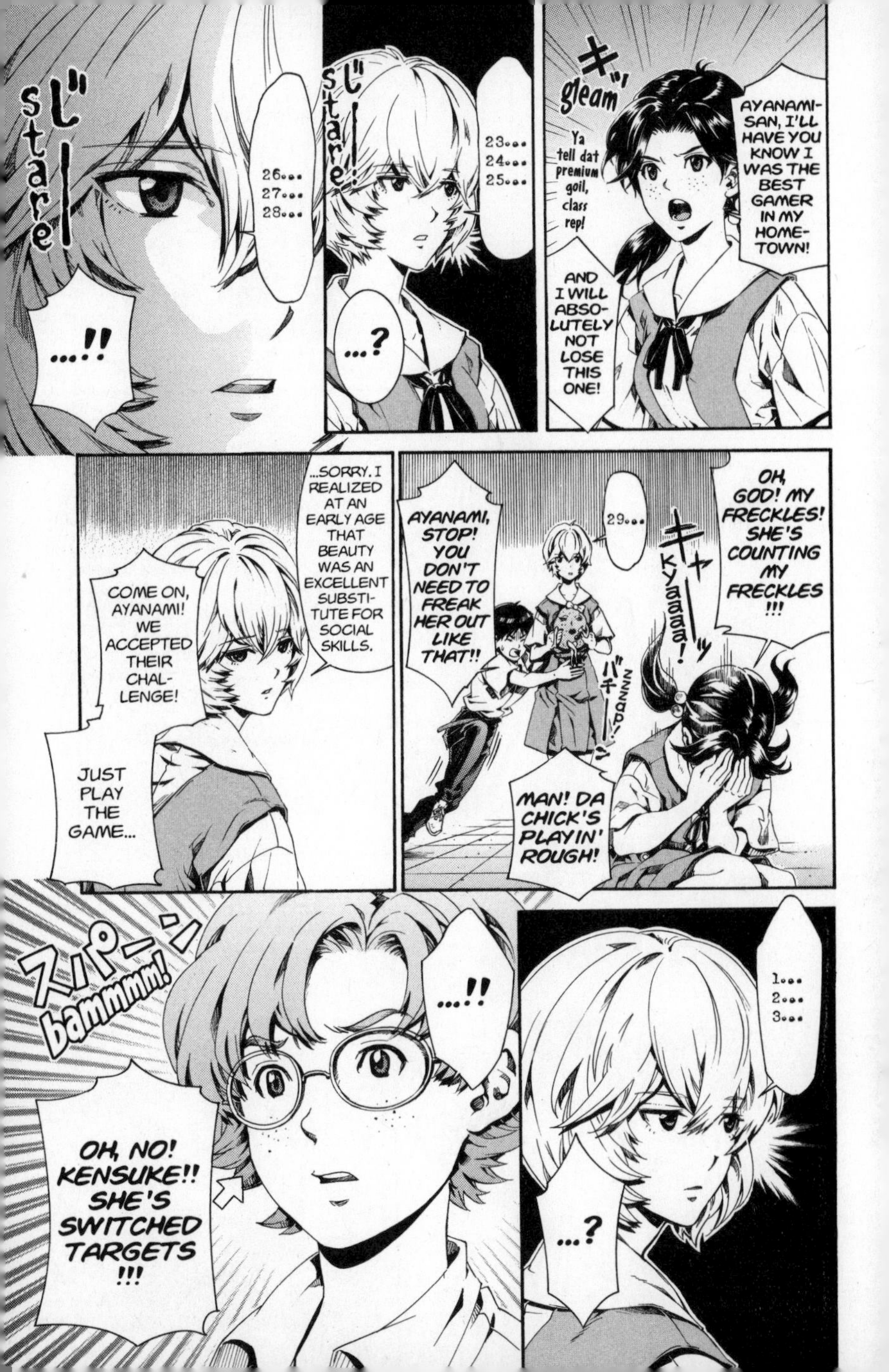
AYANAMI-SAN, I'LL HAVE YOU KNOW I WAS THE BEST GAMER IN MY HOMETOWN!
キッ gleam
Ya tell dat premium goil, class rep!
AND I WILL ABSOLUTELY NOT LOSE THIS ONE!
23... 24... 25...
じーっ stare
...?
26... 27... 28...
じーっ stare
...!!
OH, GOD! MY FRECKLES! SHE'S COUNTING MY FRECKLES!!!
29...
キャ kyaaaa!
AYANAMI, STOP! YOU DON'T NEED TO FREAK HER OUT LIKE THAT!!
バチッ zzzap!
MAN! DA CHICK'S PLAYIN' ROUGH!
...SORRY. I REALIZED AT AN EARLY AGE THAT BEAUTY WAS AN EXCELLENT SUBSTITUTE FOR SOCIAL SKILLS.
COME ON, AYANAMI! WE ACCEPTED THEIR CHALLENGE!
JUST PLAY THE GAME...
1... 2... 3...
...?
...!!
スパーン bammmm!
OH, NO! KENSUKE!! SHE'S SWITCHED TARGETS!!!

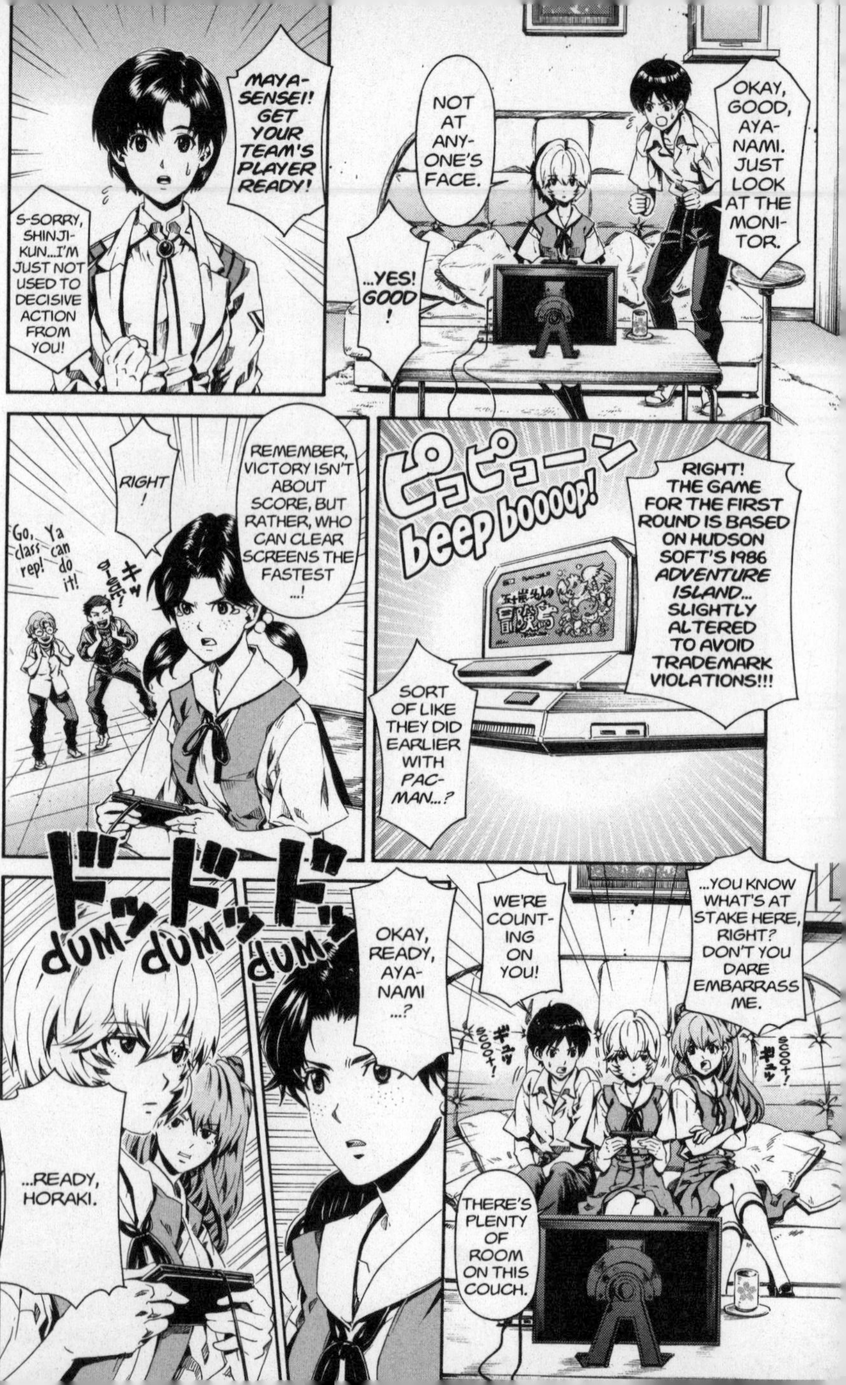

OKAY, GOOD, AYANAMI. JUST LOOK AT THE MONITOR.
NOT AT ANYONE'S FACE.
...YES! GOOD!
MAYA-SENSEI! GET YOUR TEAM'S PLAYER READY!
S-SORRY, SHINJI-KUN...I'M JUST NOT USED TO DECISIVE ACTION FROM YOU!
ぴっぴょーン
beep booooop!
RIGHT! THE GAME FOR THE FIRST ROUND IS BASED ON HUDSON SOFT'S 1986 ADVENTURE ISLAND... SLIGHTLY ALTERED TO AVOID TRADEMARK VIOLATIONS!!!
SORT OF LIKE THEY DID EARLIER WITH PAC-MAN...?
REMEMBER, VICTORY ISN'T ABOUT SCORE, BUT RATHER, WHO CAN CLEAR SCREENS THE FASTEST...!
RIGHT!
Ya can do it!
Go, class rep!
...YOU KNOW WHAT'S AT STAKE HERE, RIGHT? DON'T YOU DARE EMBARRASS ME.
WE'RE COUNTING ON YOU!
ギュッ scoot!
ギュッ scoot!
THERE'S PLENTY OF ROOM ON THIS COUCH.
ドッドッドッ
dum dum dum
OKAY, READY, AYANAMI...?
...READY, HORAKI.

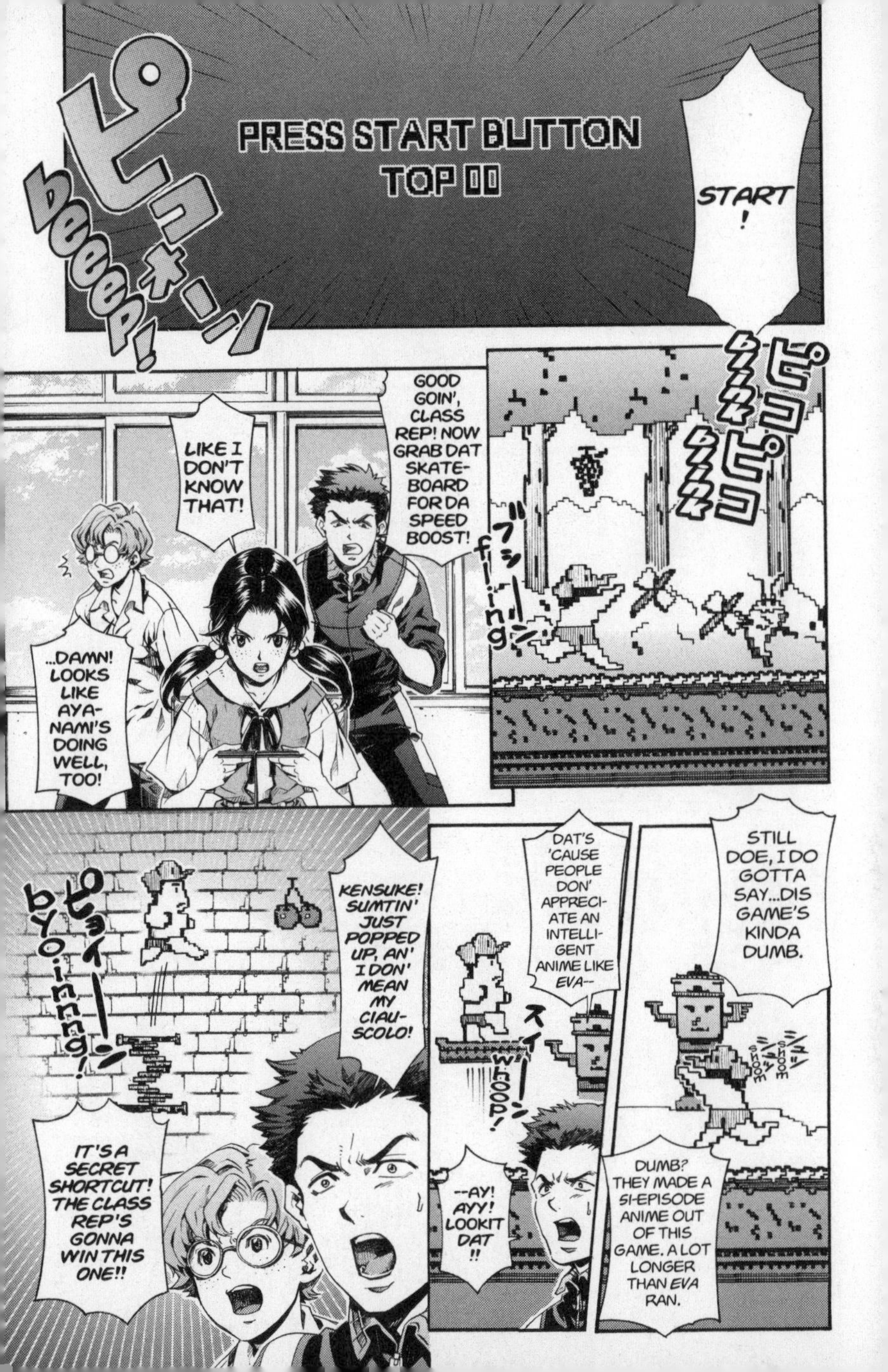
START!
PRESS START BUTTON
TOP 00
ピコオーン
beeep!
ピコピコ
pink pink
GOOD GOIN', CLASS REP! NOW GRAB DAT SKATE-BOARD FOR DA SPEED BOOST!
ブシーッ
fl-i-ing
LIKE I DON'T KNOW THAT!
...DAMN! LOOKS LIKE AYA-NAMI'S DOING WELL, TOO!
STILL DOE, I DO GOTTA SAY...DIS GAME'S KINDA DUMB.
shoom shoom
DUMB? THEY MADE A 51-EPISODE ANIME OUT OF THIS GAME. A LOT LONGER THAN EVA RAN.
DAT'S 'CAUSE PEOPLE DON' APPRECI-ATE AN INTELLI-GENT ANIME LIKE EVA--
スイーッ
whoop!
--AY! AYY! LOOKIT DAT!!
KENSUKE! SUMTIN' JUST POPPED UP, AN' I DON' MEAN MY CIAU-SCOLO!
ピョイーン
byo-inng!
IT'S A SECRET SHORTCUT! THE CLASS REP'S GONNA WIN THIS ONE!!

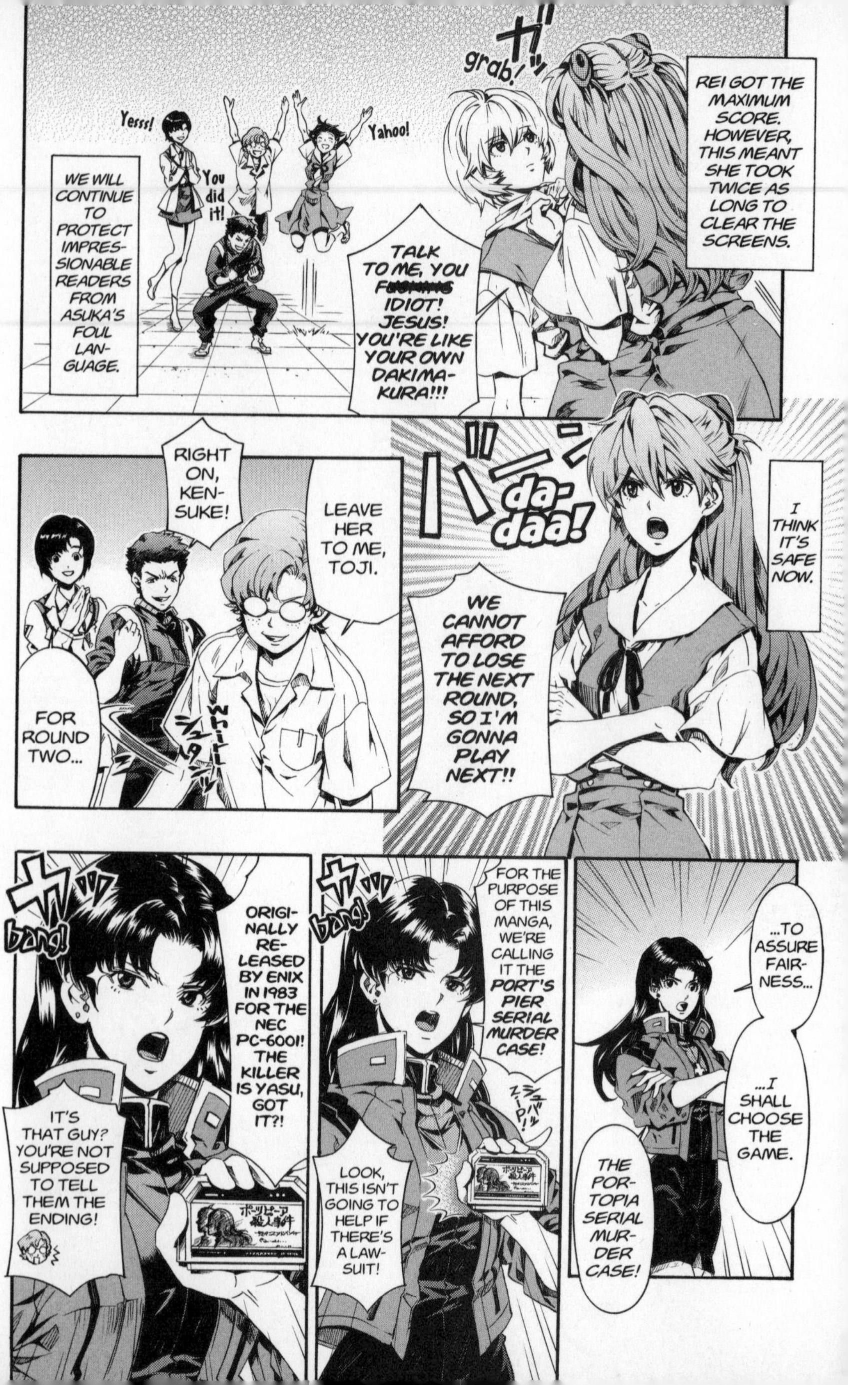

ガッ grab!
REI GOT THE MAXIMUM SCORE. HOWEVER, THIS MEANT SHE TOOK TWICE AS LONG TO CLEAR THE SCREENS.
TALK TO ME, YOU F[redacted] IDIOT! JESUS! YOU'RE LIKE YOUR OWN DAKIMAKURA!!!
Yahoo!
You did it!
Yesss!
WE WILL CONTINUE TO PROTECT IMPRESSIONABLE READERS FROM ASUKA'S FOUL LANGUAGE.
I THINK IT'S SAFE NOW.
da-daa!
WE CANNOT AFFORD TO LOSE THE NEXT ROUND, SO I'M GONNA PLAY NEXT!!
LEAVE HER TO ME, TOJI.
RIGHT ON, KENSUKE!
whirl
FOR ROUND TWO...
...TO ASSURE FAIRNESS...
...I SHALL CHOOSE THE GAME.
THE PORTOPIA SERIAL MURDER CASE!
bang!
FOR THE PURPOSE OF THIS MANGA, WE'RE CALLING IT THE PORT'S PIER SERIAL MURDER CASE!
zip!
LOOK, THIS ISN'T GOING TO HELP IF THERE'S A LAWSUIT!
bang!
ORIGINALLY RELEASED BY ENIX IN 1983 FOR THE NEC PC-6001! THE KILLER IS YASU, GOT IT?!
IT'S THAT GUY? YOU'RE NOT SUPPOSED TO TELL THEM THE ENDING!

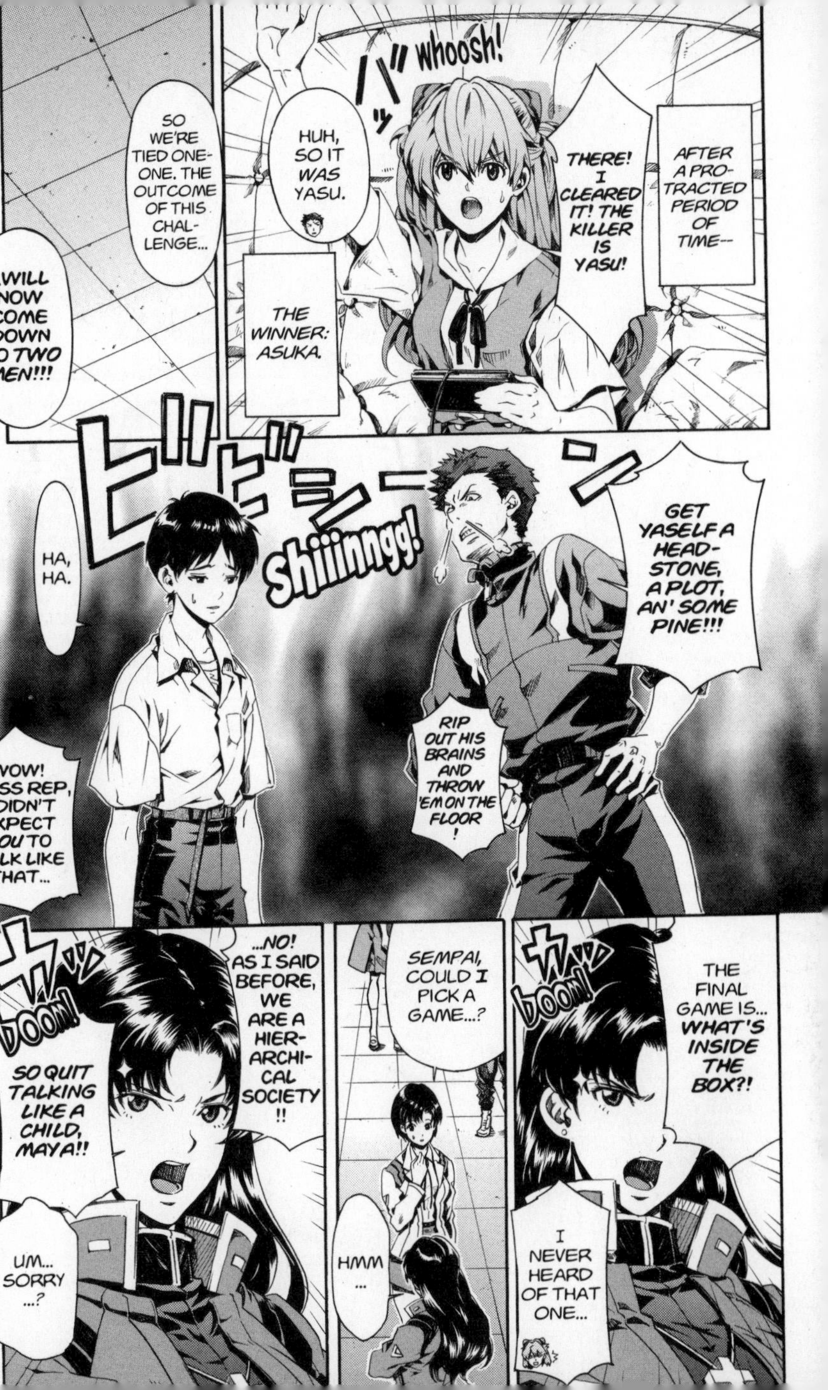
AFTER A PROTRACTED PERIOD OF TIME--
whoosh!
THERE! I CLEARED IT! THE KILLER IS YASU!
HUH, SO IT WAS YASU.
THE WINNER: ASUKA.
SO WE'RE TIED ONE-ONE. THE OUTCOME OF THIS CHALLENGE...
...WILL NOW COME DOWN TO TWO MEN!!!
Shiiinngg!
GET YASELF A HEADSTONE, A PLOT, AN' SOME PINE!!!
RIP OUT HIS BRAINS AND THROW 'EM ON THE FLOOR!
HA, HA.
WOW! CLASS REP, I DIDN'T EXPECT YOU TO TALK LIKE THAT...
boom!
THE FINAL GAME IS... WHAT'S INSIDE THE BOX?!
I NEVER HEARD OF THAT ONE...
SEMPAI, COULD I PICK A GAME...?
HMM...
boom!
...NO! AS I SAID BEFORE, WE ARE A HIERARCHICAL SOCIETY!!
SO QUIT TALKING LIKE A CHILD, MAYA!!
UM... SORRY...?

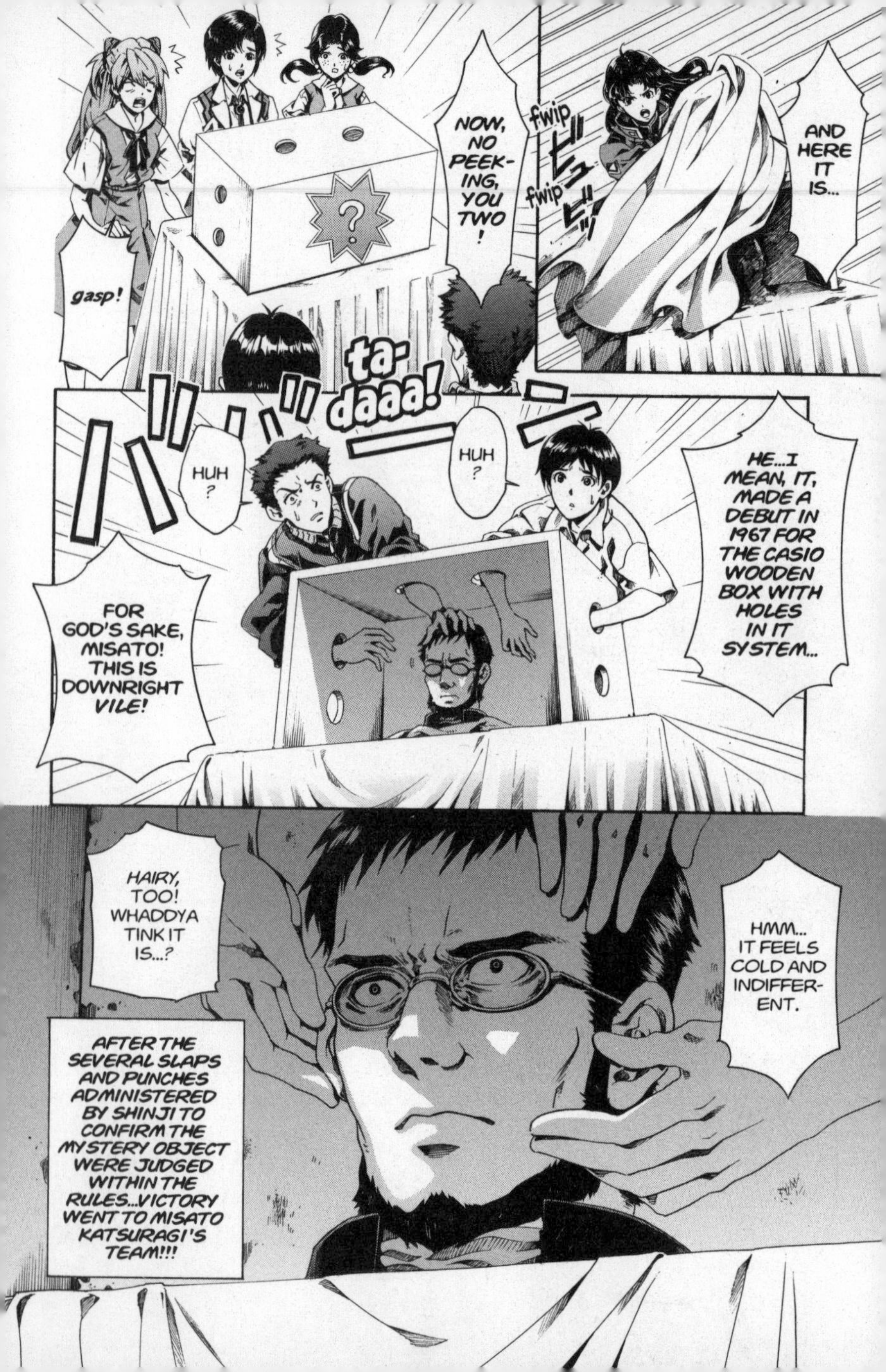
AND HERE IT IS...
fwip
fwip
NOW, NO PEEKING, YOU TWO!
gasp!
ta-daaa!
HE...I MEAN, IT, MADE A DEBUT IN 1967 FOR THE CASIO WOODEN BOX WITH HOLES IN IT SYSTEM...
HUH?
HUH?
FOR GOD'S SAKE, MISATO! THIS IS DOWNRIGHT VILE!
HMM... IT FEELS COLD AND INDIFFERENT.
HAIRY, TOO! WHADDYA TINK IT IS...?
AFTER THE SEVERAL SLAPS AND PUNCHES ADMINISTERED BY SHINJI TO CONFIRM THE MYSTERY OBJECT WERE JUDGED WITHIN THE RULES...VICTORY WENT TO MISATO KATSURAGI'S TEAM!!!

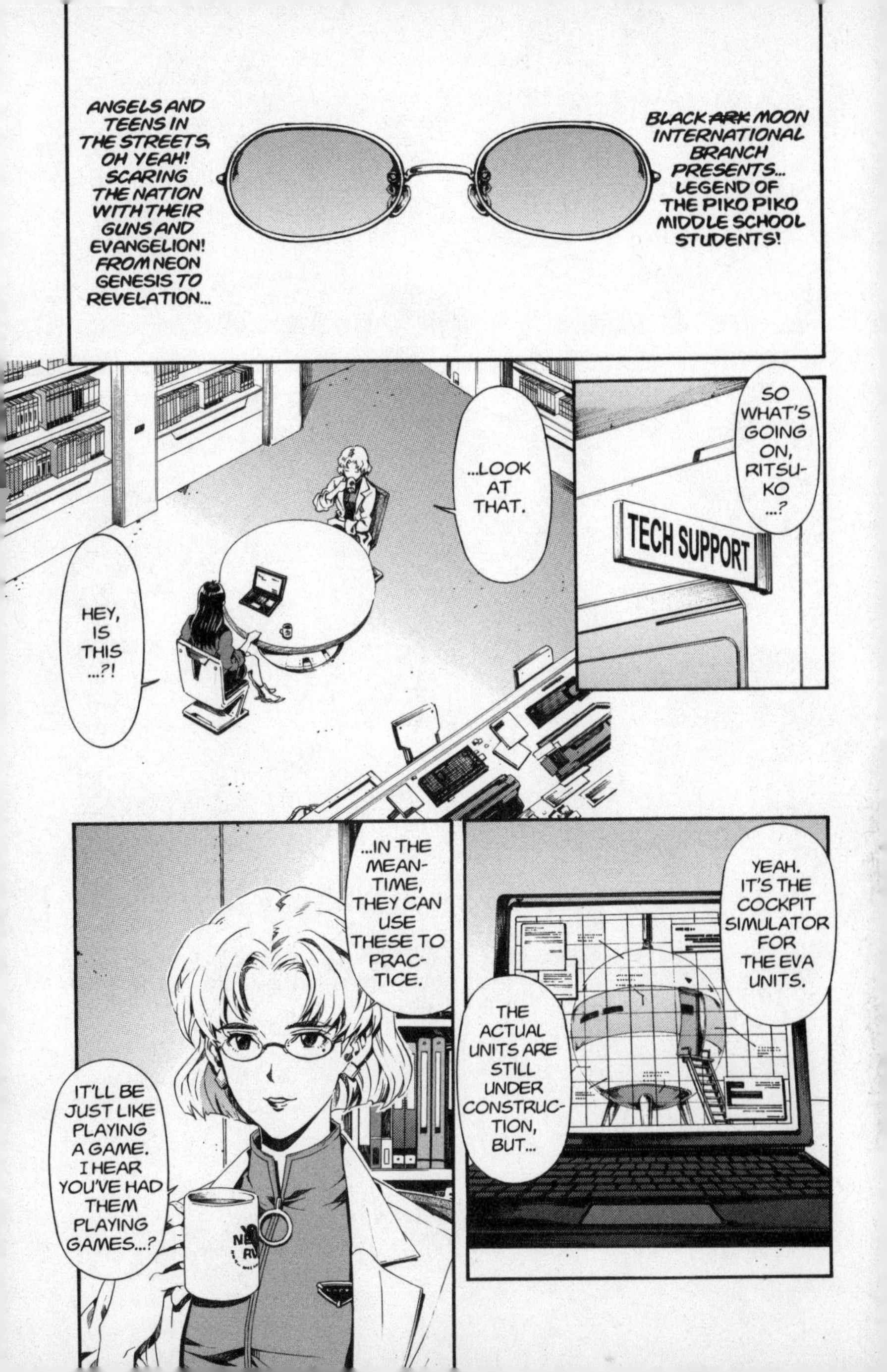
BLACK ARK MOON INTERNATIONAL BRANCH PRESENTS... LEGEND OF THE PIKO PIKO MIDDLE SCHOOL STUDENTS!
ANGELS AND TEENS IN THE STREETS, OH YEAH! SCARING THE NATION WITH THEIR GUNS AND EVANGELION! FROM NEON GENESIS TO REVELATION...
SO WHAT'S GOING ON, RITSUKO...?
TECH SUPPORT
...LOOK AT THAT.
HEY, IS THIS...?!
YEAH. IT'S THE COCKPIT SIMULATOR FOR THE EVA UNITS.
THE ACTUAL UNITS ARE STILL UNDER CONSTRUCTION, BUT...
...IN THE MEANTIME, THEY CAN USE THESE TO PRACTICE.
IT'LL BE JUST LIKE PLAYING A GAME. I HEAR YOU'VE HAD THEM PLAYING GAMES...?

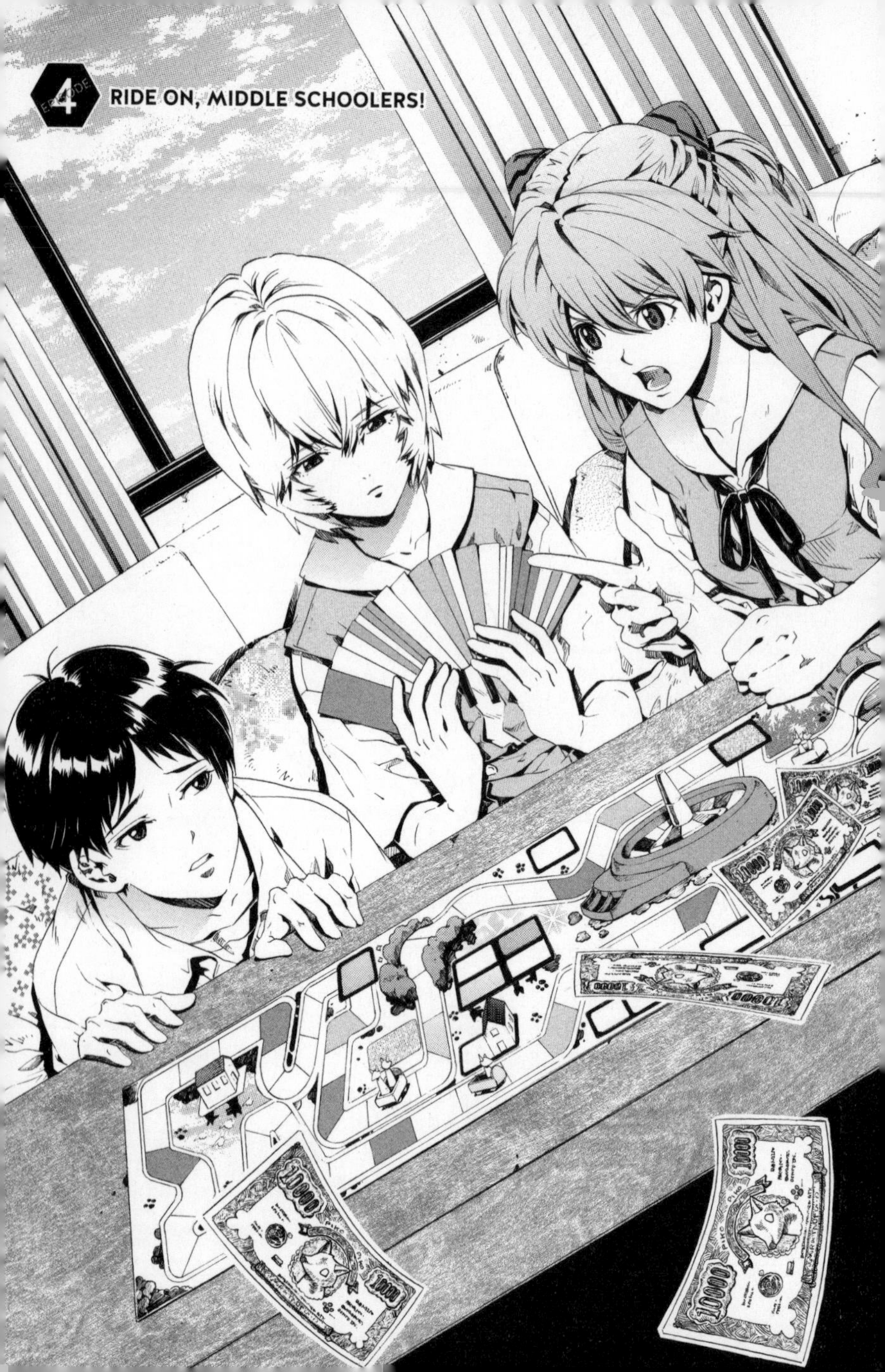
EPISODE
4
RIDE ON, MIDDLE SCHOOLERS!

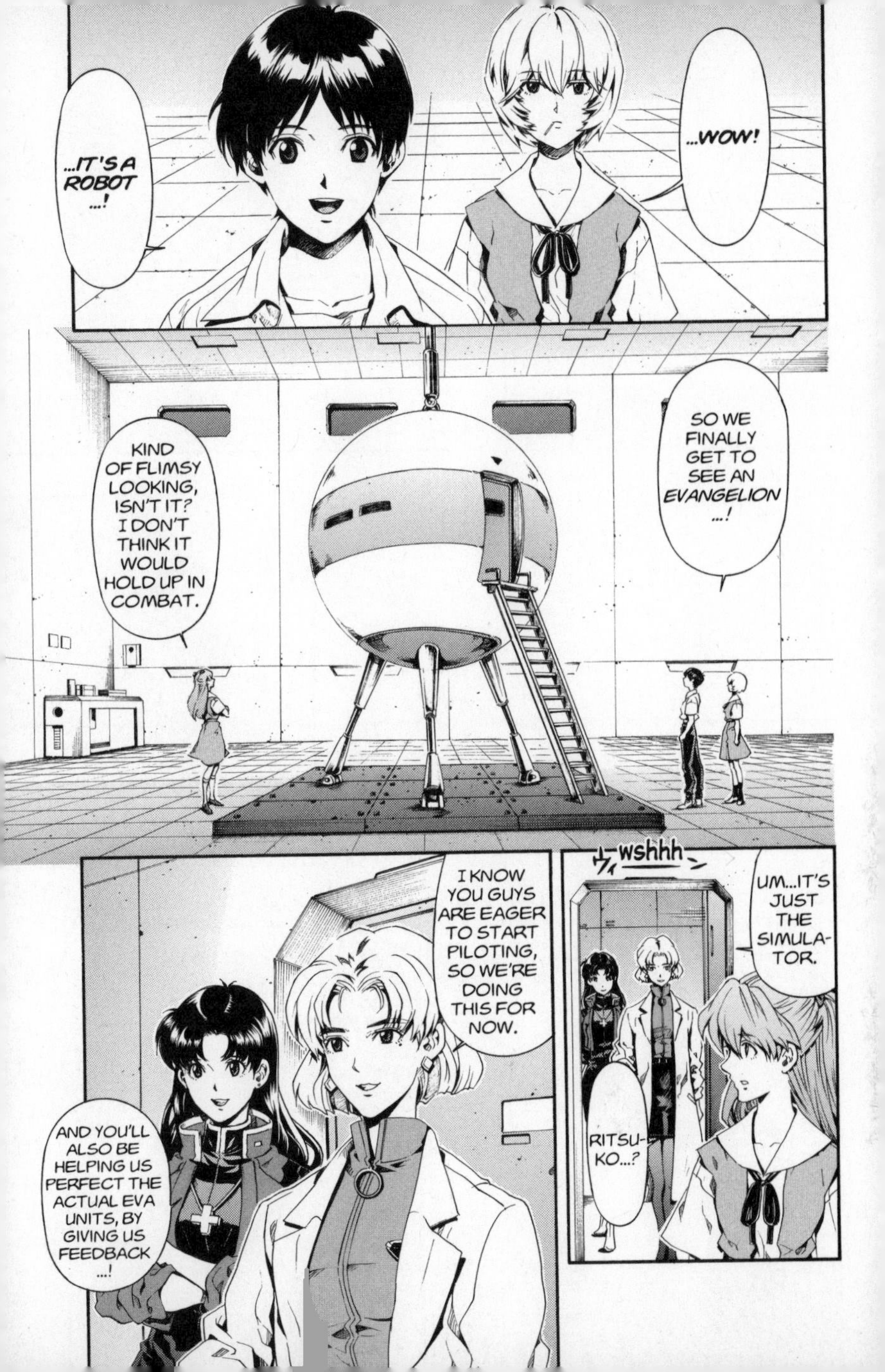
...WOW!
...IT'S A ROBOT ...!
SO WE FINALLY GET TO SEE AN EVANGELION ...!
KIND OF FLIMSY LOOKING, ISN'T IT? I DON'T THINK IT WOULD HOLD UP IN COMBAT.
wshhh
UM...IT'S JUST THE SIMULA-TOR.
RITSU-KO...?
I KNOW YOU GUYS ARE EAGER TO START PILOTING, SO WE'RE DOING THIS FOR NOW.
AND YOU'LL ALSO BE HELPING US PERFECT THE ACTUAL EVA UNITS, BY GIVING US FEEDBACK ...!

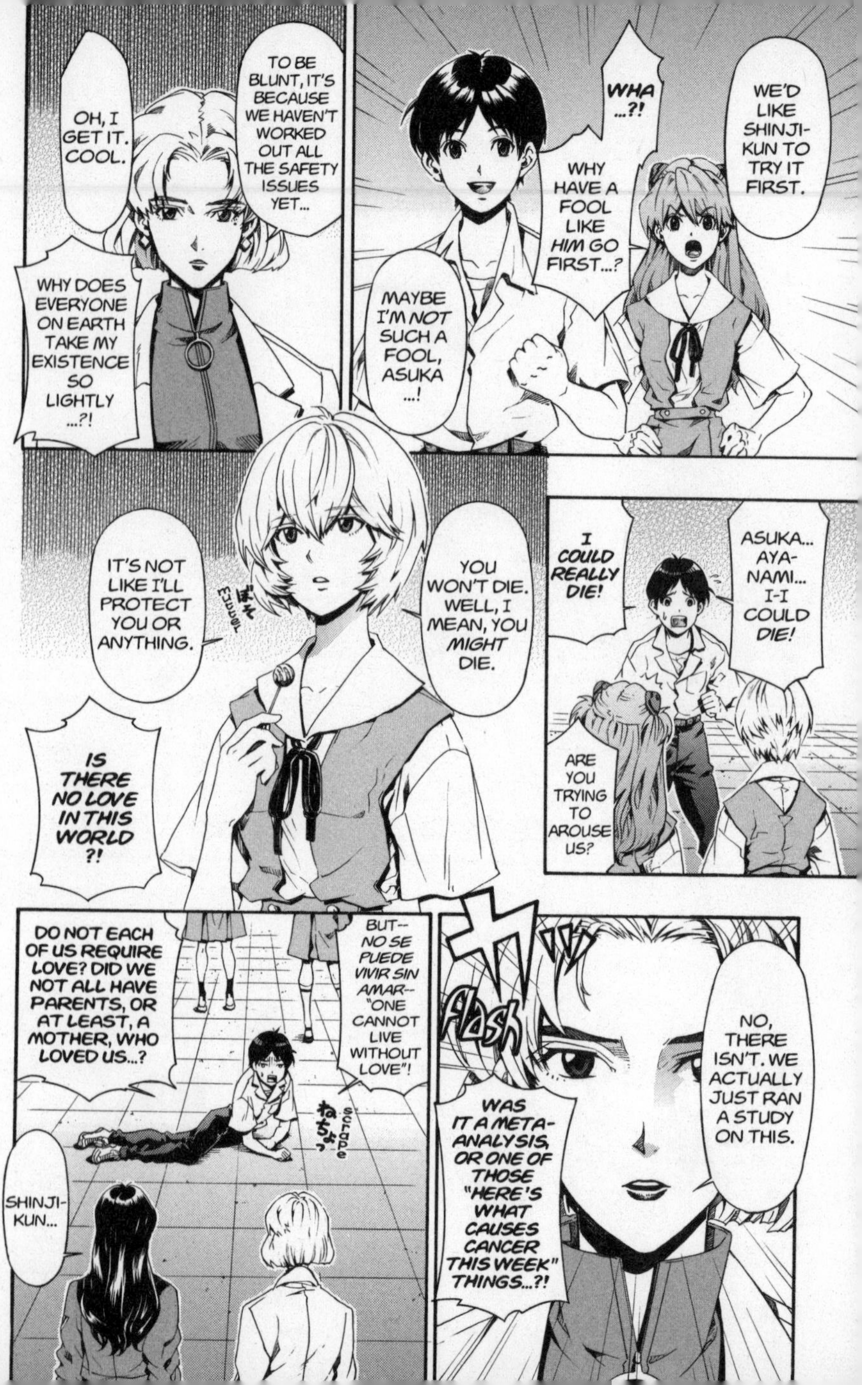
WE'D LIKE SHINJI-KUN TO TRY IT FIRST.
WHA ...?!
WHY HAVE A FOOL LIKE HIM GO FIRST...?
MAYBE I'M NOT SUCH A FOOL, ASUKA ...!
TO BE BLUNT, IT'S BECAUSE WE HAVEN'T WORKED OUT ALL THE SAFETY ISSUES YET...
OH, I GET IT. COOL.
WHY DOES EVERYONE ON EARTH TAKE MY EXISTENCE SO LIGHTLY ...?!
ASUKA... AYA-NAMI... I-I COULD DIE!
I COULD REALLY DIE!
ARE YOU TRYING TO AROUSE US?
YOU WON'T DIE. WELL, I MEAN, YOU MIGHT DIE.
ぼそ mutter
IT'S NOT LIKE I'LL PROTECT YOU OR ANYTHING.
IS THERE NO LOVE IN THIS WORLD ?!
flash
NO, THERE ISN'T. WE ACTUALLY JUST RAN A STUDY ON THIS.
WAS IT A META-ANALYSIS, OR ONE OF THOSE "HERE'S WHAT CAUSES CANCER THIS WEEK" THINGS...?!
BUT-- NO SE PUEDE VIVIR SIN AMAR-- "ONE CANNOT LIVE WITHOUT LOVE"!
DO NOT EACH OF US REQUIRE LOVE? DID WE NOT ALL HAVE PARENTS, OR AT LEAST, A MOTHER, WHO LOVED US...?
ねちょっ scrape
SHINJI-KUN...

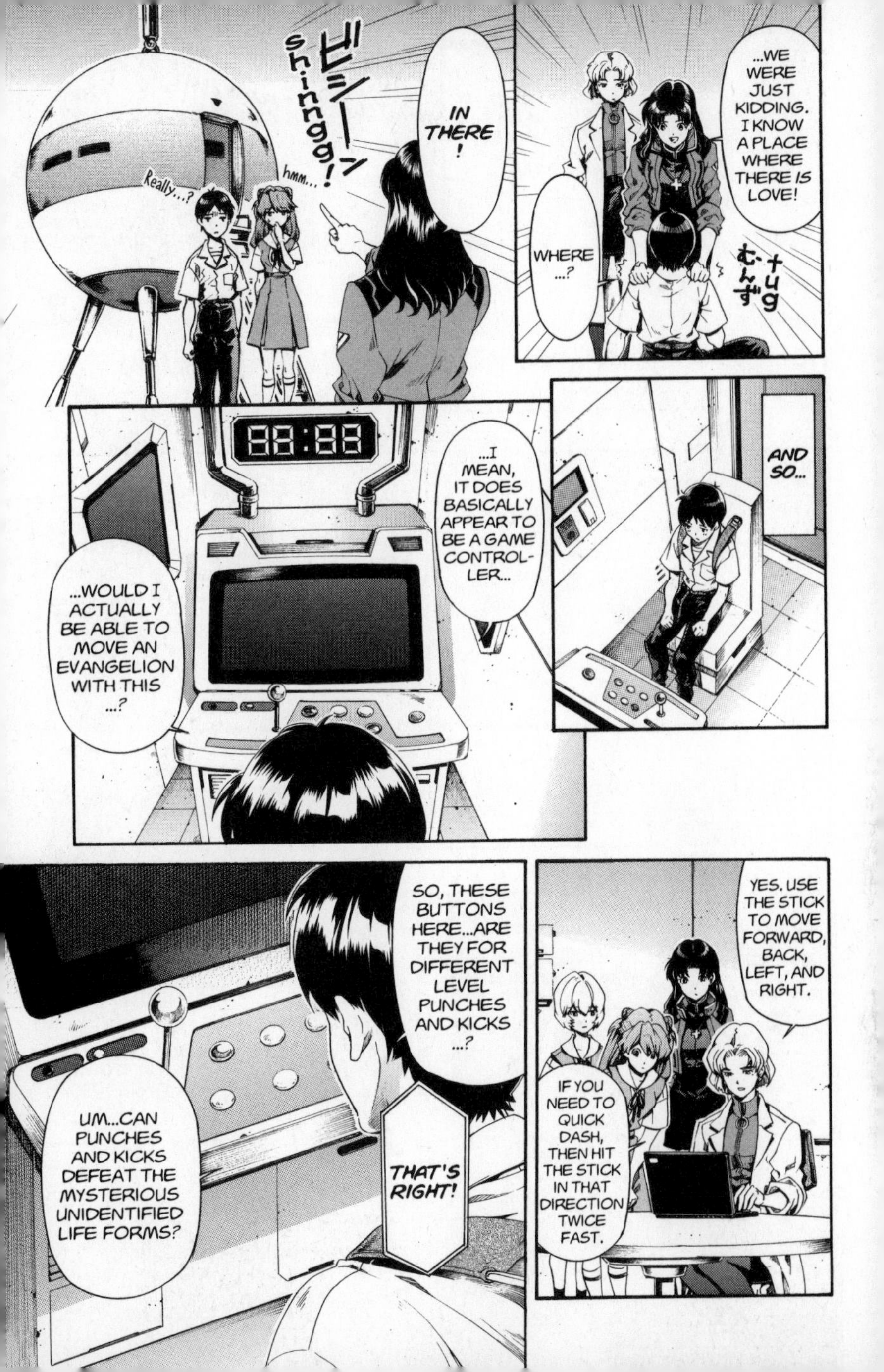
...WE WERE JUST KIDDING. I KNOW A PLACE WHERE THERE IS LOVE!
WHERE ...?
むんず tug
IN THERE!
ビシーン shinnggg!
hmm...
Really...?
AND SO...
...I MEAN, IT DOES BASICALLY APPEAR TO BE A GAME CONTROLLER...
...WOULD I ACTUALLY BE ABLE TO MOVE AN EVANGELION WITH THIS ...?
YES. USE THE STICK TO MOVE FORWARD, BACK, LEFT, AND RIGHT.
IF YOU NEED TO QUICK DASH, THEN HIT THE STICK IN THAT DIRECTION TWICE FAST.
SO, THESE BUTTONS HERE...ARE THEY FOR DIFFERENT LEVEL PUNCHES AND KICKS ...?
THAT'S RIGHT!
UM...CAN PUNCHES AND KICKS DEFEAT THE MYSTERIOUS UNIDENTIFIED LIFE FORMS?

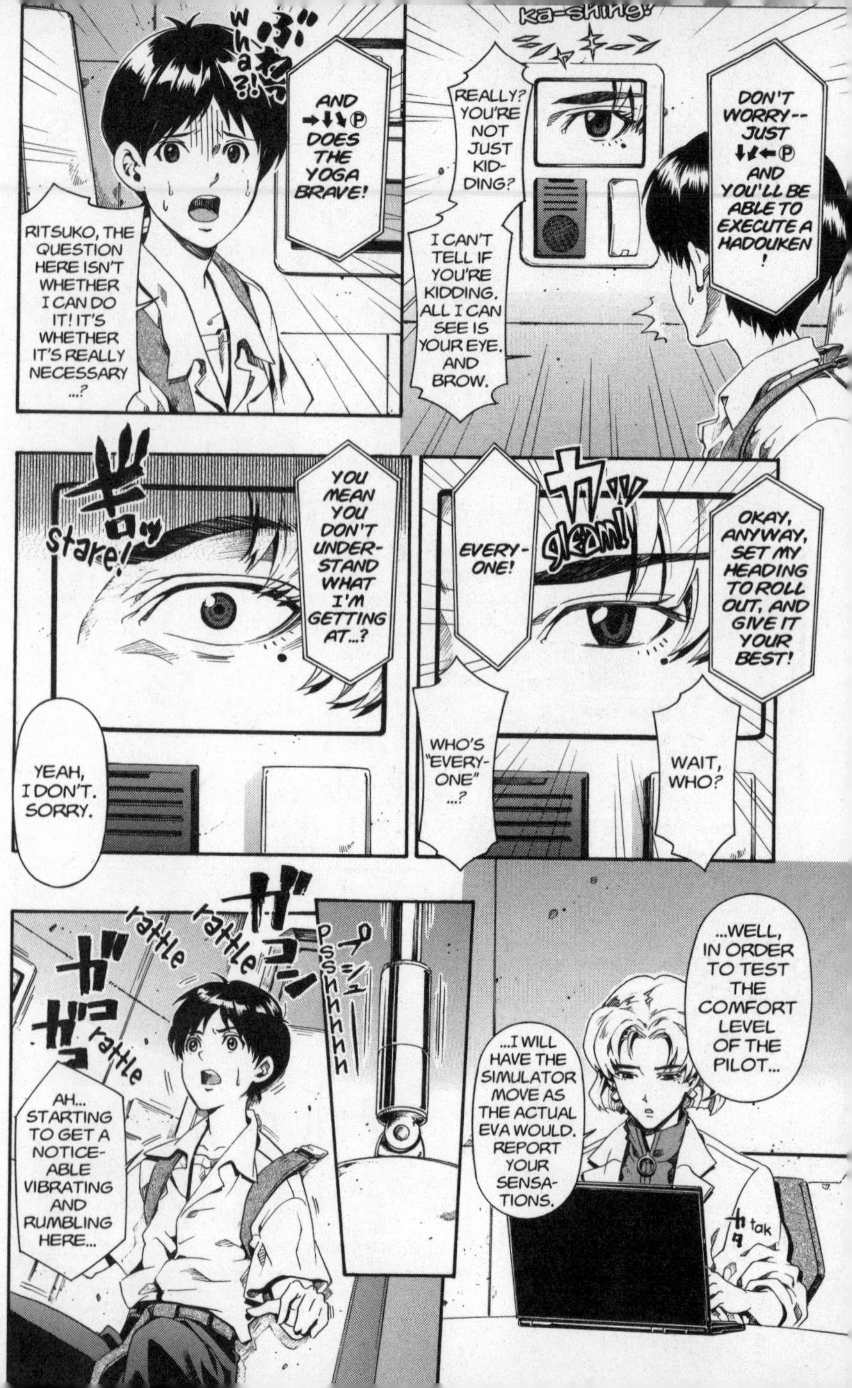
ka-shing!
DON'T WORRY-- JUST ↓↙←Ⓟ AND YOU'LL BE ABLE TO EXECUTE A HADOUKEN!
REALLY? YOU'RE NOT JUST KID-DING?
I CAN'T TELL IF YOU'RE KIDDING. ALL I CAN SEE IS YOUR EYE. AND BROW.
wha?!
AND →↓↘Ⓟ DOES THE YOGA BRAVE!
RITSUKO, THE QUESTION HERE ISN'T WHETHER I CAN DO IT! IT'S WHETHER IT'S REALLY NECESSARY ...?
gleam!
OKAY, ANYWAY, SET MY HEADING TO ROLL OUT, AND GIVE IT YOUR BEST!
EVERY-ONE!
WAIT, WHO?
WHO'S "EVERY-ONE" ...?
stare!
YOU MEAN YOU DON'T UNDER-STAND WHAT I'M GETTING AT...?
YEAH, I DON'T. SORRY.
...WELL, IN ORDER TO TEST THE COMFORT LEVEL OF THE PILOT...
...I WILL HAVE THE SIMULATOR MOVE AS THE ACTUAL EVA WOULD. REPORT YOUR SENSATIONS.
tak
psshhhhhhh
rattle
rattle
rattle
AH... STARTING TO GET A NOTICE-ABLE VIBRATING AND RUMBLING HERE...

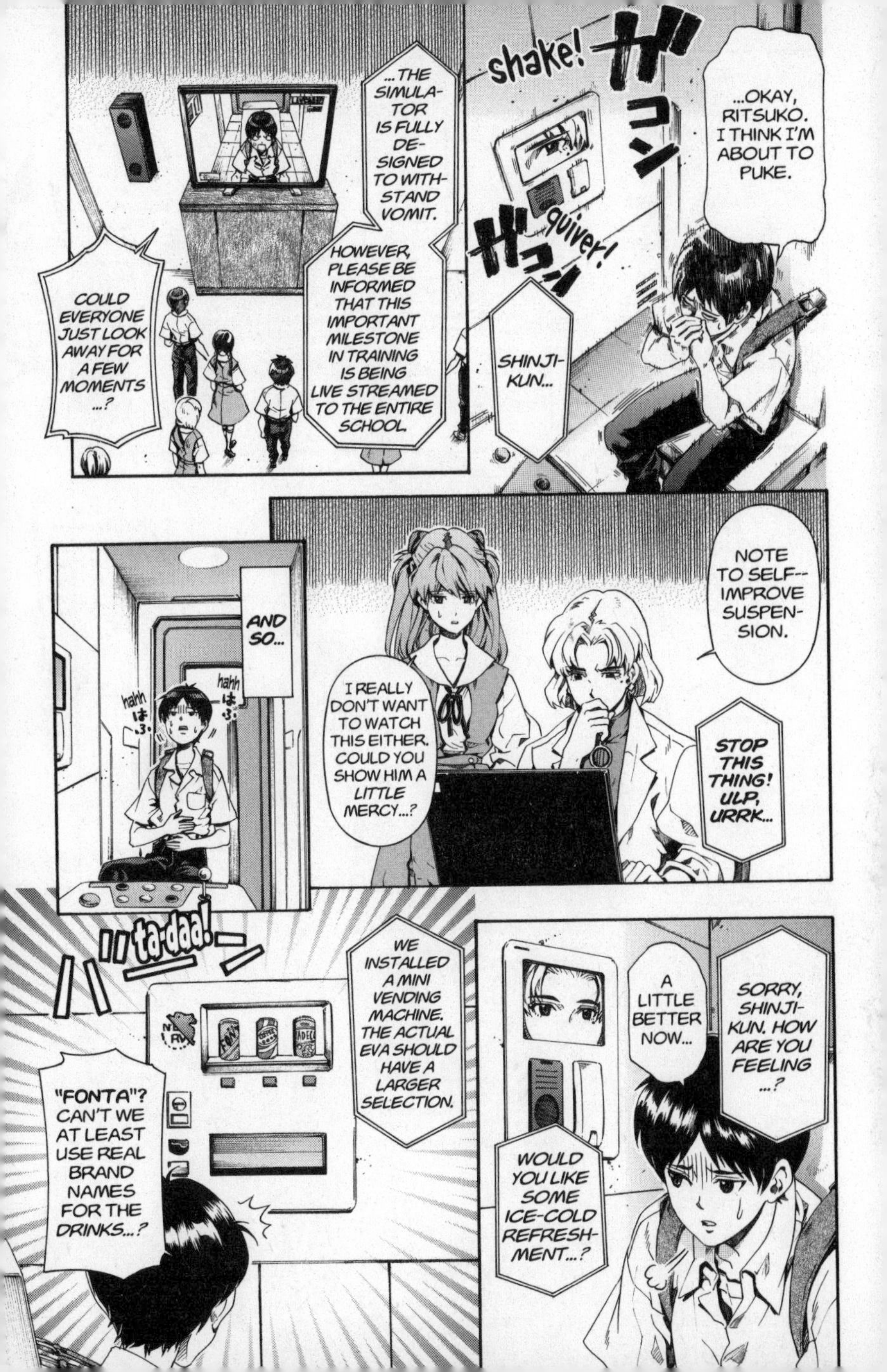
...OKAY, RITSUKO. I THINK I'M ABOUT TO PUKE.
shake!
ガコン
quiver!
ガコッ
SHINJI-KUN...
...THE SIMULATOR IS FULLY DESIGNED TO WITHSTAND VOMIT.
HOWEVER, PLEASE BE INFORMED THAT THIS IMPORTANT MILESTONE IN TRAINING IS BEING LIVE STREAMED TO THE ENTIRE SCHOOL.
COULD EVERYONE JUST LOOK AWAY FOR A FEW MOMENTS ...?
NOTE TO SELF-- IMPROVE SUSPENSION.
STOP THIS THING! ULP, URRK...
I REALLY DON'T WANT TO WATCH THIS EITHER. COULD YOU SHOW HIM A LITTLE MERCY...?
AND SO...
hahh はぁ
hahh はぁ
SORRY, SHINJI-KUN. HOW ARE YOU FEELING ...?
A LITTLE BETTER NOW...
WOULD YOU LIKE SOME ICE-COLD REFRESHMENT...?
ta-daa!
WE INSTALLED A MINI VENDING MACHINE. THE ACTUAL EVA SHOULD HAVE A LARGER SELECTION.
"FONTA"? CAN'T WE AT LEAST USE REAL BRAND NAMES FOR THE DRINKS...?

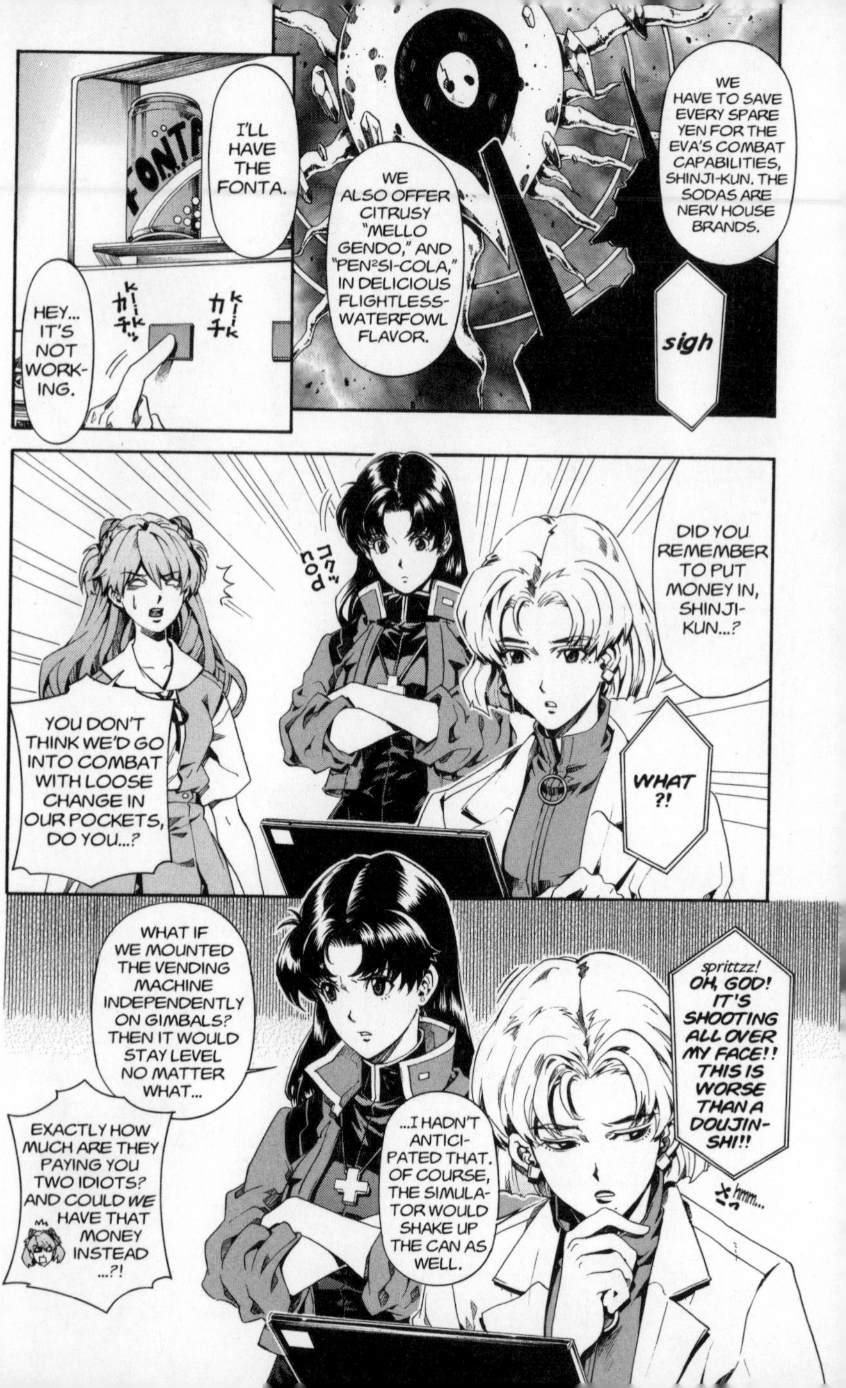
WE HAVE TO SAVE EVERY SPARE YEN FOR THE EVA'S COMBAT CAPABILITIES, SHINJI-KUN. THE SODAS ARE NERV HOUSE BRANDS.
sigh
WE ALSO OFFER CITRUSY "MELLO GENDO," AND "PEN²SI-COLA," IN DELICIOUS FLIGHTLESS-WATERFOWL FLAVOR.
FONTA
I'LL HAVE THE FONTA.
HEY... IT'S NOT WORKING.
DID YOU REMEMBER TO PUT MONEY IN, SHINJI-KUN...?
WHAT ?!
nod
YOU DON'T THINK WE'D GO INTO COMBAT WITH LOOSE CHANGE IN OUR POCKETS, DO YOU...?
spritzzz! OH, GOD! IT'S SHOOTING ALL OVER MY FACE!! THIS IS WORSE THAN A DOUJINSHI!!
hmm...
...I HADN'T ANTICIPATED THAT. OF COURSE, THE SIMULATOR WOULD SHAKE UP THE CAN AS WELL.
WHAT IF WE MOUNTED THE VENDING MACHINE INDEPENDENTLY ON GIMBALS? THEN IT WOULD STAY LEVEL NO MATTER WHAT...
EXACTLY HOW MUCH ARE THEY PAYING YOU TWO IDIOTS? AND COULD WE HAVE THAT MONEY INSTEAD ...?!

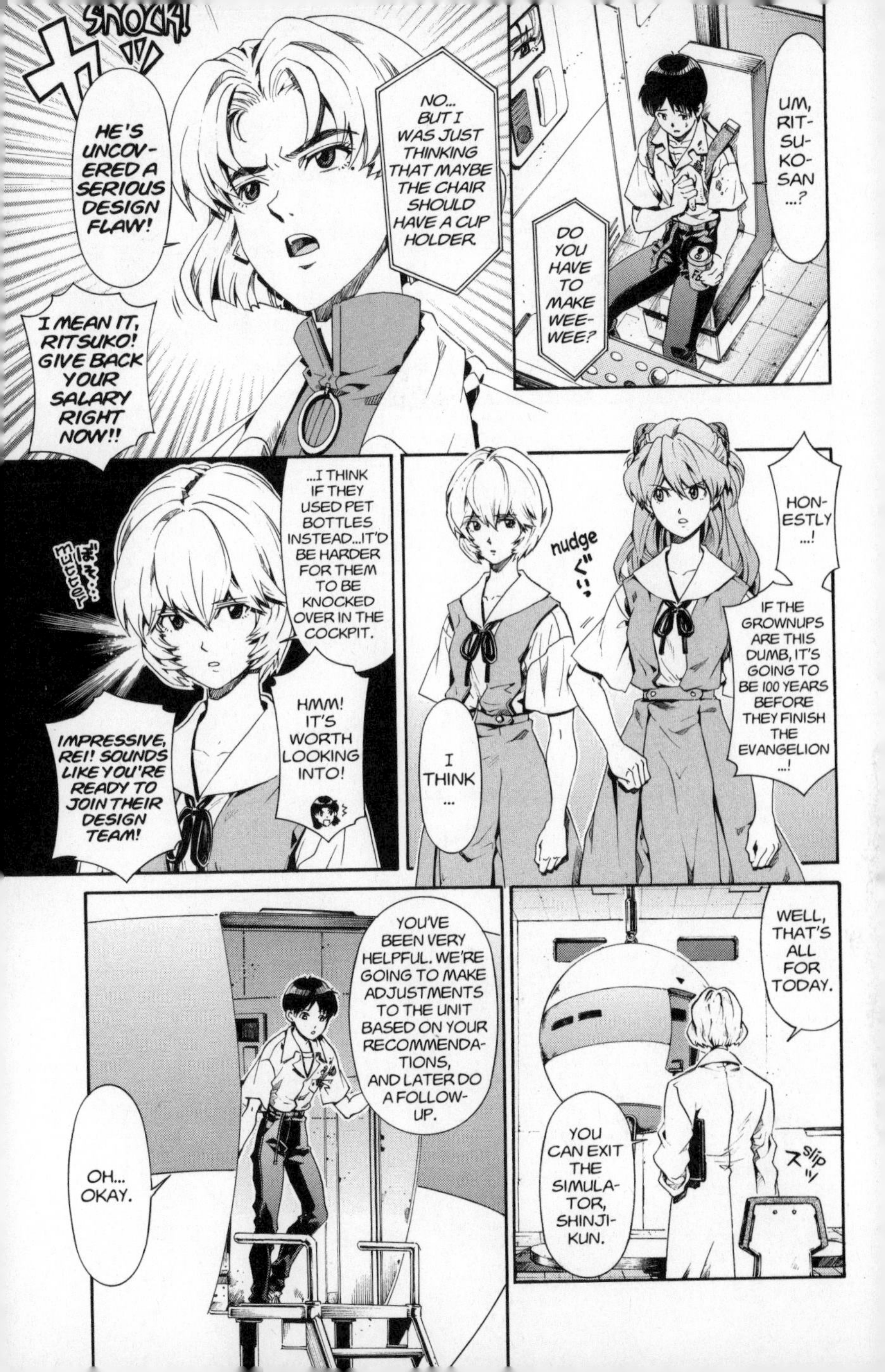

UM, RITSUKO-SAN...?
DO YOU HAVE TO MAKE WEE-WEE?
NO... BUT I WAS JUST THINKING THAT MAYBE THE CHAIR SHOULD HAVE A CUP HOLDER.
SHOCK!
HE'S UNCOVERED A SERIOUS DESIGN FLAW!
I MEAN IT, RITSUKO! GIVE BACK YOUR SALARY RIGHT NOW!!
HONESTLY...!
IF THE GROWNUPS ARE THIS DUMB, IT'S GOING TO BE 100 YEARS BEFORE THEY FINISH THE EVANGELION...!
nudge
I THINK...
...I THINK IF THEY USED PET BOTTLES INSTEAD...IT'D BE HARDER FOR THEM TO BE KNOCKED OVER IN THE COCKPIT.
HMM! IT'S WORTH LOOKING INTO!
IMPRESSIVE, REI! SOUNDS LIKE YOU'RE READY TO JOIN THEIR DESIGN TEAM!
WELL, THAT'S ALL FOR TODAY.
YOU CAN EXIT THE SIMULATOR, SHINJI-KUN.
slip
YOU'VE BEEN VERY HELPFUL. WE'RE GOING TO MAKE ADJUSTMENTS TO THE UNIT BASED ON YOUR RECOMMENDATIONS, AND LATER DO A FOLLOW-UP.
OH... OKAY.

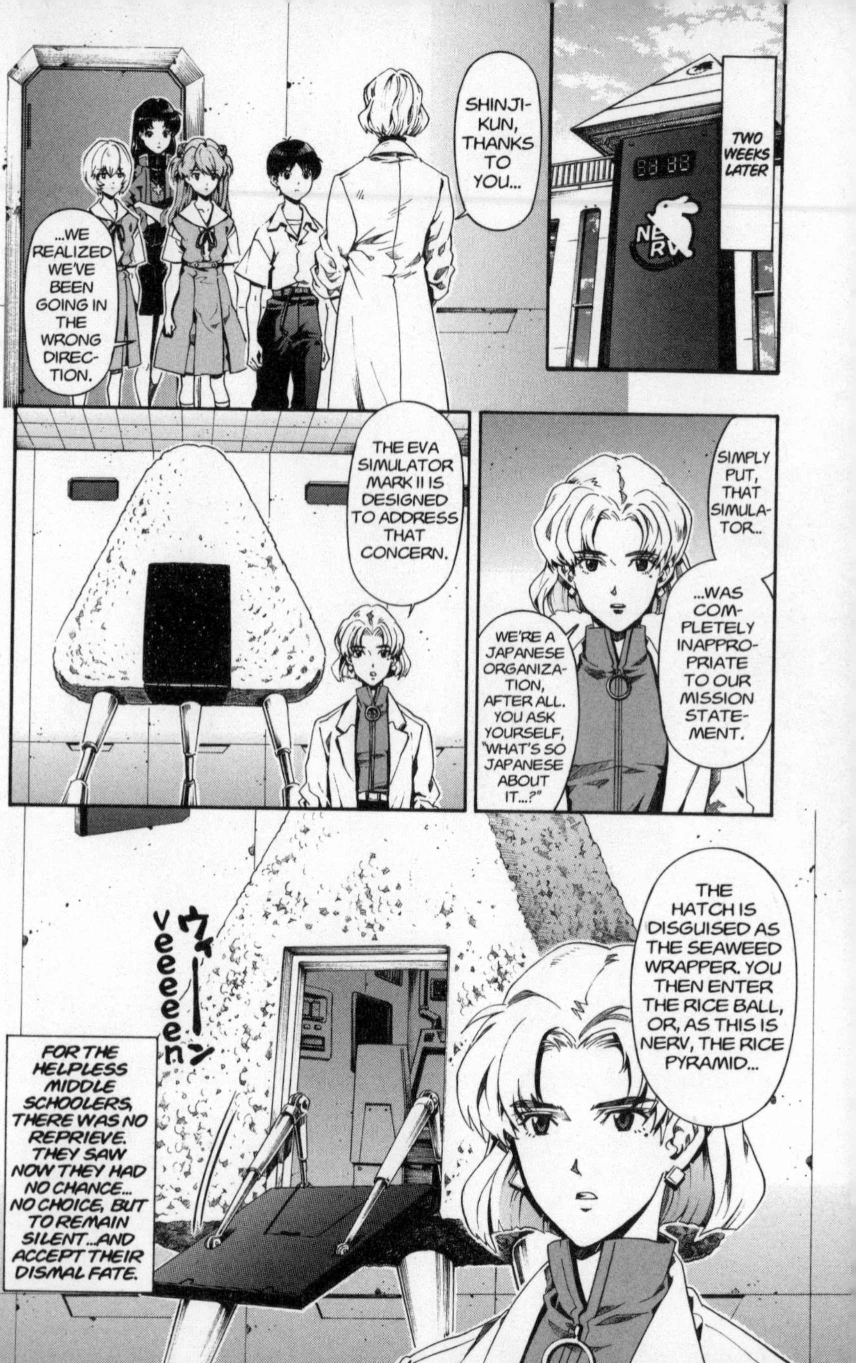
TWO WEEKS LATER
SHINJI-KUN, THANKS TO YOU...
...WE REALIZED WE'VE BEEN GOING IN THE WRONG DIRECTION.
SIMPLY PUT, THAT SIMULATOR...
...WAS COMPLETELY INAPPROPRIATE TO OUR MISSION STATEMENT.
WE'RE A JAPANESE ORGANIZATION, AFTER ALL. YOU ASK YOURSELF, "WHAT'S SO JAPANESE ABOUT IT...?"
THE EVA SIMULATOR MARK II IS DESIGNED TO ADDRESS THAT CONCERN.
THE HATCH IS DISGUISED AS THE SEAWEED WRAPPER. YOU THEN ENTER THE RICE BALL, OR, AS THIS IS NERV, THE RICE PYRAMID...
ウィーン
Veeeeeen
FOR THE HELPLESS MIDDLE SCHOOLERS, THERE WAS NO REPRIEVE. THEY SAW NOW THEY HAD NO CHANCE... NO CHOICE, BUT TO REMAIN SILENT...AND ACCEPT THEIR DISMAL FATE.

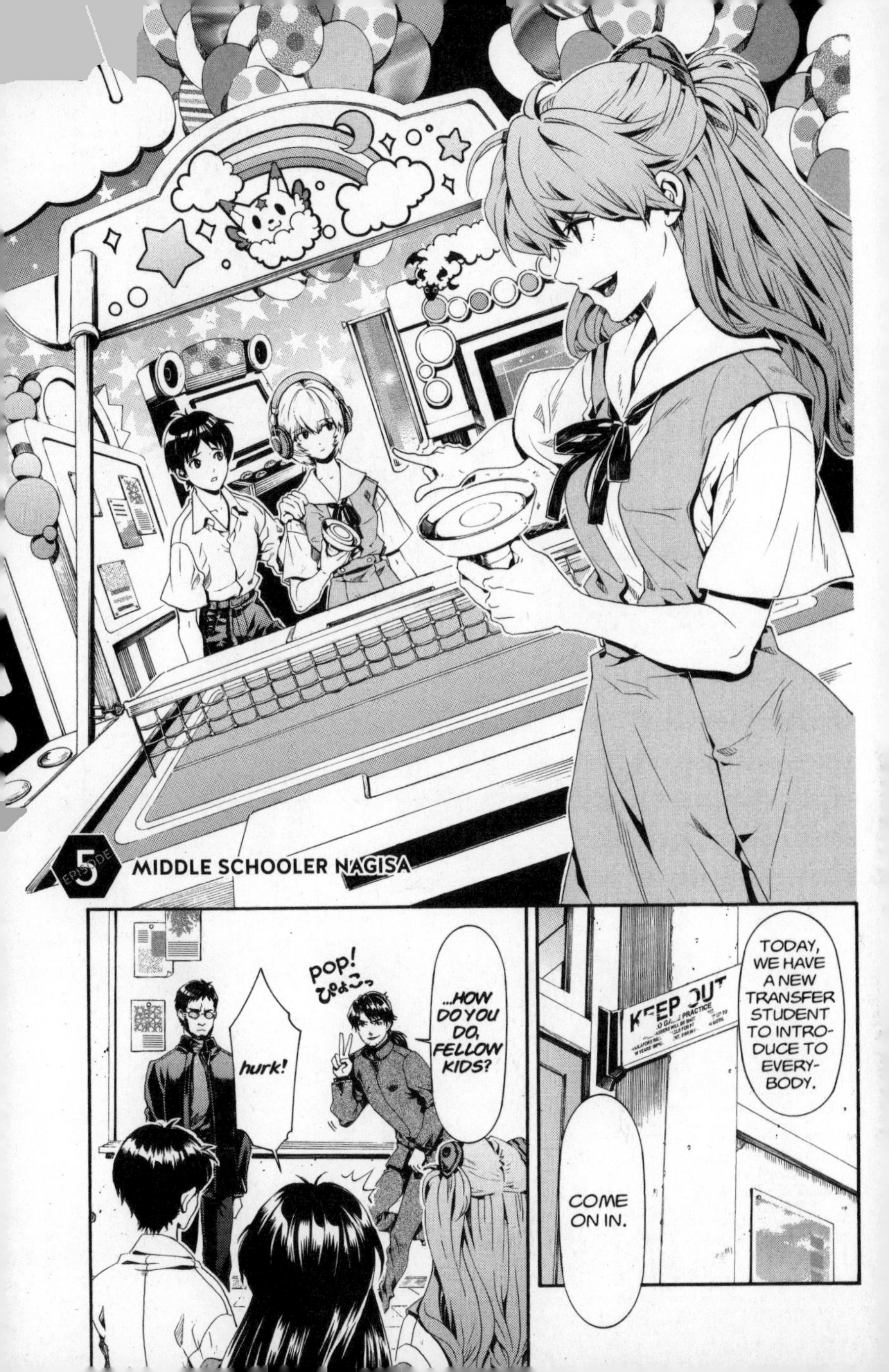
EPISODE 5
MIDDLE SCHOOLER NAGISA
TODAY, WE HAVE A NEW TRANSFER STUDENT TO INTRODUCE TO EVERYBODY.
KEEP OUT
COME ON IN.
...HOW DO YOU DO, FELLOW KIDS?
pop! ぴょこっ
hurk!

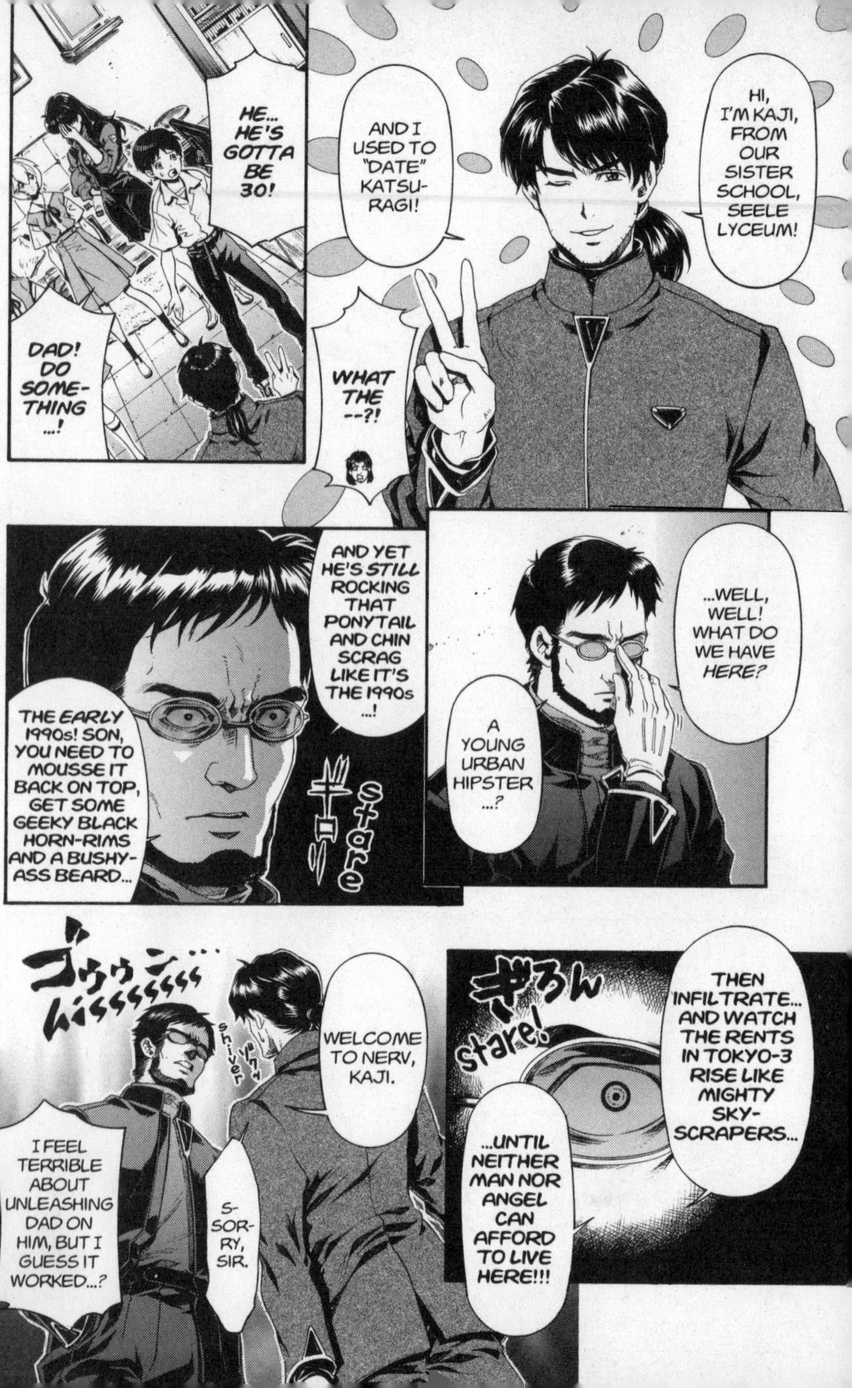
HI, I'M KAJI, FROM OUR SISTER SCHOOL, SEELE LYCEUM!
AND I USED TO "DATE" KATSURAGI!
WHAT THE --?!
HE... HE'S GOTTA BE 30!
DAD! DO SOME-THING ...!
...WELL, WELL! WHAT DO WE HAVE HERE?
A YOUNG URBAN HIPSTER ...?
AND YET HE'S STILL ROCKING THAT PONYTAIL AND CHIN SCRAG LIKE IT'S THE 1990s ...!
THE EARLY 1990s! SON, YOU NEED TO MOUSSE IT BACK ON TOP, GET SOME GEEKY BLACK HORN-RIMS AND A BUSHY-ASS BEARD...
stare
ぎろん
stare!
THEN INFILTRATE... AND WATCH THE RENTS IN TOKYO-3 RISE LIKE MIGHTY SKY-SCRAPERS...
...UNTIL NEITHER MAN NOR ANGEL CAN AFFORD TO LIVE HERE!!!
WELCOME TO NERV, KAJI.
shiver
S-SOR-RY, SIR.
I FEEL TERRIBLE ABOUT UNLEASHING DAD ON HIM, BUT I GUESS IT WORKED...?

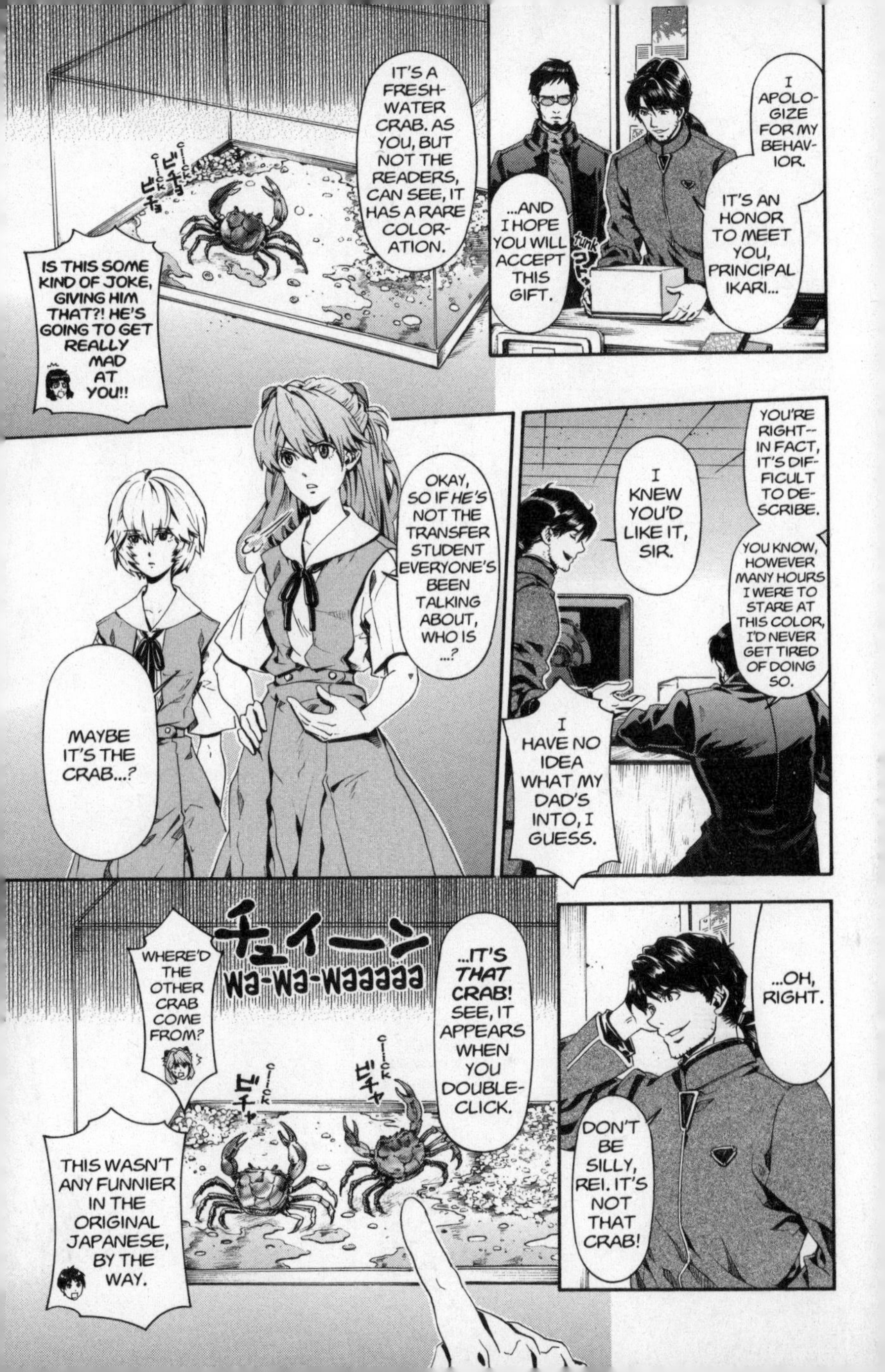
I APOLOGIZE FOR MY BEHAVIOR.
IT'S AN HONOR TO MEET YOU, PRINCIPAL IKARI...
...AND I HOPE YOU WILL ACCEPT THIS GIFT.
funk
コトッ
IT'S A FRESHWATER CRAB. AS YOU, BUT NOT THE READERS, CAN SEE, IT HAS A RARE COLORATION.
CLICK
ビチョ
CLICK
ビチョ
IS THIS SOME KIND OF JOKE, GIVING HIM THAT?! HE'S GOING TO GET REALLY MAD AT YOU!!
I KNEW YOU'D LIKE IT, SIR.
YOU'RE RIGHT-- IN FACT, IT'S DIFFICULT TO DESCRIBE.
YOU KNOW, HOWEVER MANY HOURS I WERE TO STARE AT THIS COLOR, I'D NEVER GET TIRED OF DOING SO.
I HAVE NO IDEA WHAT MY DAD'S INTO, I GUESS.
OKAY, SO IF HE'S NOT THE TRANSFER STUDENT EVERYONE'S BEEN TALKING ABOUT, WHO IS ...?
MAYBE IT'S THE CRAB...?
...OH, RIGHT.
DON'T BE SILLY, REI. IT'S NOT THAT CRAB!
...IT'S THAT CRAB! SEE, IT APPEARS WHEN YOU DOUBLE-CLICK.
チュイーン
WA-WA-WAAAAAA
WHERE'D THE OTHER CRAB COME FROM?
CLICK
ビチャ
CLICK
ビチャ
THIS WASN'T ANY FUNNIER IN THE ORIGINAL JAPANESE, BY THE WAY.

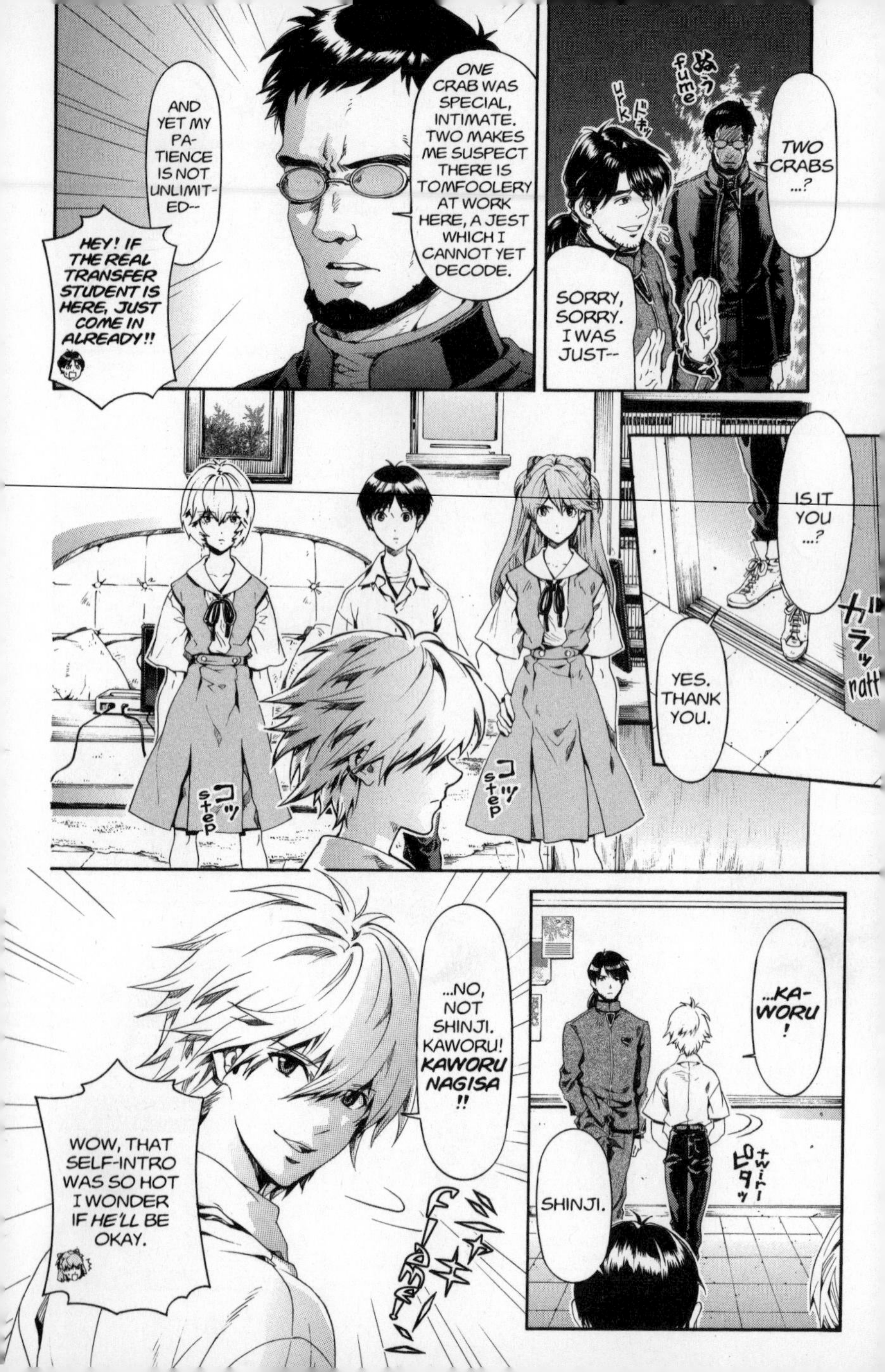
TWO CRABS ...?
ぬう fume
ドキッ urk
SORRY, SORRY. I WAS JUST--
ONE CRAB WAS SPECIAL, INTIMATE. TWO MAKES ME SUSPECT THERE IS TOMFOOLERY AT WORK HERE, A JEST WHICH I CANNOT YET DECODE.
AND YET MY PA-TIENCE IS NOT UNLIMIT-ED--
HEY! IF THE REAL TRANSFER STUDENT IS HERE, JUST COME IN ALREADY!!
ガラッ ratt
IS IT YOU ...?
YES. THANK YOU.
コッ step
コッ step
...KA-WORU!
ピタッ twirl
SHINJI.
...NO, NOT SHINJI. KAWORU! KAWORU NAGISA!!
WOW, THAT SELF-INTRO WAS SO HOT I WONDER IF HE'LL BE OKAY.

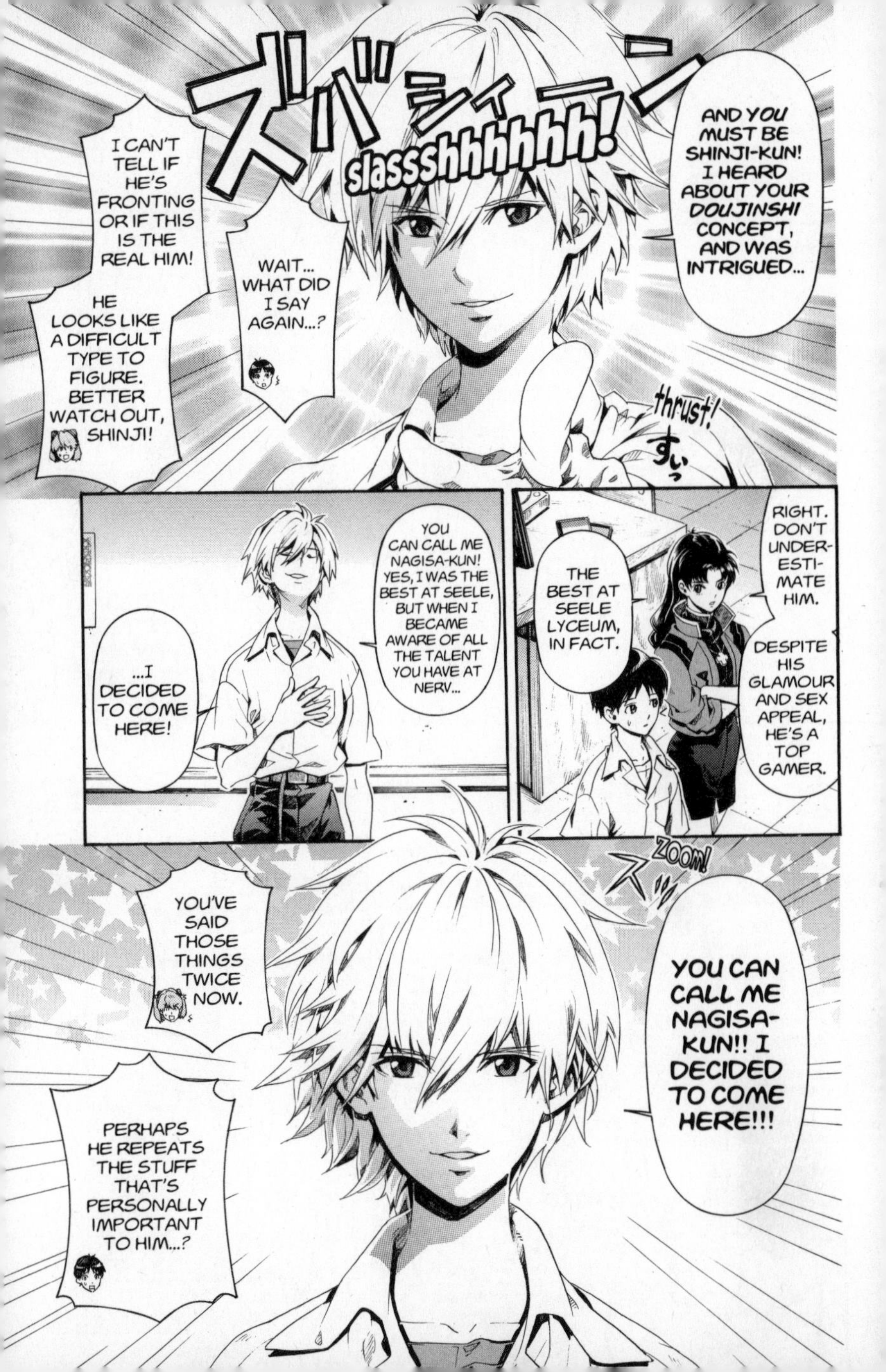
ズバシィーン
slassshhhhhh!
AND YOU MUST BE SHINJI-KUN! I HEARD ABOUT YOUR DOUJINSHI CONCEPT, AND WAS INTRIGUED...
WAIT... WHAT DID I SAY AGAIN...?
I CAN'T TELL IF HE'S FRONTING OR IF THIS IS THE REAL HIM!
HE LOOKS LIKE A DIFFICULT TYPE TO FIGURE. BETTER WATCH OUT, SHINJI!
thrust!
すいっ
RIGHT. DON'T UNDER-ESTI-MATE HIM.
THE BEST AT SEELE LYCEUM, IN FACT.
DESPITE HIS GLAMOUR AND SEX APPEAL, HE'S A TOP GAMER.
YOU CAN CALL ME NAGISA-KUN! YES, I WAS THE BEST AT SEELE, BUT WHEN I BECAME AWARE OF ALL THE TALENT YOU HAVE AT NERV...
...I DECIDED TO COME HERE!
ZOOM!
ズッ
YOU CAN CALL ME NAGISA-KUN!! I DECIDED TO COME HERE!!!
YOU'VE SAID THOSE THINGS TWICE NOW.
PERHAPS HE REPEATS THE STUFF THAT'S PERSONALLY IMPORTANT TO HIM...?

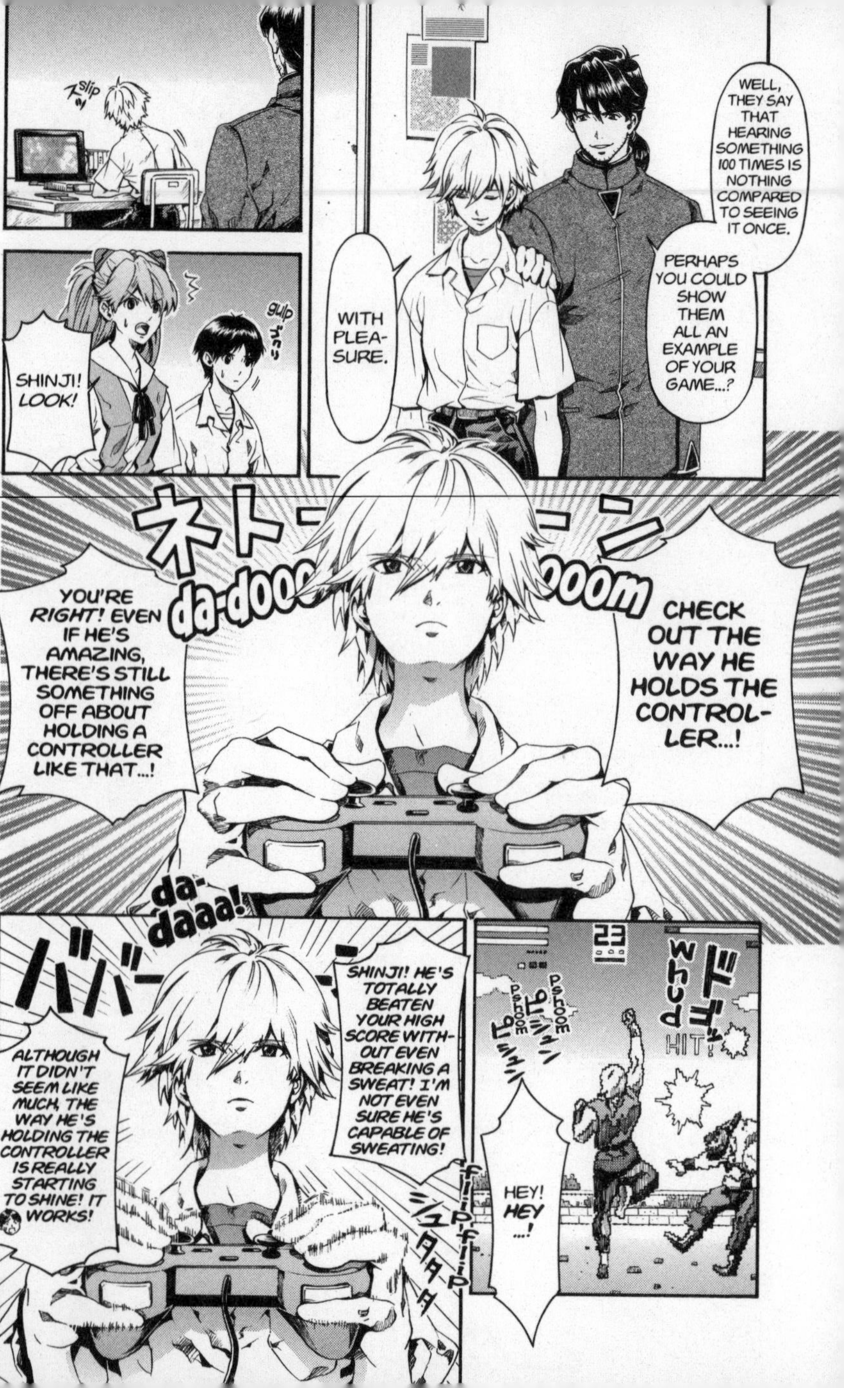
WELL, THEY SAY THAT HEARING SOMETHING 100 TIMES IS NOTHING COMPARED TO SEEING IT ONCE.
PERHAPS YOU COULD SHOW THEM ALL AN EXAMPLE OF YOUR GAME...?
WITH PLEASURE.
スッ slip
SHINJI! LOOK!
gulp ゴクリ
ネトーーン da-dooooom
CHECK OUT THE WAY HE HOLDS THE CONTROLLER...!
YOU'RE RIGHT! EVEN IF HE'S AMAZING, THERE'S STILL SOMETHING OFF ABOUT HOLDING A CONTROLLER LIKE THAT...!
23
ドゴッ
HIT!
pshoom pshoom
HEY! HEY ...!
バババーー da-daaa!
SHINJI! HE'S TOTALLY BEATEN YOUR HIGH SCORE WITHOUT EVEN BREAKING A SWEAT! I'M NOT EVEN SURE HE'S CAPABLE OF SWEATING!
シュタタタ
ALTHOUGH IT DIDN'T SEEM LIKE MUCH, THE WAY HE'S HOLDING THE CONTROLLER IS REALLY STARTING TO SHINE! IT WORKS!

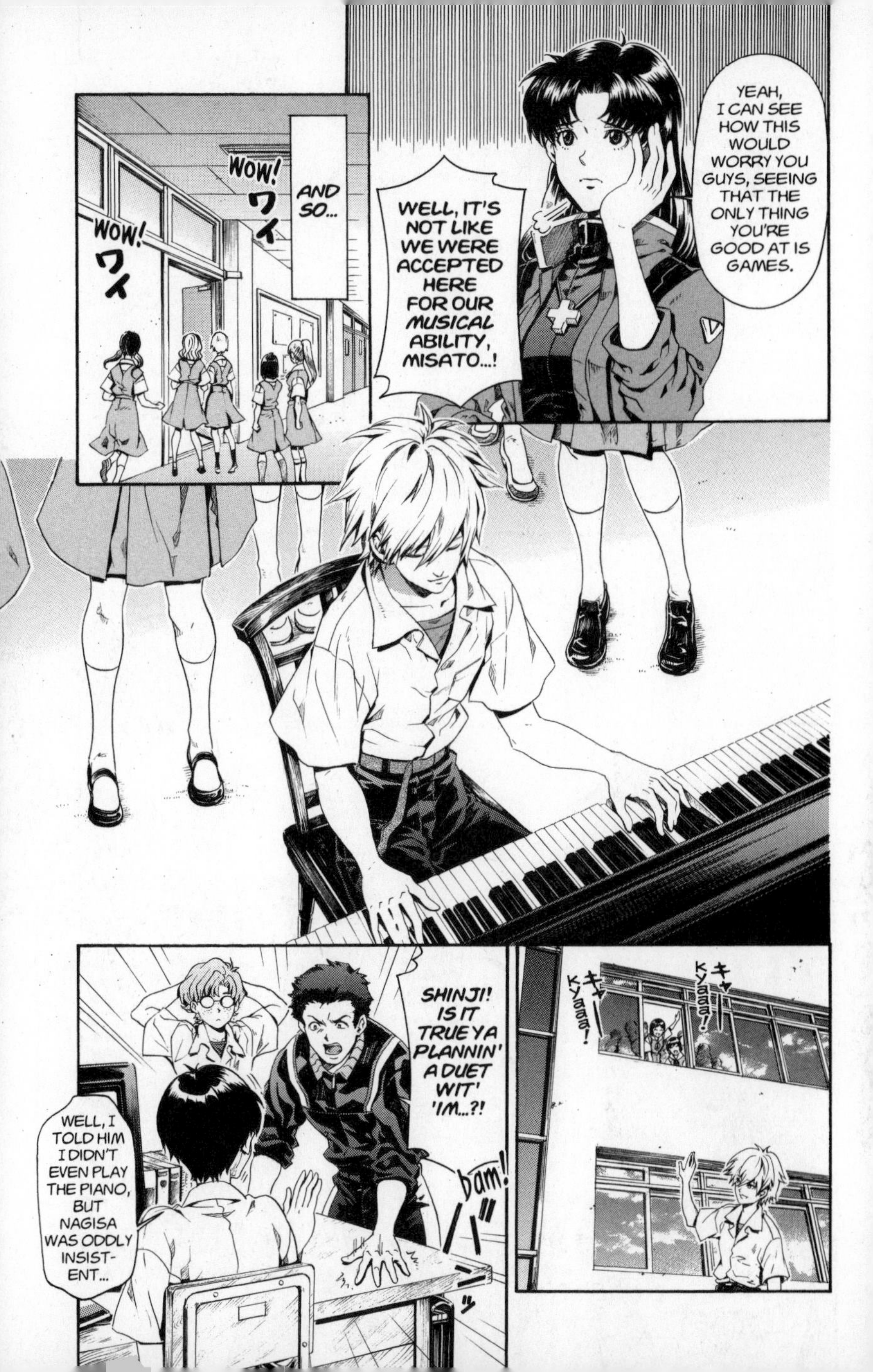
YEAH, I CAN SEE HOW THIS WOULD WORRY YOU GUYS, SEEING THAT THE ONLY THING YOU'RE GOOD AT IS GAMES.
WELL, IT'S NOT LIKE WE WERE ACCEPTED HERE FOR OUR *MUSICAL* ABILITY, MISATO...!
AND SO...
WOW! ワイ
WOW! ワイ
キャー KYAAAA!
キャー KYAAAA!
SHINJI! IS IT TRUE YA PLANNIN' A DUET WIT' 'IM...?!
bam!
WELL, I TOLD HIM I DIDN'T EVEN PLAY THE PIANO, BUT NAGISA WAS ODDLY INSIST-ENT...

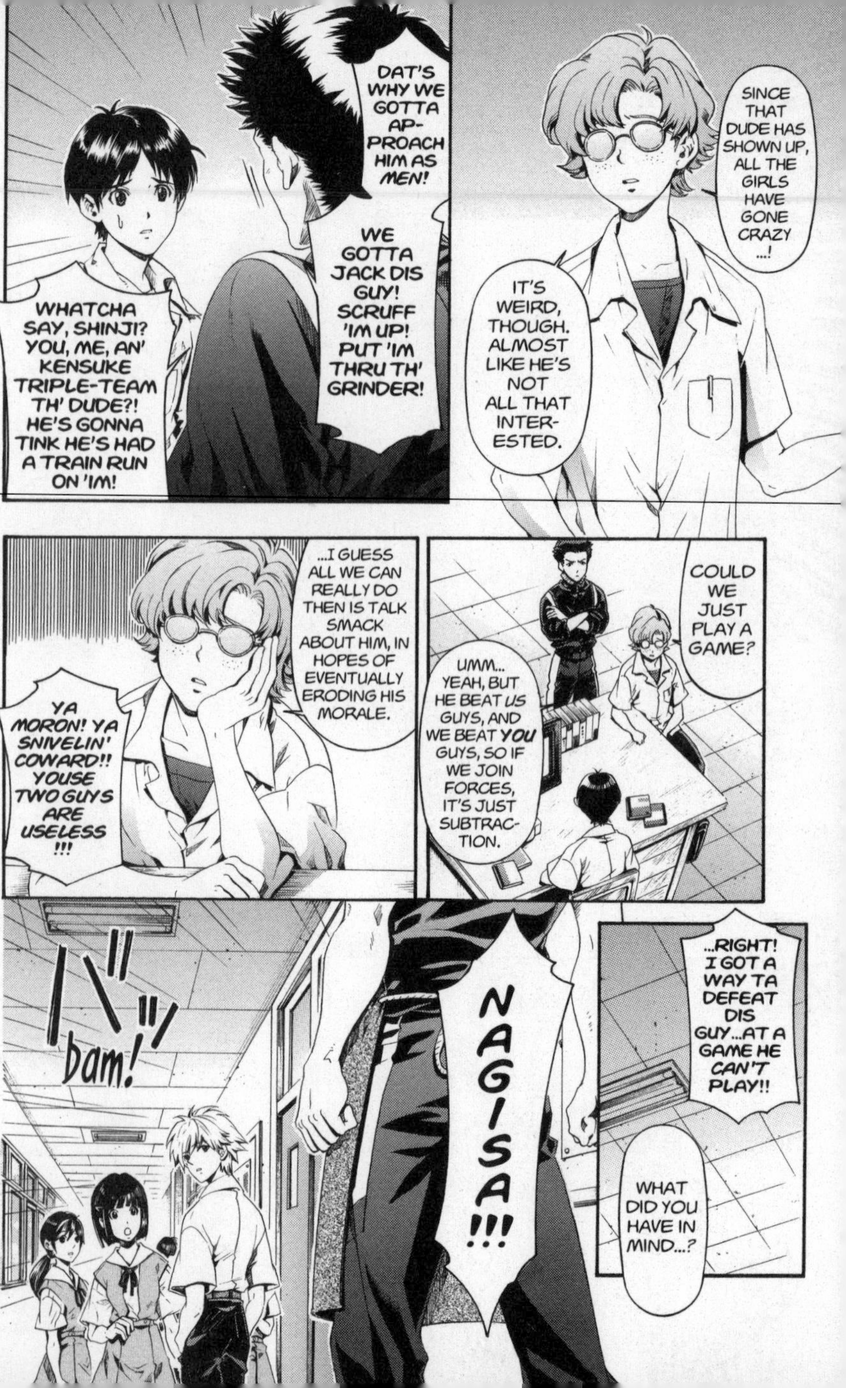
SINCE THAT DUDE HAS SHOWN UP, ALL THE GIRLS HAVE GONE CRAZY ...!
IT'S WEIRD, THOUGH. ALMOST LIKE HE'S NOT ALL THAT INTERESTED.
DAT'S WHY WE GOTTA APPROACH HIM AS MEN!
WE GOTTA JACK DIS GUY! SCRUFF 'IM UP! PUT 'IM THRU TH' GRINDER!
WHATCHA SAY, SHINJI? YOU, ME, AN' KENSUKE TRIPLE-TEAM TH' DUDE?! HE'S GONNA TINK HE'S HAD A TRAIN RUN ON 'IM!
COULD WE JUST PLAY A GAME?
UMM... YEAH, BUT HE BEAT US GUYS, AND WE BEAT YOU GUYS, SO IF WE JOIN FORCES, IT'S JUST SUBTRACTION.
...I GUESS ALL WE CAN REALLY DO THEN IS TALK SMACK ABOUT HIM, IN HOPES OF EVENTUALLY ERODING HIS MORALE.
YA MORON! YA SNIVELIN' COWARD!! YOUSE TWO GUYS ARE USELESS !!!
...RIGHT! I GOT A WAY TA DEFEAT DIS GUY...AT A GAME HE CAN'T PLAY!!
WHAT DID YOU HAVE IN MIND...?
NAGISA!!!
bam!

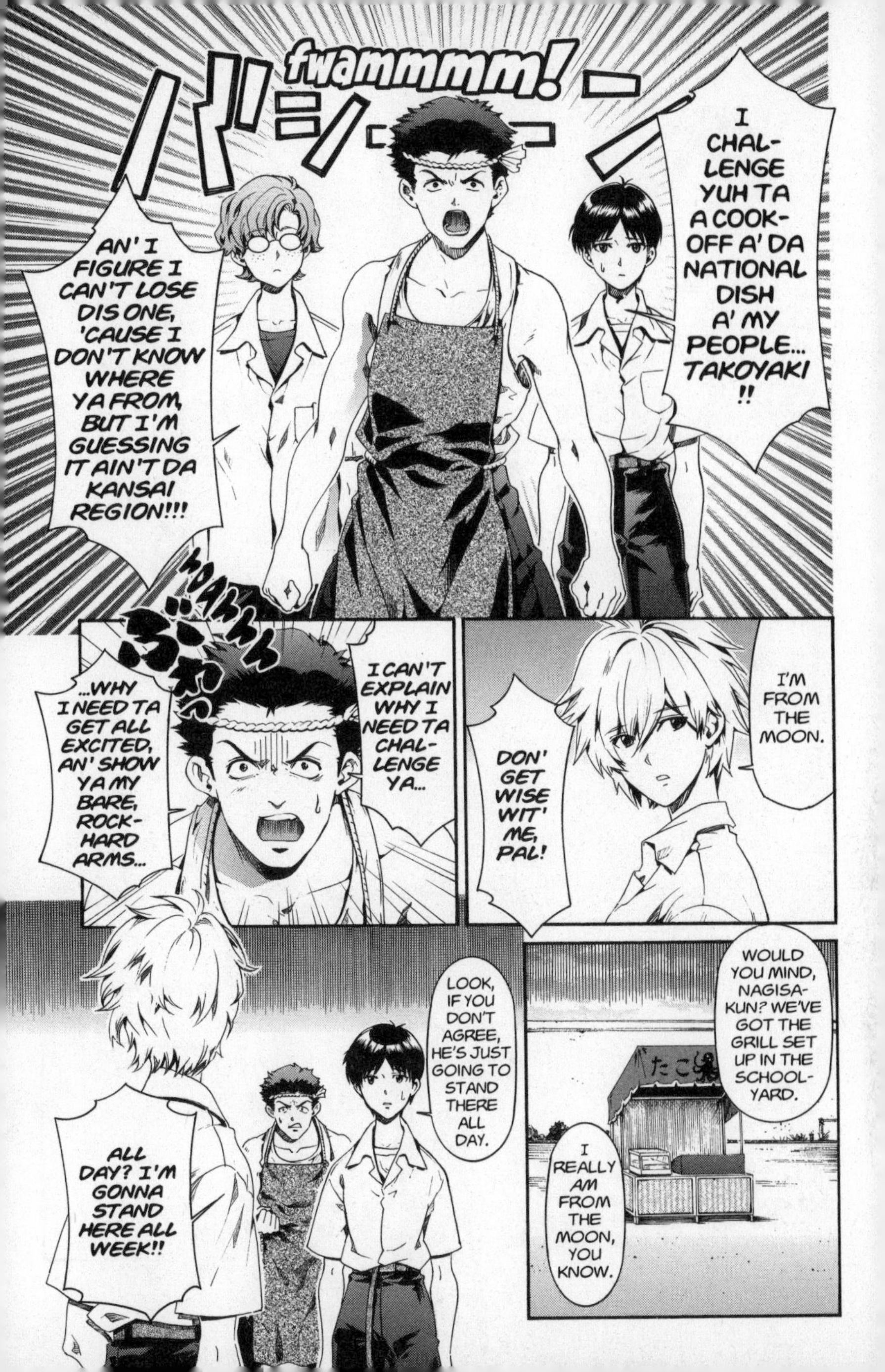
fwammmmm!
I CHALLENGE YUH TA A COOK-OFF A' DA NATIONAL DISH A' MY PEOPLE... TAKOYAKI!!
AN' I FIGURE I CAN'T LOSE DIS ONE, 'CAUSE I DON'T KNOW WHERE YA FROM, BUT I'M GUESSING IT AIN'T DA KANSAI REGION!!!
I'M FROM THE MOON.
DON' GET WISE WIT' ME, PAL!
I CAN'T EXPLAIN WHY I NEED TA CHALLENGE YA...
...WHY I NEED TA GET ALL EXCITED, AN' SHOW YA MY BARE, ROCK-HARD ARMS...
WOULD YOU MIND, NAGISA-KUN? WE'VE GOT THE GRILL SET UP IN THE SCHOOLYARD.
たこ
I REALLY AM FROM THE MOON, YOU KNOW.
LOOK, IF YOU DON'T AGREE, HE'S JUST GOING TO STAND THERE ALL DAY.
ALL DAY? I'M GONNA STAND HERE ALL WEEK!!

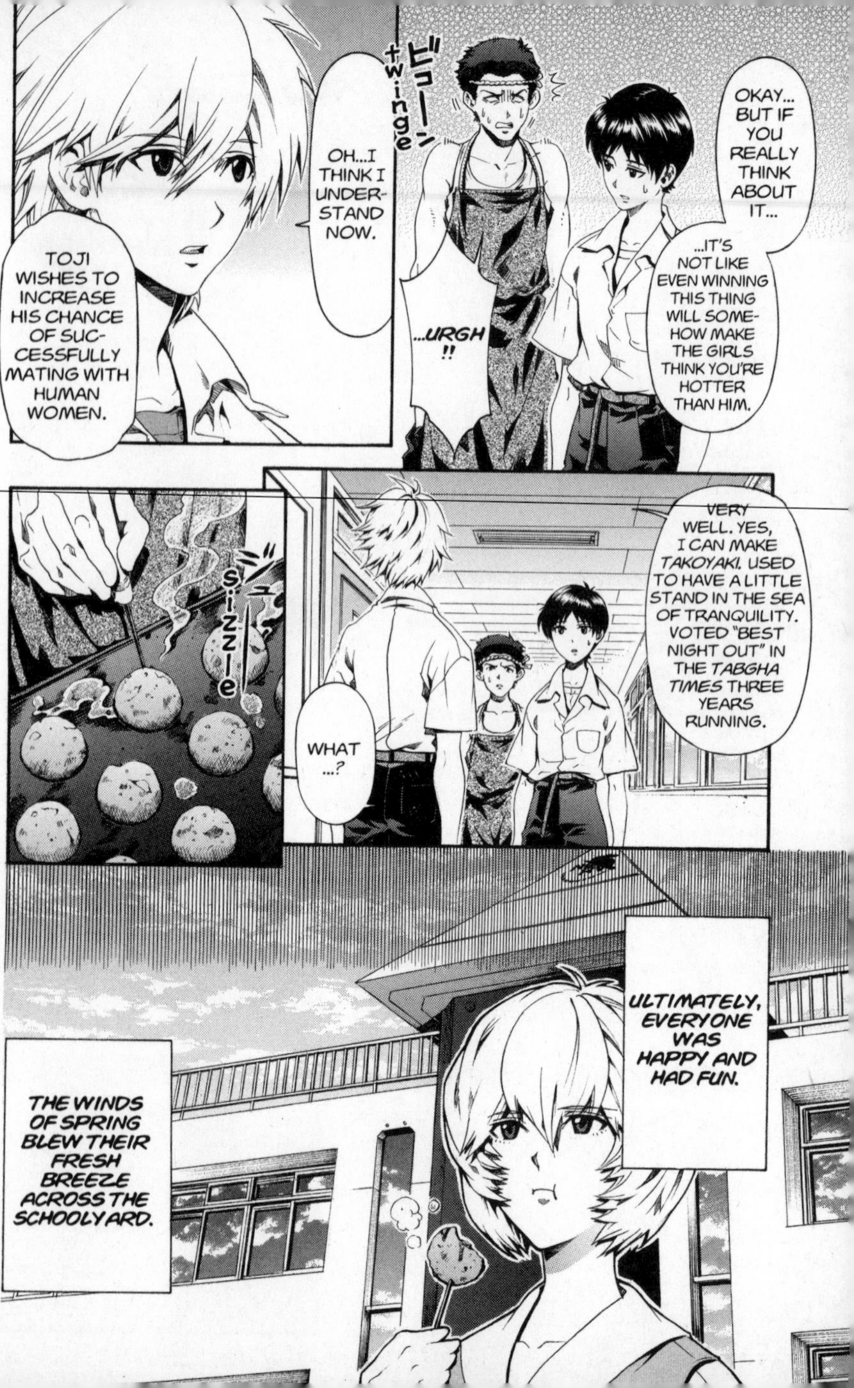
OKAY... BUT IF YOU REALLY THINK ABOUT IT...
...IT'S NOT LIKE EVEN WINNING THIS THING WILL SOME-HOW MAKE THE GIRLS THINK YOU'RE HOTTER THAN HIM.
ビコーン
twinge
...URGH!!
OH...I THINK I UNDER-STAND NOW.
TOJI WISHES TO INCREASE HIS CHANCE OF SUC-CESSFULLY MATING WITH HUMAN WOMEN.
VERY WELL. YES, I CAN MAKE *TAKOYAKI.* USED TO HAVE A LITTLE STAND IN THE SEA OF TRANQUILITY. VOTED "BEST NIGHT OUT" IN THE *TABGHA TIMES* THREE YEARS RUNNING.
WHAT...?
ジュ
sizzle
ULTIMATELY, EVERYONE WAS HAPPY AND HAD FUN.
THE WINDS OF SPRING BLEW THEIR FRESH BREEZE ACROSS THE SCHOOLYARD.

EPISODE 6 BIRTHDAY MIDDLE SCHOOLERS

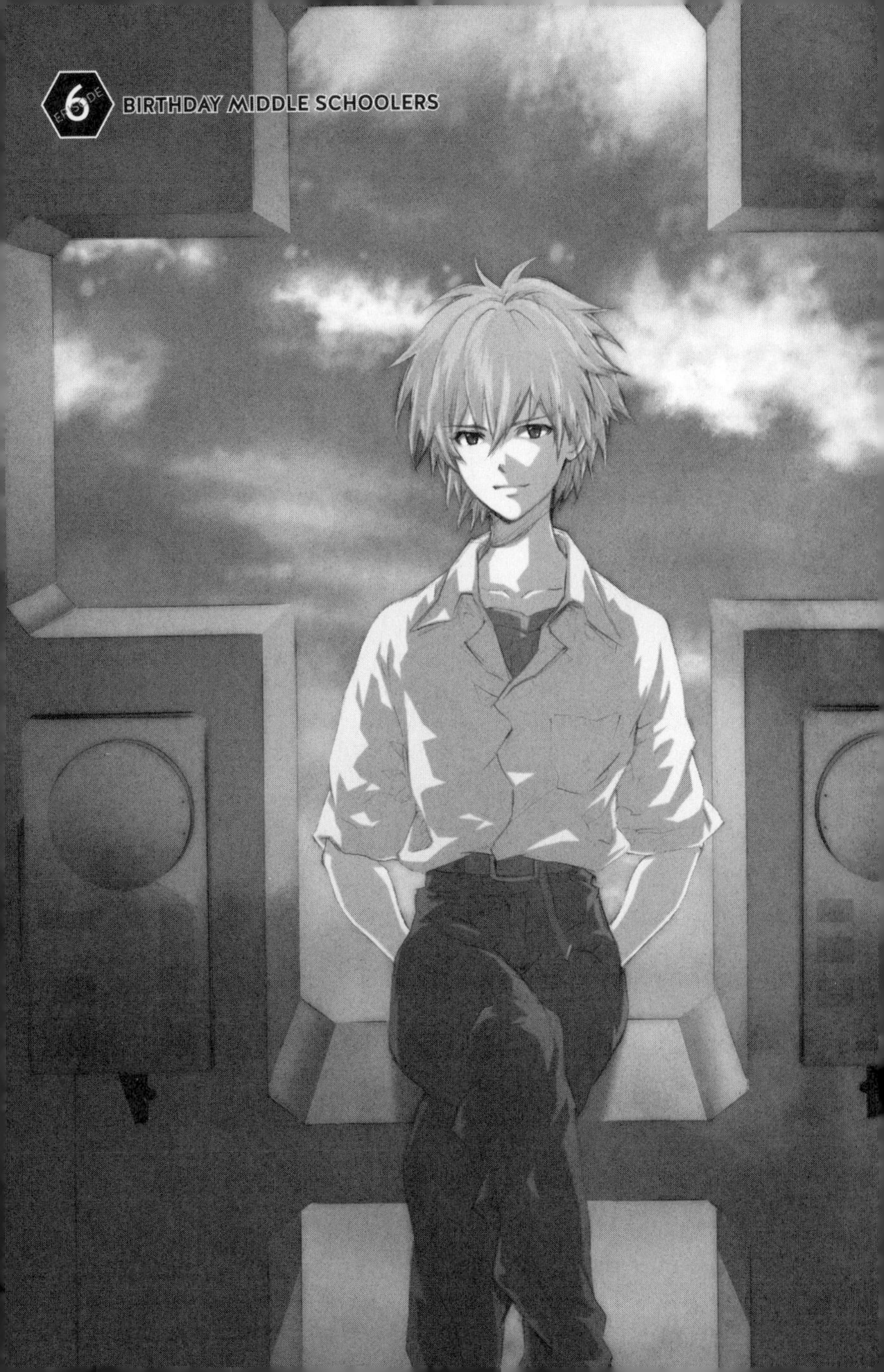

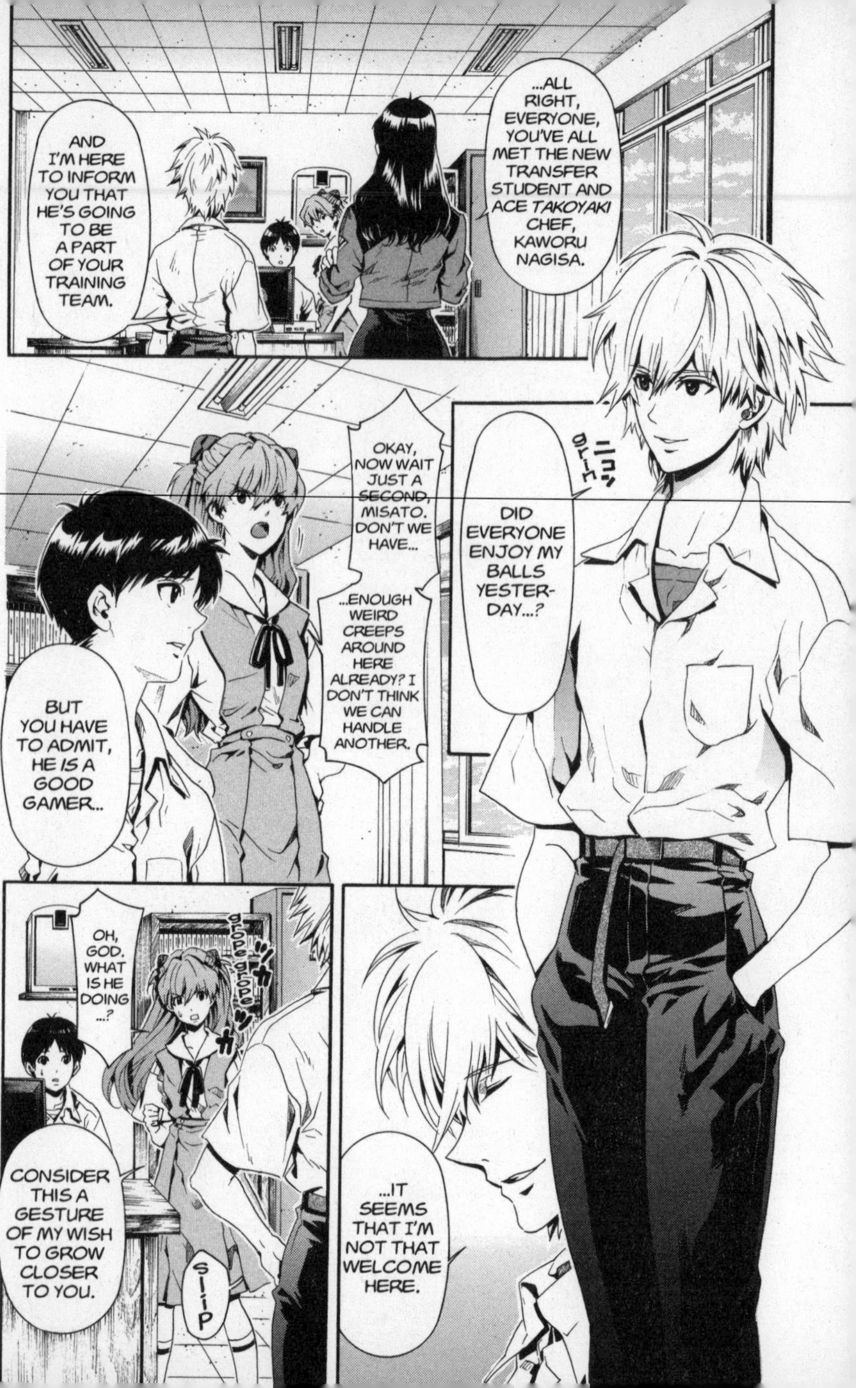
...ALL RIGHT, EVERYONE, YOU'VE ALL MET THE NEW TRANSFER STUDENT AND ACE *TAKOYAKI* CHEF, KAWORU NAGISA.
AND I'M HERE TO INFORM YOU THAT HE'S GOING TO BE A PART OF YOUR TRAINING TEAM.
grin
DID EVERYONE ENJOY MY BALLS YESTER-DAY...?
OKAY, NOW WAIT JUST A SECOND, MISATO. DON'T WE HAVE...
...ENOUGH WEIRD CREEPS AROUND HERE ALREADY? I DON'T THINK WE CAN HANDLE ANOTHER.
BUT YOU HAVE TO ADMIT, HE *IS* A GOOD GAMER...
...IT SEEMS THAT I'M NOT THAT WELCOME HERE.
grope grope
OH, GOD. WHAT IS HE DOING ...?
CONSIDER THIS A GESTURE OF MY WISH TO GROW CLOSER TO YOU.
S-L-I-P

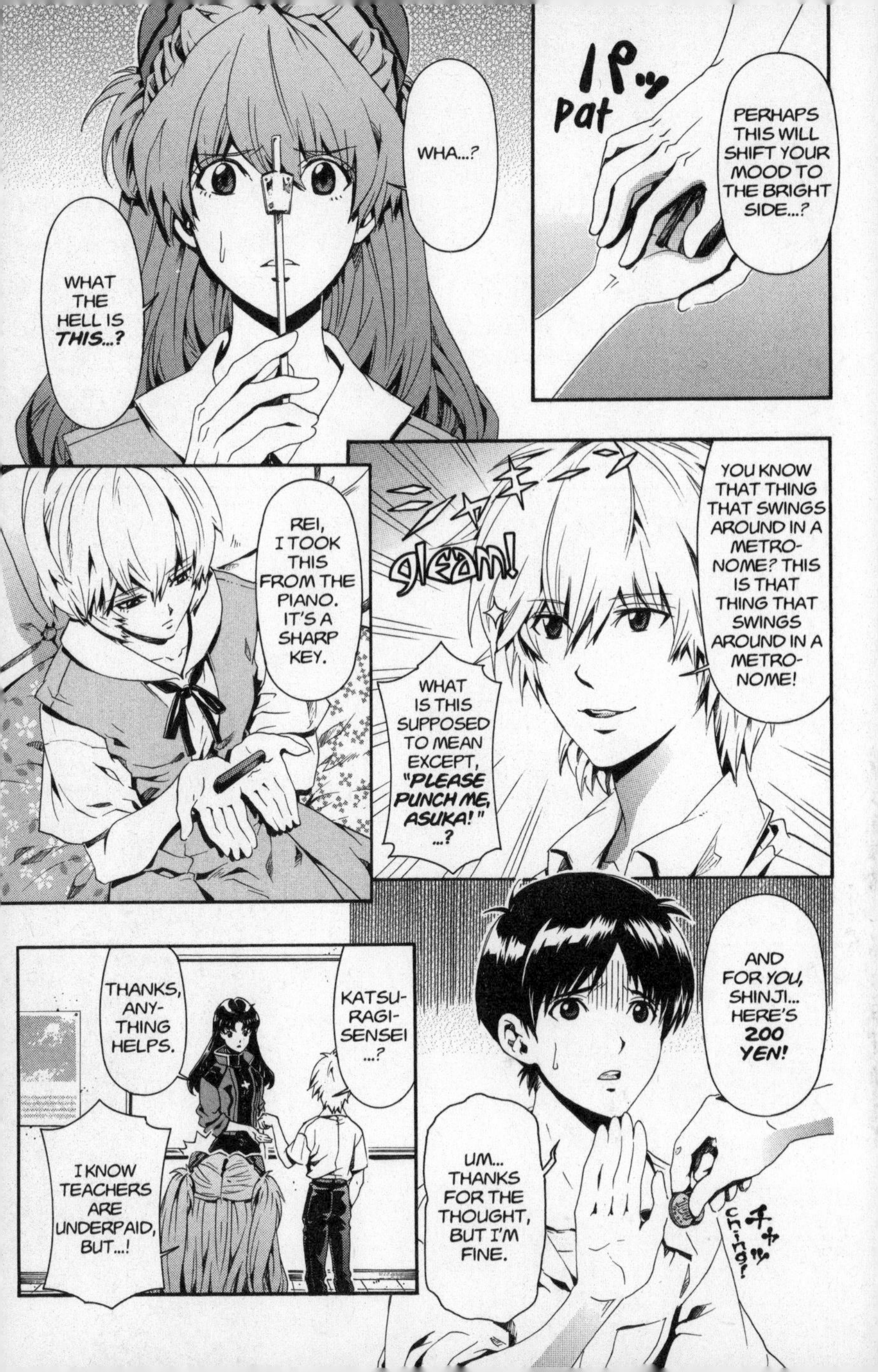
Pat
PERHAPS THIS WILL SHIFT YOUR MOOD TO THE BRIGHT SIDE...?
WHA...?
WHAT THE HELL IS *THIS...?*
YOU KNOW THAT THING THAT SWINGS AROUND IN A METRO-NOME? THIS IS THAT THING THAT SWINGS AROUND IN A METRO-NOME!
gleam!
WHAT IS THIS SUPPOSED TO MEAN EXCEPT, *"PLEASE PUNCH ME, ASUKA!"* ...?
REI, I TOOK THIS FROM THE PIANO. IT'S A SHARP KEY.
AND FOR *YOU,* SHINJI... HERE'S **200 YEN!**
UM... THANKS FOR THE THOUGHT, BUT I'M FINE.
ching!
KATSU-RAGI-SENSEI ...?
THANKS, ANY-THING HELPS.
I KNOW TEACHERS ARE UNDERPAID, BUT...!

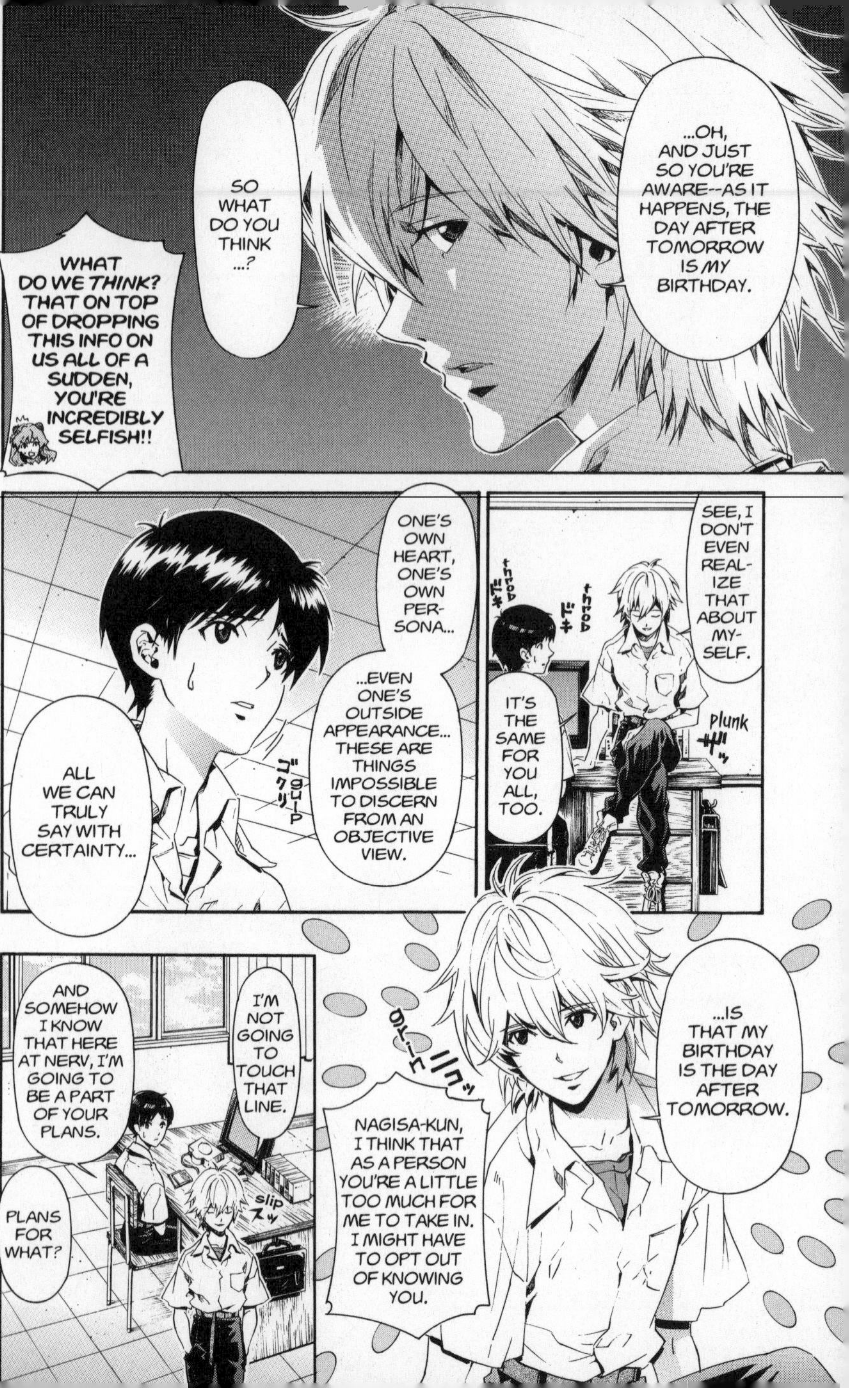
...OH, AND JUST SO YOU'RE AWARE--AS IT HAPPENS, THE DAY AFTER TOMORROW IS *MY* BIRTHDAY.
SO WHAT DO YOU THINK ...?
WHAT DO WE *THINK*? THAT ON TOP OF DROPPING THIS INFO ON US ALL OF A SUDDEN, YOU'RE INCREDIBLY SELFISH!!
SEE, I DON'T EVEN REAL-IZE THAT ABOUT MY-SELF.
throb ドキ
throb ドキ
IT'S THE SAME FOR YOU ALL, TOO.
plunk ガッ
ONE'S OWN HEART, ONE'S OWN PER-SONA...
...EVEN ONE'S OUTSIDE APPEARANCE... THESE ARE THINGS IMPOSSIBLE TO DISCERN FROM AN OBJECTIVE VIEW.
gulp ゴクリ
ALL WE CAN TRULY SAY WITH CERTAINTY...
...IS THAT MY BIRTHDAY IS THE DAY AFTER TOMORROW.
ニコッ
NAGISA-KUN, I THINK THAT AS A PERSON YOU'RE A LITTLE TOO MUCH FOR ME TO TAKE IN. I MIGHT HAVE TO OPT OUT OF KNOWING YOU.
I'M NOT GOING TO TOUCH THAT LINE.
AND SOMEHOW I KNOW THAT HERE AT NERV, I'M GOING TO BE A PART OF YOUR PLANS.
slip スッ
PLANS FOR WHAT?

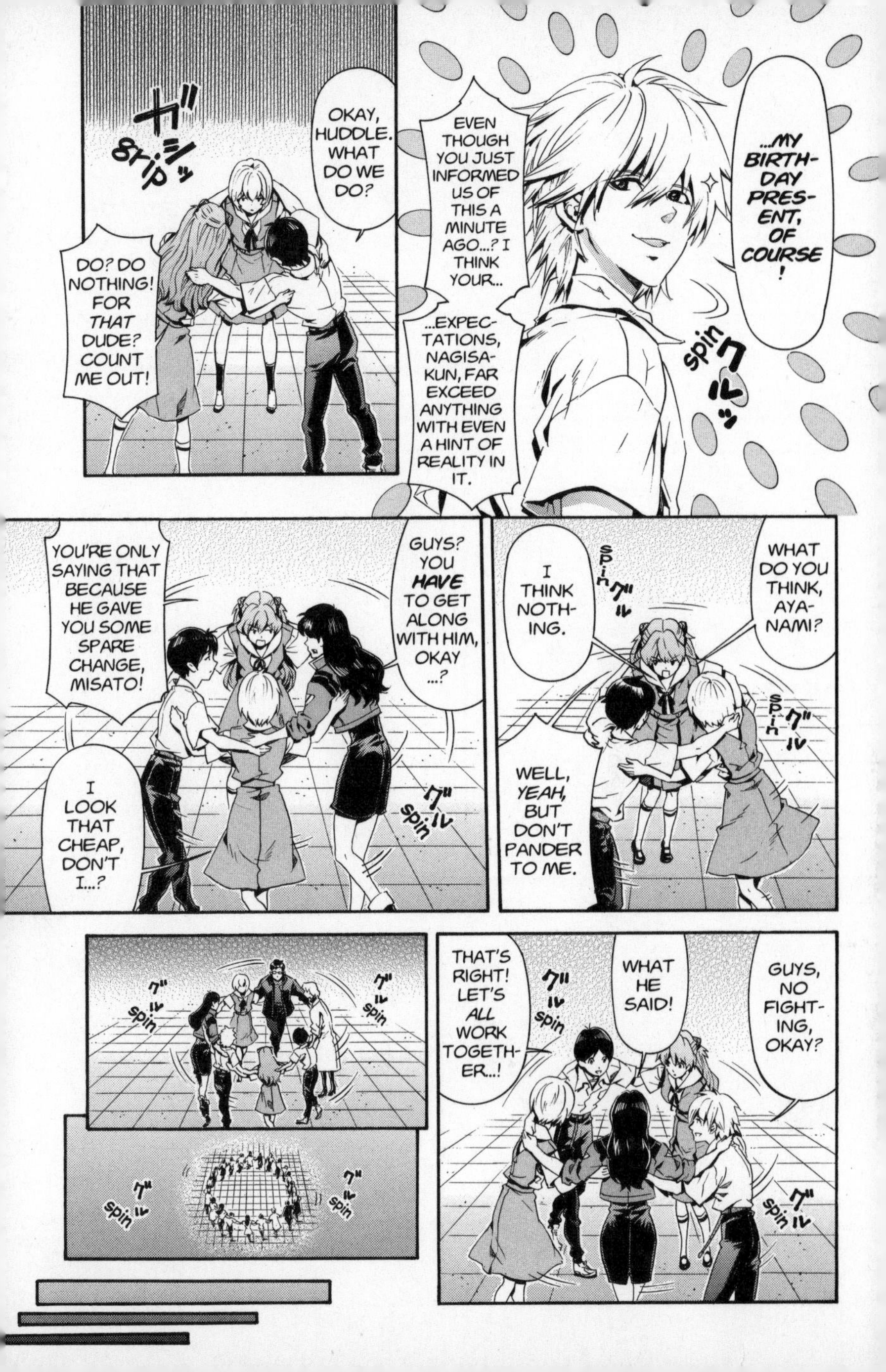
...MY BIRTHDAY PRESENT, OF COURSE!
spin クルッ
EVEN THOUGH YOU JUST INFORMED US OF THIS A MINUTE AGO...? I THINK YOUR...
...EXPECTATIONS, NAGISA-KUN, FAR EXCEED ANYTHING WITH EVEN A HINT OF REALITY IN IT.
OKAY, HUDDLE. WHAT DO WE DO?
ガシッ grip
DO? DO NOTHING! FOR *THAT* DUDE? COUNT ME OUT!
WHAT DO YOU THINK, AYANAMI?
I THINK NOTHING.
spin グル
spin グル
WELL, *YEAH,* BUT DON'T PANDER TO ME.
GUYS? YOU **HAVE** TO GET ALONG WITH HIM, OKAY ...?
YOU'RE ONLY SAYING THAT BECAUSE HE GAVE YOU SOME SPARE CHANGE, MISATO!
グル spin
I LOOK THAT CHEAP, DON'T I...?
GUYS, NO FIGHTING, OKAY?
WHAT HE SAID!
グル spin
THAT'S RIGHT! LET'S *ALL* WORK TOGETHER...!
spin グル
グル spin
グル spin
グル spin
グル spin

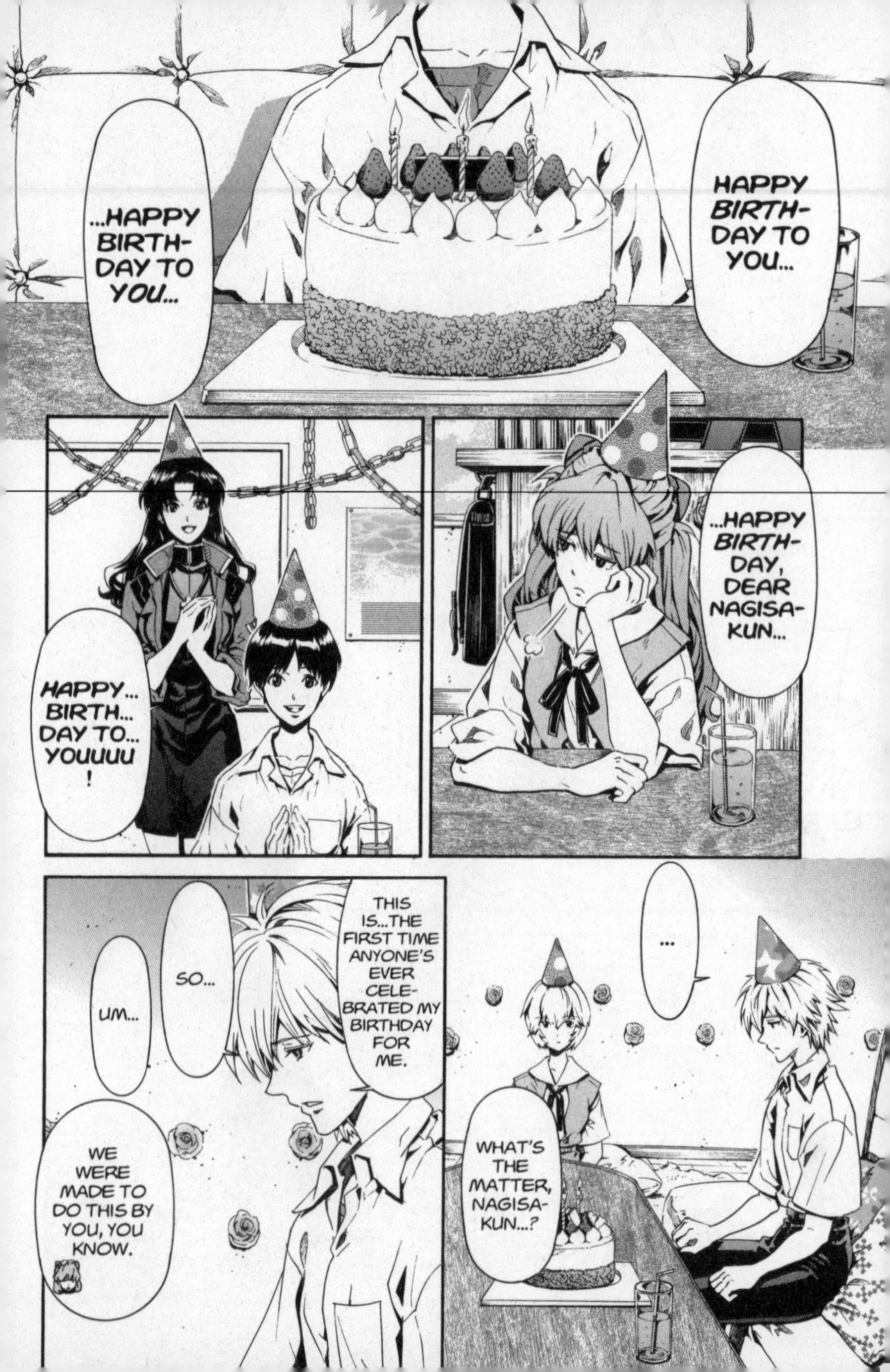
HAPPY BIRTHDAY TO YOU...
...HAPPY BIRTHDAY TO YOU...
...HAPPY BIRTHDAY, DEAR NAGISA-KUN...
HAPPY... BIRTH... DAY TO... YOUUUU!
...
WHAT'S THE MATTER, NAGISA-KUN...?
THIS IS...THE FIRST TIME ANYONE'S EVER CELEBRATED MY BIRTHDAY FOR ME.
SO...
UM...
WE WERE MADE TO DO THIS BY YOU, YOU KNOW.

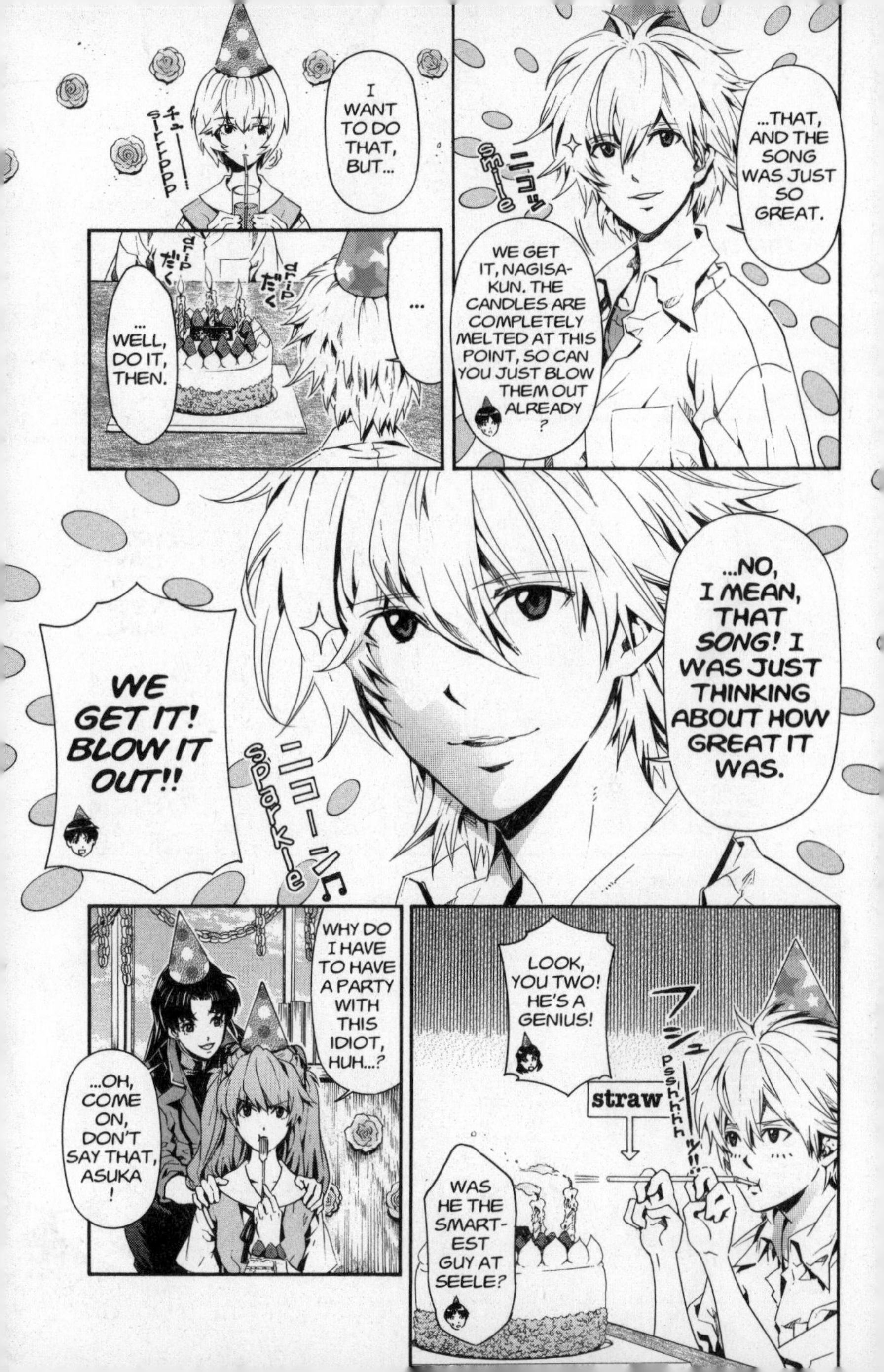
...THAT, AND THE SONG WAS JUST SO GREAT.
ニコッ smile
WE GET IT, NAGISA-KUN. THE CANDLES ARE COMPLETELY MELTED AT THIS POINT, SO CAN YOU JUST BLOW THEM OUT ALREADY?
I WANT TO DO THAT, BUT...
チュ――…!! s-rrrrppp
...
だく drip
だく drip
... WELL, DO IT, THEN.
...NO, I MEAN, THAT SONG! I WAS JUST THINKING ABOUT HOW GREAT IT WAS.
ニコーッ♫ sparkle
WE GET IT! BLOW IT OUT!!
LOOK, YOU TWO! HE'S A GENIUS!
フシュ psshhhh!!
straw
WAS HE THE SMART-EST GUY AT SEELE?
WHY DO I HAVE TO HAVE A PARTY WITH THIS IDIOT, HUH...?
...OH, COME ON, DON'T SAY THAT, ASUKA!

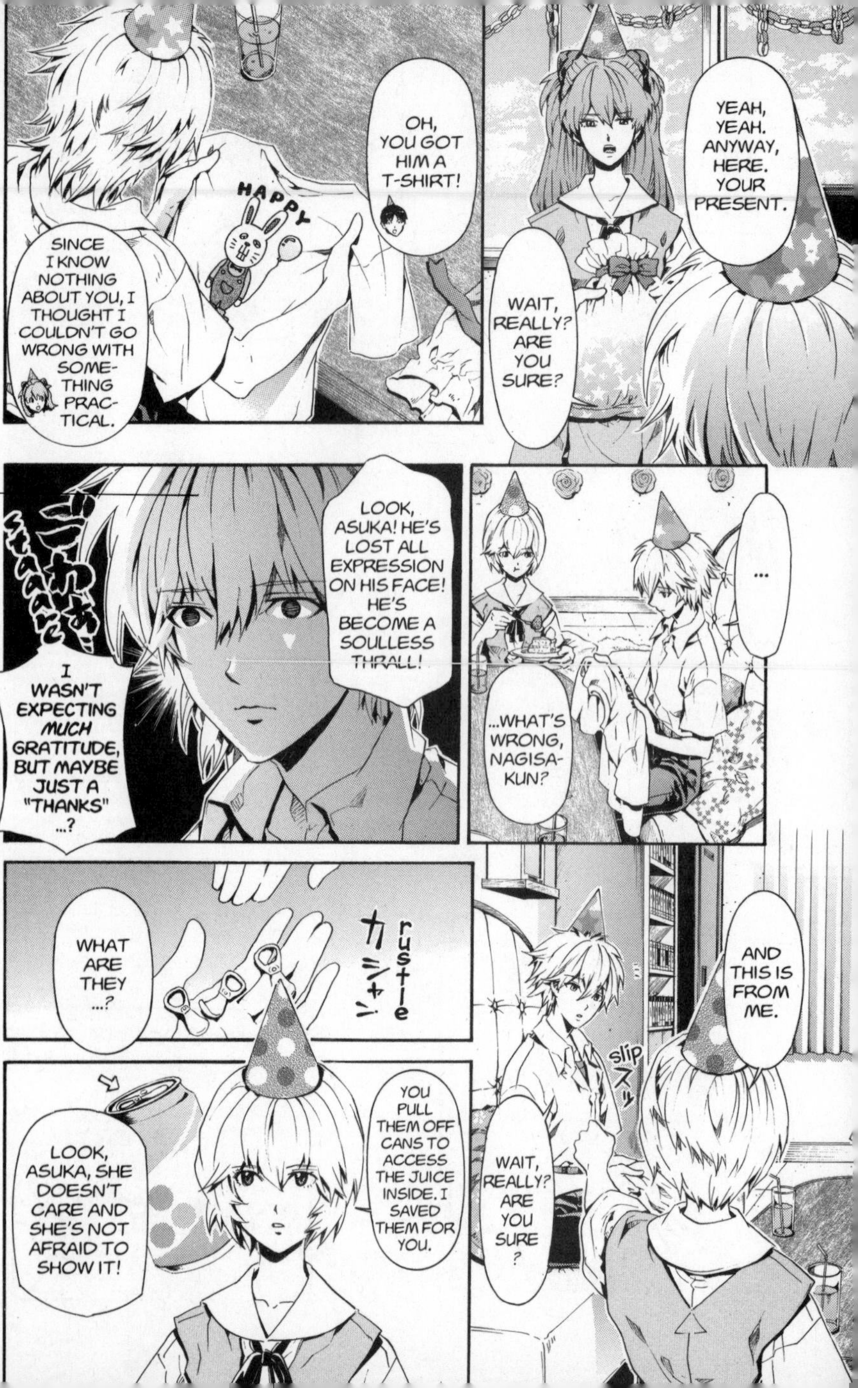
YEAH, YEAH. ANYWAY, HERE. YOUR PRESENT.
WAIT, REALLY? ARE YOU SURE?
OH, YOU GOT HIM A T-SHIRT!
HAPPY
SINCE I KNOW NOTHING ABOUT YOU, I THOUGHT I COULDN'T GO WRONG WITH SOME-THING PRAC-TICAL.
...
...WHAT'S WRONG, NAGISA-KUN?
LOOK, ASUKA! HE'S LOST ALL EXPRESSION ON HIS FACE! HE'S BECOME A SOULLESS THRALL!
I WASN'T EXPECTING *MUCH* GRATITUDE, BUT MAYBE JUST A "THANKS" ...?
AND THIS IS FROM ME.
slip
スッ
rustle
カシャン
WHAT ARE THEY ...?
WAIT, REALLY? ARE YOU SURE ?
YOU PULL THEM OFF CANS TO ACCESS THE JUICE INSIDE. I SAVED THEM FOR YOU.
LOOK, ASUKA, SHE DOESN'T CARE AND SHE'S NOT AFRAID TO SHOW IT!

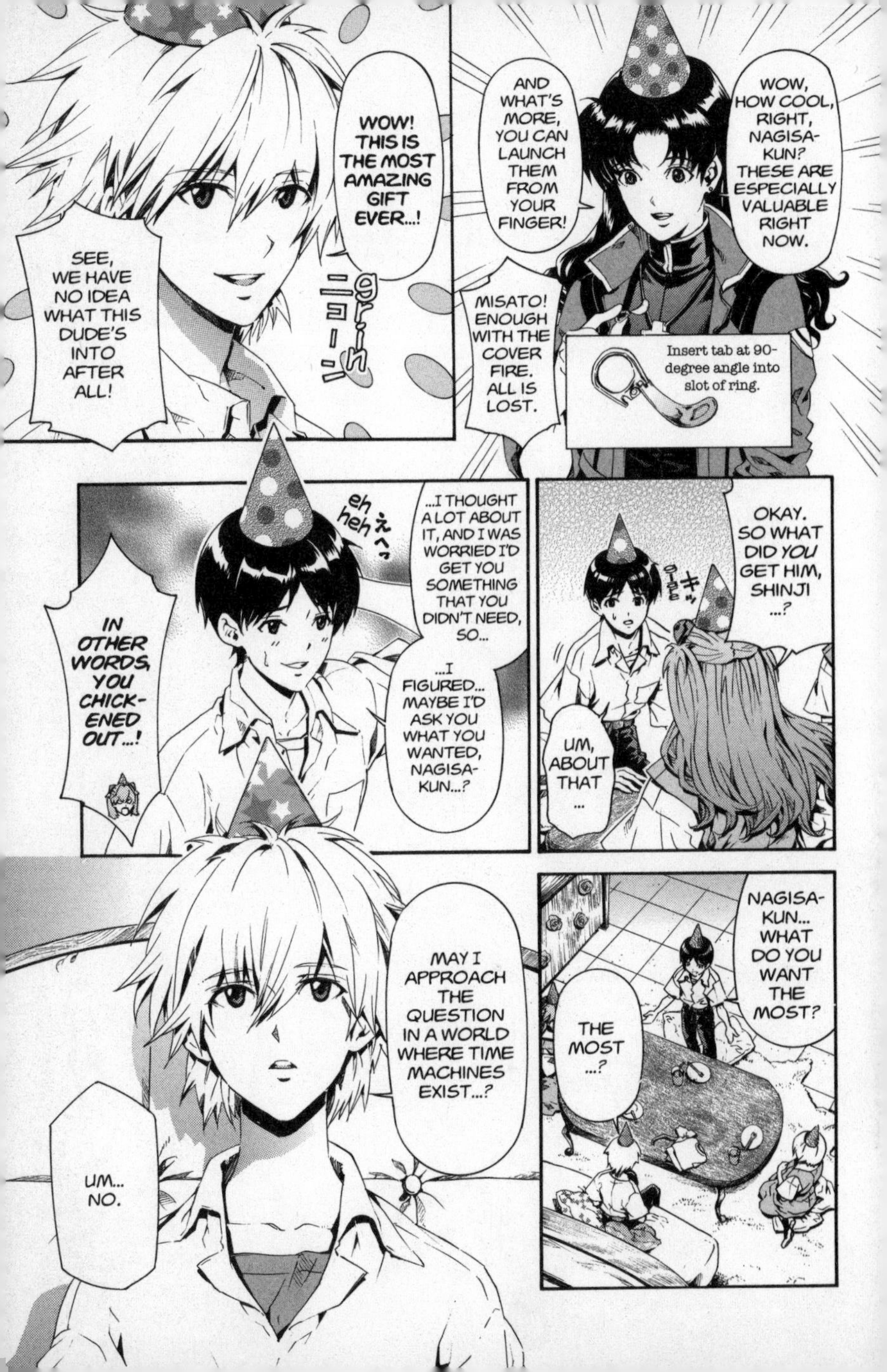
WOW, HOW COOL, RIGHT, NAGISA-KUN? THESE ARE ESPECIALLY VALUABLE RIGHT NOW.
AND WHAT'S MORE, YOU CAN LAUNCH THEM FROM YOUR FINGER!
MISATO! ENOUGH WITH THE COVER FIRE. ALL IS LOST.
Insert tab at 90-degree angle into slot of ring.
WOW! THIS IS THE MOST AMAZING GIFT EVER...!
grin ニコー
SEE, WE HAVE NO IDEA WHAT THIS DUDE'S INTO AFTER ALL!
OKAY. SO WHAT DID *YOU* GET HIM, SHINJI...?
glare キッ
UM, ABOUT THAT...
...I THOUGHT A LOT ABOUT IT, AND I WAS WORRIED I'D GET YOU SOMETHING THAT YOU DIDN'T NEED, SO...
...I FIGURED... MAYBE I'D ASK YOU WHAT YOU WANTED, NAGISA-KUN...?
eh heh えへっ
IN *OTHER WORDS*, YOU CHICKENED OUT...!
NAGISA-KUN... WHAT DO YOU WANT THE MOST?
THE MOST...?
MAY I APPROACH THE QUESTION IN A WORLD WHERE TIME MACHINES EXIST...?
UM... NO.

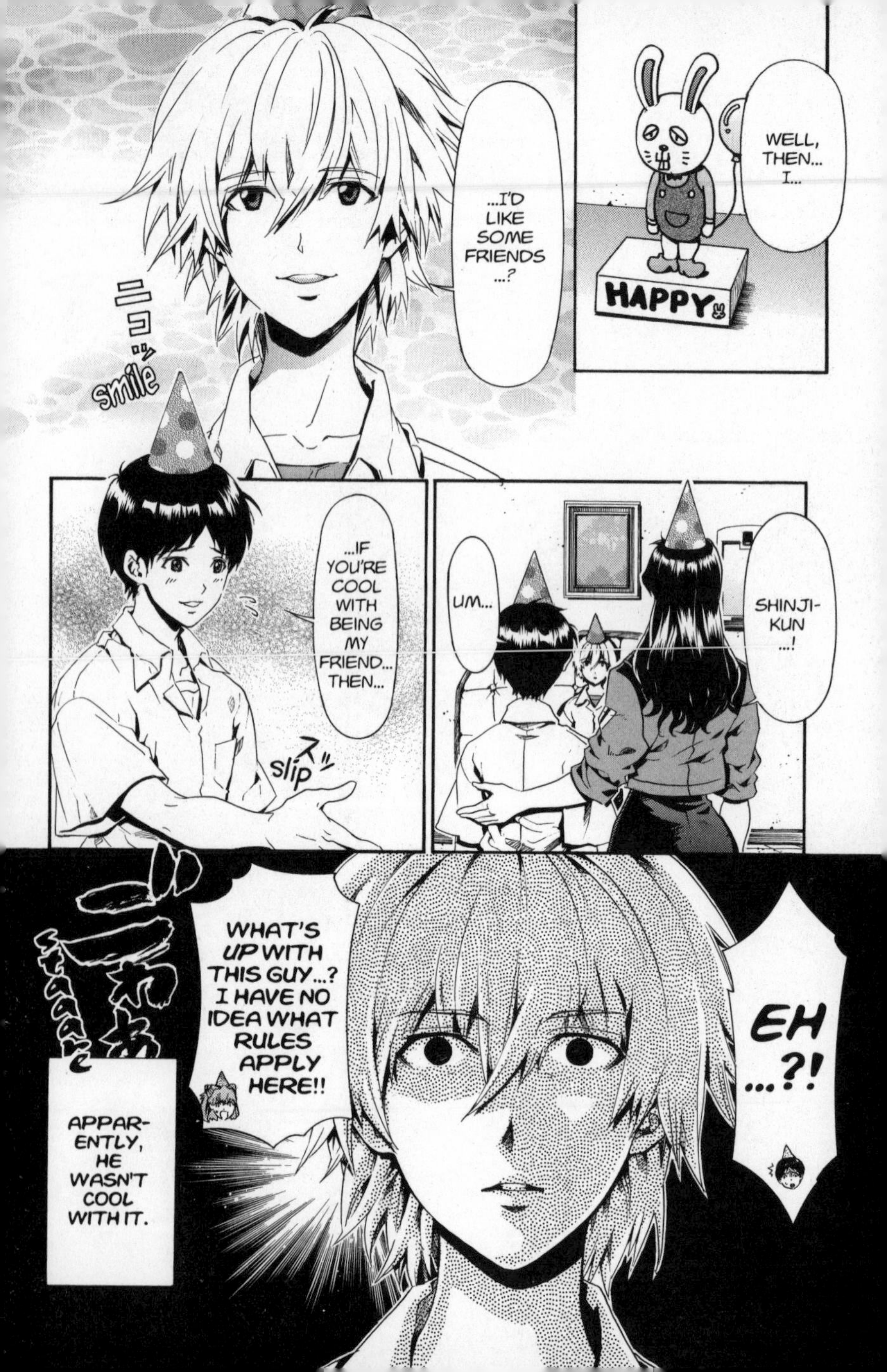
WELL, THEN... I...
...I'D LIKE SOME FRIENDS ...?
ニコッ
smile
SHINJI-KUN ...!
UM...
...IF YOU'RE COOL WITH BEING MY FRIEND... THEN...
スッ
slip
EH ...?!
WHAT'S UP WITH THIS GUY...? I HAVE NO IDEA WHAT RULES APPLY HERE!!
APPARENTLY, HE WASN'T COOL WITH IT.

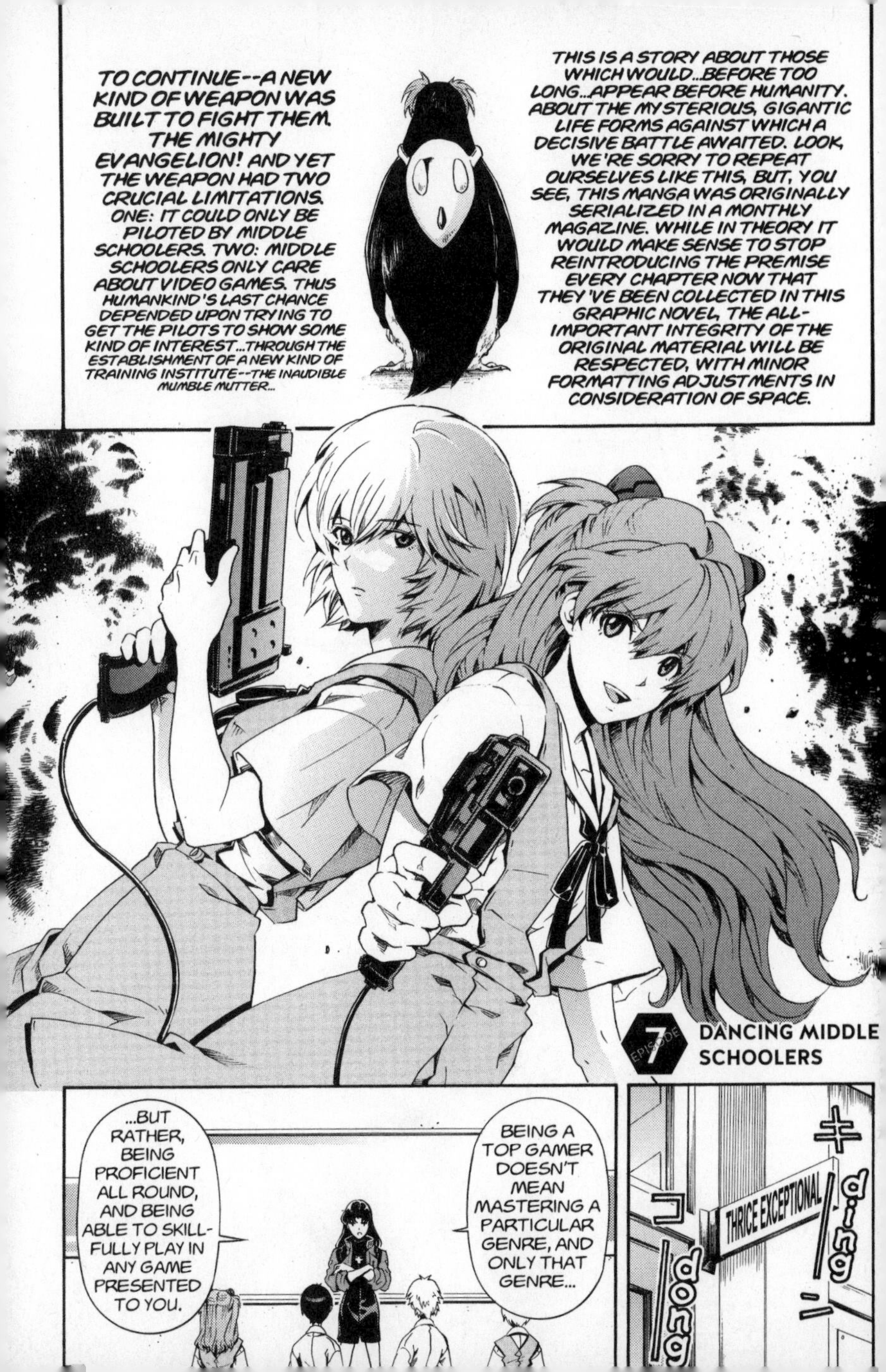
THIS IS A STORY ABOUT THOSE WHICH WOULD...BEFORE TOO LONG...APPEAR BEFORE HUMANITY. ABOUT THE MYSTERIOUS, GIGANTIC LIFE FORMS AGAINST WHICH A DECISIVE BATTLE AWAITED. LOOK, WE'RE SORRY TO REPEAT OURSELVES LIKE THIS, BUT, YOU SEE, THIS MANGA WAS ORIGINALLY SERIALIZED IN A MONTHLY MAGAZINE. WHILE IN THEORY IT WOULD MAKE SENSE TO STOP REINTRODUCING THE PREMISE EVERY CHAPTER NOW THAT THEY'VE BEEN COLLECTED IN THIS GRAPHIC NOVEL, THE ALL-IMPORTANT INTEGRITY OF THE ORIGINAL MATERIAL WILL BE RESPECTED, WITH MINOR FORMATTING ADJUSTMENTS IN CONSIDERATION OF SPACE.
TO CONTINUE--A NEW KIND OF WEAPON WAS BUILT TO FIGHT THEM. THE MIGHTY EVANGELION! AND YET THE WEAPON HAD TWO CRUCIAL LIMITATIONS. ONE: IT COULD ONLY BE PILOTED BY MIDDLE SCHOOLERS. TWO: MIDDLE SCHOOLERS ONLY CARE ABOUT VIDEO GAMES. THUS HUMANKIND'S LAST CHANCE DEPENDED UPON TRYING TO GET THE PILOTS TO SHOW SOME KIND OF INTEREST...THROUGH THE ESTABLISHMENT OF A NEW KIND OF TRAINING INSTITUTE--THE INAUDIBLE MUMBLE MUTTER...
EPISODE 7
DANCING MIDDLE SCHOOLERS
ding-dong
THRICE EXCEPTIONAL
BEING A TOP GAMER DOESN'T MEAN MASTERING A PARTICULAR GENRE, AND ONLY THAT GENRE...
...BUT RATHER, BEING PROFICIENT ALL ROUND, AND BEING ABLE TO SKILL-FULLY PLAY IN ANY GAME PRESENTED TO YOU.

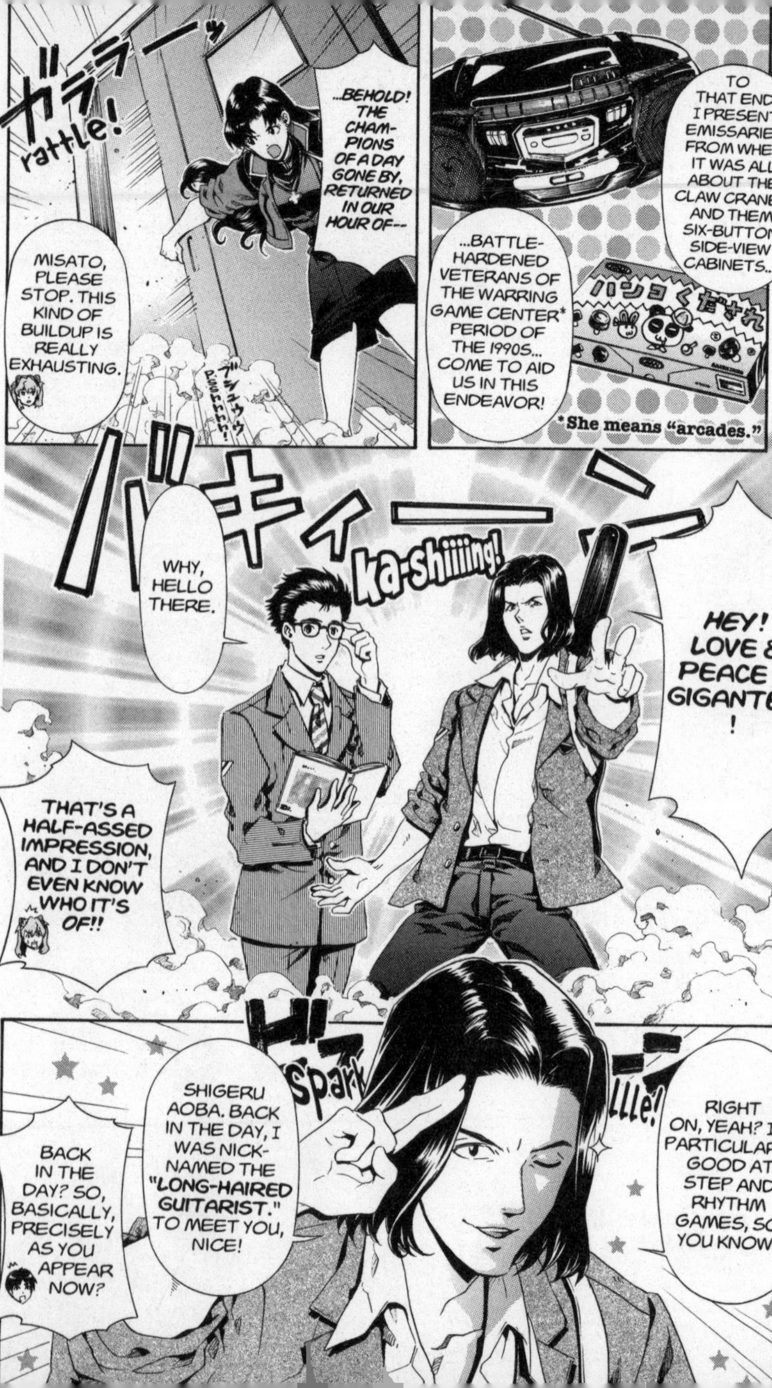
TO THAT END, I PRESENT EMISSARIES FROM WHEN IT WAS ALL ABOUT THE CLAW CRANES AND THEM SIX-BUTTON SIDE-VIEW CABINETS...
...BATTLE-HARDENED VETERANS OF THE WARRING GAME CENTER* PERIOD OF THE 1990S... COME TO AID US IN THIS ENDEAVOR!
*She means "arcades."
...BEHOLD! THE CHAMPIONS OF A DAY GONE BY, RETURNED IN OUR HOUR OF--
rattle!
MISATO, PLEASE STOP. THIS KIND OF BUILDUP IS REALLY EXHAUSTING.
pshhhh!
ka-shiiiing!
HEY! LOVE & PEACE & GIGANTES!
WHY, HELLO THERE.
THAT'S A HALF-ASSED IMPRESSION, AND I DON'T EVEN KNOW WHO IT'S OF!!
RIGHT ON, YEAH? I'M PARTICULARLY GOOD AT STEP AND RHYTHM GAMES, SO YOU KNOW.
SHIGERU AOBA. BACK IN THE DAY, I WAS NICKNAMED THE "LONG-HAIRED GUITARIST." TO MEET YOU, NICE!
sparkle!
BACK IN THE DAY? SO, BASICALLY, PRECISELY AS YOU APPEAR NOW?

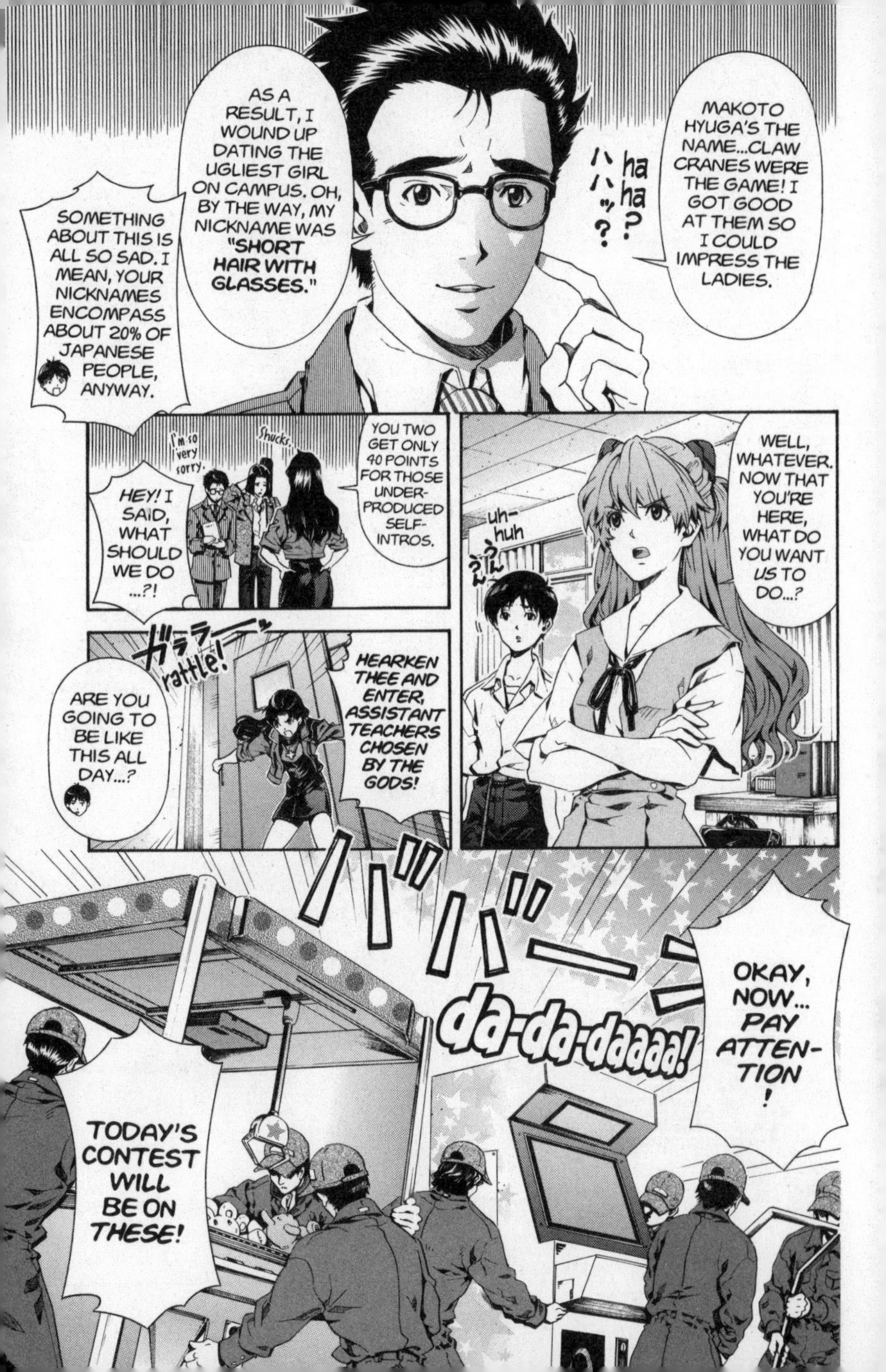
MAKOTO HYUGA'S THE NAME...CLAW CRANES WERE THE GAME! I GOT GOOD AT THEM SO I COULD IMPRESS THE LADIES.
ha ha??
ハハッ??
AS A RESULT, I WOUND UP DATING THE UGLIEST GIRL ON CAMPUS. OH, BY THE WAY, MY NICKNAME WAS "SHORT HAIR WITH GLASSES."
SOMETHING ABOUT THIS IS ALL SO SAD. I MEAN, YOUR NICKNAMES ENCOMPASS ABOUT 20% OF JAPANESE PEOPLE, ANYWAY.
WELL, WHATEVER. NOW THAT YOU'RE HERE, WHAT DO YOU WANT US TO DO...?
uh-huh
うん
YOU TWO GET ONLY 40 POINTS FOR THOSE UNDER-PRODUCED SELF-INTROS.
Shucks.
I'm so very sorry.
HEY! I SAID, WHAT SHOULD WE DO ...?!
ガララーッ
rattle!
HEARKEN THEE AND ENTER, ASSISTANT TEACHERS CHOSEN BY THE GODS!
ARE YOU GOING TO BE LIKE THIS ALL DAY...?
OKAY, NOW... PAY ATTEN-TION!
da-da-daaaa!
TODAY'S CONTEST WILL BE ON THESE!

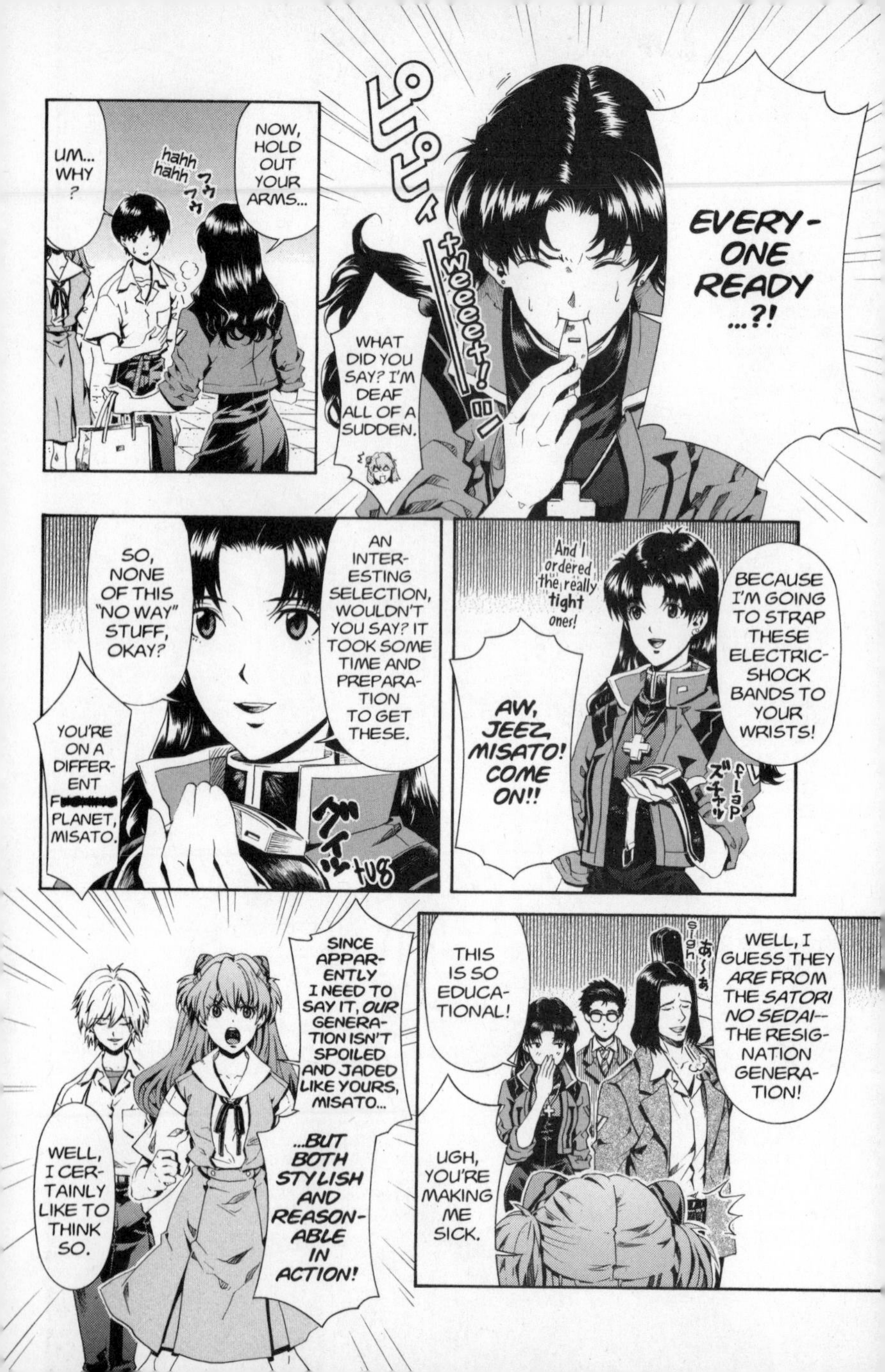
EVERY-ONE READY ...?!
ピピィ
tweeeet!
WHAT DID YOU SAY? I'M DEAF ALL OF A SUDDEN.
NOW, HOLD OUT YOUR ARMS...
hahh hahh
UM... WHY?
BECAUSE I'M GOING TO STRAP THESE ELECTRIC-SHOCK BANDS TO YOUR WRISTS!
And I ordered the really tight ones!
flap
AW, JEEZ, MISATO! COME ON!!
AN INTERESTING SELECTION, WOULDN'T YOU SAY? IT TOOK SOME TIME AND PREPARATION TO GET THESE.
SO, NONE OF THIS "NO WAY" STUFF, OKAY?
tug
YOU'RE ON A DIFFERENT F[redacted] PLANET, MISATO.
WELL, I GUESS THEY ARE FROM THE SATORI NO SEDAI--THE RESIGNATION GENERATION!
sigh
あ～ぁ
THIS IS SO EDUCATIONAL!
UGH, YOU'RE MAKING ME SICK.
SINCE APPARENTLY I NEED TO SAY IT, OUR GENERATION ISN'T SPOILED AND JADED LIKE YOURS, MISATO...
...BUT BOTH STYLISH AND REASONABLE IN ACTION!
WELL, I CERTAINLY LIKE TO THINK SO.

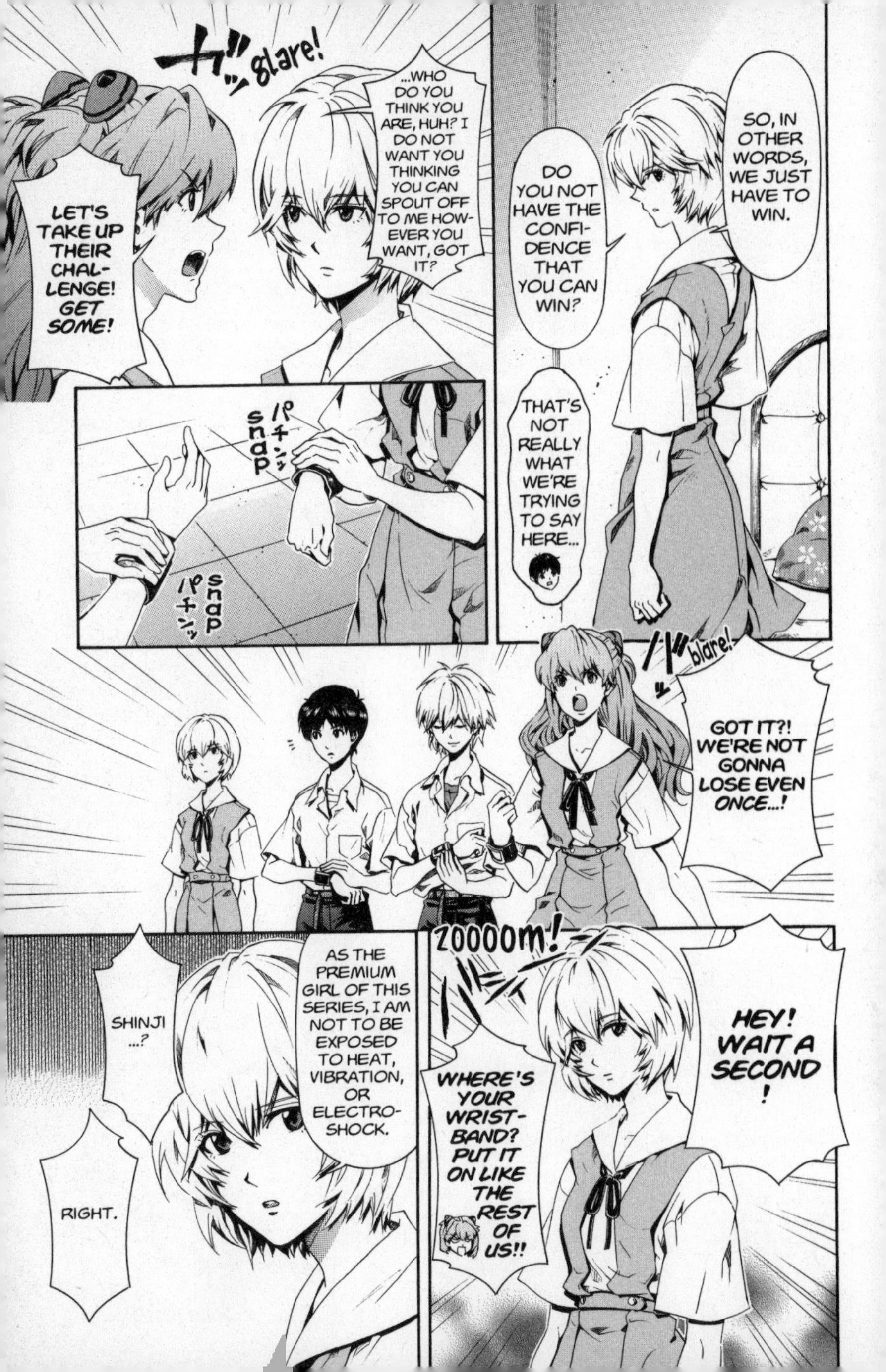
SO, IN OTHER WORDS, WE JUST HAVE TO WIN.
DO YOU NOT HAVE THE CONFIDENCE THAT YOU CAN WIN?
THAT'S NOT REALLY WHAT WE'RE TRYING TO SAY HERE...
ガッ glare!
...WHO DO YOU THINK YOU ARE, HUH? I DO NOT WANT YOU THINKING YOU CAN SPOUT OFF TO ME HOWEVER YOU WANT, GOT IT?
LET'S TAKE UP THEIR CHALLENGE! GET SOME!
パチンッ snap
パチンッ snap
バッ blare!
GOT IT?! WE'RE NOT GONNA LOSE EVEN ONCE...!
HEY! WAIT A SECOND!
zooooM!
WHERE'S YOUR WRISTBAND? PUT IT ON LIKE THE REST OF US!!
AS THE PREMIUM GIRL OF THIS SERIES, I AM NOT TO BE EXPOSED TO HEAT, VIBRATION, OR ELECTROSHOCK.
SHINJI ...?
RIGHT.

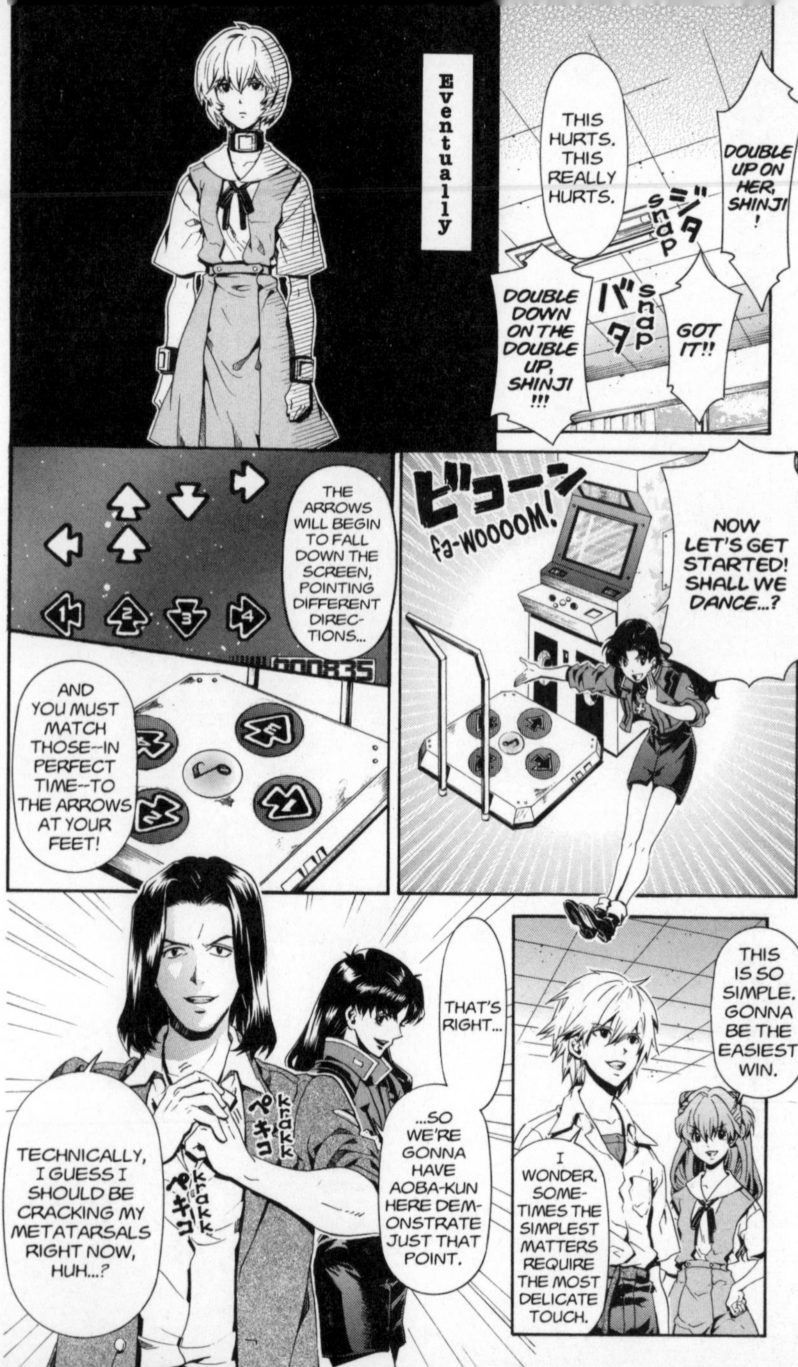
DOUBLE UP ON HER, SHINJI!
THIS HURTS. THIS REALLY HURTS.
snap
GOT IT!!
DOUBLE DOWN ON THE DOUBLE UP, SHINJI!!!
snap
Eventually
NOW LET'S GET STARTED! SHALL WE DANCE...?
fa-WOOOOM!
THE ARROWS WILL BEGIN TO FALL DOWN THE SCREEN, POINTING DIFFERENT DIREC-TIONS...
AND YOU MUST MATCH THOSE--IN PERFECT TIME--TO THE ARROWS AT YOUR FEET!
THIS IS SO SIMPLE. GONNA BE THE EASIEST WIN.
I WONDER. SOME-TIMES THE SIMPLEST MATTERS REQUIRE THE MOST DELICATE TOUCH.
THAT'S RIGHT...
...SO WE'RE GONNA HAVE AOBA-KUN HERE DEM-ONSTRATE JUST THAT POINT.
krakk
krakk
TECHNICALLY, I GUESS I SHOULD BE CRACKING MY METATARSALS RIGHT NOW, HUH...?

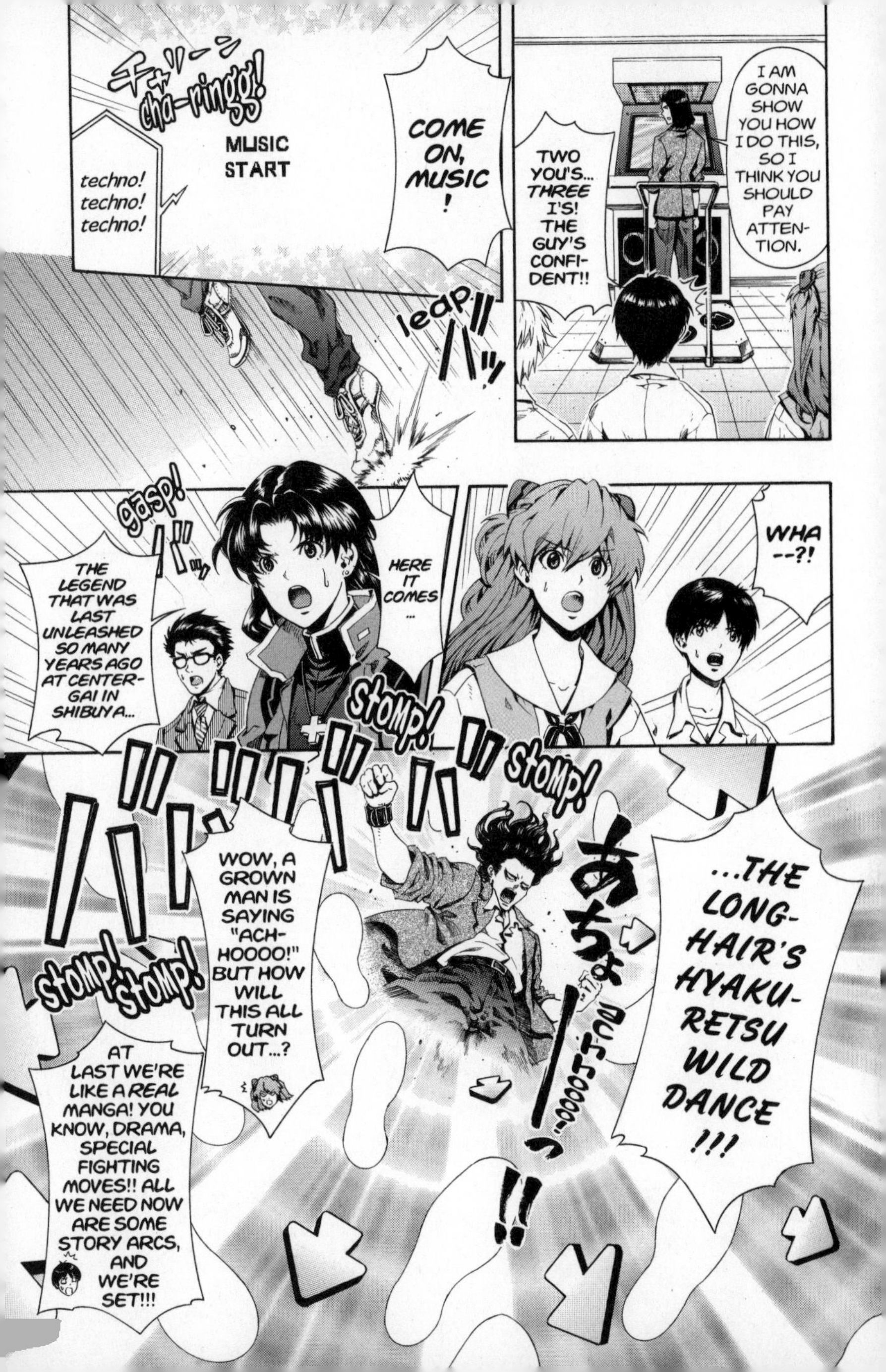

I AM GONNA SHOW YOU HOW I DO THIS, SO I THINK YOU SHOULD PAY ATTENTION.
TWO YOU'S... THREE I'S! THE GUY'S CONFIDENT!!
COME ON, MUSIC!
チャリーン cha-ringg!
MUSIC START
techno! techno! techno!
leap
バッ
WHA--?!
HERE IT COMES...
gasp!
バッ
THE LEGEND THAT WAS LAST UNLEASHED SO MANY YEARS AGO AT CENTER-GAI IN SHIBUYA...
stomp! stomp!
...THE LONG-HAIR'S HYAKU-RETSU WILD DANCE!!!
あちょーっ!!
achoooo...
WOW, A GROWN MAN IS SAYING "ACH-HOOOO!" BUT HOW WILL THIS ALL TURN OUT...?
stomp! stomp!
AT LAST WE'RE LIKE A REAL MANGA! YOU KNOW, DRAMA, SPECIAL FIGHTING MOVES!! ALL WE NEED NOW ARE SOME STORY ARCS, AND WE'RE SET!!!

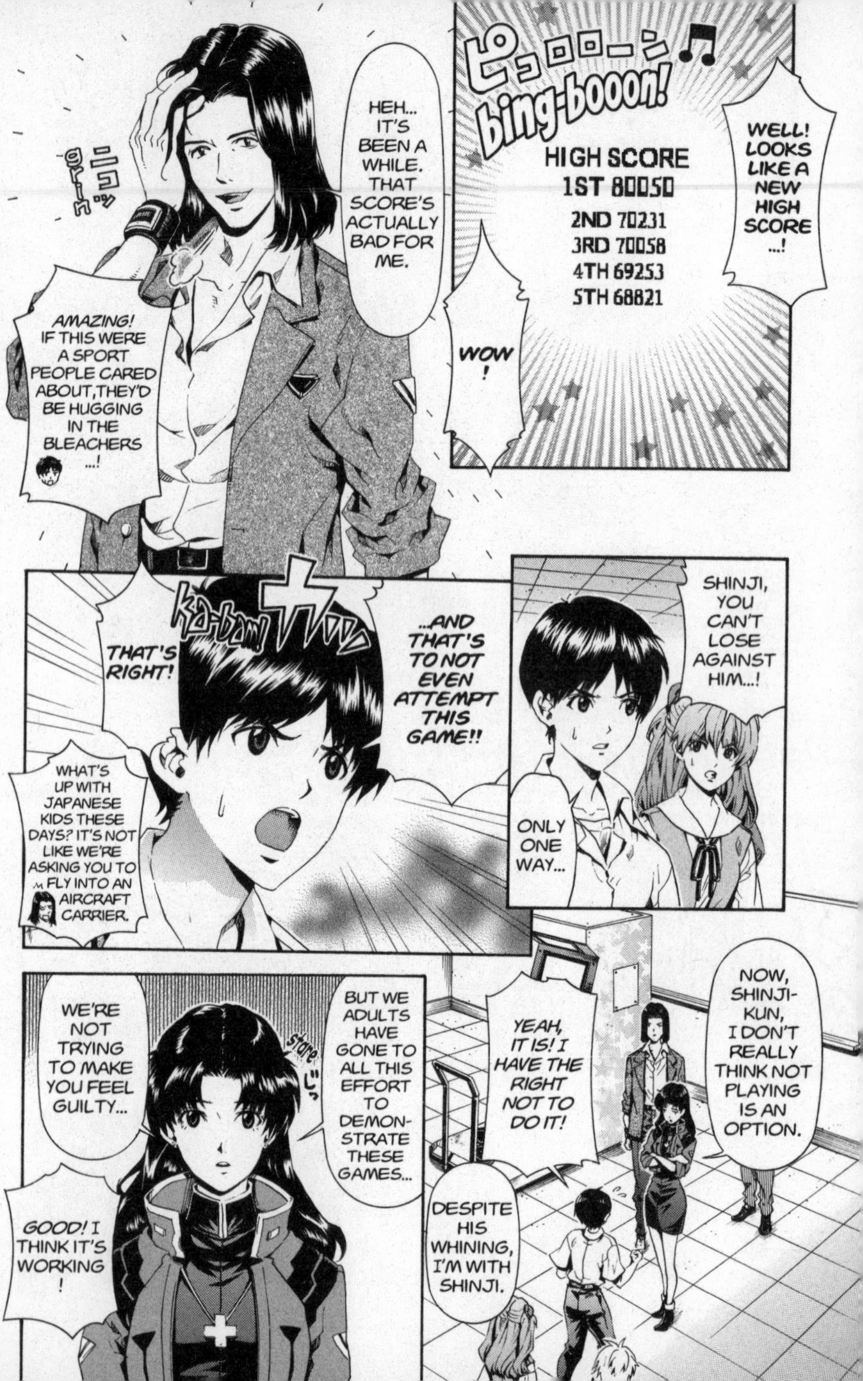
bing-booon!
HIGH SCORE
1ST 80050
2ND 70231
3RD 70058
4TH 69253
5TH 68821
WELL! LOOKS LIKE A NEW HIGH SCORE ...!
WOW!
grin
HEH... IT'S BEEN A WHILE. THAT SCORE'S ACTUALLY BAD FOR ME.
AMAZING! IF THIS WERE A SPORT PEOPLE CARED ABOUT, THEY'D BE HUGGING IN THE BLEACHERS ...!
SHINJI, YOU CAN'T LOSE AGAINST HIM...!
ONLY ONE WAY...
...AND THAT'S TO NOT EVEN ATTEMPT THIS GAME!!
ka-bam!
THAT'S RIGHT!
WHAT'S UP WITH JAPANESE KIDS THESE DAYS? IT'S NOT LIKE WE'RE ASKING YOU TO FLY INTO AN AIRCRAFT CARRIER.
NOW, SHINJI-KUN, I DON'T REALLY THINK NOT PLAYING IS AN OPTION.
YEAH, IT IS! I HAVE THE RIGHT NOT TO DO IT!
DESPITE HIS WHINING, I'M WITH SHINJI.
BUT WE ADULTS HAVE GONE TO ALL THIS EFFORT TO DEMON-STRATE THESE GAMES...
stare
WE'RE NOT TRYING TO MAKE YOU FEEL GUILTY...
GOOD! I THINK IT'S WORKING!

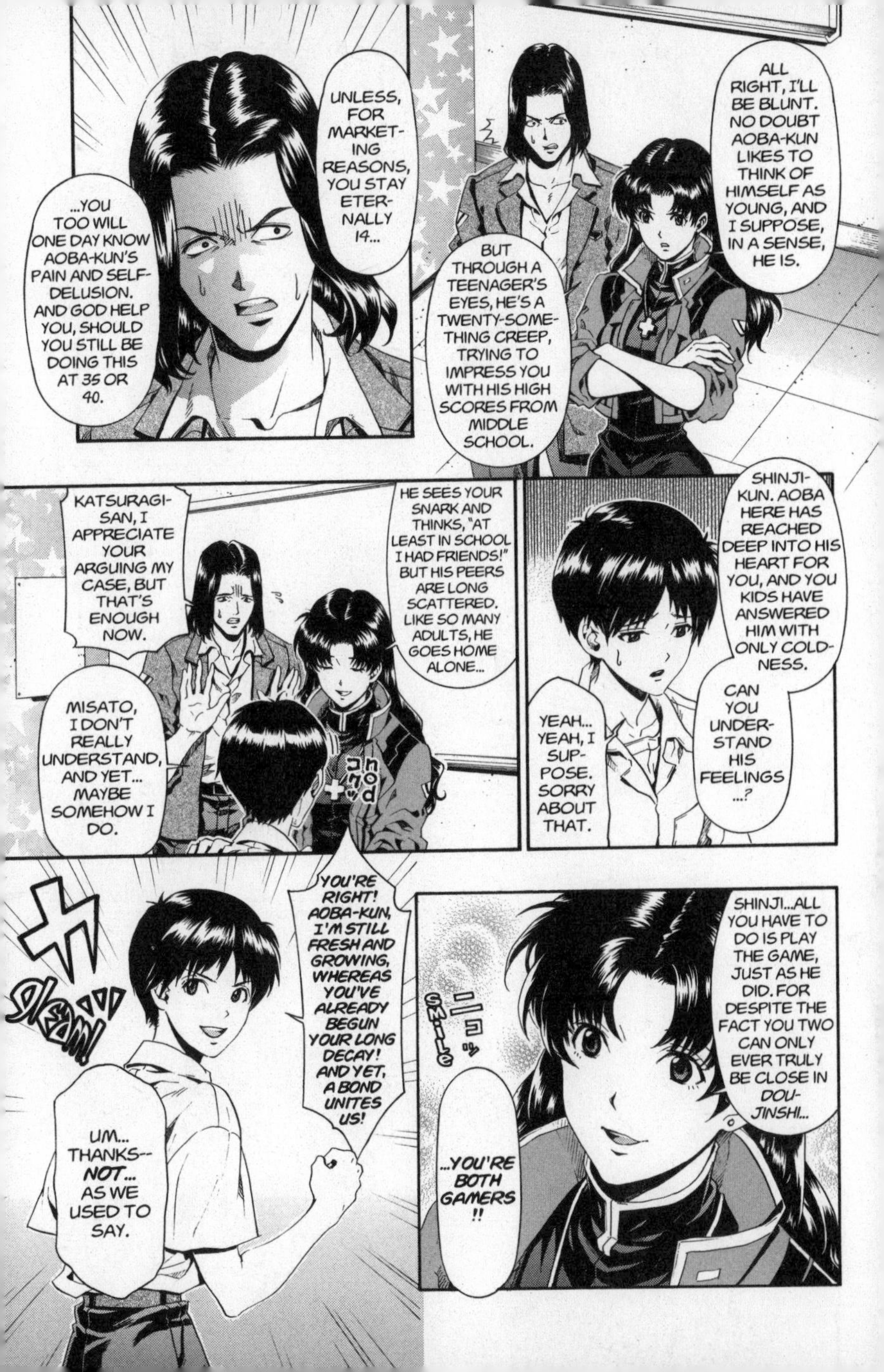
ALL RIGHT, I'LL BE BLUNT. NO DOUBT AOBA-KUN LIKES TO THINK OF HIMSELF AS YOUNG, AND I SUPPOSE, IN A SENSE, HE IS.
BUT THROUGH A TEENAGER'S EYES, HE'S A TWENTY-SOMETHING CREEP, TRYING TO IMPRESS YOU WITH HIS HIGH SCORES FROM MIDDLE SCHOOL.
UNLESS, FOR MARKETING REASONS, YOU STAY ETERNALLY 14...
...YOU TOO WILL ONE DAY KNOW AOBA-KUN'S PAIN AND SELF-DELUSION. AND GOD HELP YOU, SHOULD YOU STILL BE DOING THIS AT 35 OR 40.
SHINJI-KUN. AOBA HERE HAS REACHED DEEP INTO HIS HEART FOR YOU, AND YOU KIDS HAVE ANSWERED HIM WITH ONLY COLDNESS.
CAN YOU UNDERSTAND HIS FEELINGS...?
YEAH... YEAH, I SUPPOSE. SORRY ABOUT THAT.
HE SEES YOUR SNARK AND THINKS, "AT LEAST IN SCHOOL I HAD FRIENDS!" BUT HIS PEERS ARE LONG SCATTERED. LIKE SO MANY ADULTS, HE GOES HOME ALONE...
KATSURAGI-SAN, I APPRECIATE YOUR ARGUING MY CASE, BUT THAT'S ENOUGH NOW.
nod
MISATO, I DON'T REALLY UNDERSTAND, AND YET... MAYBE SOMEHOW I DO.
SHINJI...ALL YOU HAVE TO DO IS PLAY THE GAME, JUST AS HE DID. FOR DESPITE THE FACT YOU TWO CAN ONLY EVER TRULY BE CLOSE IN DOUJINSHI...
smile
...YOU'RE BOTH GAMERS!!
YOU'RE RIGHT! AOBA-KUN, I'M STILL FRESH AND GROWING, WHEREAS YOU'VE ALREADY BEGUN YOUR LONG DECAY! AND YET, A BOND UNITES US!
gleam
UM... THANKS--NOT... AS WE USED TO SAY.

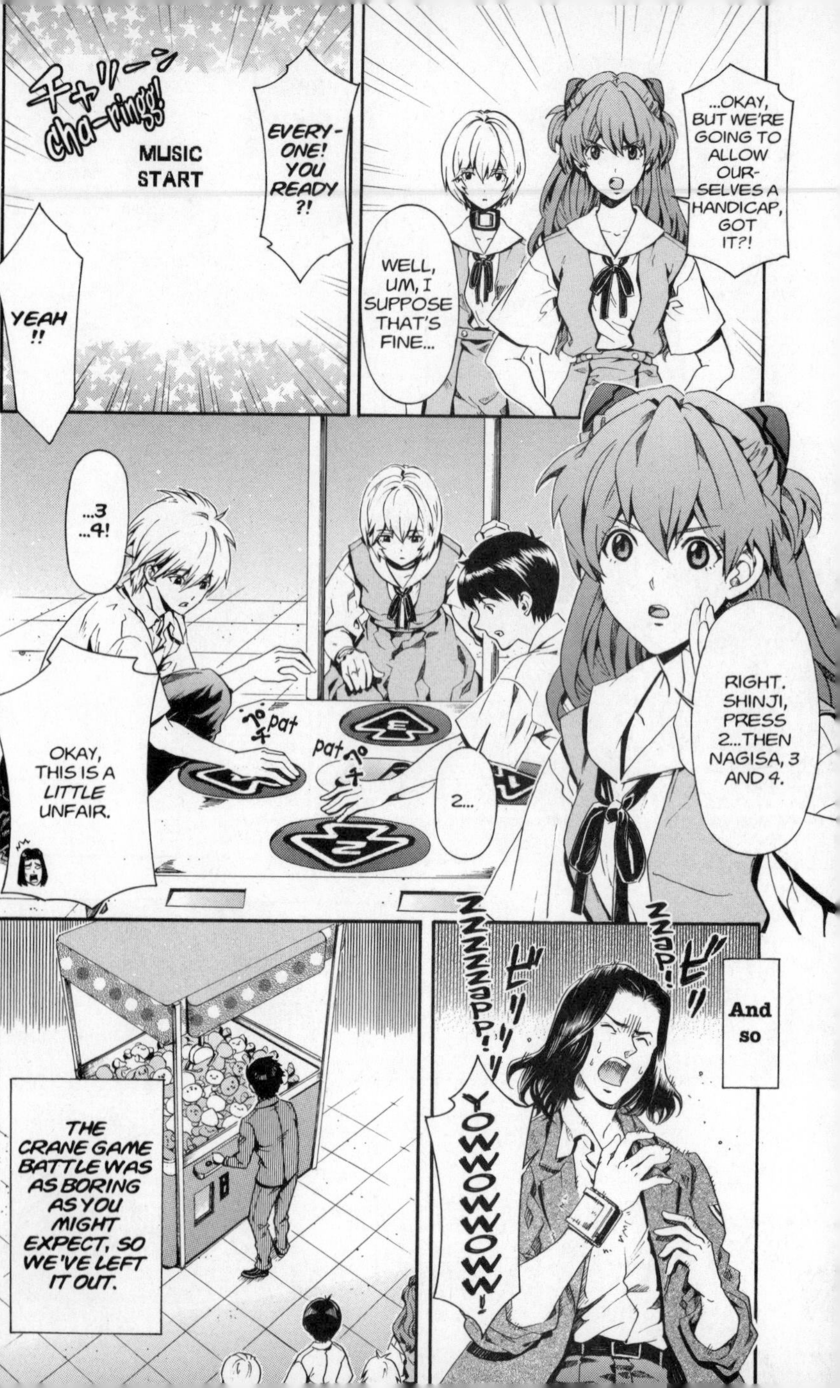
...OKAY, BUT WE'RE GOING TO ALLOW OUR-SELVES A HANDICAP, GOT IT?!
WELL, UM, I SUPPOSE THAT'S FINE...
EVERY-ONE! YOU READY ?!
チャリーン cha-ringg!
MUSIC START
YEAH !!
RIGHT. SHINJI, PRESS 2...THEN NAGISA, 3 AND 4.
2...
pat ペチ
...3 ...4!
ペチ pat
OKAY, THIS IS A LITTLE UNFAIR.
And so
ビリ zzap!
ビリリ ZZZZZZAPP!!
YOWWOWWOWW!
THE CRANE GAME BATTLE WAS AS BORING AS YOU MIGHT EXPECT, SO WE'VE LEFT IT OUT.

Why is it just me? Whenever I feel down and out, whenever I fall into the depression of thinking, "Why'd I even have to be born?" I'm of the opinion that I should really try to combat that feeling by making this into a manga that says to you what I'd say if I were a really positive American, you know, something like, "Hey brother, don't let it get you down!" And see how that works.

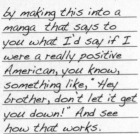

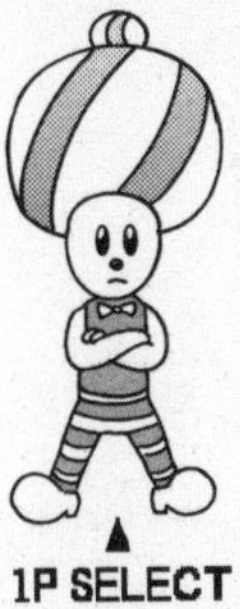
1P SELECT

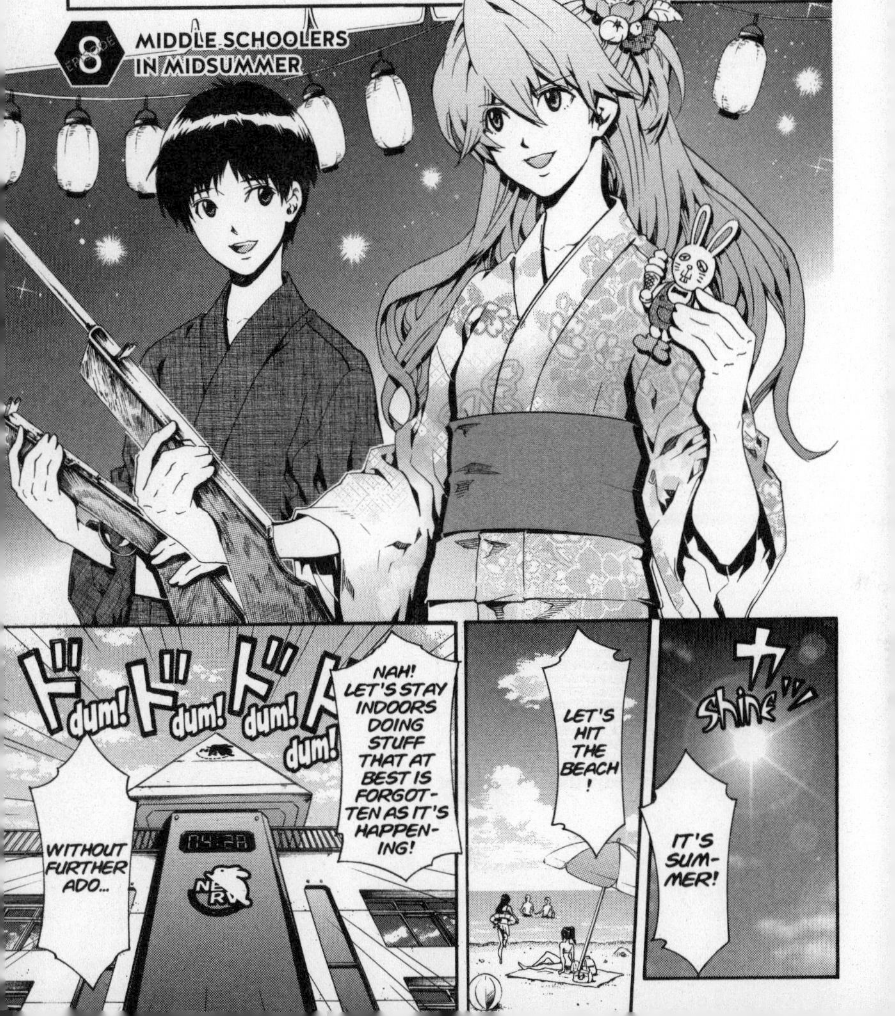
EPISODE 8
MIDDLE SCHOOLERS IN MIDSUMMER
shine
IT'S SUMMER!
LET'S HIT THE BEACH!
NAH! LET'S STAY INDOORS DOING STUFF THAT AT BEST IS FORGOTTEN AS IT'S HAPPENING!
dum! dum! dum! dum!
WITHOUT FURTHER ADO...

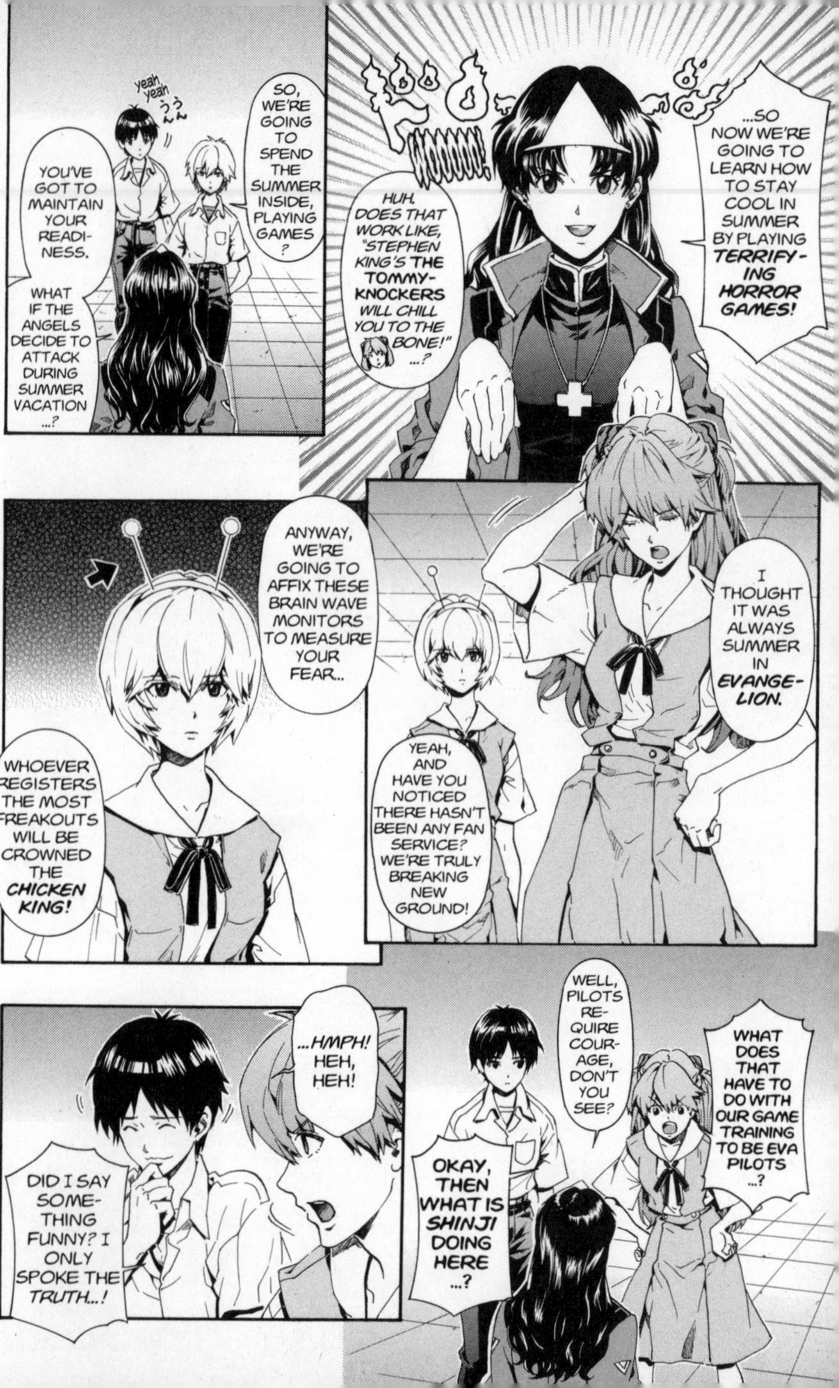
...SO NOW WE'RE GOING TO LEARN HOW TO STAY COOL IN SUMMER BY PLAYING **TERRIFYING HORROR GAMES!**
WOOOOOO!
HUH. DOES THAT WORK LIKE, "STEPHEN KING'S **THE TOMMYKNOCKERS** WILL CHILL YOU TO THE BONE!" ...?
SO, WE'RE GOING TO SPEND THE SUMMER INSIDE, PLAYING GAMES?
yeah yeah
うぅん
YOU'VE GOT TO MAINTAIN YOUR READINESS.
WHAT IF THE ANGELS DECIDE TO ATTACK DURING SUMMER VACATION...?
I THOUGHT IT WAS ALWAYS SUMMER IN ***EVANGELION.***
YEAH, AND HAVE YOU NOTICED THERE HASN'T BEEN ANY FAN SERVICE? WE'RE TRULY BREAKING NEW GROUND!
ANYWAY, WE'RE GOING TO AFFIX THESE BRAIN WAVE MONITORS TO MEASURE YOUR FEAR...
WHOEVER REGISTERS THE MOST FREAKOUTS WILL BE CROWNED THE ***CHICKEN KING!***
WHAT DOES THAT HAVE TO DO WITH OUR GAME TRAINING TO BE EVA PILOTS...?
WELL, PILOTS REQUIRE COURAGE, DON'T YOU SEE?
OKAY, THEN WHAT IS *SHINJI* DOING HERE...?
...HMPH! HEH, HEH!
DID I SAY SOMETHING FUNNY? I ONLY SPOKE THE *TRUTH...!*

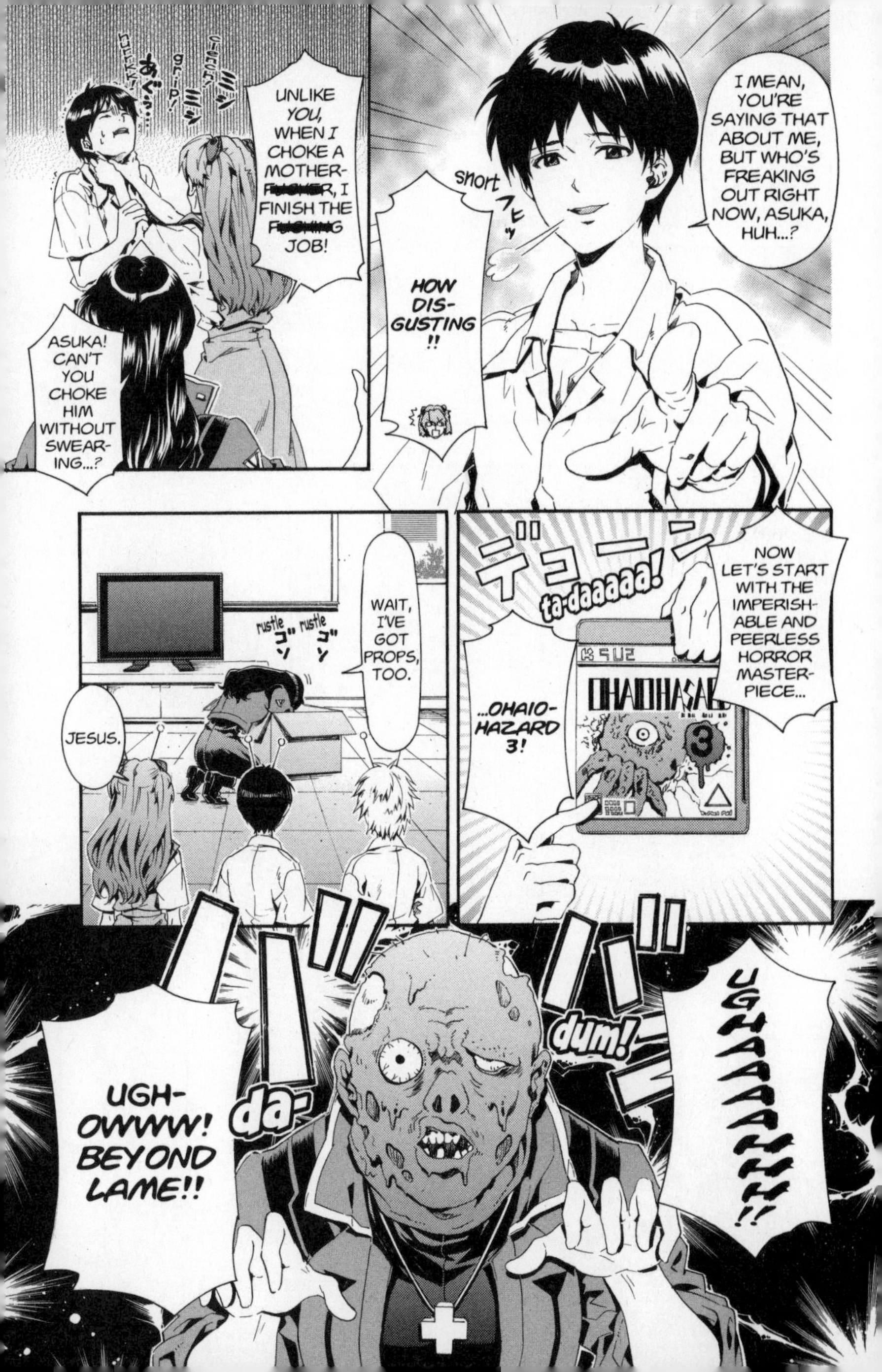
I MEAN, YOU'RE SAYING THAT ABOUT ME, BUT WHO'S FREAKING OUT RIGHT NOW, ASUKA, HUH...?
snort フヒッ
HOW DIS-GUSTING!!
UNLIKE YOU, WHEN I CHOKE A MOTHER-[redacted], I FINISH THE [redacted] JOB!
clench! ミシ
grip! ミシ
hurkk! あぐぅ…
ASUKA! CAN'T YOU CHOKE HIM WITHOUT SWEARING...?
デューン ta-daaaaa!
NOW LET'S START WITH THE IMPERISH-ABLE AND PEERLESS HORROR MASTER-PIECE...
...OHAIO-HAZARD 3!
WAIT, I'VE GOT PROPS, TOO.
rustle ゴソ rustle ゴソ
JESUS.
UGHAAAAAHH!!
dum!
da-
UGH-OWWW! BEYOND LAME!!

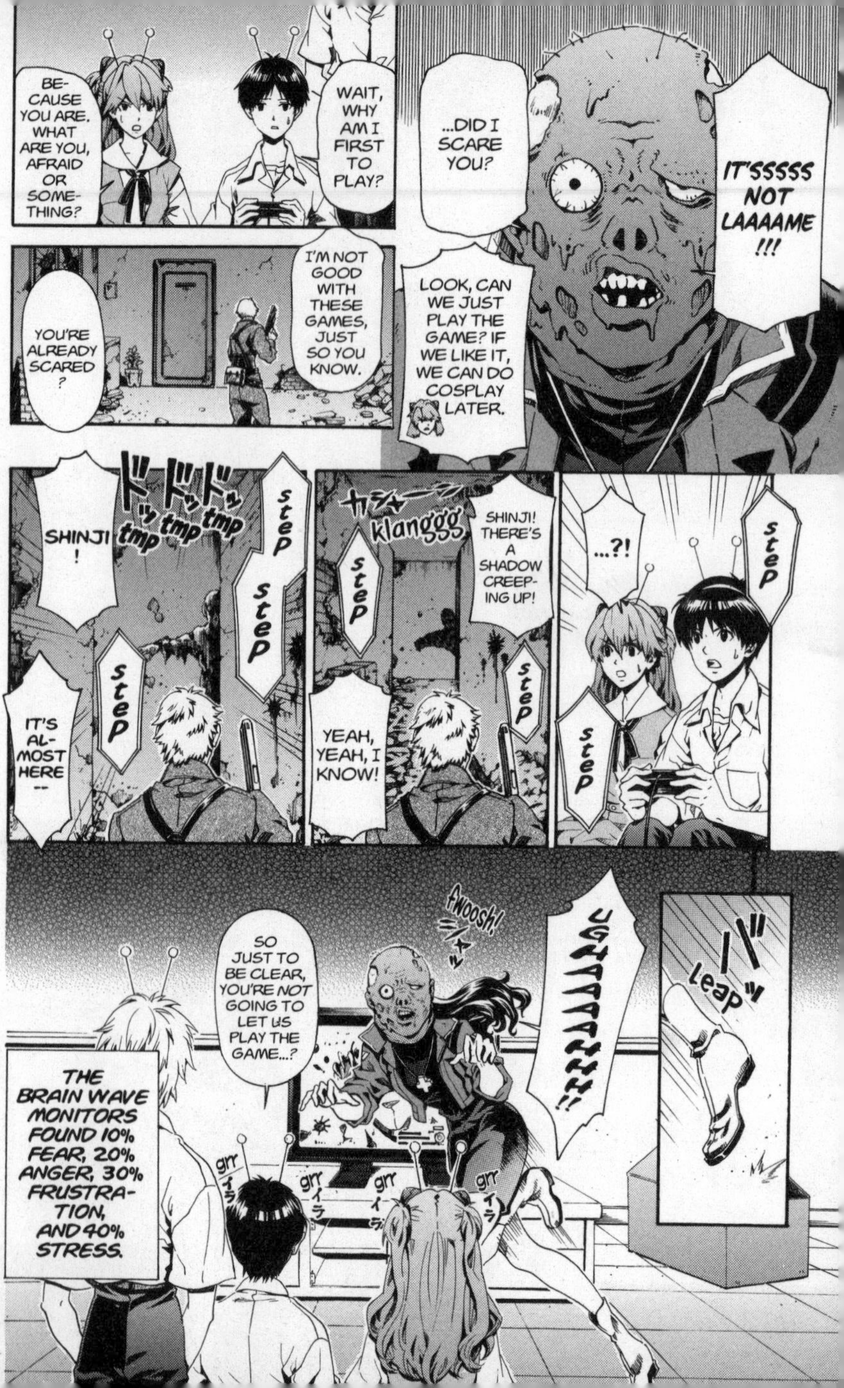
IT'SSSSS NOT LAAAAME!!!
...DID I SCARE YOU?
LOOK, CAN WE JUST PLAY THE GAME? IF WE LIKE IT, WE CAN DO COSPLAY LATER.
WAIT, WHY AM I FIRST TO PLAY?
BE-CAUSE YOU ARE. WHAT ARE YOU, AFRAID OR SOME-THING?
I'M NOT GOOD WITH THESE GAMES, JUST SO YOU KNOW.
YOU'RE ALREADY SCARED?
step
...?!
step
SHINJI! THERE'S A SHADOW CREEPING UP!
カシャーン
klanggg
step
step
YEAH, YEAH, I KNOW!
step
step
ドドドッ
tmp tmp tmp
SHINJI!
step
IT'S AL-MOST HERE--
バッ
leap
UGHAAAAAHHH!!
fwoosh!
シャッ
SO JUST TO BE CLEAR, YOU'RE NOT GOING TO LET US PLAY THE GAME...?
grr
イラ
grr
イラ
grr
イラ
grr
イラ
THE BRAIN WAVE MONITORS FOUND 10% FEAR, 20% ANGER, 30% FRUSTRA-TION, AND 40% STRESS.

Maybe there will come a time when I can look back fondly as an adult on all those days as a kid when things seemed so out of control. This is a manga about boys and girls in that exact same situation.

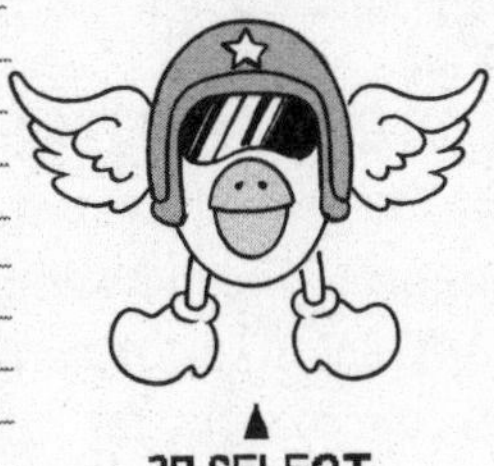
2P SELECT

There are some days when I think tomorrow can't come any sooner, and there are some days when I hope that tomorrow never comes at all.

EPISODE 9 NOTEBOOK OF THE WANDERING MIDDLE SCHOOLERS (PART 1)

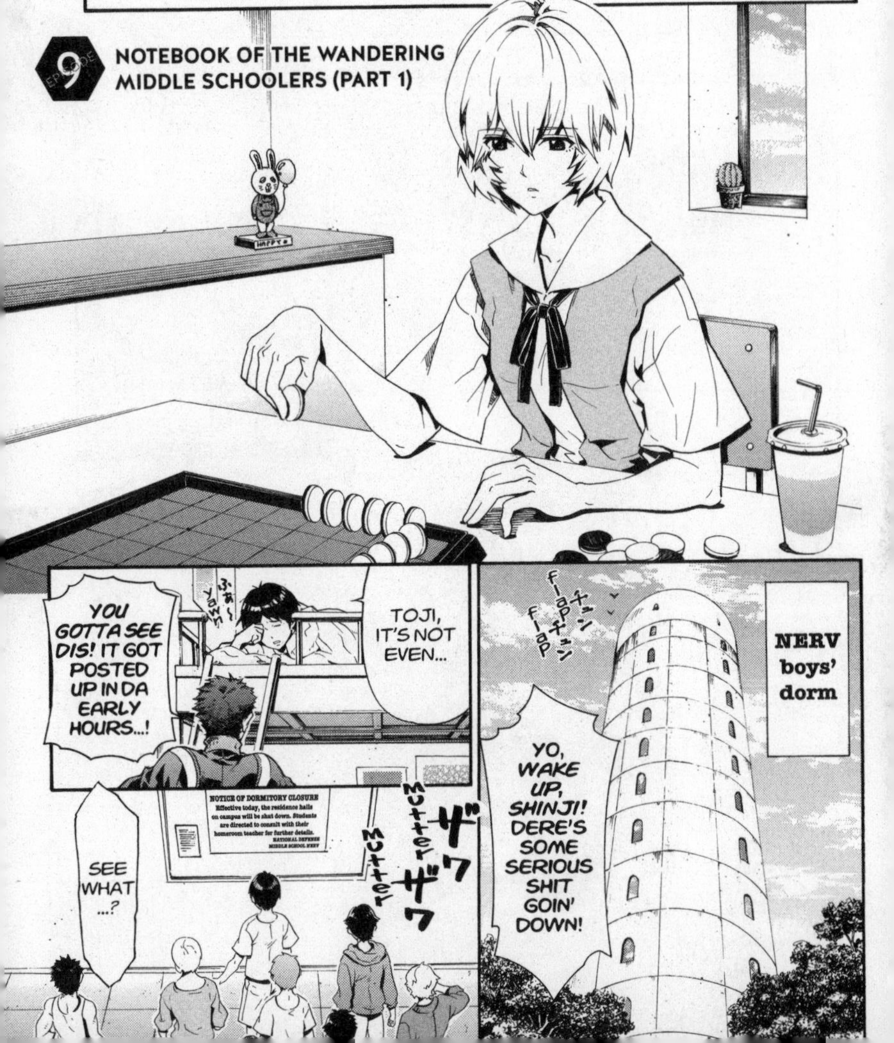
NERV boys' dorm
flap チュン flap チュン flap
YO, WAKE UP, SHINJI! DERE'S SOME SERIOUS SHIT GOIN' DOWN!
TOJI, IT'S NOT EVEN...
ふあ~ yawn
YOU GOTTA SEE DIS! IT GOT POSTED UP IN DA EARLY HOURS...!
NOTICE OF DORMITORY CLOSURE
Effective today, the residence halls on campus will be shut down. Students are directed to consult with their homeroom teacher for further details.
NATIONAL DEFENSE MIDDLE SCHOOL NERV
MUTTER ザワ MUTTER ザワ
SEE WHAT ...?

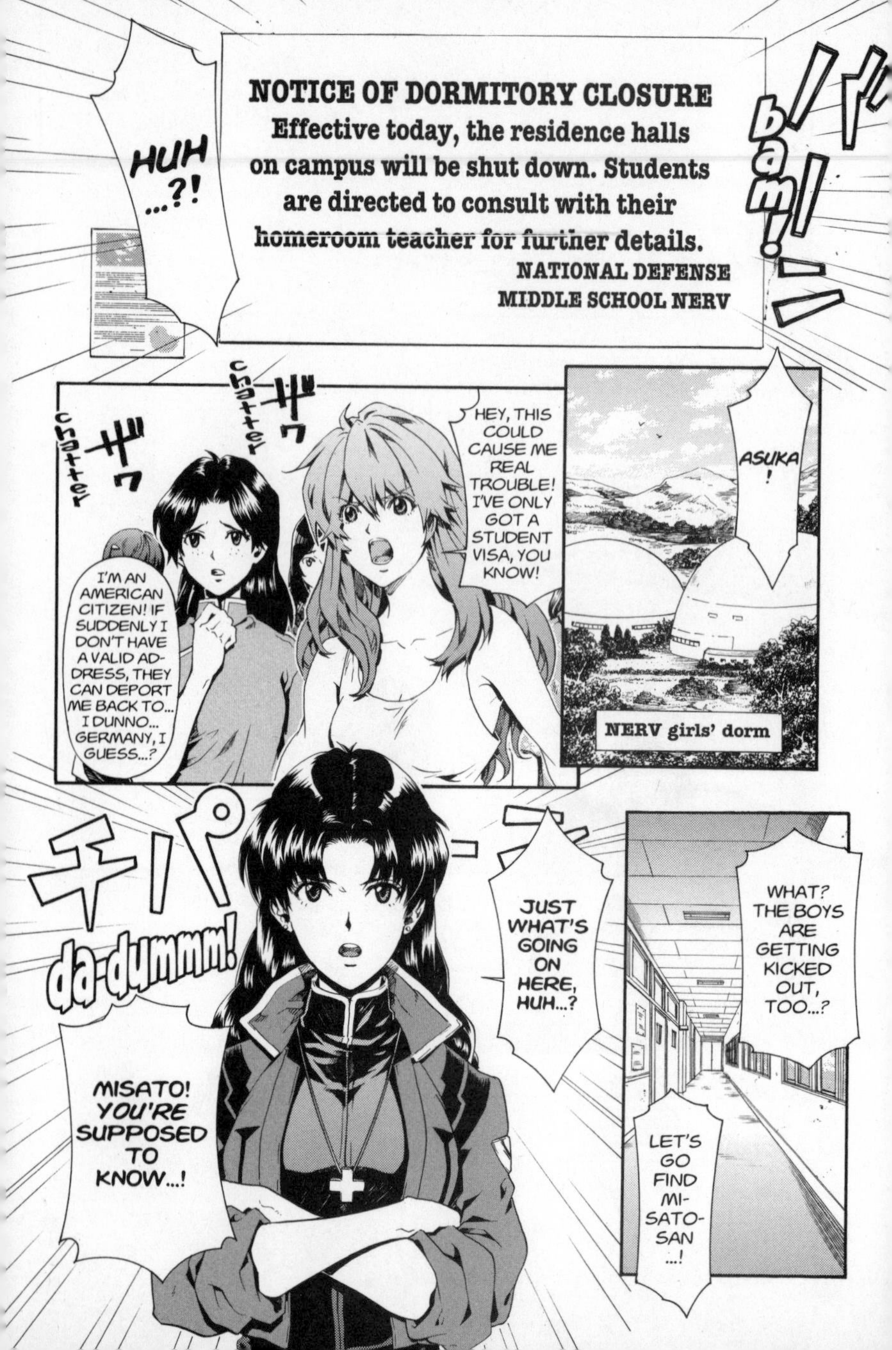
bam!
NOTICE OF DORMITORY CLOSURE
Effective today, the residence halls on campus will be shut down. Students are directed to consult with their homeroom teacher for further details.
NATIONAL DEFENSE MIDDLE SCHOOL NERV
HUH ...?!
ASUKA!
NERV girls' dorm
chatter
chatter
HEY, THIS COULD CAUSE ME REAL TROUBLE! I'VE ONLY GOT A STUDENT VISA, YOU KNOW!
I'M AN AMERICAN CITIZEN! IF SUDDENLY I DON'T HAVE A VALID ADDRESS, THEY CAN DEPORT ME BACK TO... I DUNNO... GERMANY, I GUESS...?
WHAT? THE BOYS ARE GETTING KICKED OUT, TOO...?
LET'S GO FIND MISATO-SAN...!
JUST WHAT'S GOING ON HERE, HUH...?
da-dummm!
MISATO! YOU'RE SUPPOSED TO KNOW...!

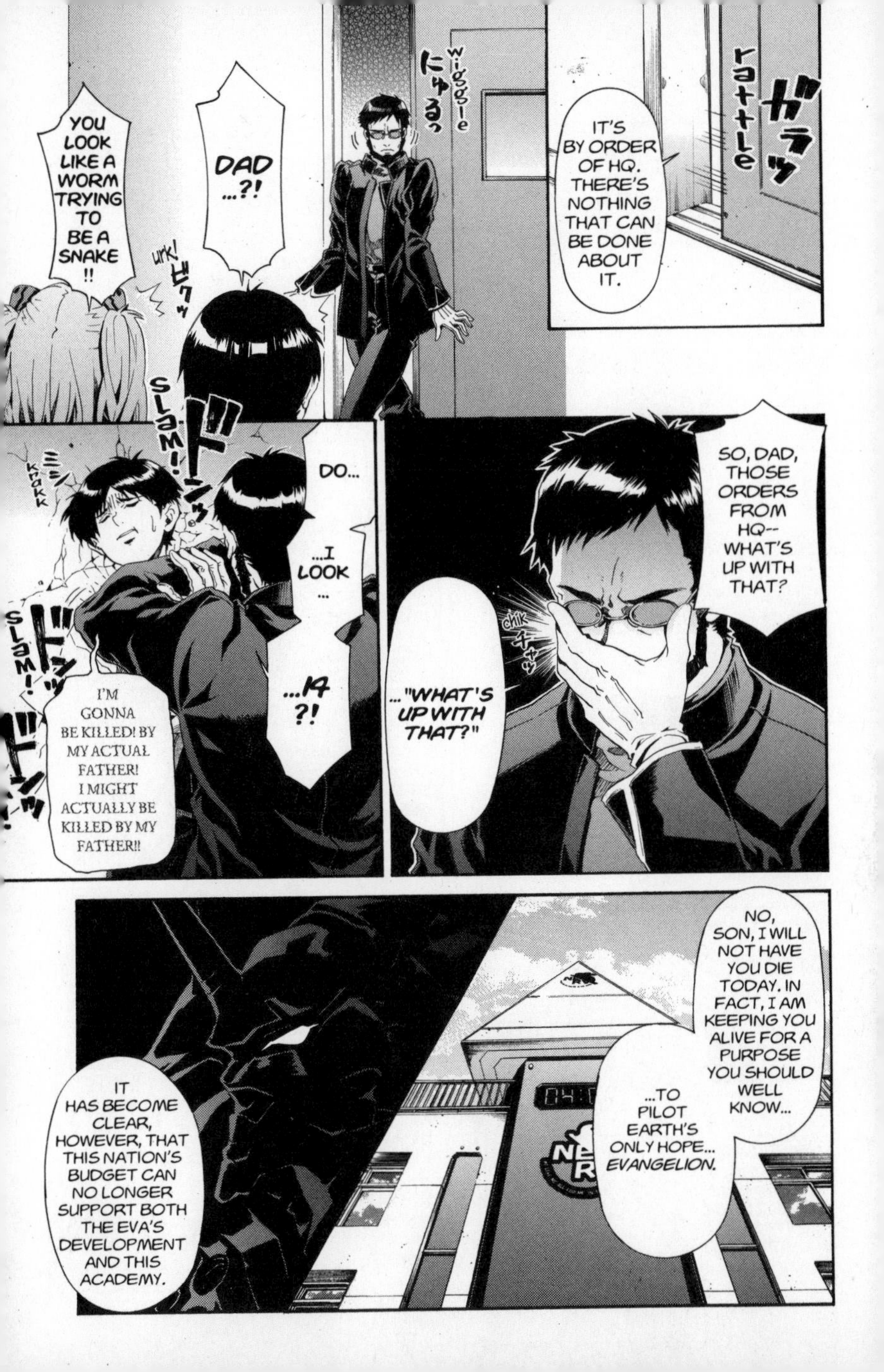

rattle
ガラッ
IT'S BY ORDER OF HQ. THERE'S NOTHING THAT CAN BE DONE ABOUT IT.
wiggle
にゅるっ
DAD ...?!
YOU LOOK LIKE A WORM TRYING TO BE A SNAKE !!
urk!
ビクッ
SLAM!
SO, DAD, THOSE ORDERS FROM HQ-- WHAT'S UP WITH THAT?
chik
チャッ
..."WHAT'S UP WITH THAT?"
DO...
...I LOOK ...
...14 ?!
krakk
ミシ
SLAM!
I'M GONNA BE KILLED! BY MY ACTUAL FATHER! I MIGHT ACTUALLY BE KILLED BY MY FATHER!!
NO, SON, I WILL NOT HAVE YOU DIE TODAY. IN FACT, I AM KEEPING YOU ALIVE FOR A PURPOSE YOU SHOULD WELL KNOW...
...TO PILOT EARTH'S ONLY HOPE... EVANGELION.
IT HAS BECOME CLEAR, HOWEVER, THAT THIS NATION'S BUDGET CAN NO LONGER SUPPORT BOTH THE EVA'S DEVELOPMENT AND THIS ACADEMY.

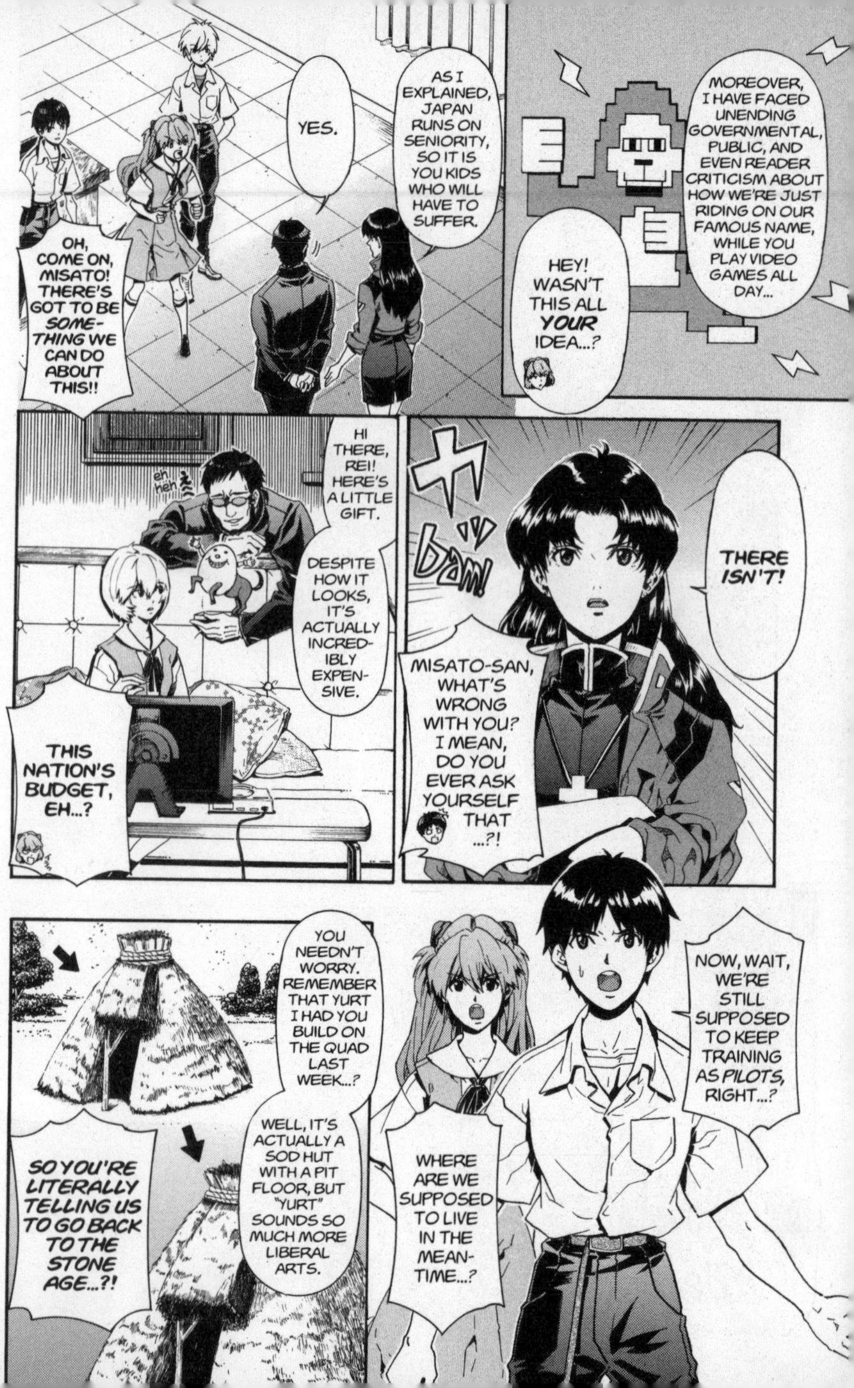
MOREOVER, I HAVE FACED UNENDING GOVERNMENTAL, PUBLIC, AND EVEN READER CRITICISM ABOUT HOW WE'RE JUST RIDING ON OUR FAMOUS NAME, WHILE YOU PLAY VIDEO GAMES ALL DAY...
HEY! WASN'T THIS ALL YOUR IDEA...?
AS I EXPLAINED, JAPAN RUNS ON SENIORITY, SO IT IS YOU KIDS WHO WILL HAVE TO SUFFER.
YES.
OH, COME ON, MISATO! THERE'S GOT TO BE SOMETHING WE CAN DO ABOUT THIS!!
bam!
THERE ISN'T!
MISATO-SAN, WHAT'S WRONG WITH YOU? I MEAN, DO YOU EVER ASK YOURSELF THAT ...?!
eh heh
HI THERE, REI! HERE'S A LITTLE GIFT.
DESPITE HOW IT LOOKS, IT'S ACTUALLY INCREDIBLY EXPENSIVE.
THIS NATION'S BUDGET, EH...?
NOW, WAIT, WE'RE STILL SUPPOSED TO KEEP TRAINING AS PILOTS, RIGHT...?
YOU NEEDN'T WORRY. REMEMBER THAT YURT I HAD YOU BUILD ON THE QUAD LAST WEEK...?
WHERE ARE WE SUPPOSED TO LIVE IN THE MEANTIME...?
WELL, IT'S ACTUALLY A SOD HUT WITH A PIT FLOOR, BUT "YURT" SOUNDS SO MUCH MORE LIBERAL ARTS.
SO YOU'RE LITERALLY TELLING US TO GO BACK TO THE STONE AGE...?!

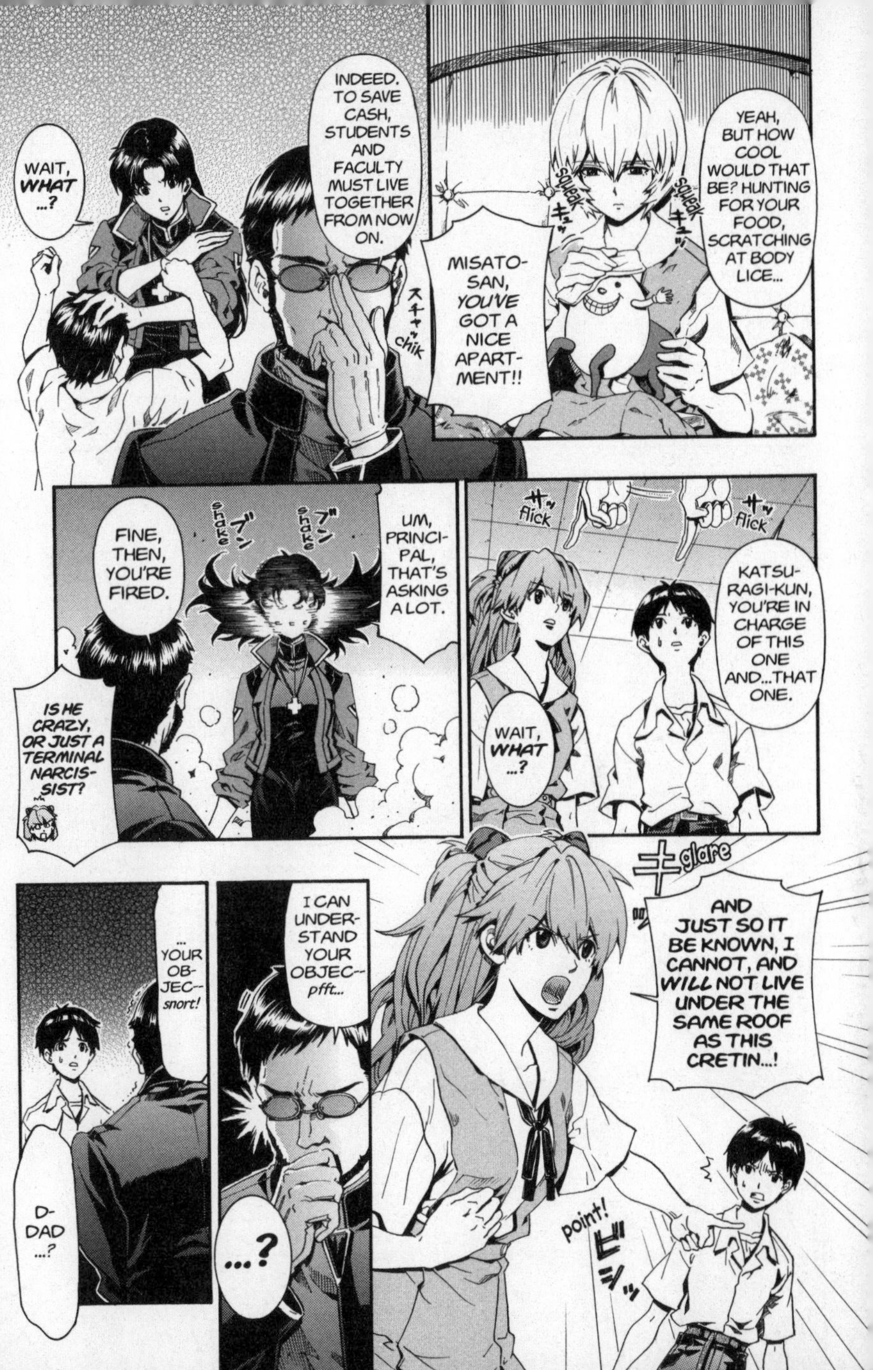

YEAH, BUT HOW COOL WOULD THAT BE? HUNTING FOR YOUR FOOD, SCRATCHING AT BODY LICE...
squeak
squeak
MISATO-SAN, YOU'VE GOT A NICE APARTMENT!!
INDEED. TO SAVE CASH, STUDENTS AND FACULTY MUST LIVE TOGETHER FROM NOW ON.
chik
WAIT, WHAT ...?
flick
flick
KATSURAGI-KUN, YOU'RE IN CHARGE OF THIS ONE AND...THAT ONE.
WAIT, WHAT ...?
UM, PRINCIPAL, THAT'S ASKING A LOT.
shake
shake
FINE, THEN, YOU'RE FIRED.
IS HE CRAZY, OR JUST A TERMINAL NARCIS-SIST?
glare
AND JUST SO IT BE KNOWN, I CANNOT, AND WILL NOT LIVE UNDER THE SAME ROOF AS THIS CRETIN...!
point!
I CAN UNDER-STAND YOUR OBJEC-- pfft...
...?
... YOUR OB-JEC-- snort!
D-DAD ...?

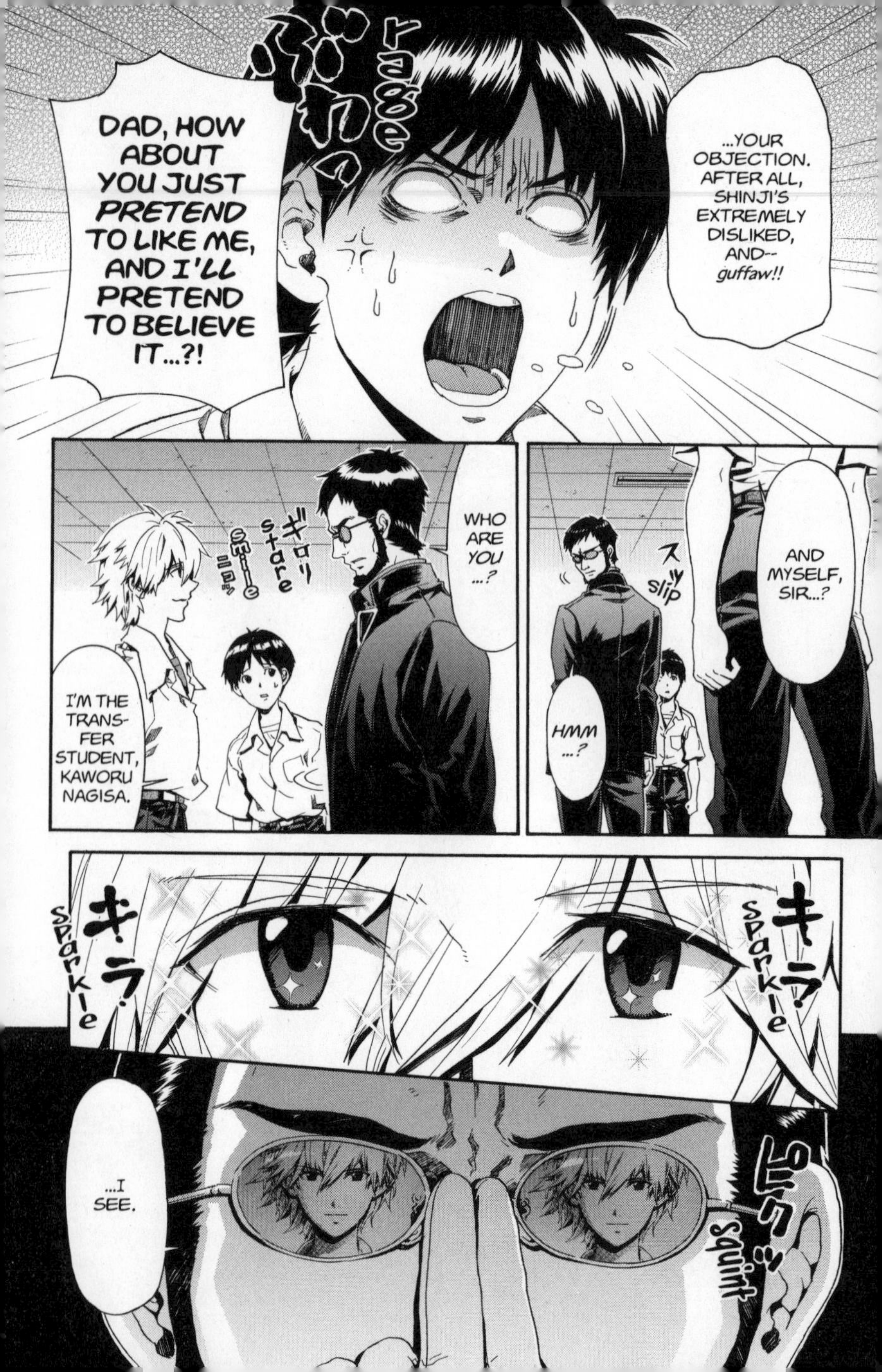
...YOUR OBJECTION. AFTER ALL, SHINJI'S EXTREMELY DISLIKED, AND-- *guffaw!!*
ぶわっ
rage
DAD, HOW ABOUT YOU JUST *PRETEND* TO LIKE ME, AND I'LL PRETEND TO BELIEVE IT...?!
AND MYSELF, SIR...?
スッ
slip
HMM...?
WHO ARE *YOU*...?
ギロリ
stare
ニコッ
smile
I'M THE TRANSFER STUDENT, KAWORU NAGISA.
キラ
sparkle
キラ
sparkle
ピクッ
squint
...I SEE.

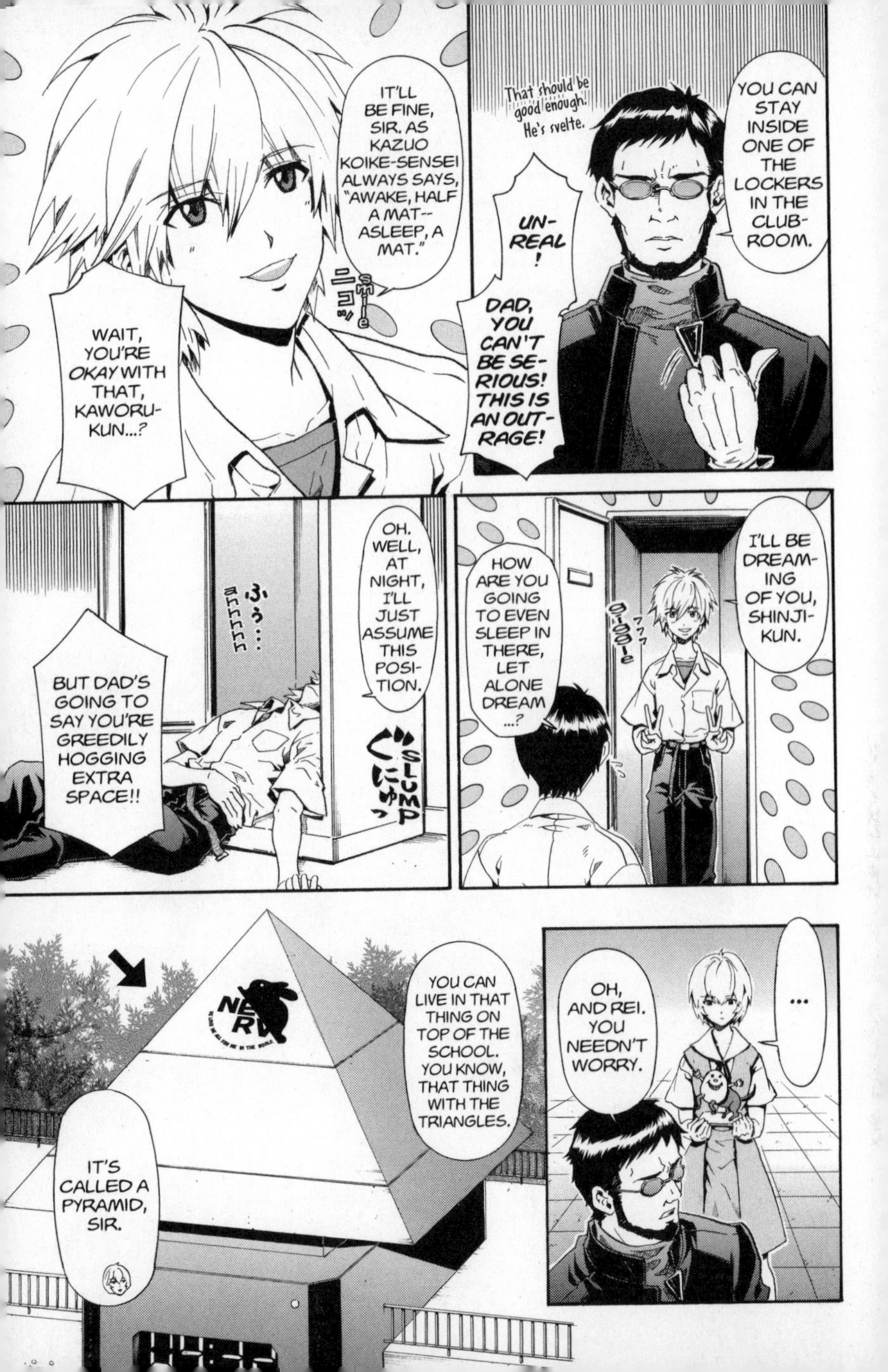
YOU CAN STAY INSIDE ONE OF THE LOCKERS IN THE CLUB-ROOM.
That should be good enough! He's svelte.
UN-REAL!
DAD, YOU CAN'T BE SE-RIOUS! THIS IS AN OUT-RAGE!
IT'LL BE FINE, SIR. AS KAZUO KOIKE-SENSEI ALWAYS SAYS, "AWAKE, HALF A MAT-- ASLEEP, A MAT."
smile
WAIT, YOU'RE OKAY WITH THAT, KAWORU-KUN...?
I'LL BE DREAM-ING OF YOU, SHINJI-KUN.
giggle
HOW ARE YOU GOING TO EVEN SLEEP IN THERE, LET ALONE DREAM ...?
OH. WELL, AT NIGHT, I'LL JUST ASSUME THIS POSI-TION.
SLUMP
ahhhhh
BUT DAD'S GOING TO SAY YOU'RE GREEDILY HOGGING EXTRA SPACE!!
...
OH, AND REI. YOU NEEDN'T WORRY.
YOU CAN LIVE IN THAT THING ON TOP OF THE SCHOOL. YOU KNOW, THAT THING WITH THE TRIANGLES.
NERV
IT'S CALLED A PYRAMID, SIR.

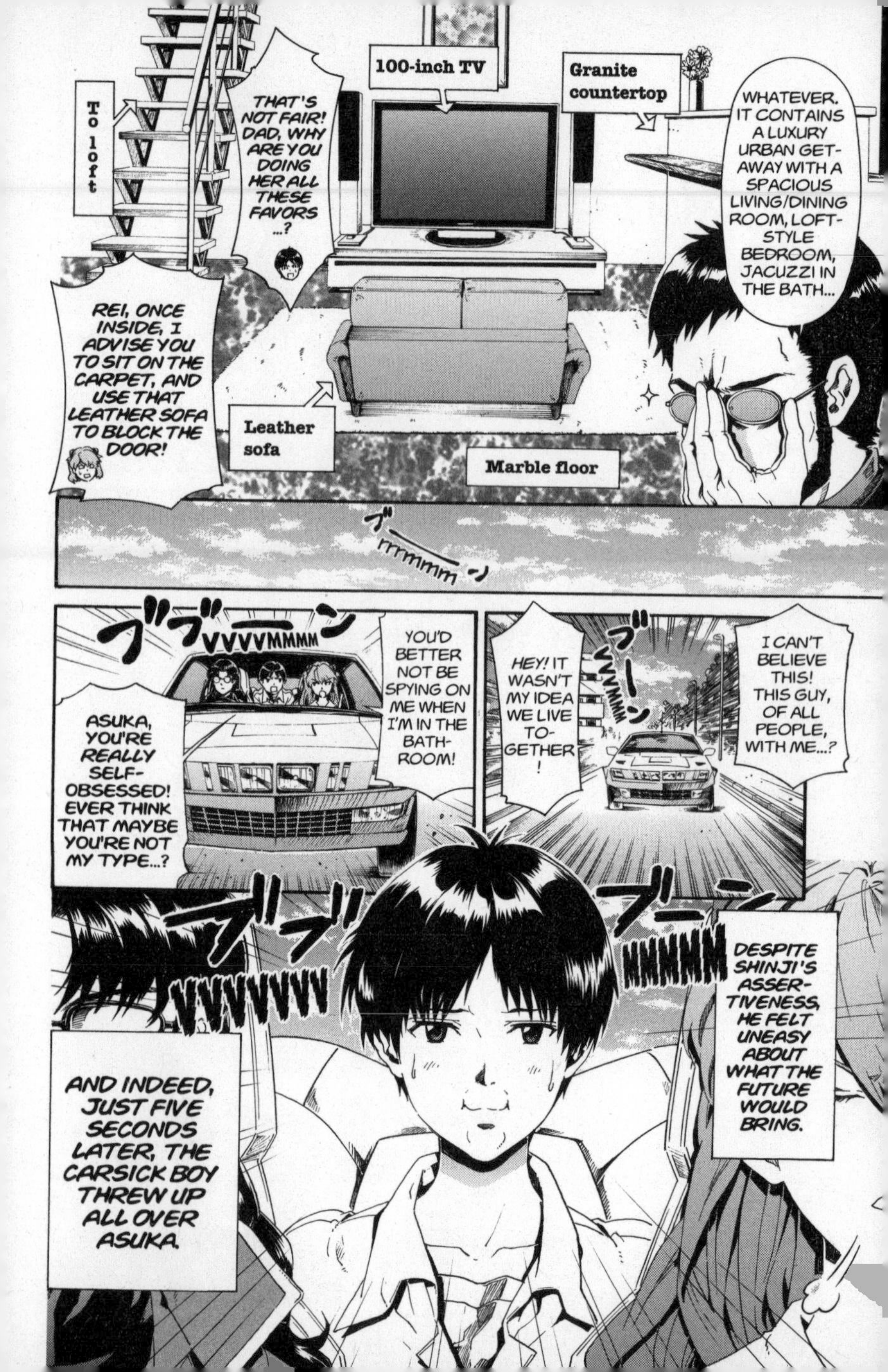
WHATEVER. IT CONTAINS A LUXURY URBAN GET-AWAY WITH A SPACIOUS LIVING/DINING ROOM, LOFT-STYLE BEDROOM, JACUZZI IN THE BATH...
Granite countertop
100-inch TV
THAT'S NOT FAIR! DAD, WHY ARE YOU DOING HER ALL THESE FAVORS ...?
To loft
REI, ONCE INSIDE, I ADVISE YOU TO SIT ON THE CARPET, AND USE THAT LEATHER SOFA TO BLOCK THE DOOR!
Leather sofa
Marble floor
ブー rrrrmmm ン
I CAN'T BELIEVE THIS! THIS GUY, OF ALL PEOPLE, WITH ME...?
HEY! IT WASN'T MY IDEA WE LIVE TO-GETHER!
ブーン VVVMMM
ブブーーン VVVVMMMM
YOU'D BETTER NOT BE SPYING ON ME WHEN I'M IN THE BATH-ROOM!
ASUKA, YOU'RE REALLY SELF-OBSESSED! EVER THINK THAT MAYBE YOU'RE NOT MY TYPE...?
DESPITE SHINJI'S ASSER-TIVENESS, HE FELT UNEASY ABOUT WHAT THE FUTURE WOULD BRING.
ブブブーー VVVVVVVV MMMMM
AND INDEED, JUST FIVE SECONDS LATER, THE CARSICK BOY THREW UP ALL OVER ASUKA.

9.5 NOTEBOOK OF THE WANDERING MIDDLE SCHOOLERS (PART 2)

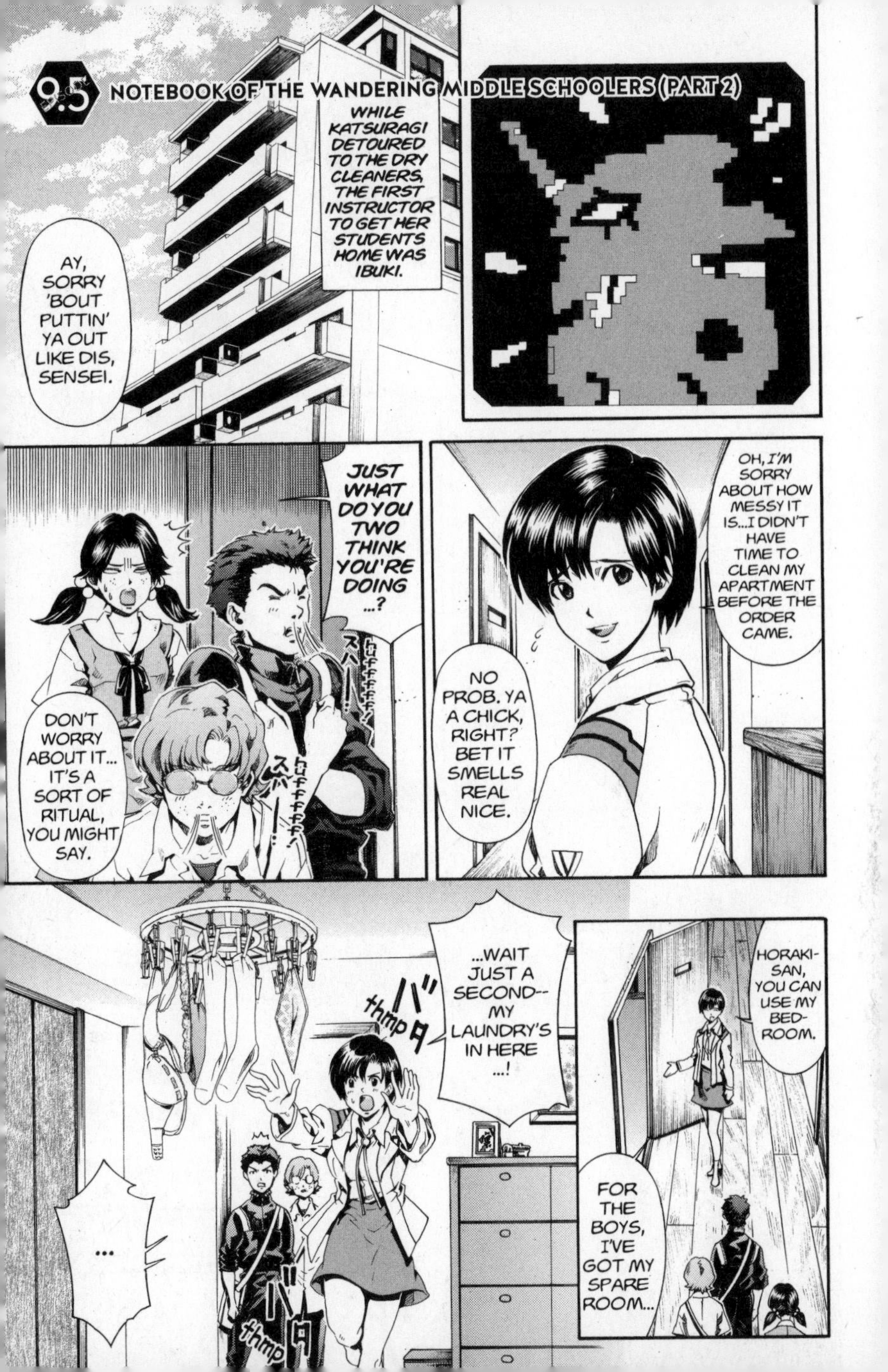

WHILE KATSURAGI DETOURED TO THE DRY CLEANERS, THE FIRST INSTRUCTOR TO GET HER STUDENTS HOME WAS IBUKI.
AY, SORRY 'BOUT PUTTIN' YA OUT LIKE DIS, SENSEI.
OH, I'M SORRY ABOUT HOW MESSY IT IS...I DIDN'T HAVE TIME TO CLEAN MY APARTMENT BEFORE THE ORDER CAME.
NO PROB. YA A CHICK, RIGHT? BET IT SMELLS REAL NICE.
JUST WHAT DO YOU TWO THINK YOU'RE DOING ...?
DON'T WORRY ABOUT IT... IT'S A SORT OF RITUAL, YOU MIGHT SAY.
HORAKI-SAN, YOU CAN USE MY BED-ROOM.
FOR THE BOYS, I'VE GOT MY SPARE ROOM...
...WAIT JUST A SECOND-- MY LAUNDRY'S IN HERE ...!
thmp
...
thmp

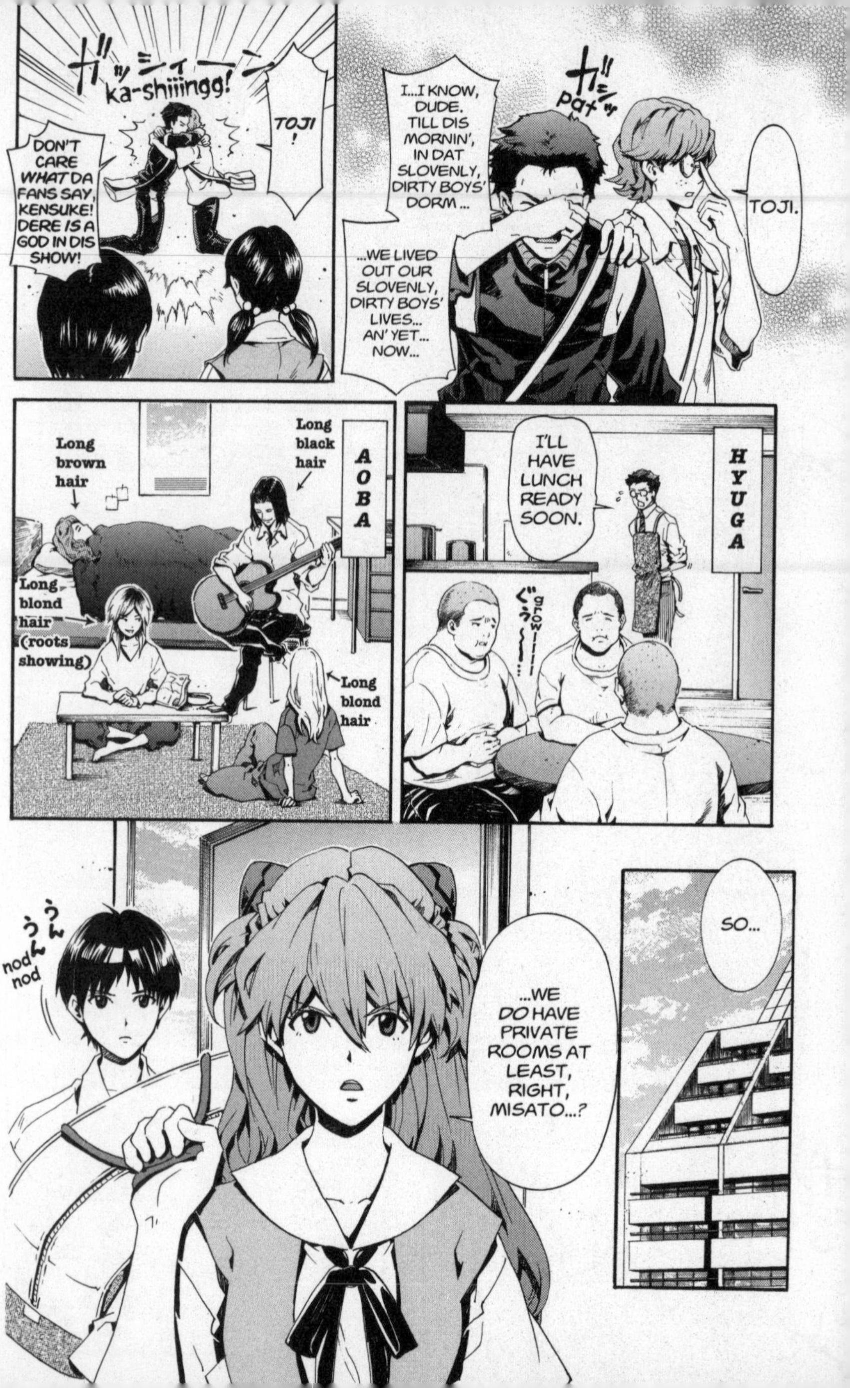
TOJI.
ガッ!! pat
I...I KNOW, DUDE. TILL DIS MORNIN', IN DAT SLOVENLY, DIRTY BOYS' DORM...
...WE LIVED OUT OUR SLOVENLY, DIRTY BOYS' LIVES... AN' YET... NOW...
ガッシィーン ka-shiiingg!
TOJI!
DON'T CARE WHAT DA FANS SAY, KENSUKE! DERE IS A GOD IN DIS SHOW!
HYUGA
I'LL HAVE LUNCH READY SOON.
ぐう~ grow!!!
AOBA
Long black hair
Long brown hair
Long blond hair (roots showing)
Long blond hair
SO...
...WE DO HAVE PRIVATE ROOMS AT LEAST, RIGHT, MISATO...?
うんうん nod nod

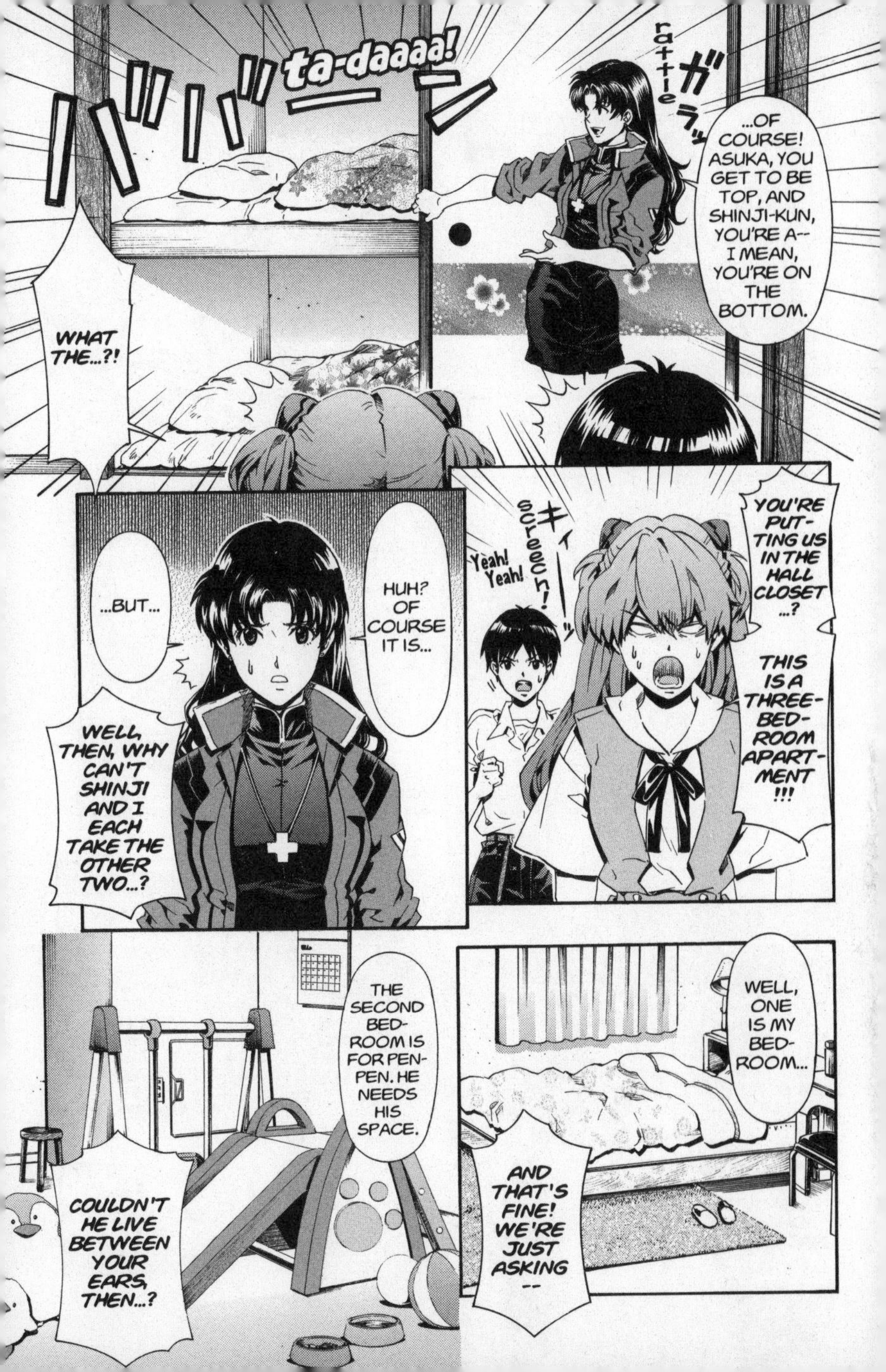

ガラッ
rattle
...OF COURSE! ASUKA, YOU GET TO BE TOP, AND SHINJI-KUN, YOU'RE A-- I MEAN, YOU'RE ON THE BOTTOM.
ta-daaaa!
WHAT THE...?!
YOU'RE PUT-TING US IN THE HALL CLOSET ...?
キィ
screech!
Yeah! Yeah!
THIS IS A THREE-BED-ROOM APART-MENT !!!
HUH? OF COURSE IT IS...
...BUT...
WELL, THEN, WHY CAN'T SHINJI AND I EACH TAKE THE OTHER TWO...?
WELL, ONE IS MY BED-ROOM...
AND THAT'S FINE! WE'RE JUST ASKING --
THE SECOND BED-ROOM IS FOR PEN-PEN. HE NEEDS HIS SPACE.
COULDN'T HE LIVE BETWEEN YOUR EARS, THEN...?

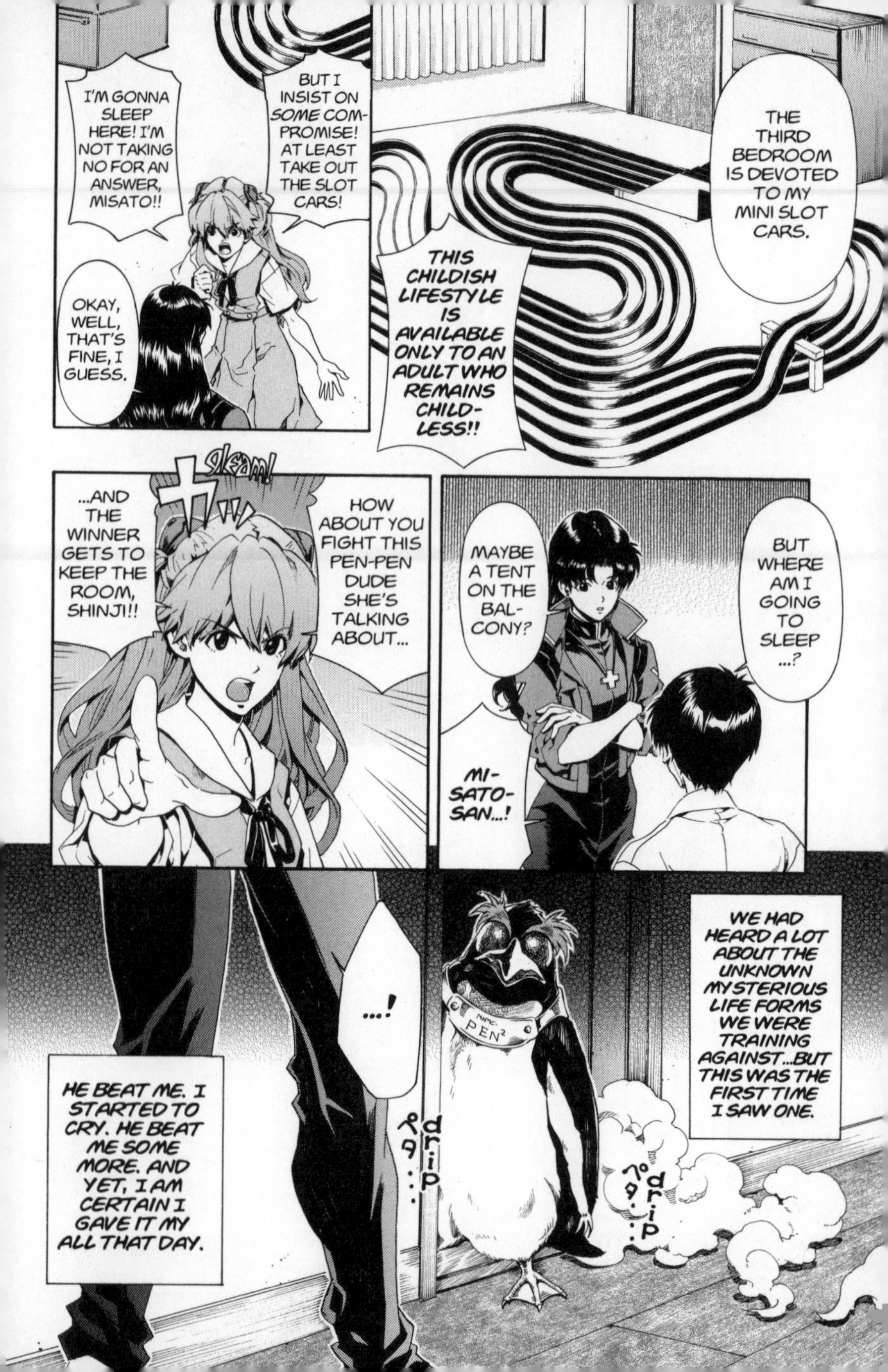
THE THIRD BEDROOM IS DEVOTED TO MY MINI SLOT CARS.
THIS CHILDISH LIFESTYLE IS AVAILABLE ONLY TO AN ADULT WHO REMAINS CHILD-LESS!!
BUT I INSIST ON SOME COM-PROMISE! AT LEAST TAKE OUT THE SLOT CARS!
I'M GONNA SLEEP HERE! I'M NOT TAKING NO FOR AN ANSWER, MISATO!!
OKAY, WELL, THAT'S FINE, I GUESS.
BUT WHERE AM I GOING TO SLEEP ...?
MAYBE A TENT ON THE BAL-CONY?
MI-SATO-SAN...!
gleam!
HOW ABOUT YOU FIGHT THIS PEN-PEN DUDE SHE'S TALKING ABOUT...
...AND THE WINNER GETS TO KEEP THE ROOM, SHINJI!!
WE HAD HEARD A LOT ABOUT THE UNKNOWN MYSTERIOUS LIFE FORMS WE WERE TRAINING AGAINST...BUT THIS WAS THE FIRST TIME I SAW ONE.
drip
NAME: PEN²
...!
drip
HE BEAT ME. I STARTED TO CRY. HE BEAT ME SOME MORE. AND YET, I AM CERTAIN I GAVE IT MY ALL THAT DAY.

EPISODE 10 MORNING, MIDDLE SCHOOLERS

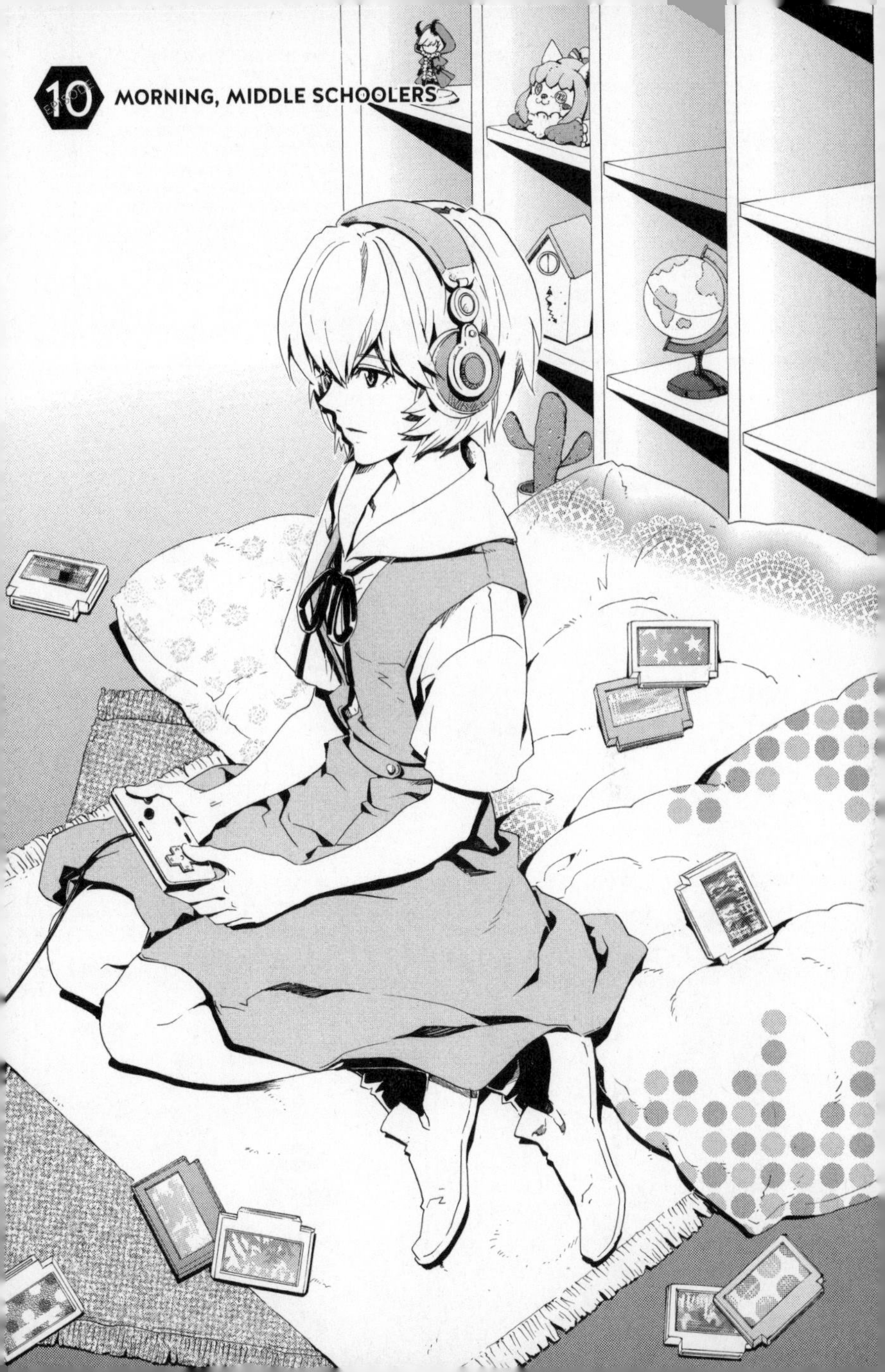

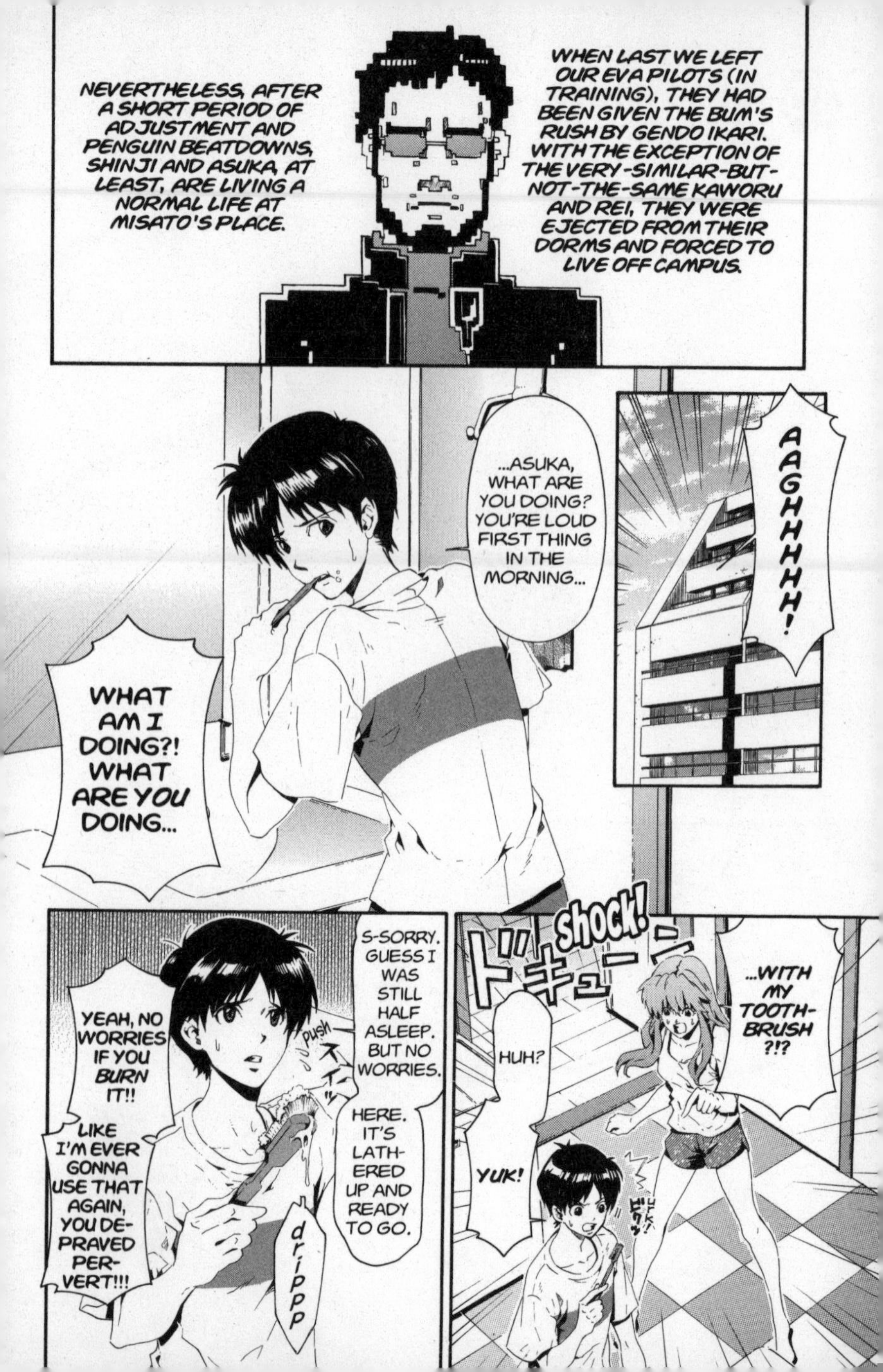

WHEN LAST WE LEFT OUR EVA PILOTS (IN TRAINING), THEY HAD BEEN GIVEN THE BUM'S RUSH BY GENDO IKARI. WITH THE EXCEPTION OF THE VERY-SIMILAR-BUT-NOT-THE-SAME KAWORU AND REI, THEY WERE EJECTED FROM THEIR DORMS AND FORCED TO LIVE OFF CAMPUS.
NEVERTHELESS, AFTER A SHORT PERIOD OF ADJUSTMENT AND PENGUIN BEATDOWNS, SHINJI AND ASUKA, AT LEAST, ARE LIVING A NORMAL LIFE AT MISATO'S PLACE.
AAGHHHHHH!
...ASUKA, WHAT ARE YOU DOING? YOU'RE LOUD FIRST THING IN THE MORNING...
WHAT AM I DOING?! WHAT ARE YOU DOING...
...WITH MY TOOTH-BRUSH ?!?
shock!
HUH?
YUK!
S-SORRY. GUESS I WAS STILL HALF ASLEEP. BUT NO WORRIES.
push
HERE. IT'S LATH-ERED UP AND READY TO GO.
YEAH, NO WORRIES IF YOU BURN IT!!
LIKE I'M EVER GONNA USE THAT AGAIN, YOU DE-PRAVED PER-VERT!!!
drippp

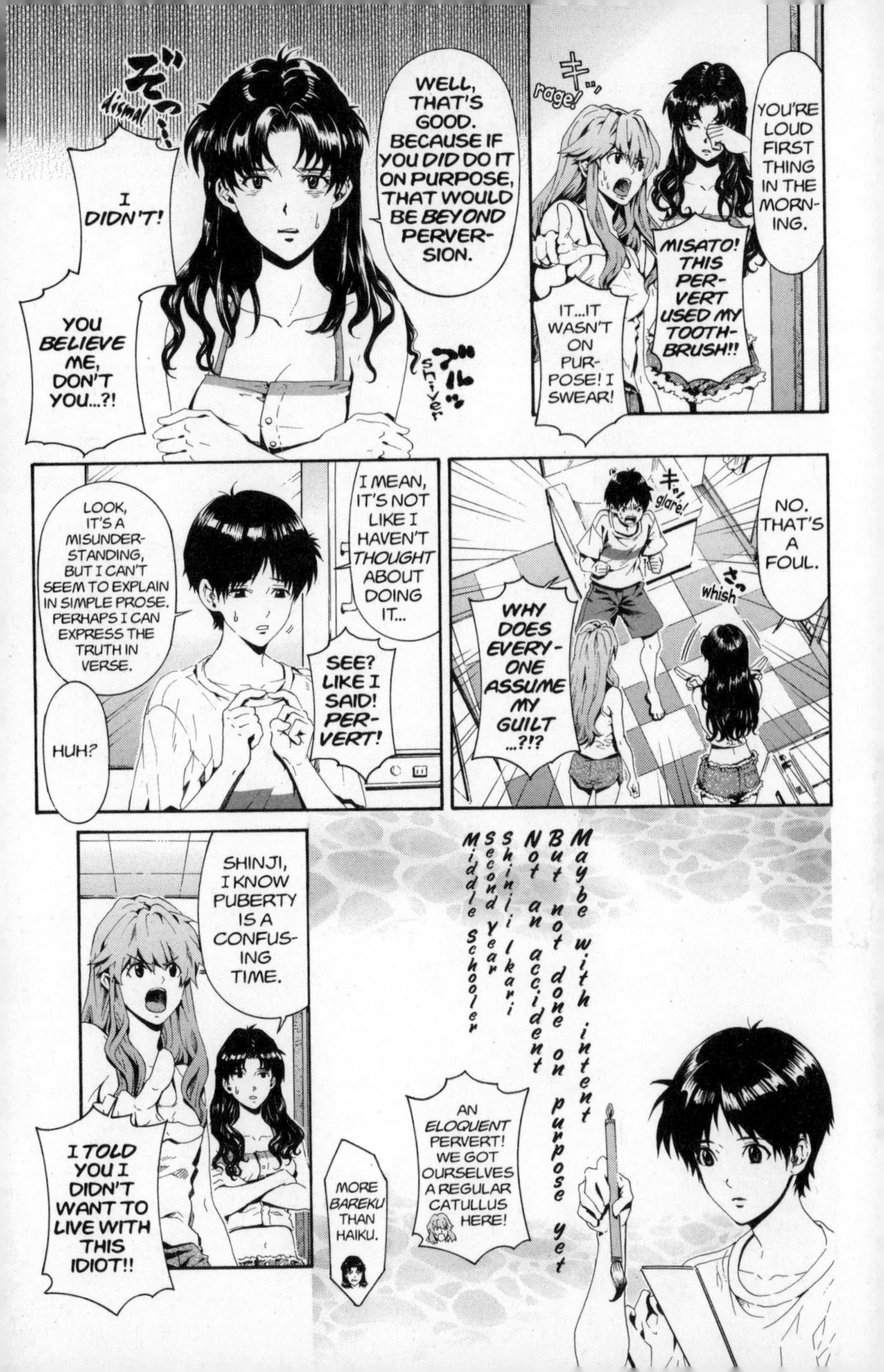
rage!
YOU'RE LOUD FIRST THING IN THE MORNING.
MISATO! THIS PERVERT USED MY TOOTHBRUSH!!
IT...IT WASN'T ON PURPOSE! I SWEAR!
WELL, THAT'S GOOD. BECAUSE IF YOU *DID* DO IT ON PURPOSE, THAT WOULD BE *BEYOND* PERVERSION.
dismal
I DIDN'T!
YOU *BELIEVE* ME, DON'T YOU...?!
shiver
glare!
NO. THAT'S A FOUL.
whish
WHY DOES EVERYONE ASSUME MY GUILT...?!?
I MEAN, IT'S NOT LIKE I HAVEN'T *THOUGHT* ABOUT DOING IT...
LOOK, IT'S A MISUNDERSTANDING, BUT I CAN'T SEEM TO EXPLAIN IN SIMPLE PROSE. PERHAPS I CAN EXPRESS THE TRUTH IN VERSE.
SEE? LIKE I SAID! PERVERT!
HUH?
Maybe with intent
But not done on purpose yet
Not an accident
Shinji Ikari
Second Year
Middle Schooler
AN *ELOQUENT* PERVERT! WE GOT OURSELVES A REGULAR CATULLUS HERE!
MORE *BAREKU* THAN HAIKU.
SHINJI, I KNOW PUBERTY IS A CONFUSING TIME.
I TOLD YOU I DIDN'T WANT TO LIVE WITH THIS IDIOT!!

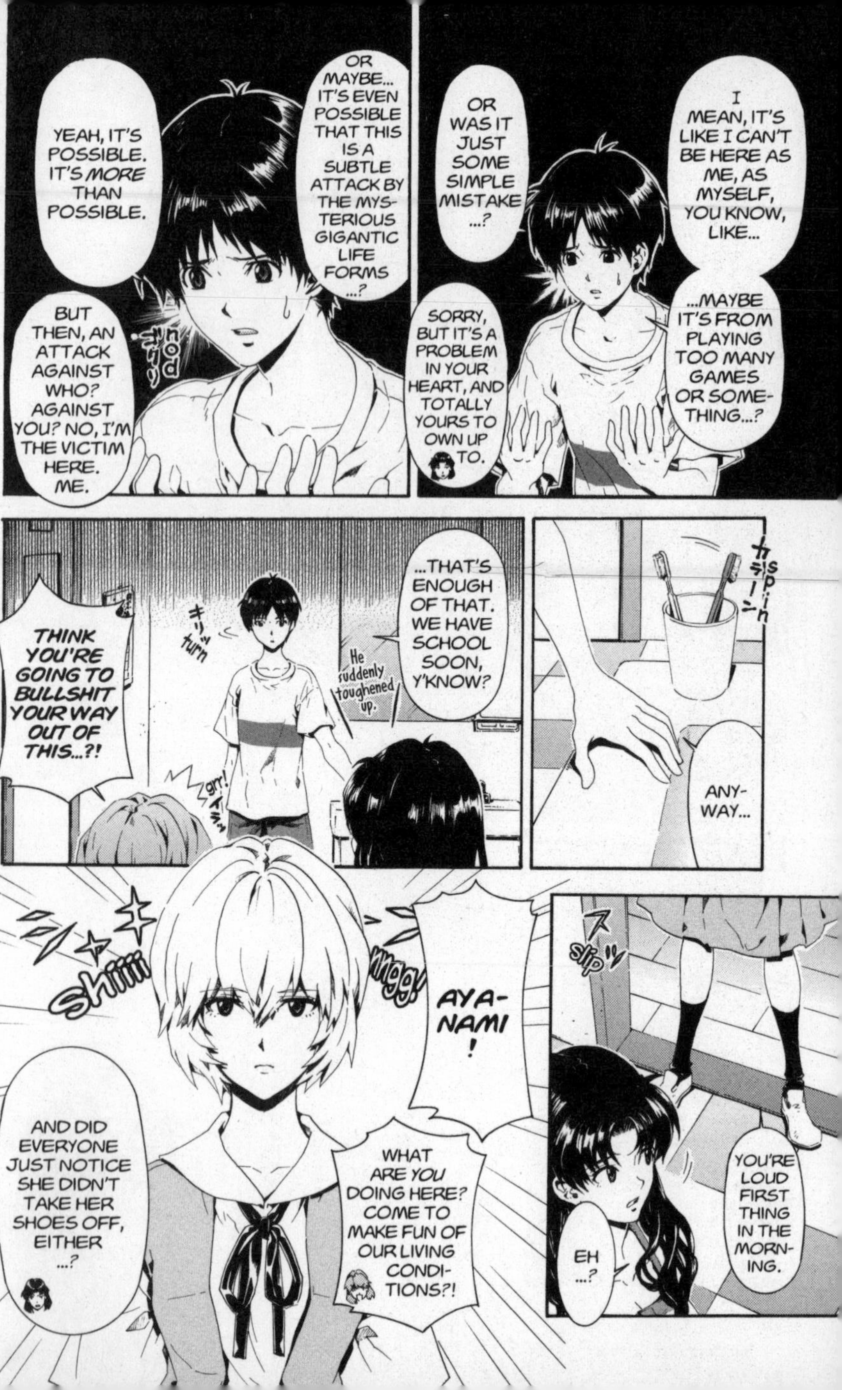
I MEAN, IT'S LIKE I CAN'T BE HERE AS ME, AS MYSELF, YOU KNOW, LIKE...
...MAYBE IT'S FROM PLAYING TOO MANY GAMES OR SOMETHING...?
OR WAS IT JUST SOME SIMPLE MISTAKE ...?
SORRY, BUT IT'S A PROBLEM IN YOUR HEART, AND TOTALLY YOURS TO OWN UP TO.
OR MAYBE... IT'S EVEN POSSIBLE THAT THIS IS A SUBTLE ATTACK BY THE MYSTERIOUS GIGANTIC LIFE FORMS ...?
YEAH, IT'S POSSIBLE. IT'S *MORE* THAN POSSIBLE.
nod
BUT THEN, AN ATTACK AGAINST WHO? AGAINST YOU? NO, I'M THE VICTIM HERE. ME.
spin
ANY-WAY...
...THAT'S ENOUGH OF THAT. WE HAVE SCHOOL SOON, Y'KNOW?
He suddenly toughened up.
turn
grr!
THINK YOU'RE GOING TO BULLSHIT YOUR WAY OUT OF THIS...?!
slip
YOU'RE LOUD FIRST THING IN THE MORN-ING.
EH ...?
AYA-NAMI !
nngg!
Shiiii
WHAT ARE *YOU* DOING HERE? COME TO MAKE FUN OF OUR LIVING CONDI-TIONS?!
AND DID EVERYONE JUST NOTICE SHE DIDN'T TAKE HER SHOES OFF, EITHER ...?

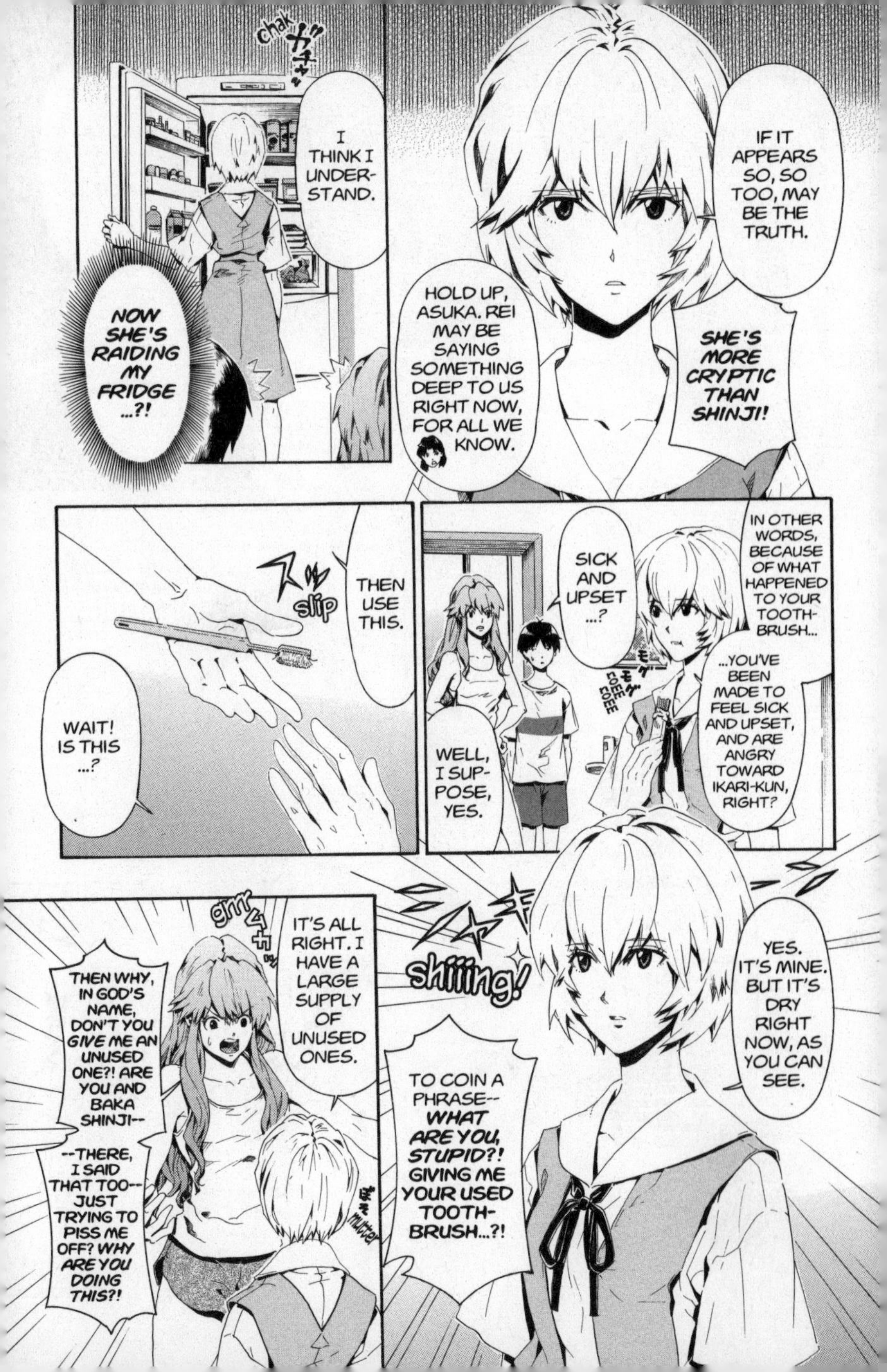
IF IT APPEARS SO, SO TOO, MAY BE THE TRUTH.
SHE'S MORE CRYPTIC THAN SHINJI!
HOLD UP, ASUKA. REI MAY BE SAYING SOMETHING DEEP TO US RIGHT NOW, FOR ALL WE KNOW.
chak
I THINK I UNDER-STAND.
NOW SHE'S RAIDING MY FRIDGE ...?!
IN OTHER WORDS, BECAUSE OF WHAT HAPPENED TO YOUR TOOTH-BRUSH...
...YOU'VE BEEN MADE TO FEEL SICK AND UPSET, AND ARE ANGRY TOWARD IKARI-KUN, RIGHT?
EOEE EOEE
SICK AND UPSET ...?
WELL, I SUP-POSE, YES.
slip
THEN USE THIS.
WAIT! IS THIS ...?
YES. IT'S MINE. BUT IT'S DRY RIGHT NOW, AS YOU CAN SEE.
shiiing!
TO COIN A PHRASE-- WHAT ARE YOU, STUPID?! GIVING ME YOUR USED TOOTH-BRUSH...?!
IT'S ALL RIGHT. I HAVE A LARGE SUPPLY OF UNUSED ONES.
grrr
THEN WHY, IN GOD'S NAME, DON'T YOU GIVE ME AN UNUSED ONE?! ARE YOU AND BAKA SHINJI--
--THERE, I SAID THAT TOO-- JUST TRYING TO PISS ME OFF? WHY ARE YOU DOING THIS?!
mutter

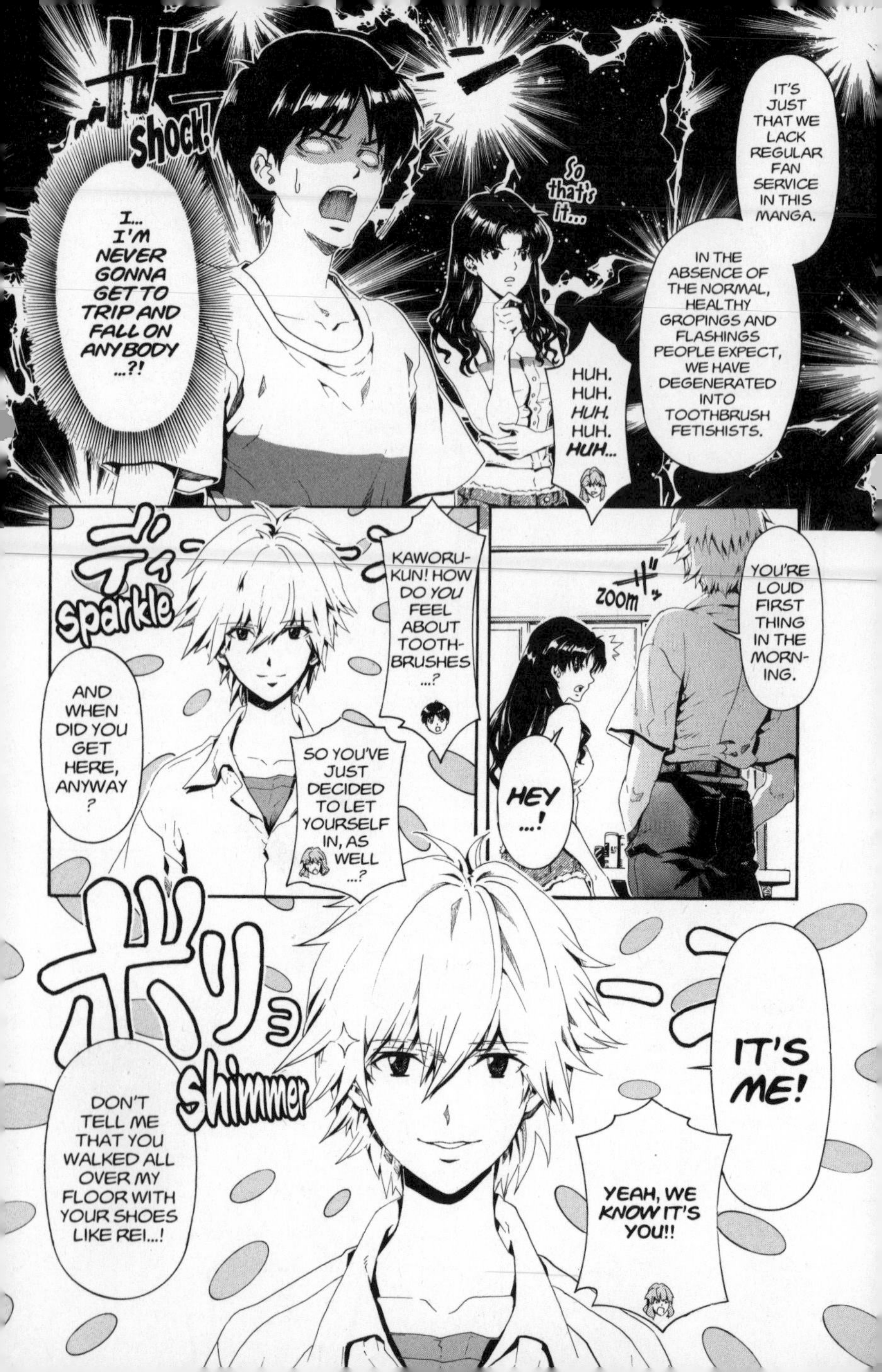
IT'S JUST THAT WE LACK REGULAR FAN SERVICE IN THIS MANGA.
IN THE ABSENCE OF THE NORMAL, HEALTHY GROPINGS AND FLASHINGS PEOPLE EXPECT, WE HAVE DEGENERATED INTO TOOTHBRUSH FETISHISTS.
So that's it...
HUH. HUH. HUH. HUH. HUH...
shock!
I... I'M NEVER GONNA GET TO TRIP AND FALL ON ANYBODY ...?!
zoom
YOU'RE LOUD FIRST THING IN THE MORNING.
HEY ...!
KAWORU-KUN! HOW DO YOU FEEL ABOUT TOOTH-BRUSHES ...?
sparkle
SO YOU'VE JUST DECIDED TO LET YOURSELF IN, AS WELL ...?
AND WHEN DID YOU GET HERE, ANYWAY ?
IT'S ME!
shimmer
YEAH, WE KNOW IT'S YOU!!
DON'T TELL ME THAT YOU WALKED ALL OVER MY FLOOR WITH YOUR SHOES LIKE REI...!

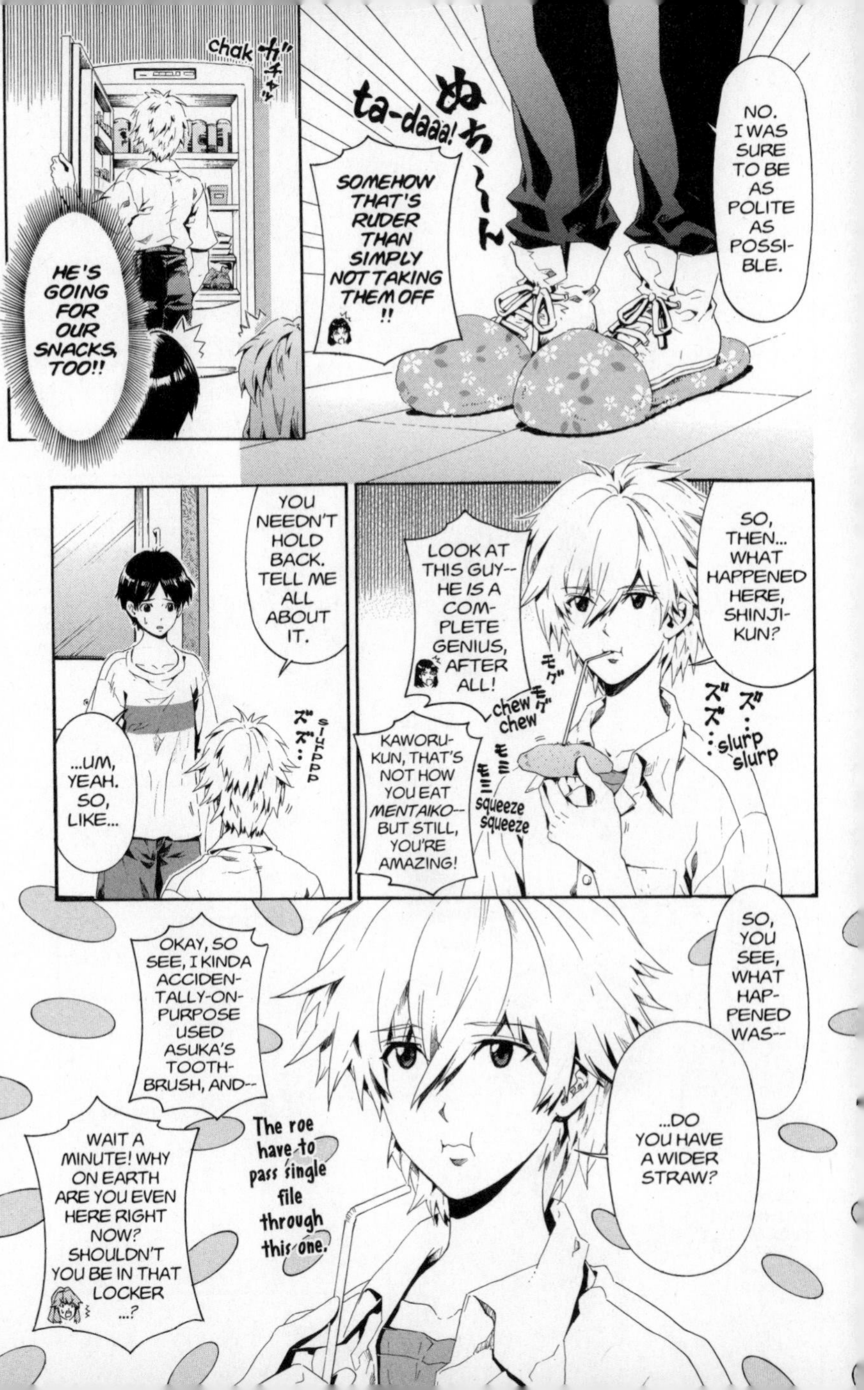
NO. I WAS SURE TO BE AS POLITE AS POSSIBLE.
ぬちーん
ta-daaa!
SOMEHOW THAT'S RUDER THAN SIMPLY NOT TAKING THEM OFF!!
chak ガチャ
HE'S GOING FOR OUR SNACKS, TOO!!
SO, THEN... WHAT HAPPENED HERE, SHINJI-KUN?
ズズ…
slurp slurp
LOOK AT THIS GUY-- HE IS A COMPLETE GENIUS, AFTER ALL!
モグモグ
chew chew
モミモミ
squeeze squeeze
KAWORU-KUN, THAT'S NOT HOW YOU EAT MENTAIKO-- BUT STILL, YOU'RE AMAZING!
YOU NEEDN'T HOLD BACK. TELL ME ALL ABOUT IT.
ズズ…
SLURPPP
...UM, YEAH. SO, LIKE...
SO, YOU SEE, WHAT HAPPENED WAS--
OKAY, SO SEE, I KINDA ACCIDENTALLY-ON-PURPOSE USED ASUKA'S TOOTHBRUSH, AND--
...DO YOU HAVE A WIDER STRAW?
The roe have to pass single file through this one.
WAIT A MINUTE! WHY ON EARTH ARE YOU EVEN HERE RIGHT NOW? SHOULDN'T YOU BE IN THAT LOCKER ...?

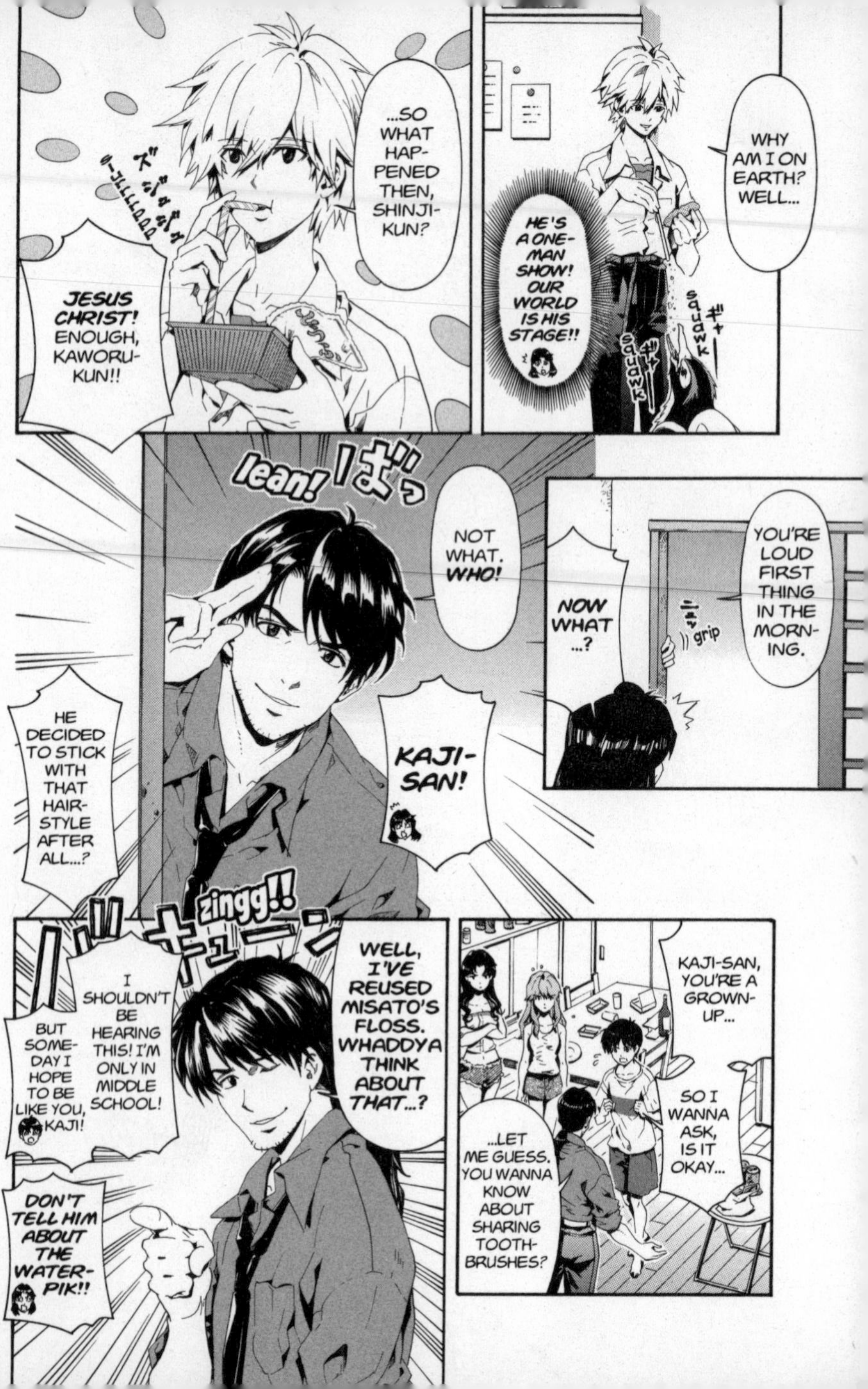
WHY AM I ON EARTH? WELL...
HE'S A ONE-MAN SHOW! OUR WORLD IS HIS STAGE!!
squawk
squawk
...SO WHAT HAPPENED THEN, SHINJI-KUN?
JESUS CHRIST! ENOUGH, KAWORU-KUN!!
YOU'RE LOUD FIRST THING IN THE MORNING.
grip
NOW WHAT ...?
lean!
NOT WHAT. WHO!
KAJI-SAN!
HE DECIDED TO STICK WITH THAT HAIRSTYLE AFTER ALL...?
KAJI-SAN, YOU'RE A GROWN-UP...
SO I WANNA ASK, IS IT OKAY...
...LET ME GUESS. YOU WANNA KNOW ABOUT SHARING TOOTHBRUSHES?
zingg!!
WELL, I'VE REUSED MISATO'S FLOSS. WHADDYA THINK ABOUT THAT...?
I SHOULDN'T BE HEARING THIS! I'M ONLY IN MIDDLE SCHOOL!
BUT SOMEDAY I HOPE TO BE LIKE YOU, KAJI!
DON'T TELL HIM ABOUT THE WATER-PIK!!

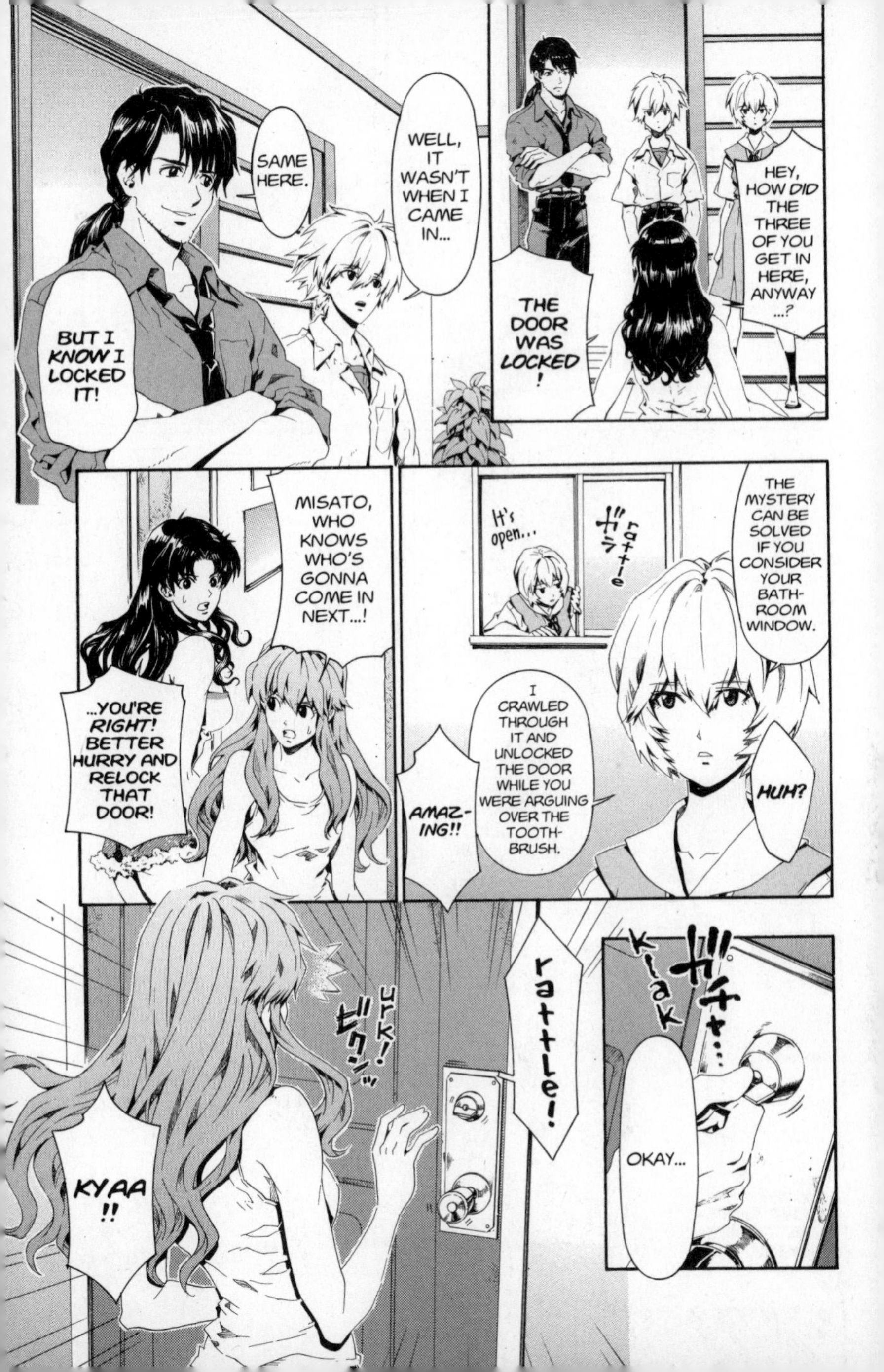
HEY, HOW DID THE THREE OF YOU GET IN HERE, ANYWAY ...?
THE DOOR WAS LOCKED!
WELL, IT WASN'T WHEN I CAME IN...
SAME HERE.
BUT I KNOW I LOCKED IT!
THE MYSTERY CAN BE SOLVED IF YOU CONSIDER YOUR BATH-ROOM WINDOW.
ガラ rattle
It's open...
HUH?
I CRAWLED THROUGH IT AND UNLOCKED THE DOOR WHILE YOU WERE ARGUING OVER THE TOOTH-BRUSH.
AMAZ-ING!!
MISATO, WHO KNOWS WHO'S GONNA COME IN NEXT...!
...YOU'RE RIGHT! BETTER HURRY AND RELOCK THAT DOOR!
ガチャ... klak
OKAY...
rattle!
ビクン URK!
KYAA!!

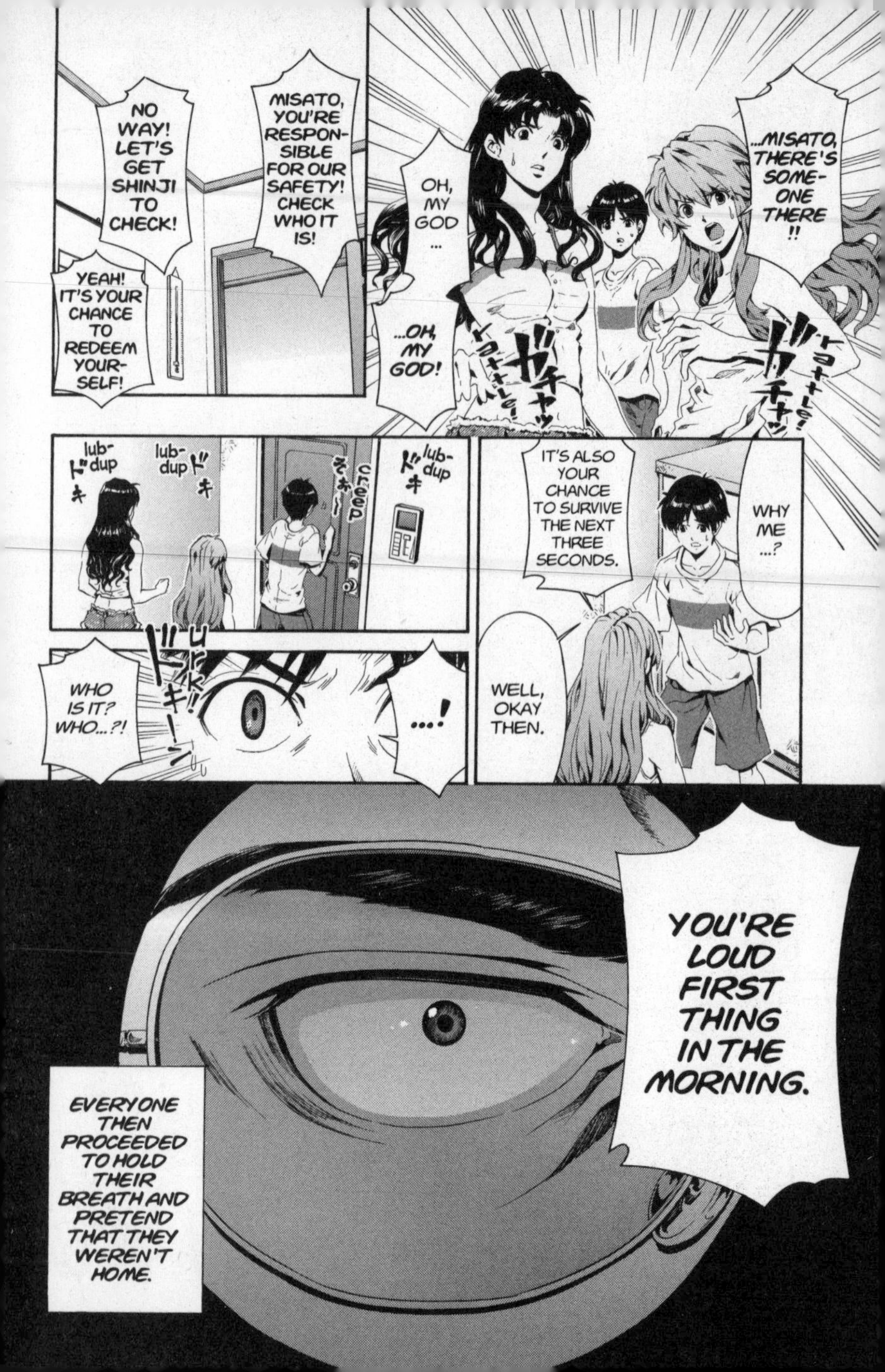
...MISATO, THERE'S SOME-ONE THERE!!
OH, MY GOD...
...OH, MY GOD!
MISATO, YOU'RE RESPON-SIBLE FOR OUR SAFETY! CHECK WHO IT IS!
NO WAY! LET'S GET SHINJI TO CHECK!
YEAH! IT'S YOUR CHANCE TO REDEEM YOUR-SELF!
WHY ME...?
IT'S ALSO YOUR CHANCE TO SURVIVE THE NEXT THREE SECONDS.
WELL, OKAY THEN.
lub-dup
creep
lub-dup
lub-dup
...!
URK!!
WHO IS IT? WHO...?!
YOU'RE LOUD FIRST THING IN THE MORNING.
EVERYONE THEN PROCEEDED TO HOLD THEIR BREATH AND PRETEND THAT THEY WEREN'T HOME.

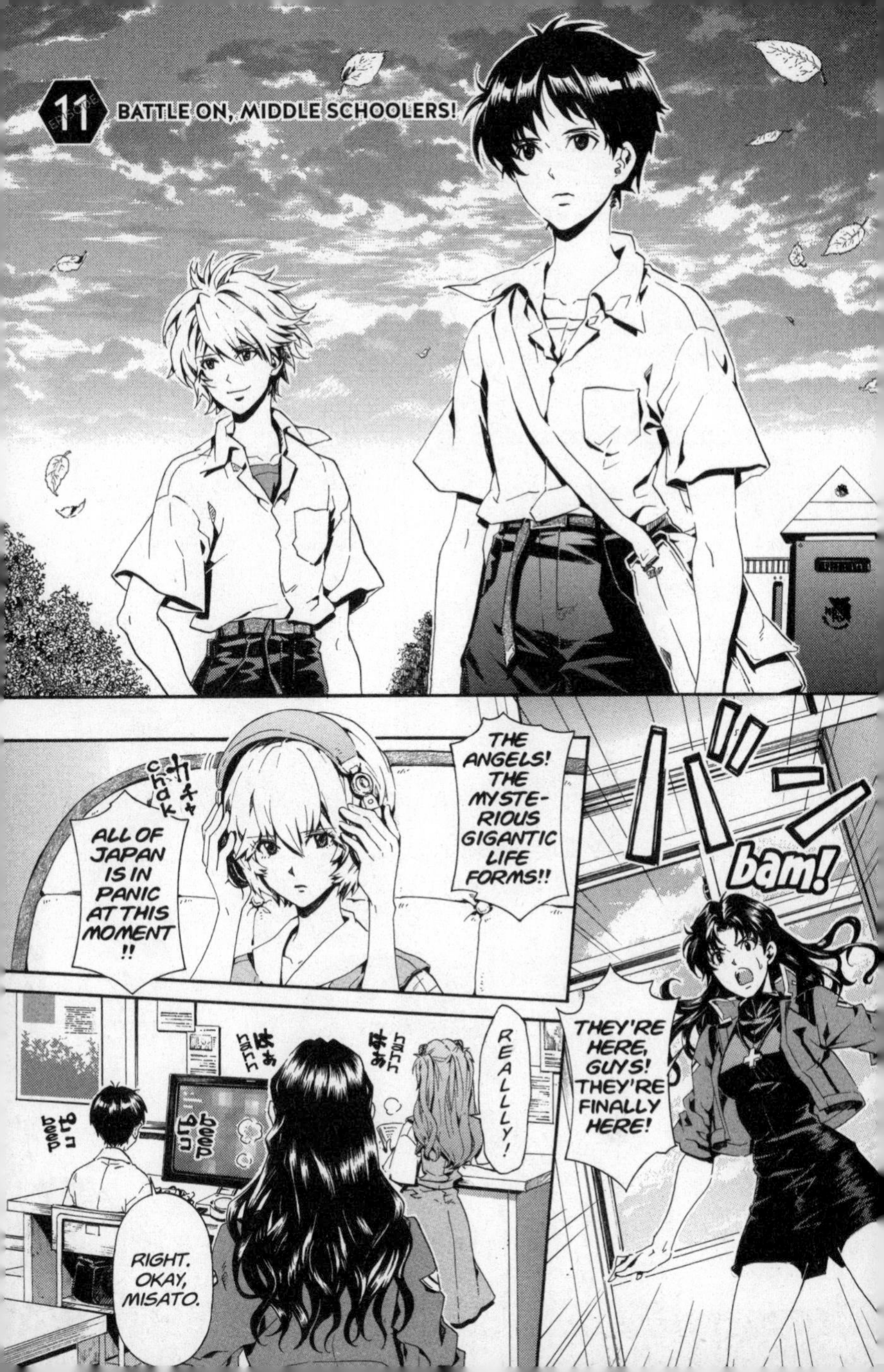
EPISODE 11
BATTLE ON, MIDDLE SCHOOLERS!
bam!
THEY'RE HERE, GUYS! THEY'RE FINALLY HERE!
カチャ chak
THE ANGELS! THE MYSTE-RIOUS GIGANTIC LIFE FORMS!!
ALL OF JAPAN IS IN PANIC AT THIS MOMENT!!
REALLLY!
はぁ hahh
はぁ hahh
beep
beep
RIGHT. OKAY, MISATO.

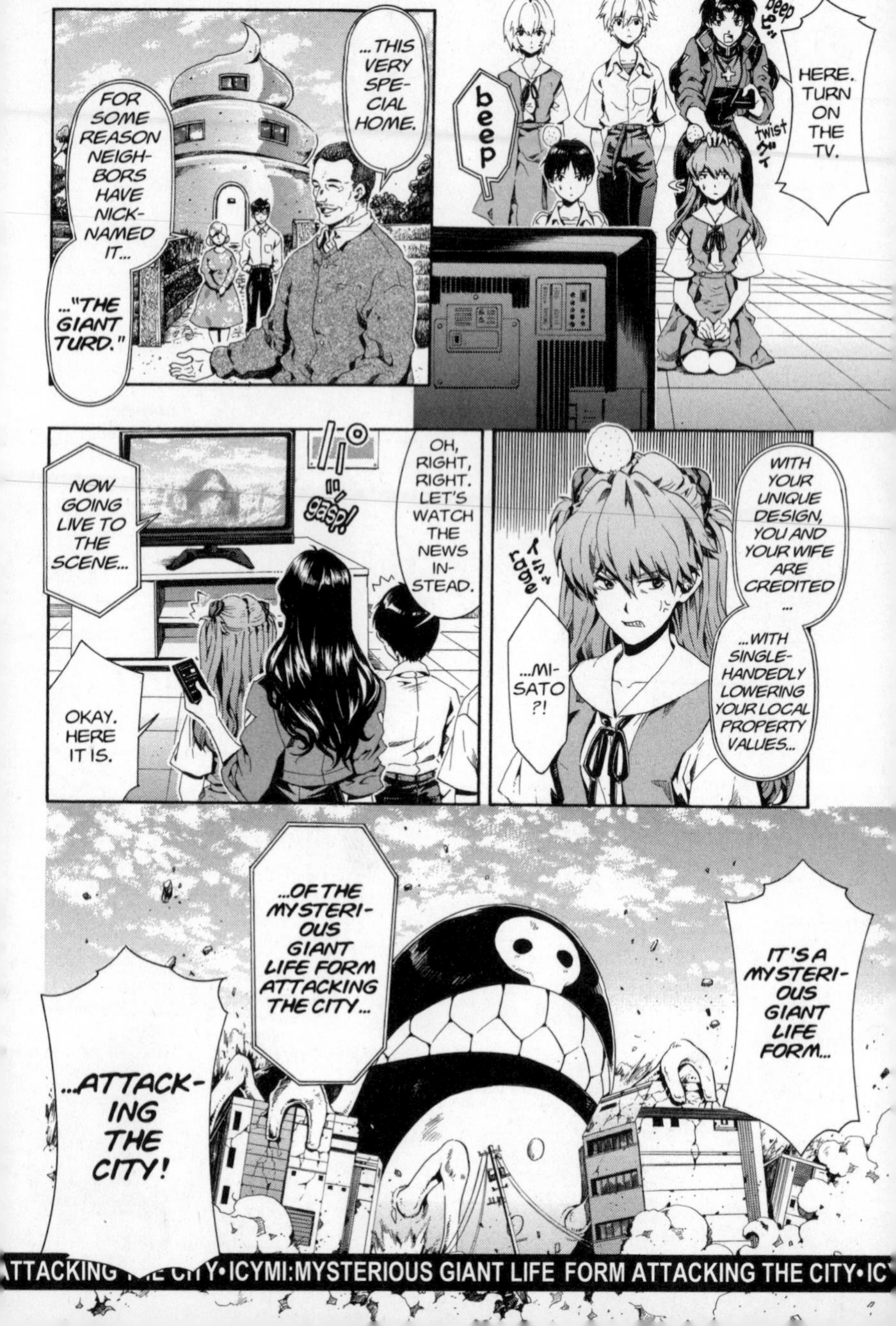
beep
HERE. TURN ON THE TV.
twist
beep
...THIS VERY SPE-CIAL HOME.
FOR SOME REASON NEIGH-BORS HAVE NICK-NAMED IT...
..."THE GIANT TURD."
WITH YOUR UNIQUE DESIGN, YOU AND YOUR WIFE ARE CREDITED ...
...WITH SINGLE-HANDEDLY LOWERING YOUR LOCAL PROPERTY VALUES...
rage
...MI-SATO ?!
OH, RIGHT, RIGHT. LET'S WATCH THE NEWS IN-STEAD.
gasp!
NOW GOING LIVE TO THE SCENE...
OKAY. HERE IT IS.
IT'S A MYSTERIOUS GIANT LIFE FORM...
...OF THE MYSTERIOUS GIANT LIFE FORM ATTACKING THE CITY...
...ATTACK-ING THE CITY!
TTACKING THE CITY• ICYMI: MYSTERIOUS GIANT LIFE FORM ATTACKING THE CITY• IC

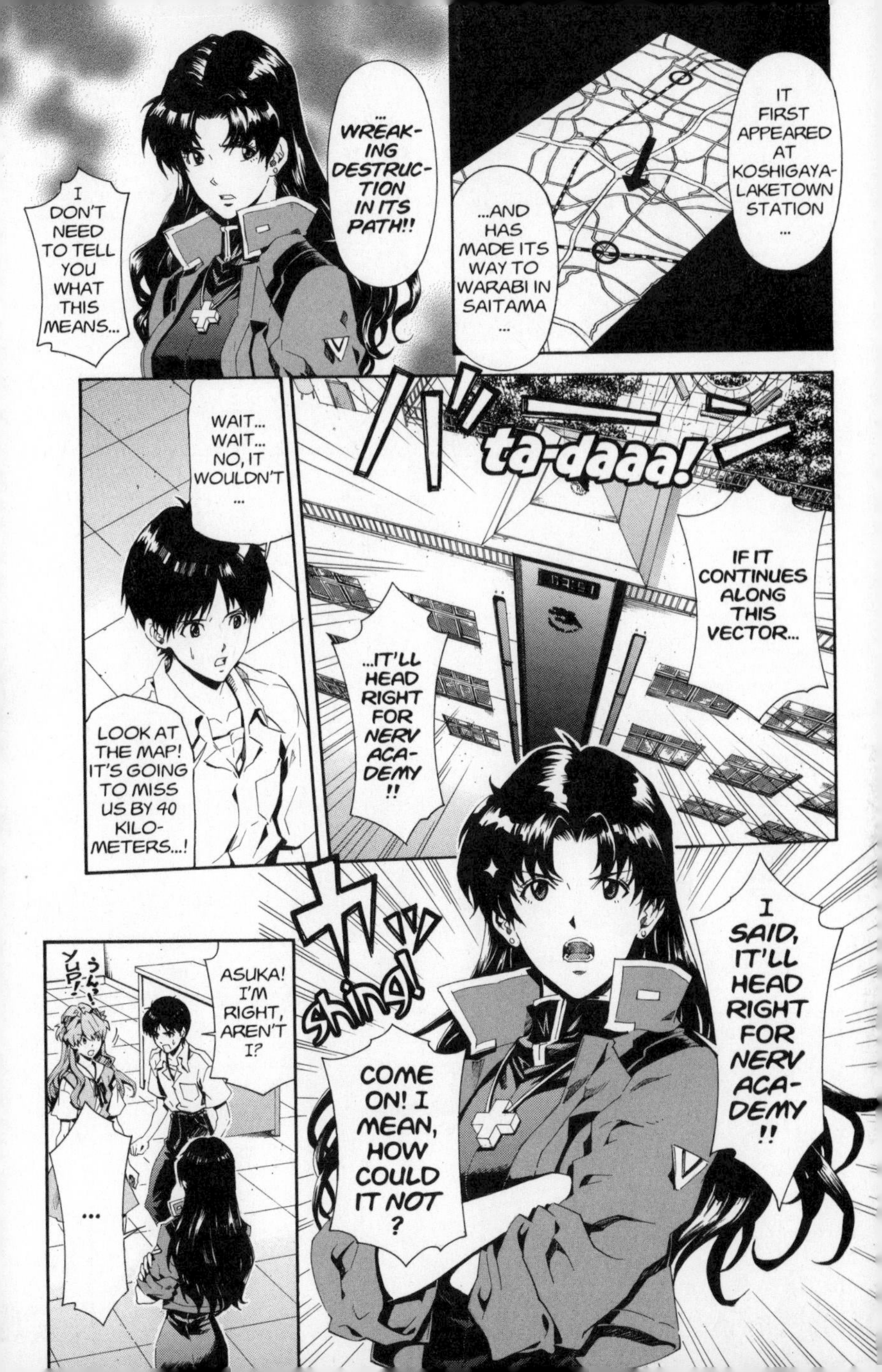
IT FIRST APPEARED AT KOSHIGAYA-LAKETOWN STATION ...
...AND HAS MADE ITS WAY TO WARABI IN SAITAMA ...
... WREAKING DESTRUCTION IN ITS PATH!!
I DON'T NEED TO TELL YOU WHAT THIS MEANS...
ta-daaa!
IF IT CONTINUES ALONG THIS VECTOR...
...IT'LL HEAD RIGHT FOR NERV ACADEMY!!
WAIT... WAIT... NO, IT WOULDN'T ...
LOOK AT THE MAP! IT'S GOING TO MISS US BY 40 KILOMETERS...!
I SAID, IT'LL HEAD RIGHT FOR NERV ACADEMY!!
shing!
COME ON! I MEAN, HOW COULD IT NOT ?
ASUKA! I'M RIGHT, AREN'T I?
YUP!!
...

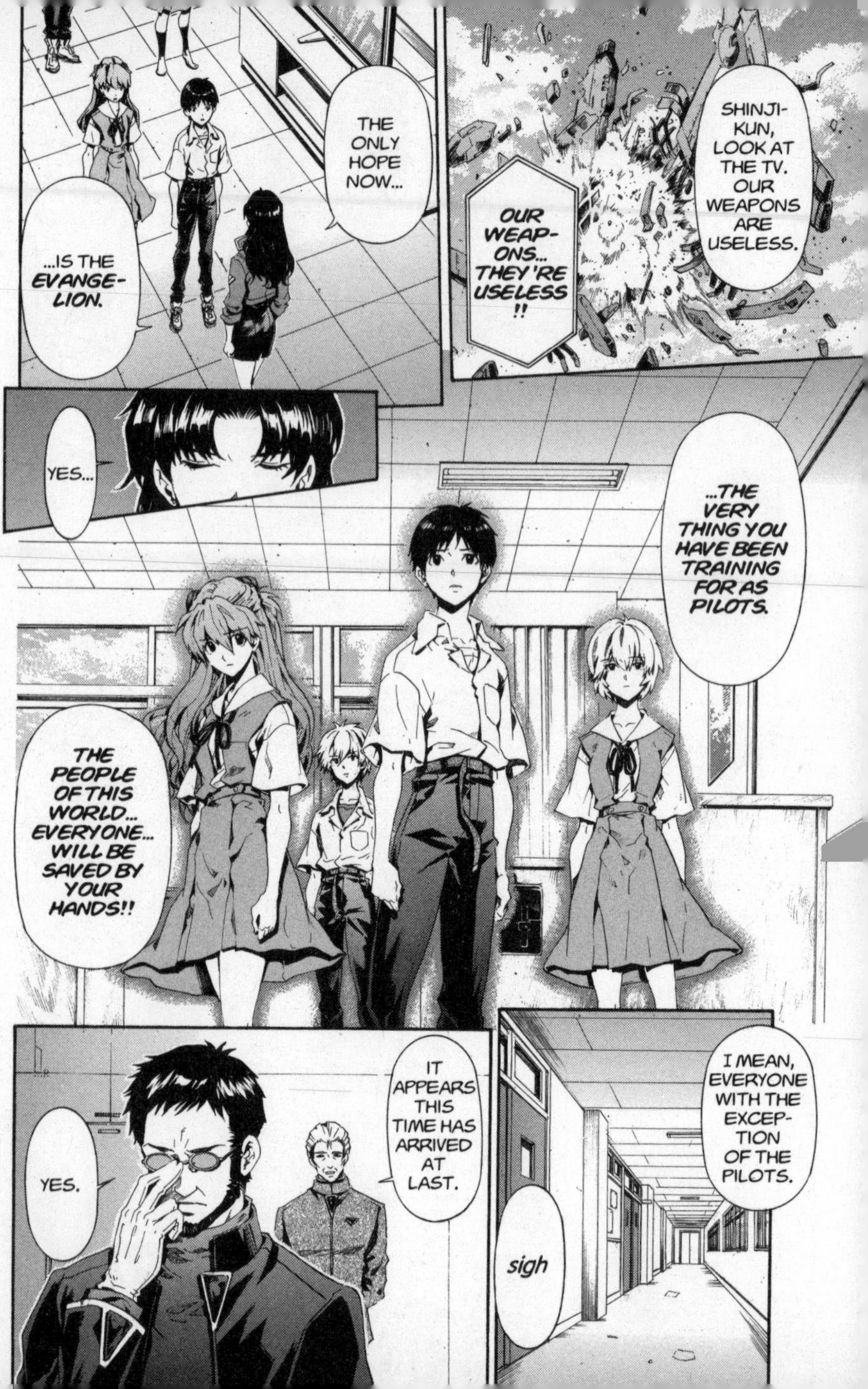
SHINJI-KUN, LOOK AT THE TV. OUR WEAPONS ARE USELESS.
OUR WEAPONS... THEY'RE USELESS!!
THE ONLY HOPE NOW...
...IS THE EVANGELION.
YES...
...THE VERY THING YOU HAVE BEEN TRAINING FOR AS PILOTS.
THE PEOPLE OF THIS WORLD... EVERYONE... WILL BE SAVED BY YOUR HANDS!!
I MEAN, EVERYONE WITH THE EXCEPTION OF THE PILOTS.
sigh
IT APPEARS THIS TIME HAS ARRIVED AT LAST.
YES.

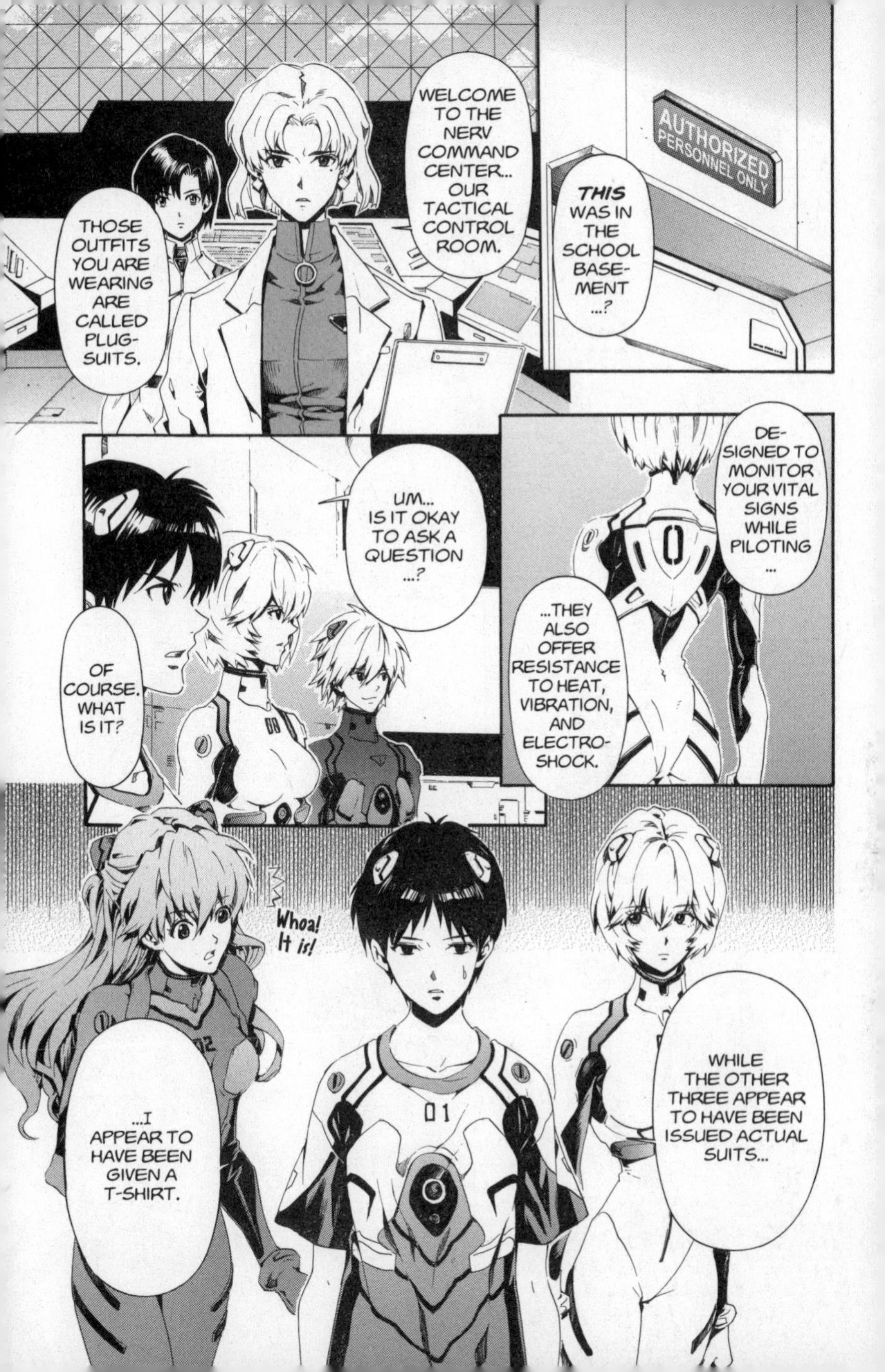
AUTHORIZED PERSONNEL ONLY
THIS WAS IN THE SCHOOL BASEMENT...?
WELCOME TO THE NERV COMMAND CENTER... OUR TACTICAL CONTROL ROOM.
THOSE OUTFITS YOU ARE WEARING ARE CALLED PLUG-SUITS.
DE-SIGNED TO MONITOR YOUR VITAL SIGNS WHILE PILOTING...
...THEY ALSO OFFER RESISTANCE TO HEAT, VIBRATION, AND ELECTRO-SHOCK.
UM... IS IT OKAY TO ASK A QUESTION...?
OF COURSE. WHAT IS IT?
WHILE THE OTHER THREE APPEAR TO HAVE BEEN ISSUED ACTUAL SUITS...
Whoa! It is!
...I APPEAR TO HAVE BEEN GIVEN A T-SHIRT.

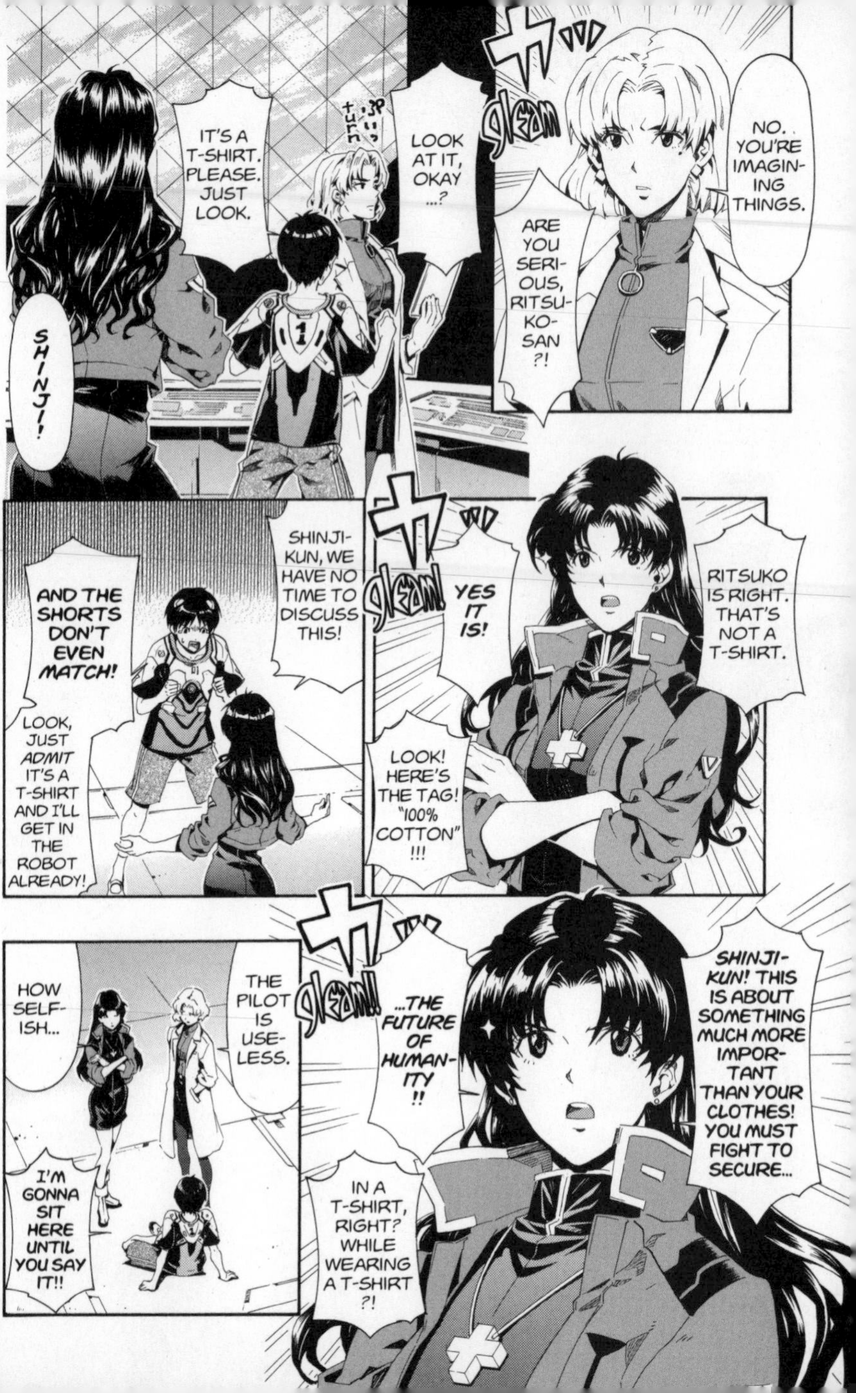
gleam
NO. YOU'RE IMAGINING THINGS.
ARE YOU SERIOUS, RITSUKO-SAN?!
turn
LOOK AT IT, OKAY ...?
IT'S A T-SHIRT. PLEASE. JUST LOOK.
SHINJI!
gleam!
RITSUKO IS RIGHT. THAT'S NOT A T-SHIRT.
YES IT IS!
LOOK! HERE'S THE TAG! "100% COTTON" !!!
SHINJI-KUN, WE HAVE NO TIME TO DISCUSS THIS!
AND THE SHORTS DON'T EVEN MATCH!
LOOK, JUST ADMIT IT'S A T-SHIRT AND I'LL GET IN THE ROBOT ALREADY!
gleam!!
SHINJI-KUN! THIS IS ABOUT SOMETHING MUCH MORE IMPORTANT THAN YOUR CLOTHES! YOU MUST FIGHT TO SECURE...
...THE FUTURE OF HUMANITY!!
IN A T-SHIRT, RIGHT? WHILE WEARING A T-SHIRT?!
THE PILOT IS USELESS.
HOW SELFISH...
I'M GONNA SIT HERE UNTIL YOU SAY IT!!

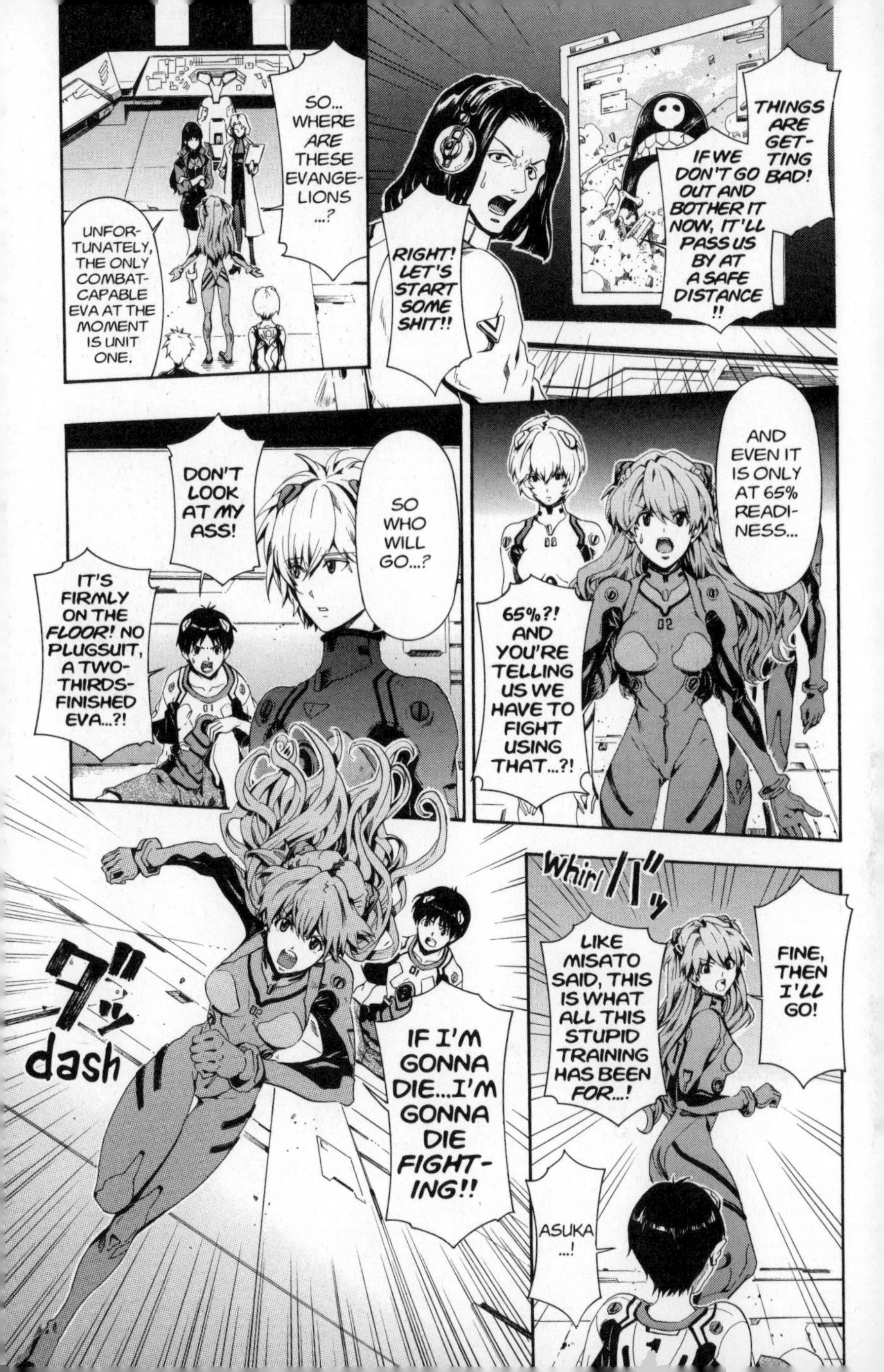

THINGS ARE GETTING BAD!
IF WE DON'T GO OUT AND BOTHER IT NOW, IT'LL PASS US BY AT A SAFE DISTANCE!!
RIGHT! LET'S START SOME SHIT!!
SO... WHERE ARE THESE EVANGELIONS ...?
UNFORTUNATELY, THE ONLY COMBAT-CAPABLE EVA AT THE MOMENT IS UNIT ONE.
AND EVEN IT IS ONLY AT 65% READINESS...
65%?! AND YOU'RE TELLING US WE HAVE TO FIGHT USING THAT...?!
SO WHO WILL GO...?
DON'T LOOK AT MY ASS!
IT'S FIRMLY ON THE FLOOR! NO PLUGSUIT, A TWO-THIRDS-FINISHED EVA...?!
バッ Whirl
FINE, THEN I'LL GO!
LIKE MISATO SAID, THIS IS WHAT ALL THIS STUPID TRAINING HAS BEEN FOR...!
ASUKA ...!
IF I'M GONNA DIE...I'M GONNA DIE FIGHTING!!
ダッ dash

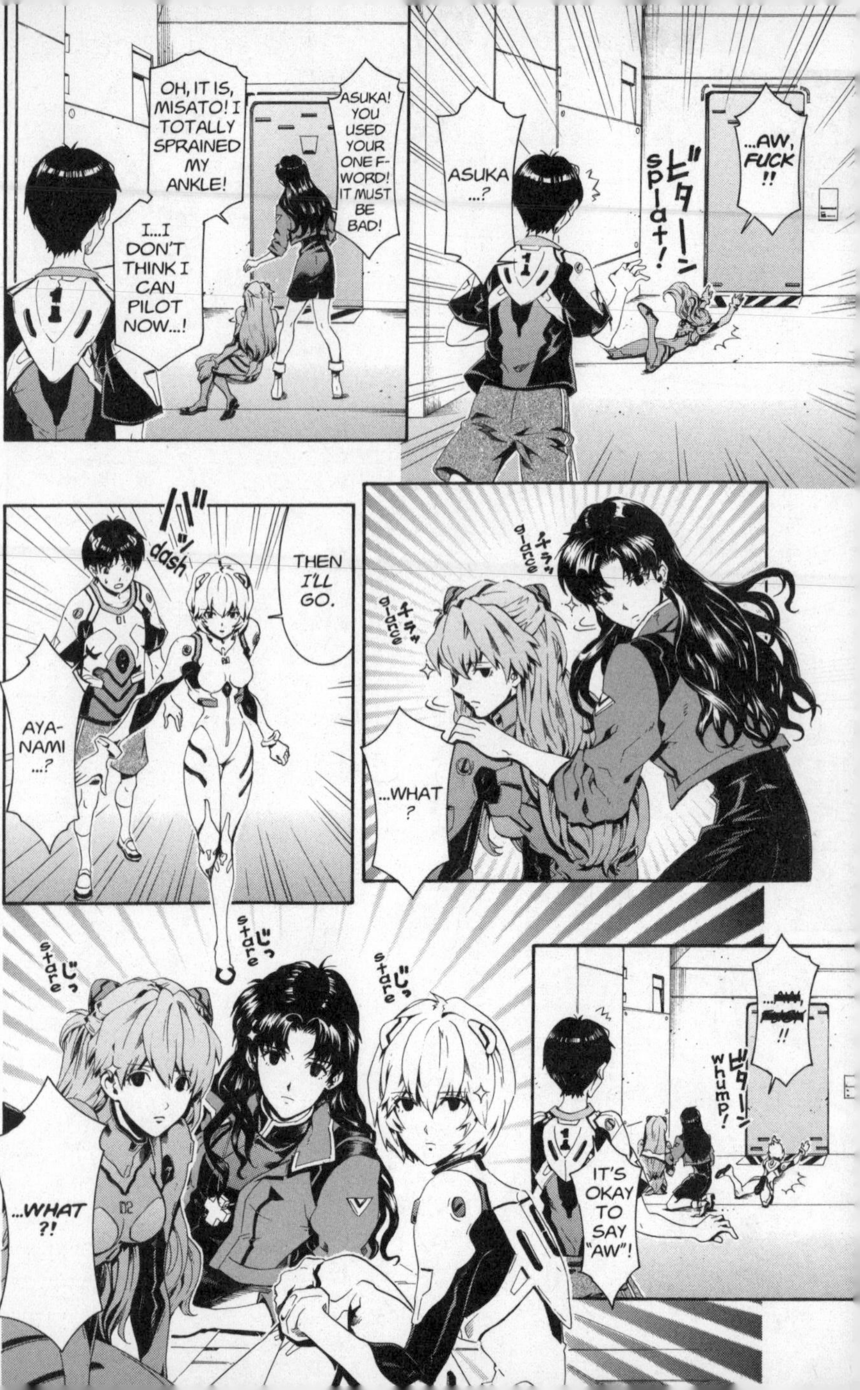
...AW, FUCK !!
ビターン
splat!
ASUKA ...?
ASUKA! YOU USED YOUR ONE F-WORD! IT MUST BE BAD!
OH, IT IS, MISATO! I TOTALLY SPRAINED MY ANKLE!
I...I DON'T THINK I CAN PILOT NOW...!
チラッ
glance
チラッ
glance
...WHAT ?
THEN I'LL GO.
バッ
dash
AYA-NAMI ...?
...[redacted] !!
ビターン
whump!
IT'S OKAY TO SAY "AW"!
じっ
stare
じっ
stare
じっ
stare
...WHAT ?!

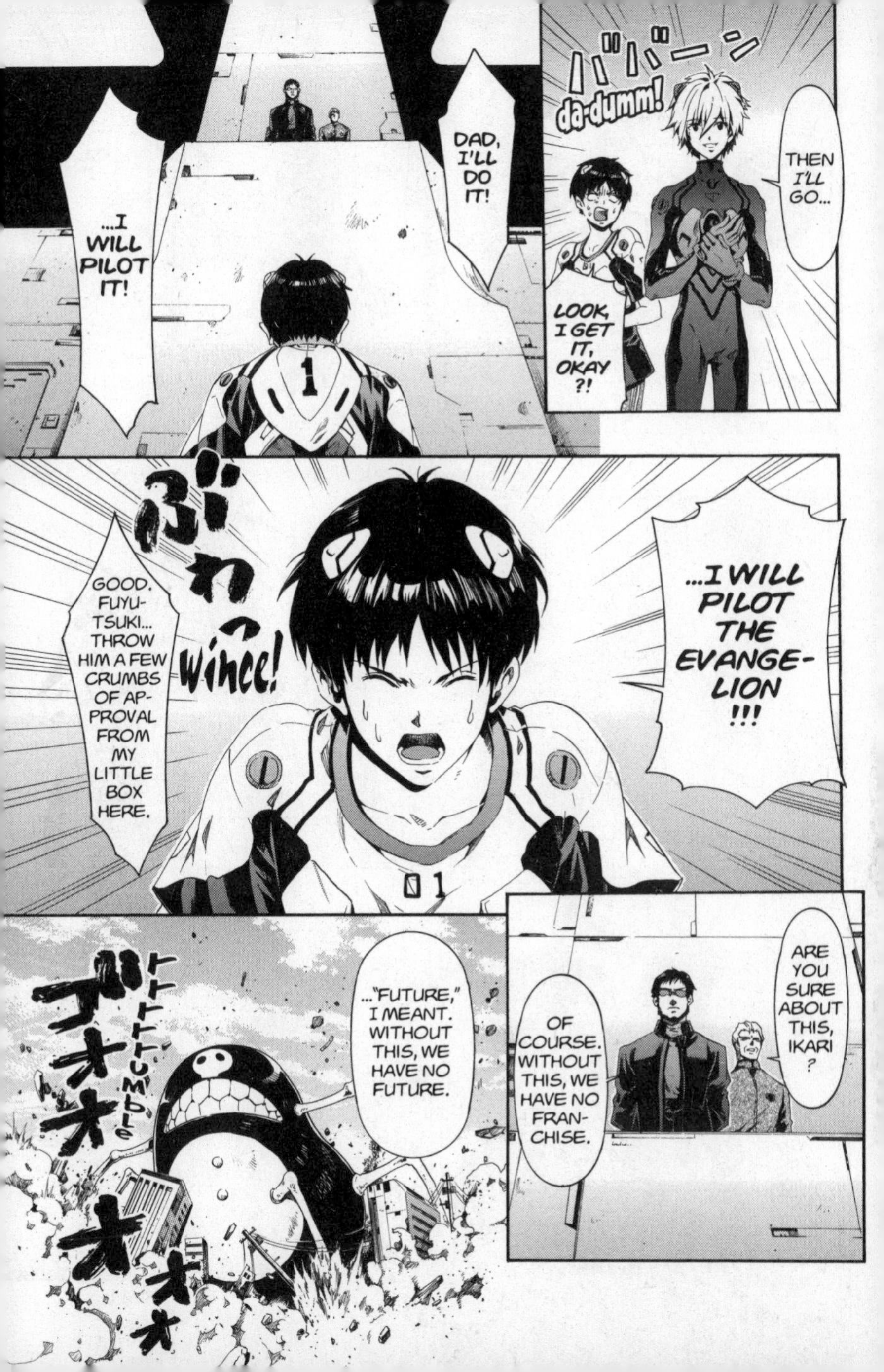
da-dumm!
THEN I'LL GO...
LOOK, I GET IT, OKAY?!
DAD, I'LL DO IT!
...I WILL PILOT IT!
...I WILL PILOT THE EVANGELION!!!
wince!
GOOD. FUYU-TSUKI... THROW HIM A FEW CRUMBS OF APPROVAL FROM MY LITTLE BOX HERE.
ARE YOU SURE ABOUT THIS, IKARI?
OF COURSE. WITHOUT THIS, WE HAVE NO FRANCHISE.
..."FUTURE," I MEANT. WITHOUT THIS, WE HAVE NO FUTURE.
rumble

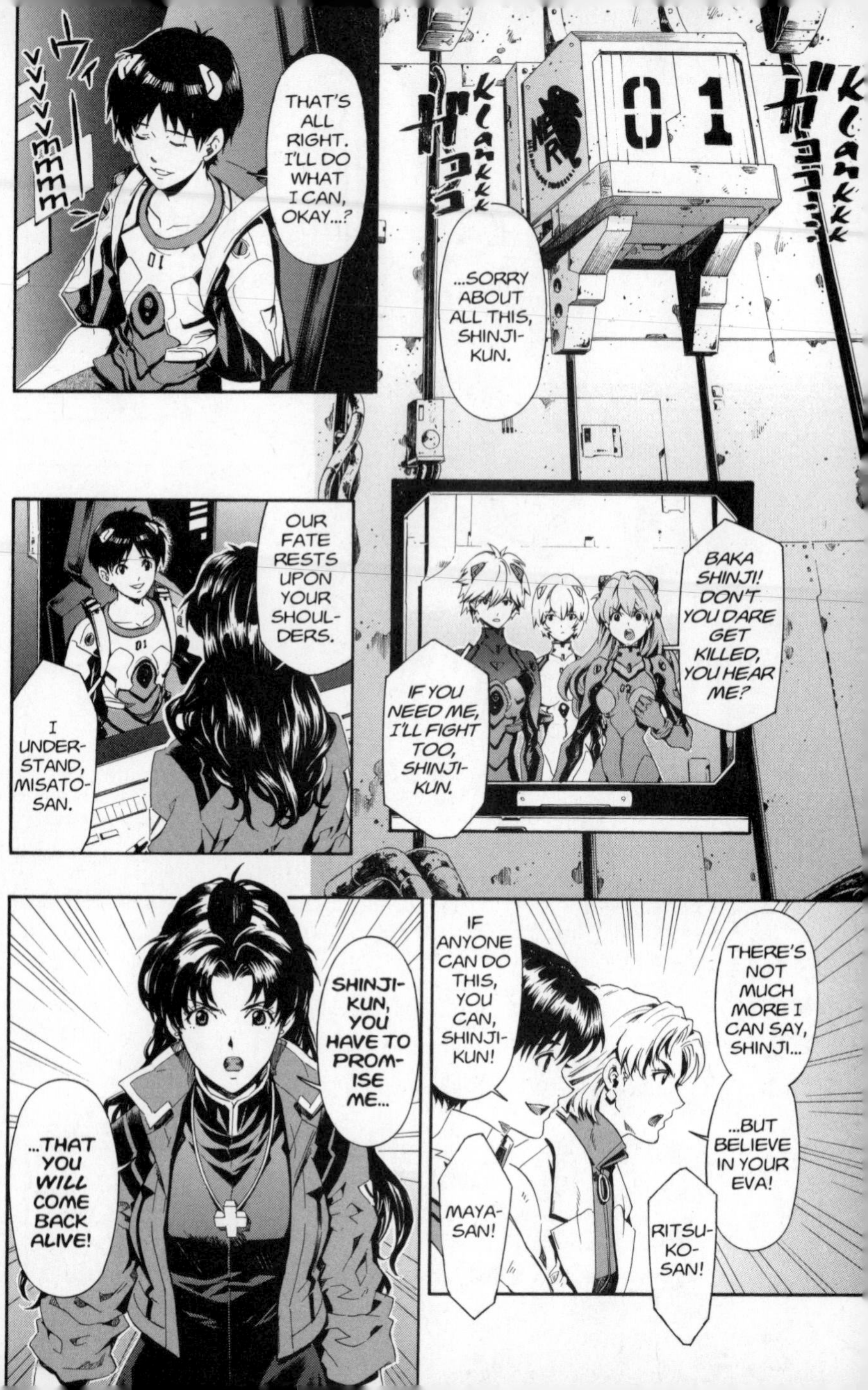
klankkk
klankkk
...SORRY ABOUT ALL THIS, SHINJI-KUN.
vvvvvvvmmmm
THAT'S ALL RIGHT. I'LL DO WHAT I CAN, OKAY...?
BAKA SHINJI! DON'T YOU DARE GET KILLED, YOU HEAR ME?
IF YOU NEED ME, I'LL FIGHT TOO, SHINJI-KUN.
OUR FATE RESTS UPON YOUR SHOULDERS.
I UNDERSTAND, MISATO-SAN.
THERE'S NOT MUCH MORE I CAN SAY, SHINJI...
...BUT BELIEVE IN YOUR EVA!
RITSUKO-SAN!
IF ANYONE CAN DO THIS, YOU CAN, SHINJI-KUN!
MAYA-SAN!
SHINJI-KUN, YOU HAVE TO PROMISE ME...
...THAT YOU WILL COME BACK ALIVE!

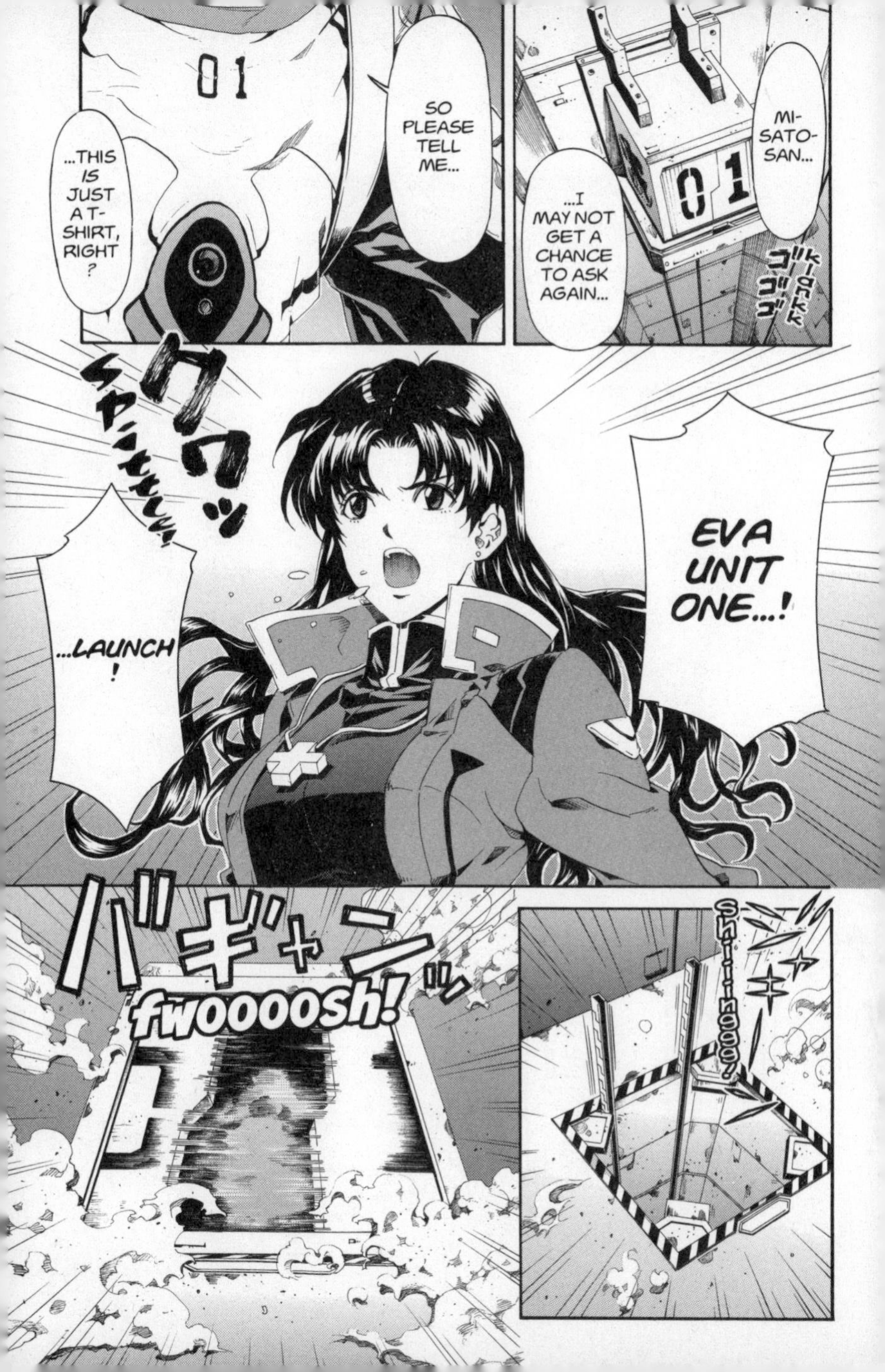
MI-SATO-SAN...
...I MAY NOT GET A CHANCE TO ASK AGAIN...
ゴゴゴ k-lankk
SO PLEASE TELL ME...
...THIS IS JUST A T-SHIRT, RIGHT?
EVA UNIT ONE...!
...LAUNCH!
Shi-i-i-nggg!
fwoooosh!

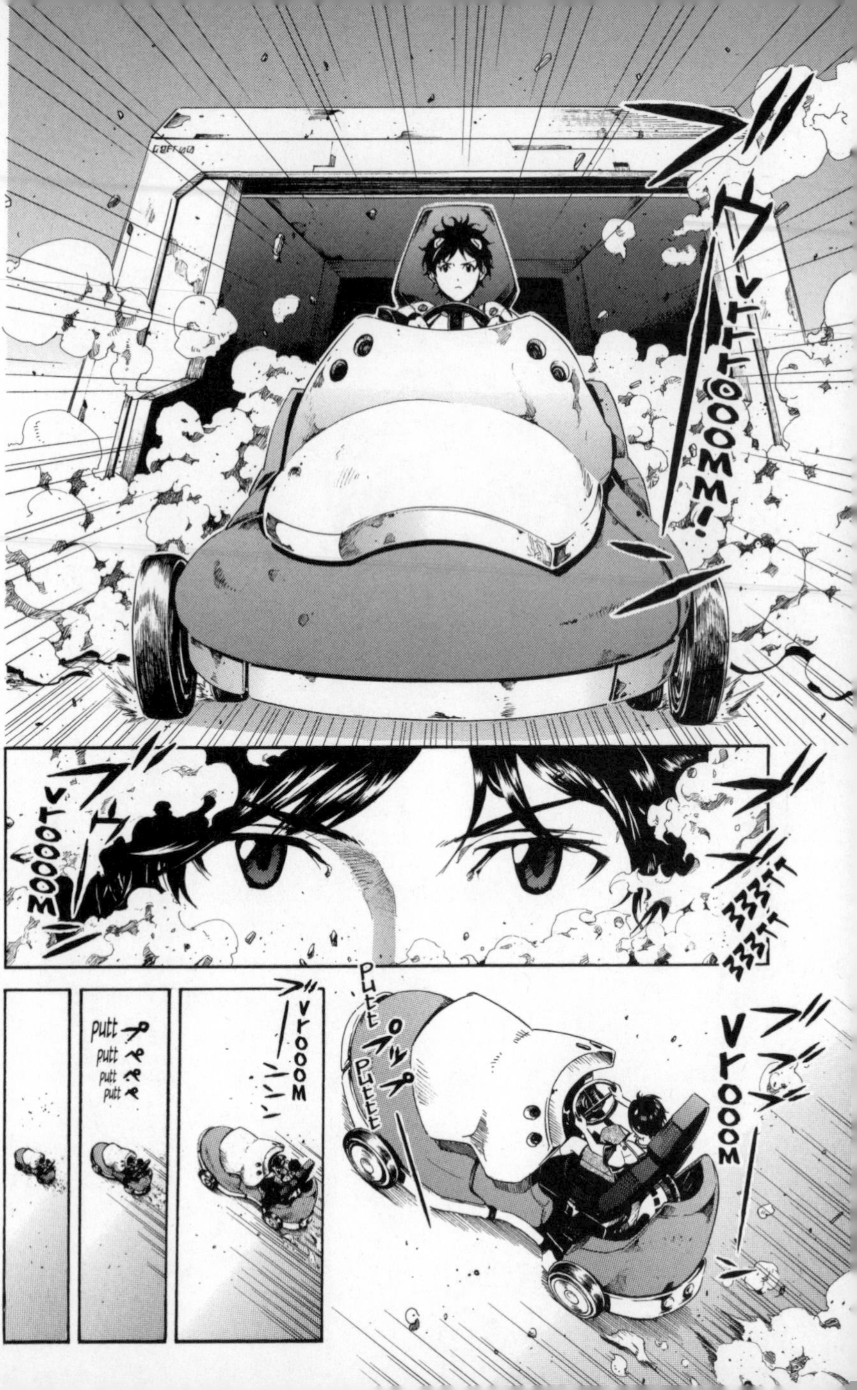
VRRRROOOOMM!
VROOOOM
VROOOOM
Putt
Putt
VROOOOM
putt
putt
putt
putt

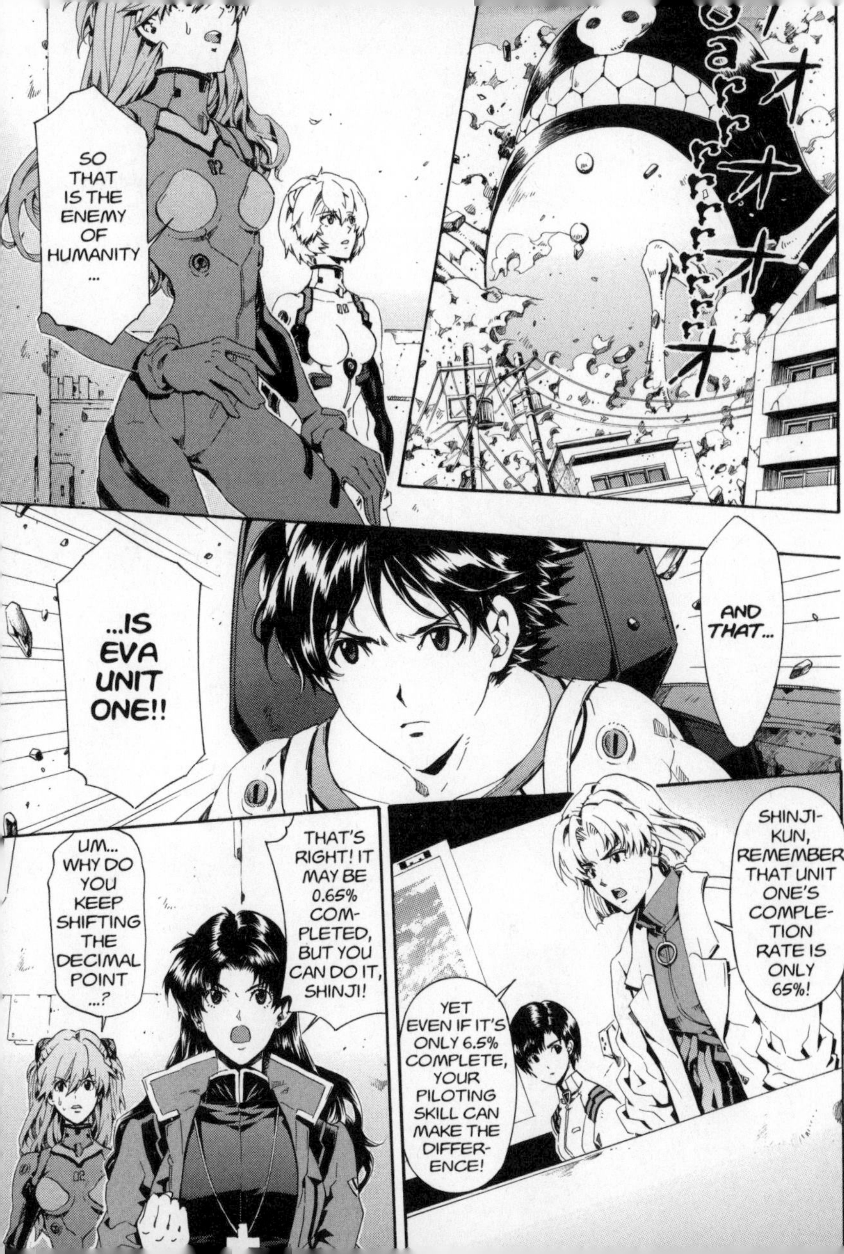
SO THAT IS THE ENEMY OF HUMANITY ...
AND THAT...
...IS EVA UNIT ONE!!
SHINJI-KUN, REMEMBER THAT UNIT ONE'S COMPLETION RATE IS ONLY 65%!
YET EVEN IF IT'S ONLY 6.5% COMPLETE, YOUR PILOTING SKILL CAN MAKE THE DIFFERENCE!
THAT'S RIGHT! IT MAY BE 0.65% COMPLETED, BUT YOU CAN DO IT, SHINJI!
UM... WHY DO YOU KEEP SHIFTING THE DECIMAL POINT ...?

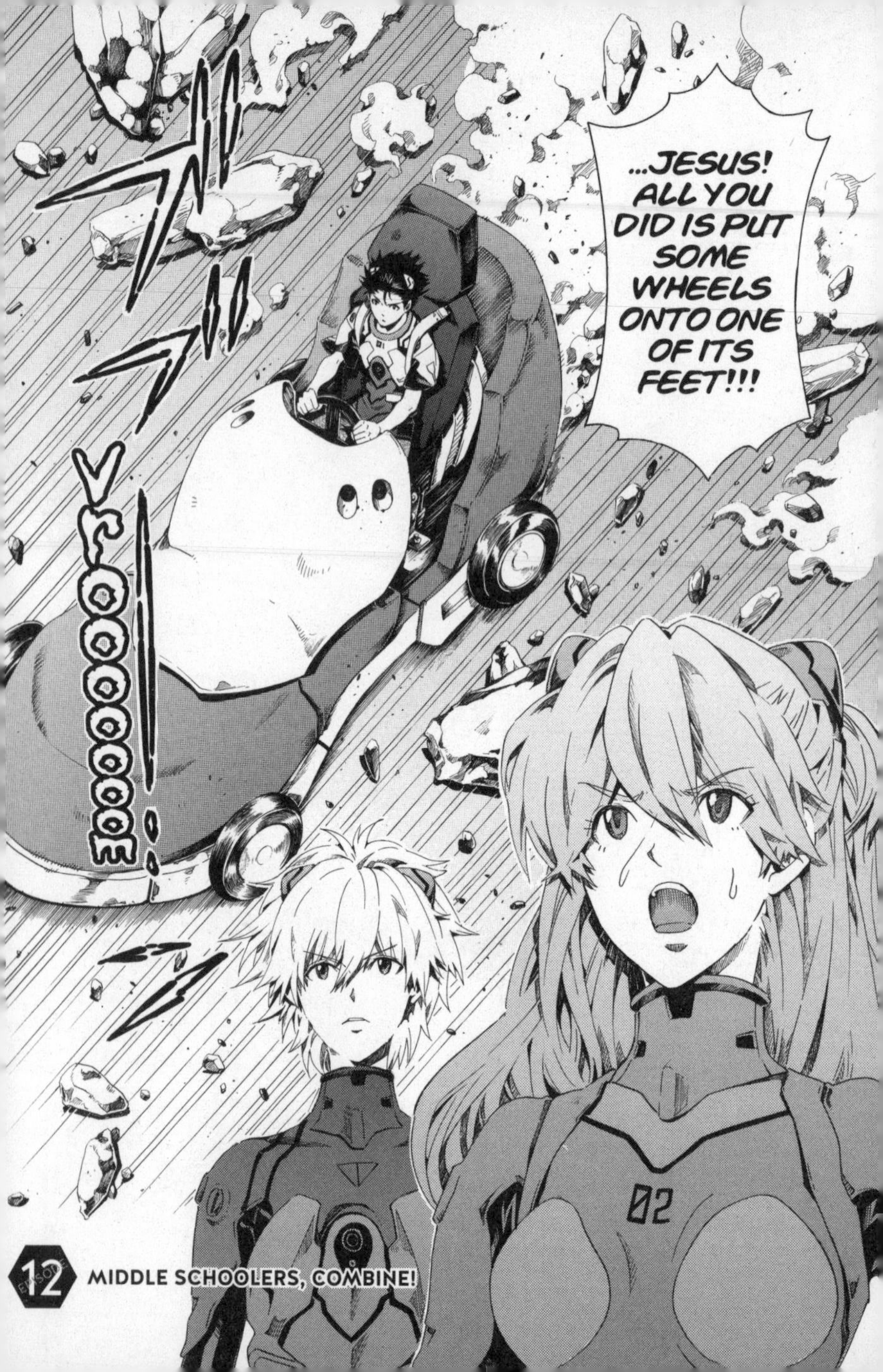
...JESUS! ALL YOU DID IS PUT SOME WHEELS ONTO ONE OF ITS FEET!!!
Vroooooom!

EPISODE 12 MIDDLE SCHOOLERS, COMBINE!

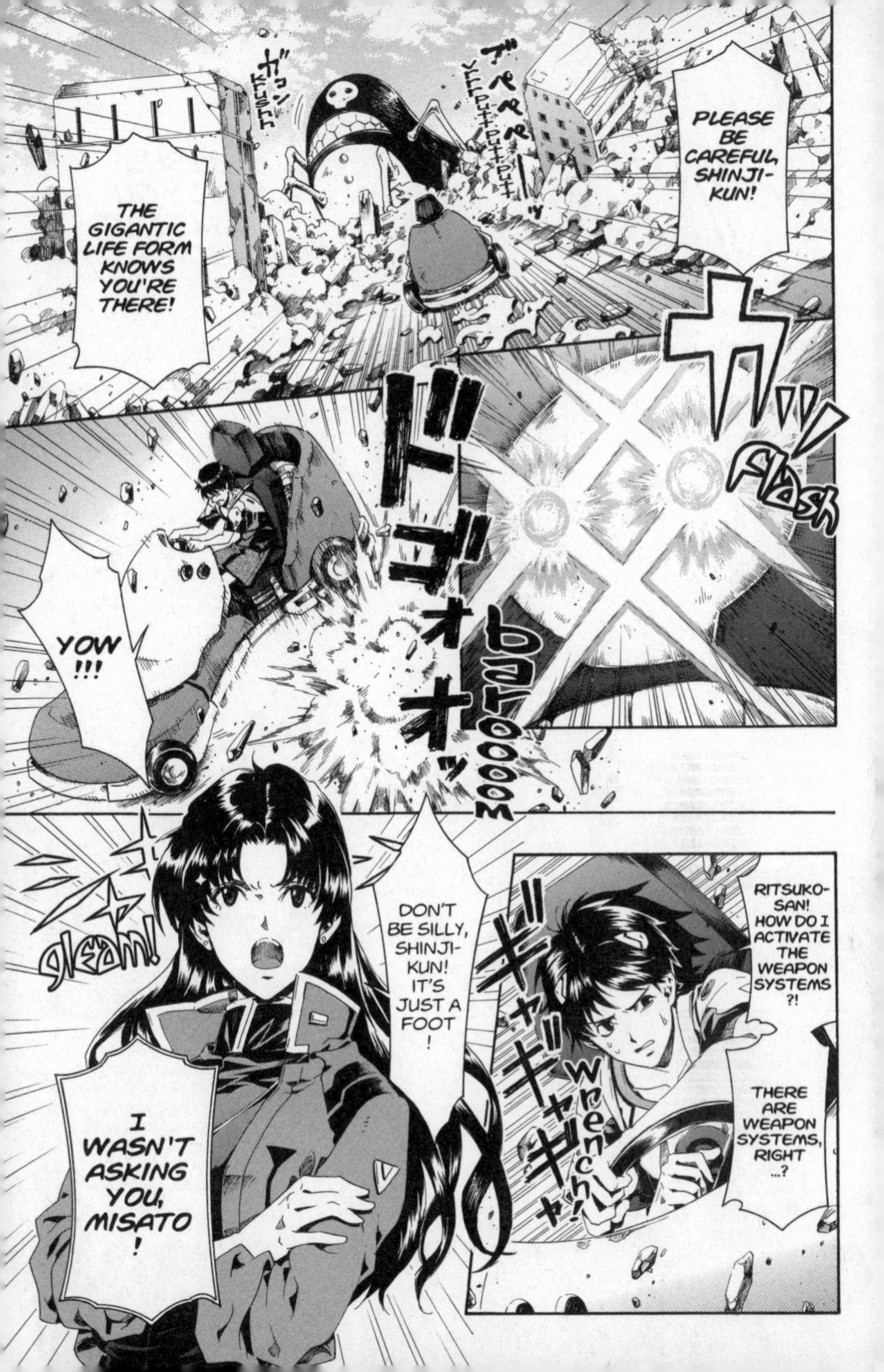
PLEASE BE CAREFUL, SHINJI-KUN!
vrrr putt putt putt
krush
THE GIGANTIC LIFE FORM KNOWS YOU'RE THERE!
flash
baROOOOOM
YOW !!!
RITSUKO-SAN! HOW DO I ACTIVATE THE WEAPON SYSTEMS ?!
wrench!
THERE ARE WEAPON SYSTEMS, RIGHT ...?
DON'T BE SILLY, SHINJI-KUN! IT'S JUST A FOOT !
gleam!
I WASN'T ASKING YOU, MISATO !

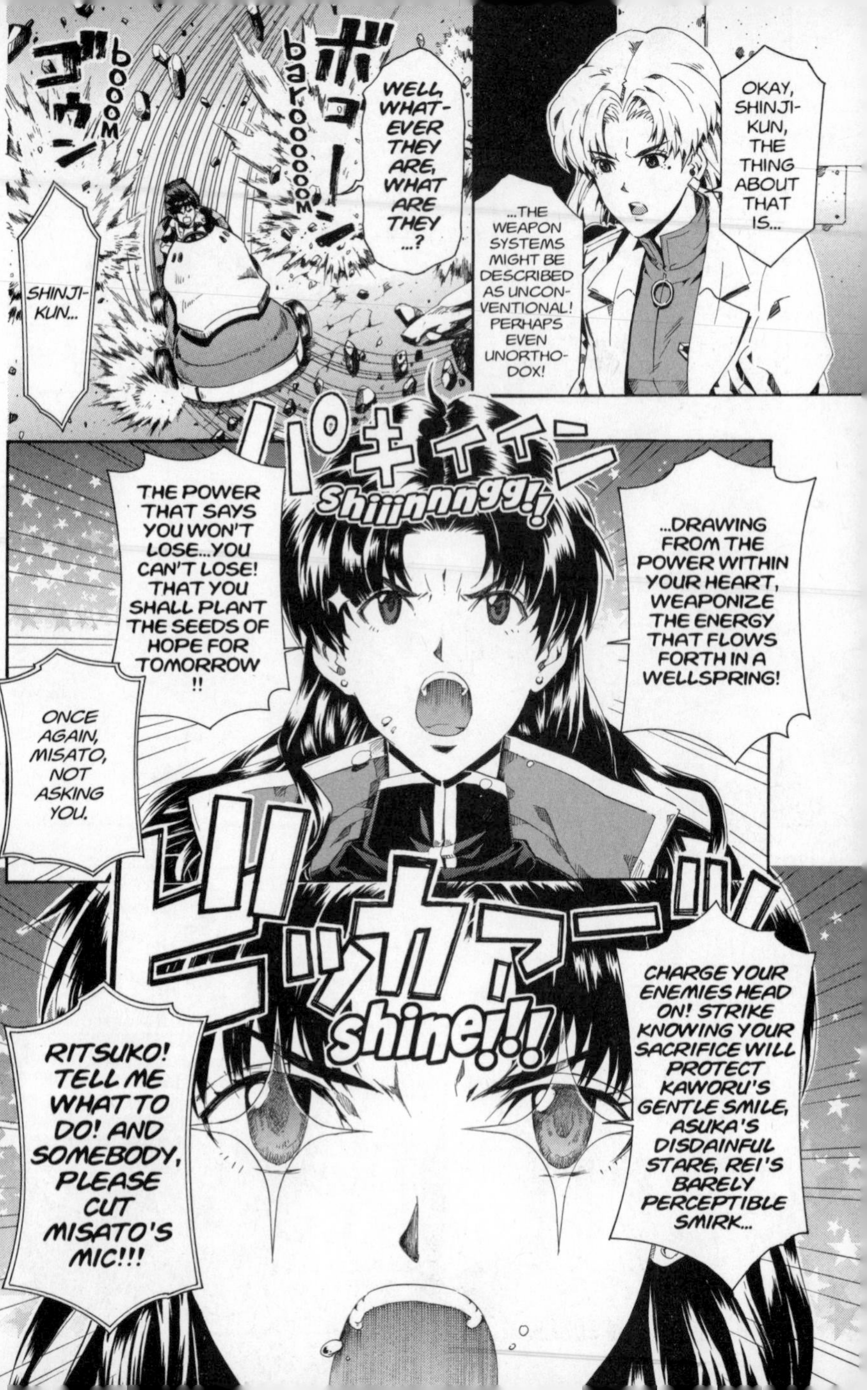
OKAY, SHINJI-KUN, THE THING ABOUT THAT IS...
...THE WEAPON SYSTEMS MIGHT BE DESCRIBED AS UNCONVENTIONAL! PERHAPS EVEN UNORTHODOX!
ボコーン
bakoooooooom
WELL, WHATEVER THEY ARE, WHAT ARE THEY ...?
ゴウン
boooom
SHINJI-KUN...
パキイィン
Shiiinnnngg!!
THE POWER THAT SAYS YOU WON'T LOSE...YOU CAN'T LOSE! THAT YOU SHALL PLANT THE SEEDS OF HOPE FOR TOMORROW !!
...DRAWING FROM THE POWER WITHIN YOUR HEART, WEAPONIZE THE ENERGY THAT FLOWS FORTH IN A WELLSPRING!
ONCE AGAIN, MISATO, NOT ASKING YOU.
ピッカァーン
shine!!!
CHARGE YOUR ENEMIES HEAD ON! STRIKE KNOWING YOUR SACRIFICE WILL PROTECT KAWORU'S GENTLE SMILE, ASUKA'S DISDAINFUL STARE, REI'S BARELY PERCEPTIBLE SMIRK...
RITSUKO! TELL ME WHAT TO DO! AND SOMEBODY, PLEASE CUT MISATO'S MIC!!!

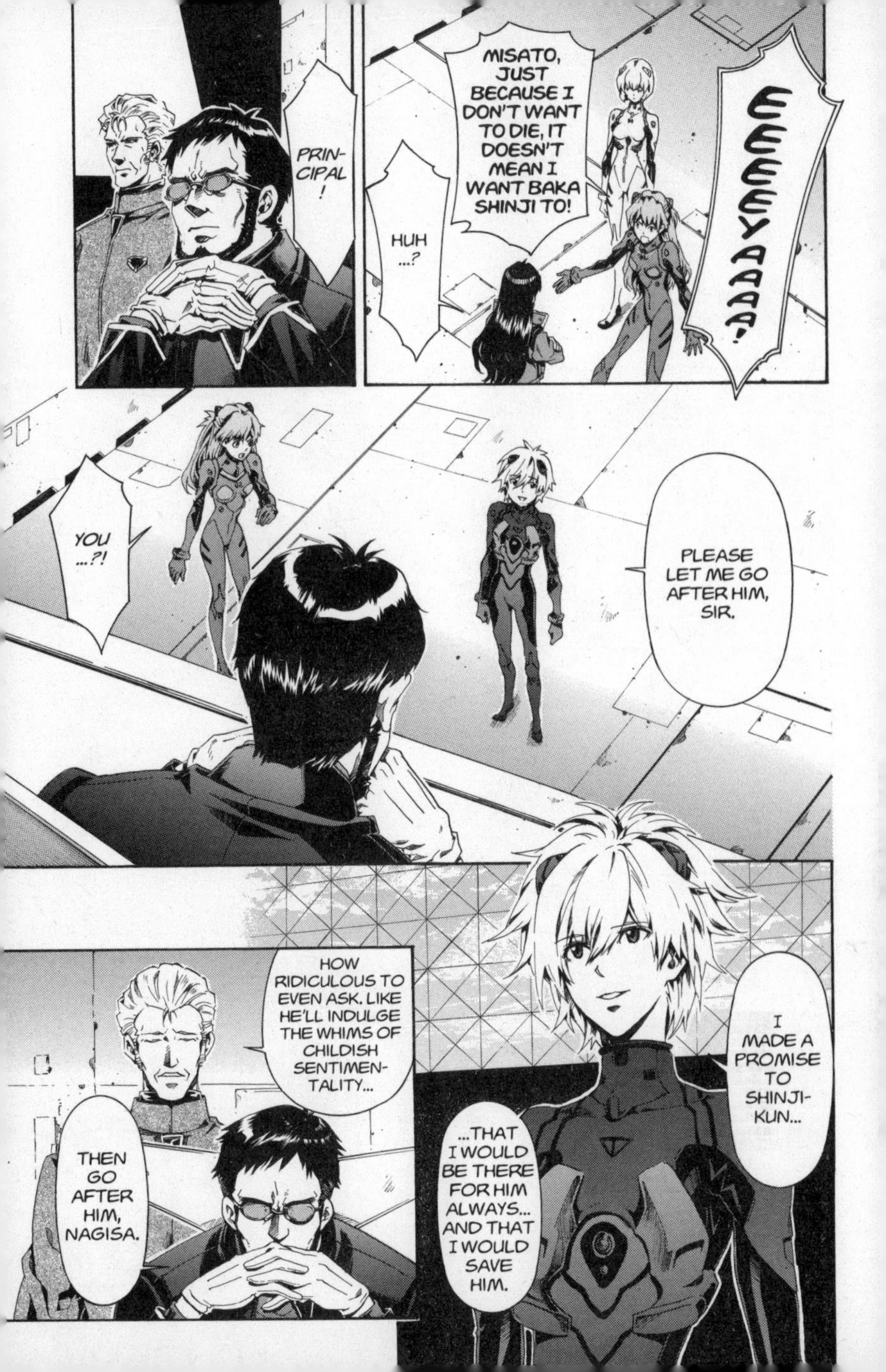
EEEEYAAAAA!
MISATO, JUST BECAUSE I DON'T WANT TO DIE, IT DOESN'T MEAN I WANT BAKA SHINJI TO!
HUH ...?
PRIN-CIPAL!
PLEASE LET ME GO AFTER HIM, SIR.
YOU ...?!
I MADE A PROMISE TO SHINJI-KUN...
...THAT I WOULD BE THERE FOR HIM ALWAYS... AND THAT I WOULD SAVE HIM.
HOW RIDICULOUS TO EVEN ASK. LIKE HE'LL INDULGE THE WHIMS OF CHILDISH SENTIMEN-TALITY...
THEN GO AFTER HIM, NAGISA.

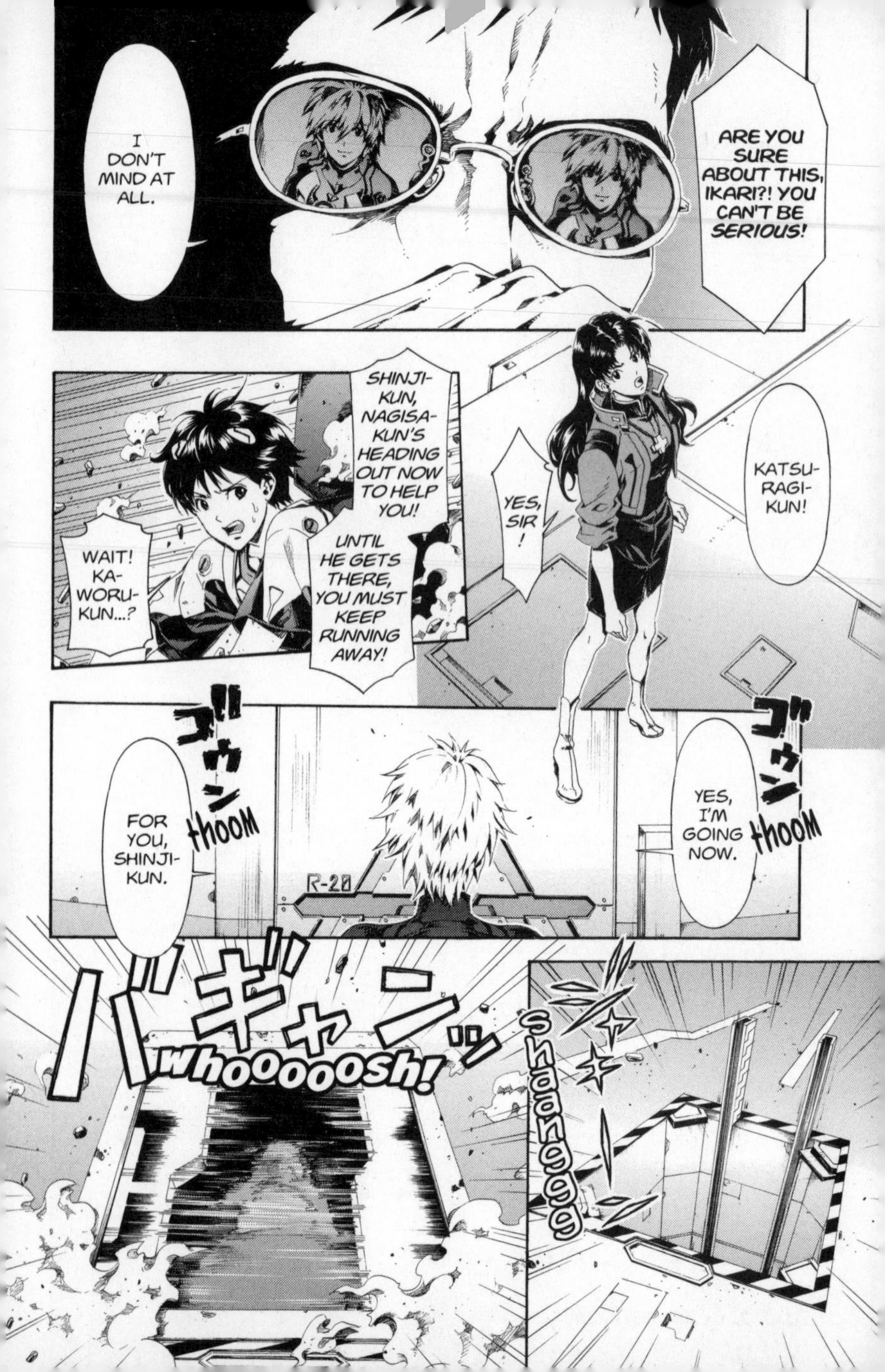
ARE YOU SURE ABOUT THIS, IKARI?! YOU CAN'T BE SERIOUS!
I DON'T MIND AT ALL.
KATSURAGI-KUN!
YES, SIR!
SHINJI-KUN, NAGISA-KUN'S HEADING OUT NOW TO HELP YOU!
UNTIL HE GETS THERE, YOU MUST KEEP RUNNING AWAY!
WAIT! KAWORU-KUN...?
ゴゥン thoom
YES, I'M GOING NOW.
R-20
FOR YOU, SHINJI-KUN.
ゴゥン thoom
shaanggg
バギャーッ
whoooooosh!

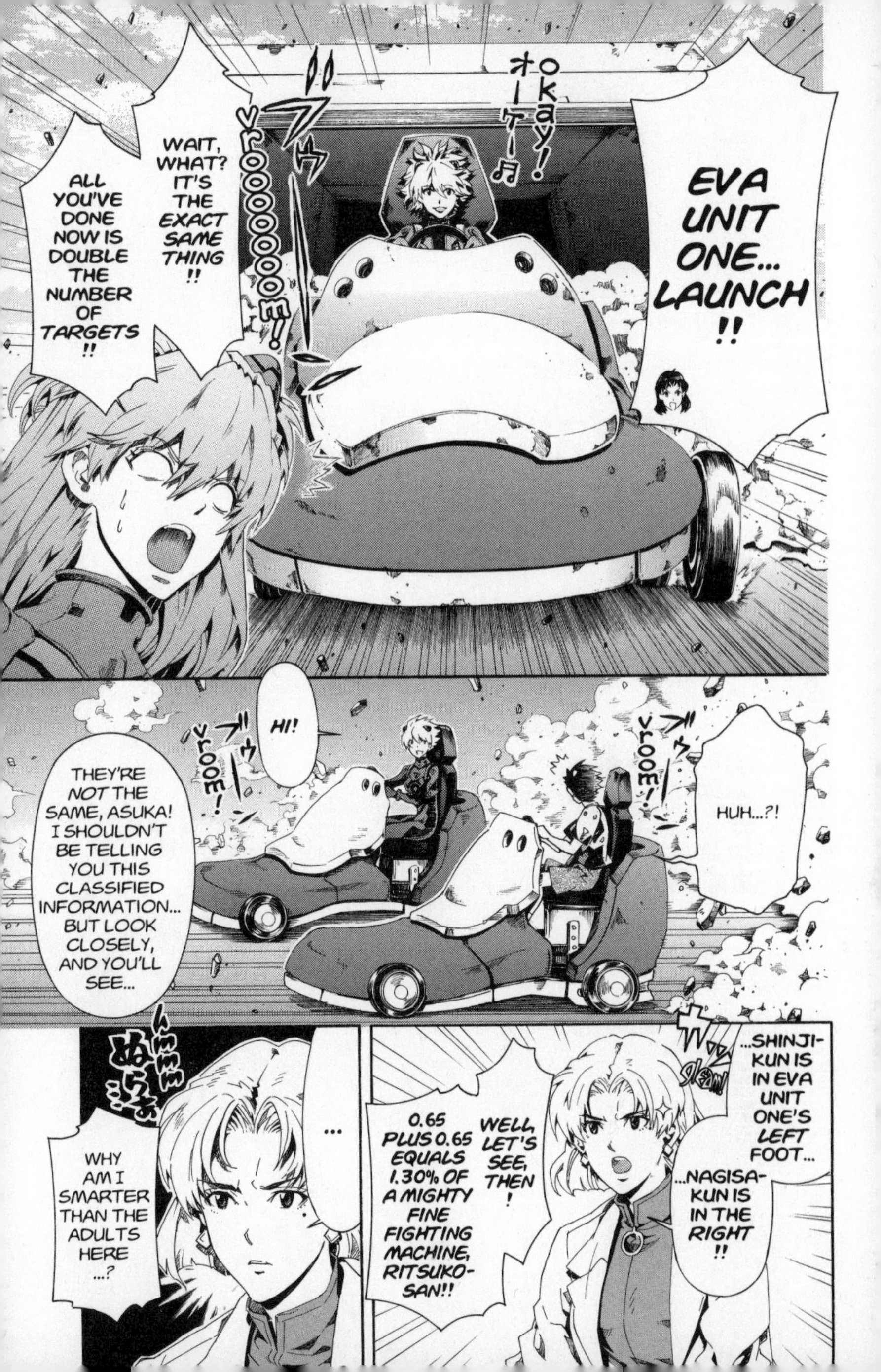
EVA UNIT ONE... LAUNCH!!
okay!
vroooooooom!
WAIT, WHAT? IT'S THE EXACT SAME THING!!
ALL YOU'VE DONE NOW IS DOUBLE THE NUMBER OF TARGETS!!
HUH...?!
vroom!
HI!
vroom!
THEY'RE NOT THE SAME, ASUKA! I SHOULDN'T BE TELLING YOU THIS CLASSIFIED INFORMATION... BUT LOOK CLOSELY, AND YOU'LL SEE...
SLAM!
...SHINJI-KUN IS IN EVA UNIT ONE'S LEFT FOOT...
...NAGISA-KUN IS IN THE RIGHT!!
WELL, LET'S SEE, THEN!
0.65 PLUS 0.65 EQUALS 1.30% OF A MIGHTY FINE FIGHTING MACHINE, RITSUKO-SAN!!
...
WHY AM I SMARTER THAN THE ADULTS HERE...?

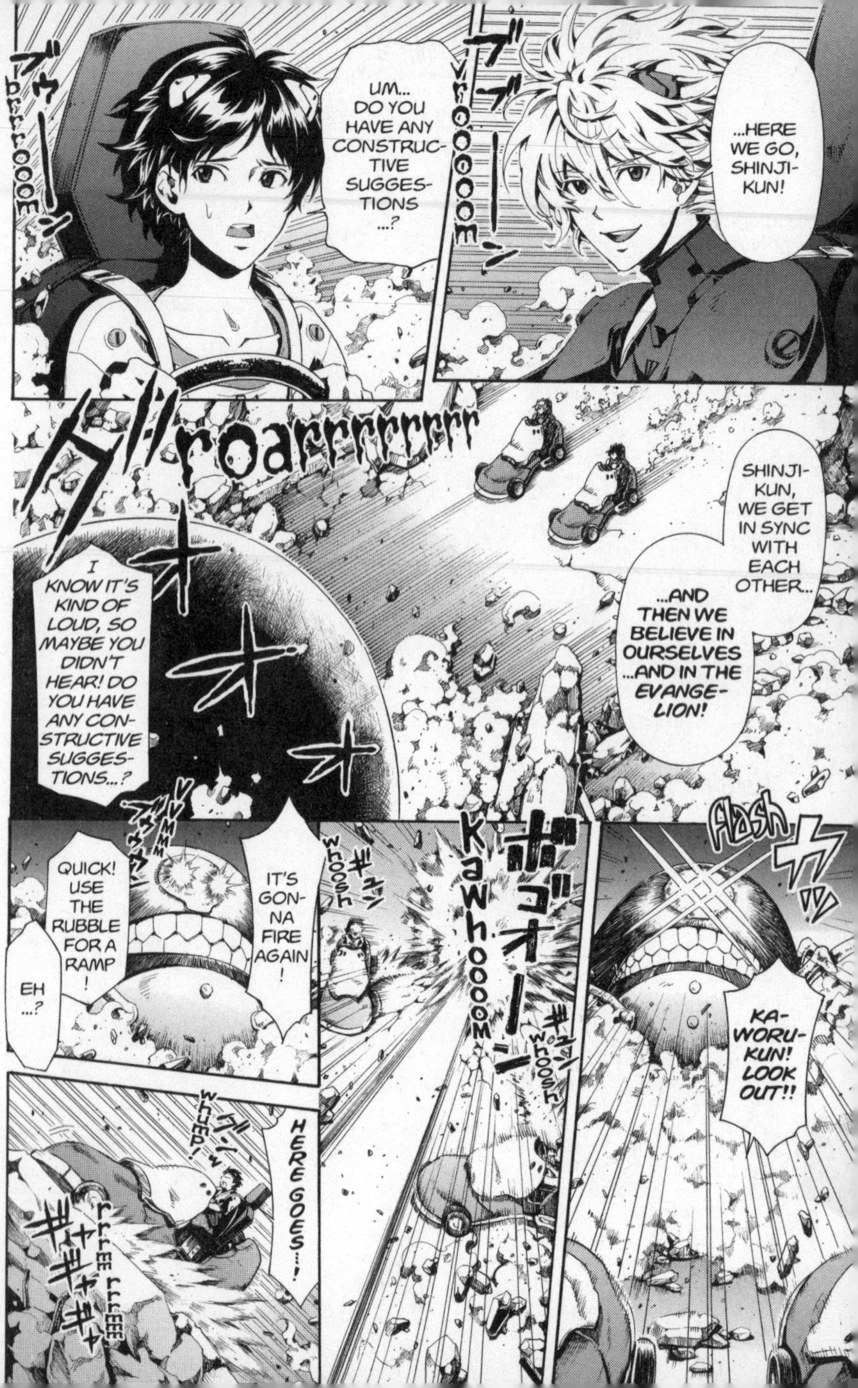
vrooooooom
...HERE WE GO, SHINJI-KUN!
vrrroooom
UM... DO YOU HAVE ANY CONSTRUC-TIVE SUGGES-TIONS ...?
roarrrrrrrr
SHINJI-KUN, WE GET IN SYNC WITH EACH OTHER...
...AND THEN WE BELIEVE IN OURSELVES ...AND IN THE EVANGE-LION!
I KNOW IT'S KIND OF LOUD, SO MAYBE YOU DIDN'T HEAR! DO YOU HAVE ANY CON-STRUCTIVE SUGGES-TIONS...?
flash
KA-WORU-KUN! LOOK OUT!!
kawhooooom
whoosh
whoosh
IT'S GON-NA FIRE AGAIN!
vvmmm
QUICK! USE THE RUBBLE FOR A RAMP!
EH ...?
whump!
HERE GOES...!
rrrrm rrrrmmm

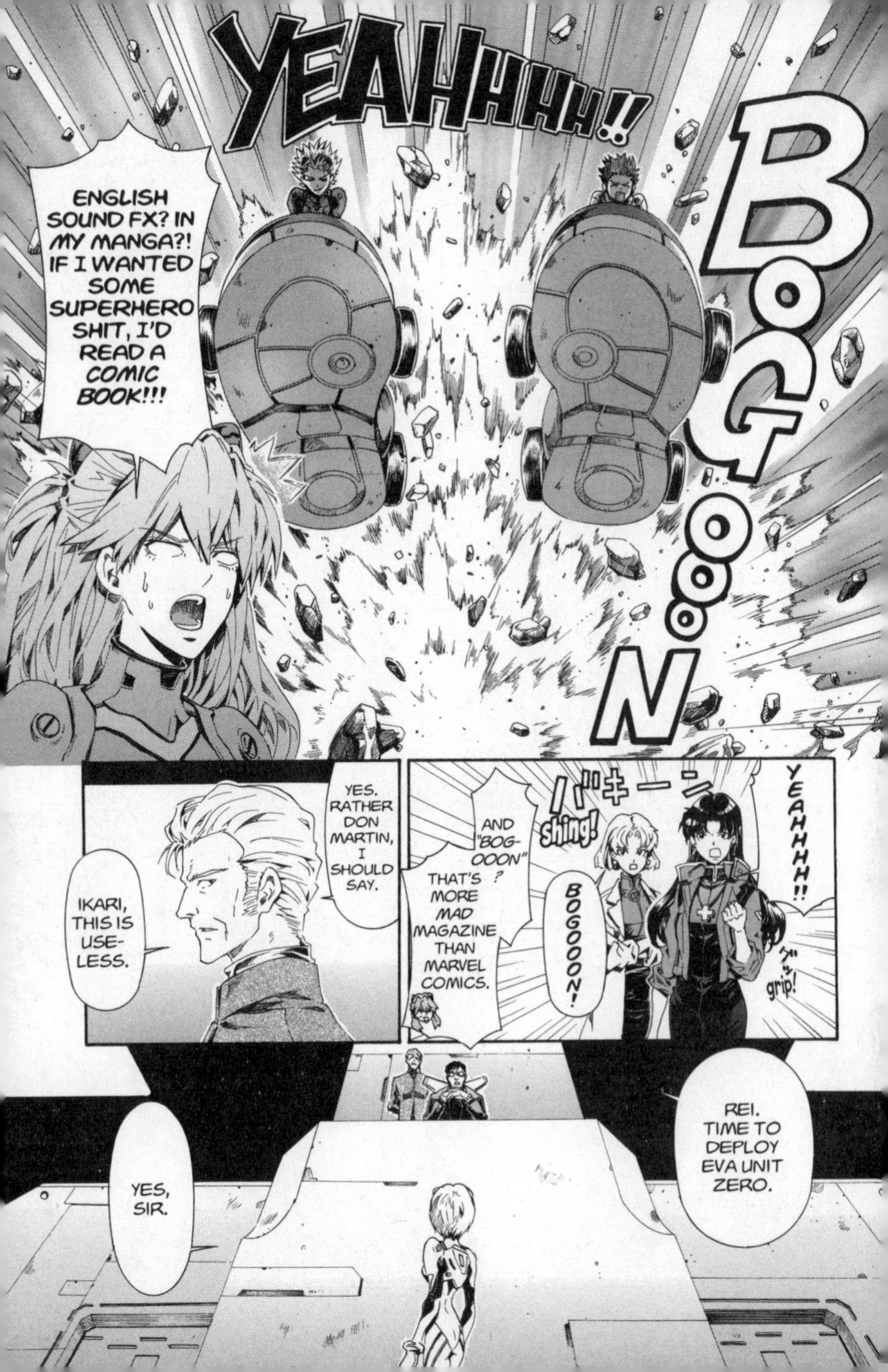
YEAHHHH!!
BOGOOON
ENGLISH SOUND FX? IN MY MANGA?! IF I WANTED SOME SUPERHERO SHIT, I'D READ A COMIC BOOK!!!
YEAHHHH!!
shing!
BOGOOOON!
grip!
AND "BOG-OOON"? THAT'S MORE MAD MAGAZINE THAN MARVEL COMICS.
YES. RATHER DON MARTIN, I SHOULD SAY.
IKARI, THIS IS USE-LESS.
REI. TIME TO DEPLOY EVA UNIT ZERO.
YES, SIR.

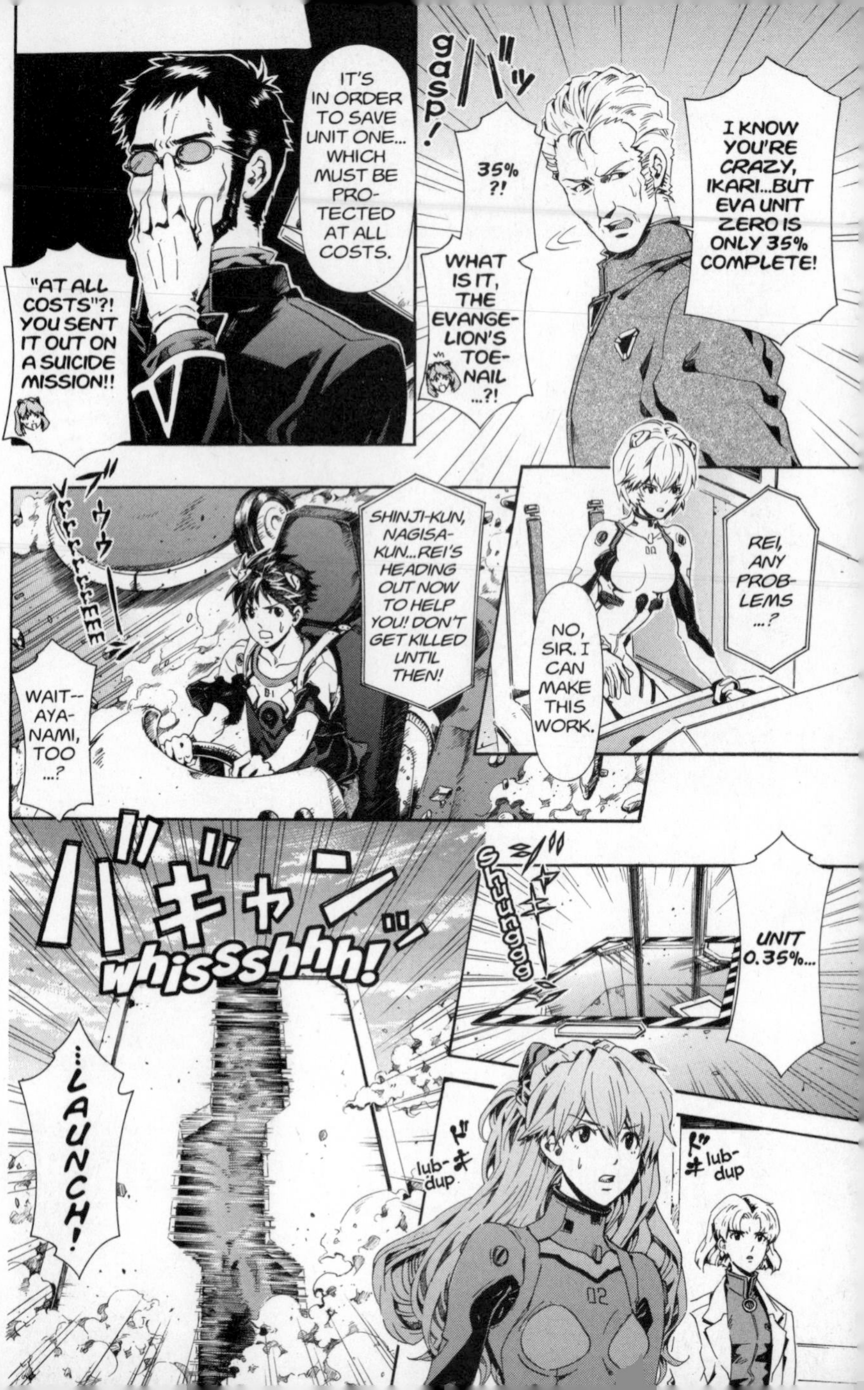
I KNOW YOU'RE CRAZY, IKARI...BUT EVA UNIT ZERO IS ONLY 35% COMPLETE!
バッ
gasp!
35% ?!
WHAT IS IT, THE EVANGELION'S TOE-NAIL ...?!
IT'S IN ORDER TO SAVE UNIT ONE... WHICH MUST BE PRO-TECTED AT ALL COSTS.
"AT ALL COSTS"?! YOU SENT IT OUT ON A SUICIDE MISSION!!
REI, ANY PROB-LEMS ...?
NO, SIR. I CAN MAKE THIS WORK.
SHINJI-KUN, NAGISA-KUN...REI'S HEADING OUT NOW TO HELP YOU! DON'T GET KILLED UNTIL THEN!
ブウウー
WAIT-- AYA-NAMI, TOO ...?
UNIT 0.35%...
ドキ lub-dup
ドキ lub-dup
バギャーン
whissshhh!
...LAUNCH!

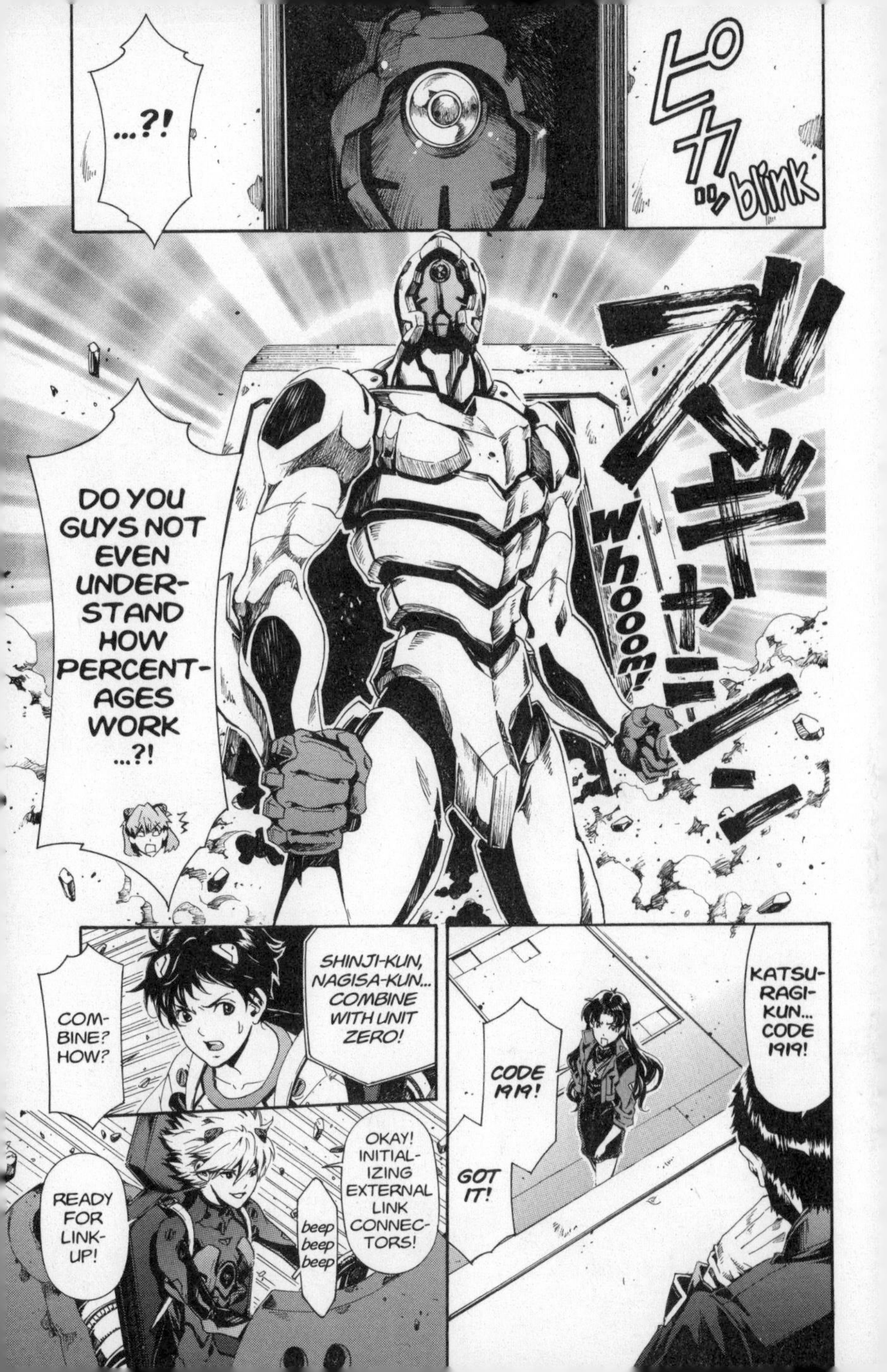

ピカッ blink
...?!
whoooom!
DO YOU GUYS NOT EVEN UNDER-STAND HOW PERCENT-AGES WORK ...?!
KATSU-RAGI-KUN... CODE 1919!
CODE 1919!
GOT IT!
SHINJI-KUN, NAGISA-KUN... COMBINE WITH UNIT ZERO!
COM-BINE? HOW?
OKAY! INITIAL-IZING EXTERNAL LINK CONNEC-TORS!
beep beep beep
READY FOR LINK-UP!

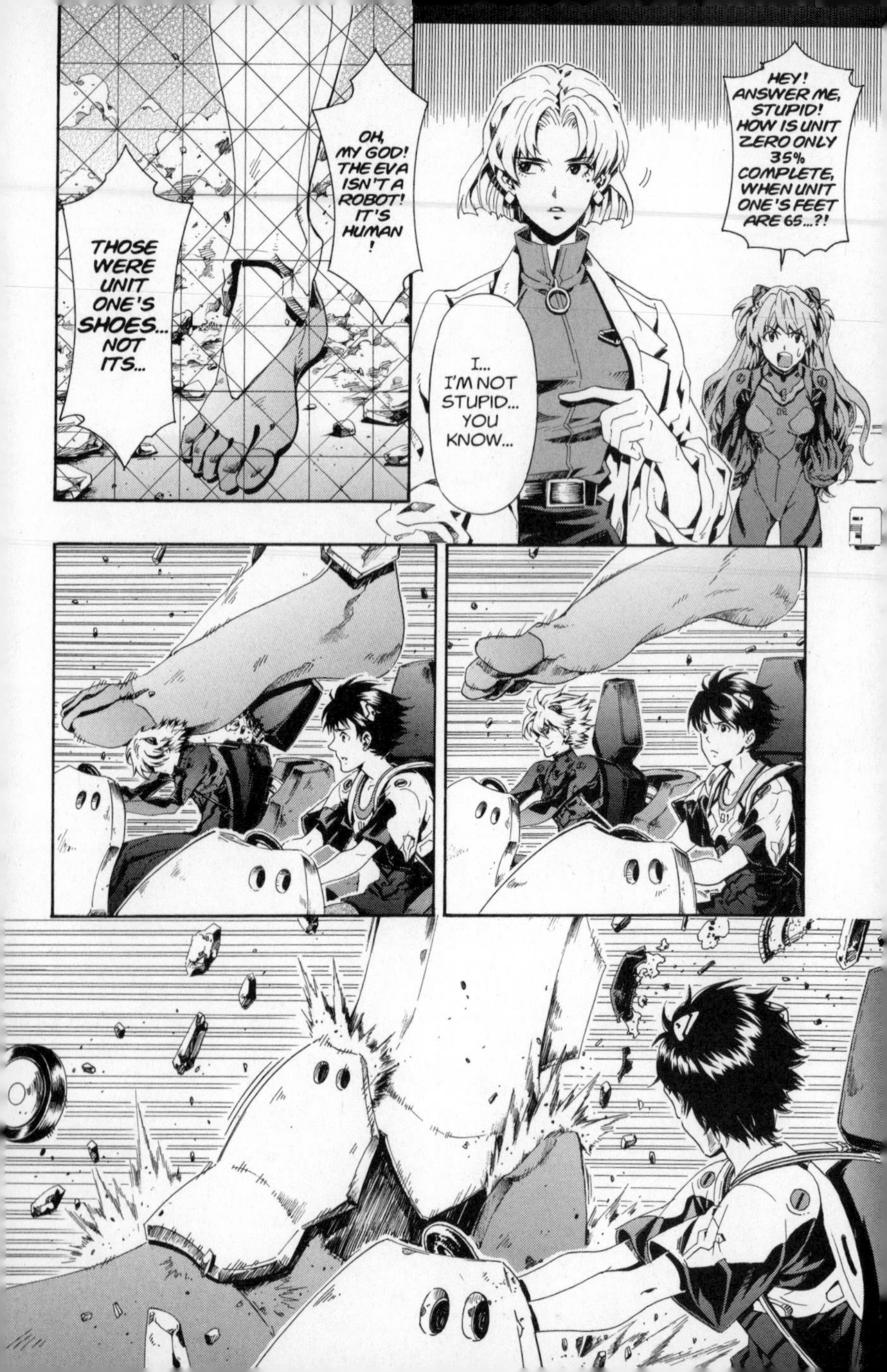
HEY! ANSWER ME, STUPID! HOW IS UNIT ZERO ONLY 35% COMPLETE, WHEN UNIT ONE'S FEET ARE 65...?!
I... I'M NOT STUPID... YOU KNOW...
OH, MY GOD! THE EVA ISN'T A ROBOT! IT'S HUMAN!
THOSE WERE UNIT ONE'S SHOES... NOT ITS...

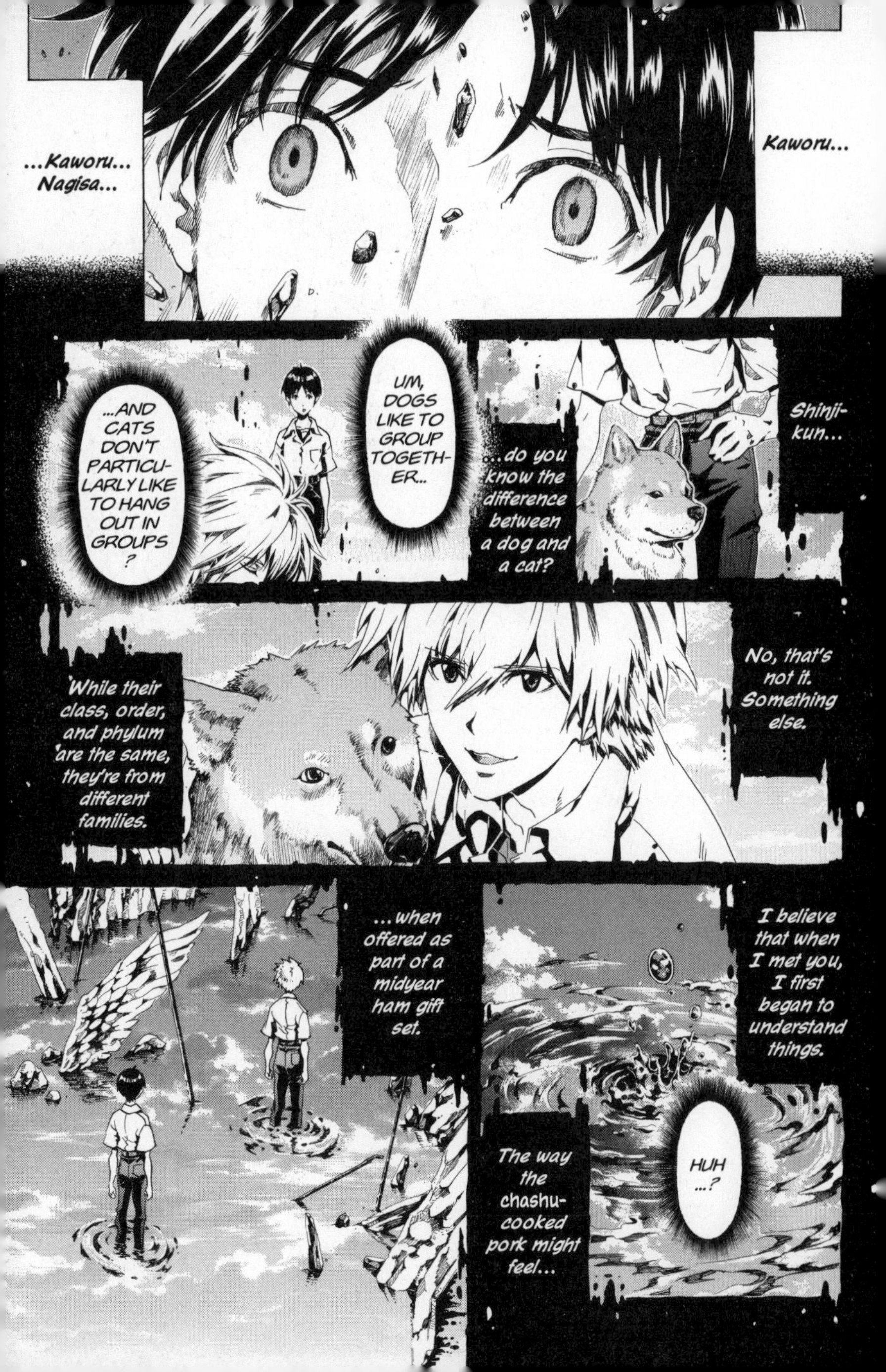
Kaworu...
...Kaworu... Nagisa...
Shinji-kun...
...do you know the difference between a dog and a cat?
UM, DOGS LIKE TO GROUP TOGETHER...
...AND CATS DON'T PARTICULARLY LIKE TO HANG OUT IN GROUPS?
No, that's not it. Something else.
While their class, order, and phylum are the same, they're from different families.
I believe that when I met you, I first began to understand things.
HUH ...?
The way the chashu-cooked pork might feel...
...when offered as part of a midyear ham gift set.

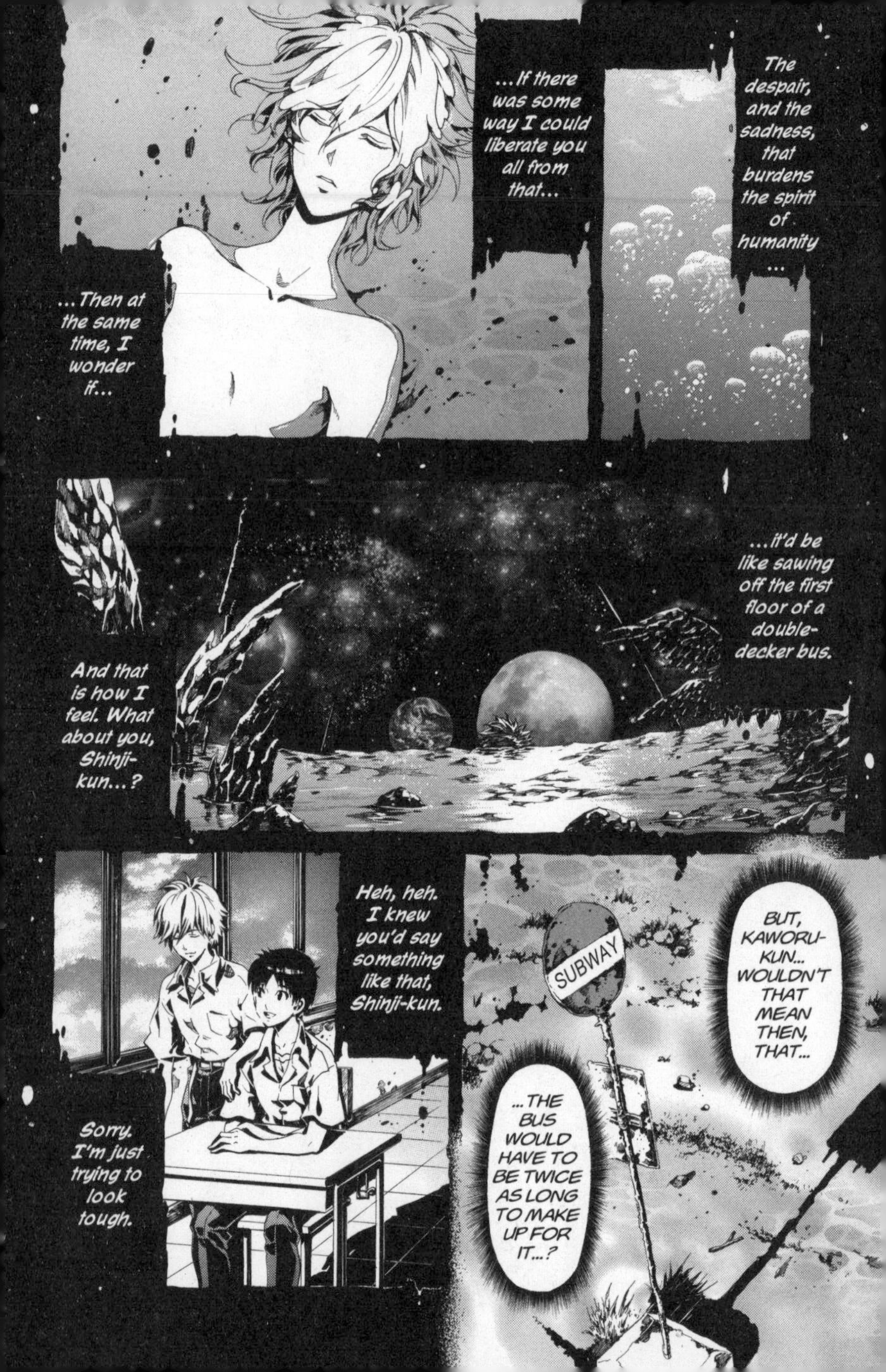
The despair, and the sadness, that burdens the spirit of humanity ...
...If there was some way I could liberate you all from that...
...Then at the same time, I wonder if...
...it'd be like sawing off the first floor of a double-decker bus.
And that is how I feel. What about you, Shinji-kun...?
BUT, KAWORU-KUN... WOULDN'T THAT MEAN THEN, THAT...
SUBWAY
...THE BUS WOULD HAVE TO BE TWICE AS LONG TO MAKE UP FOR IT...?
Heh, heh. I knew you'd say something like that, Shinji-kun.
Sorry. I'm just trying to look tough.

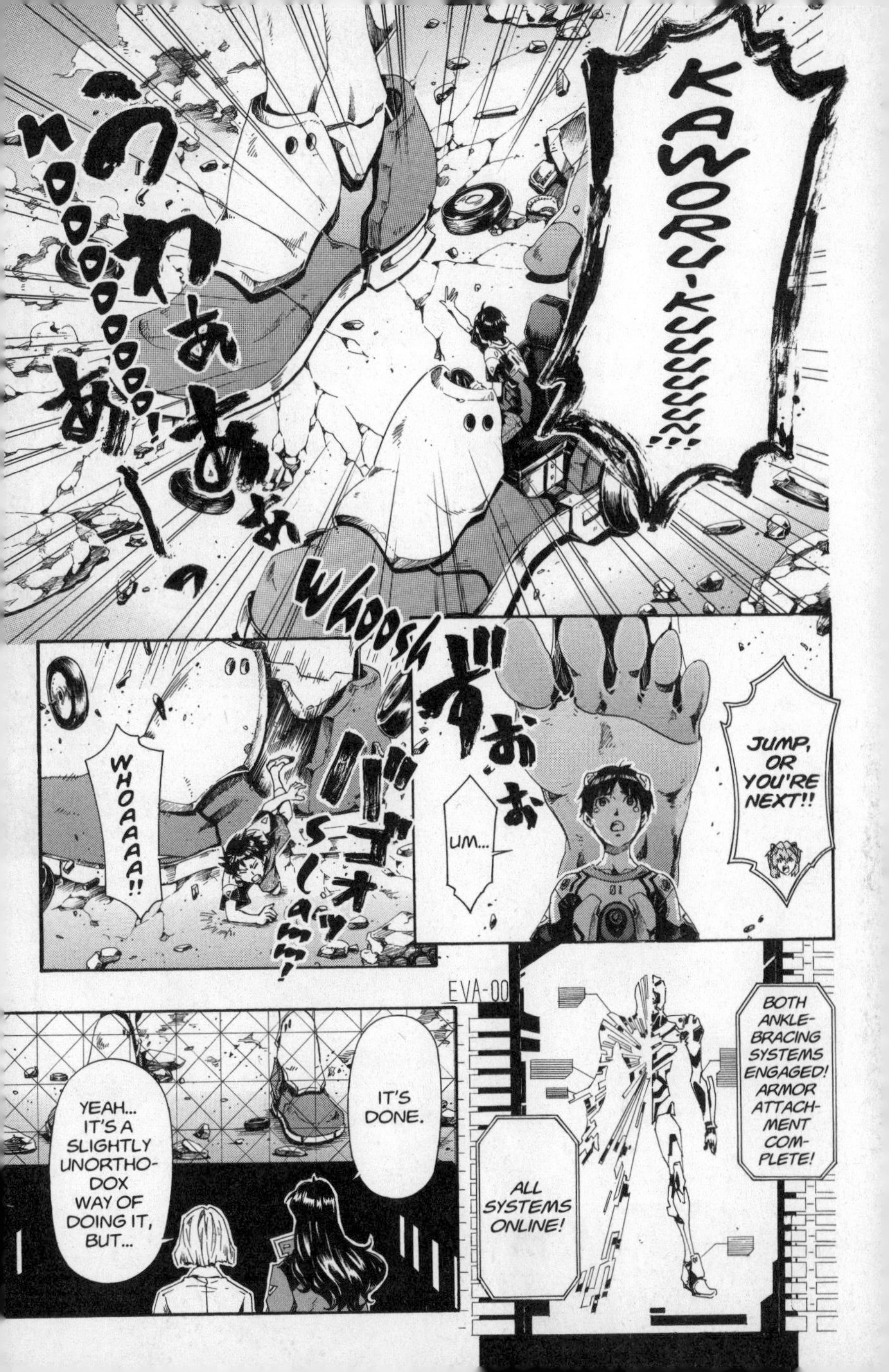

KAWORU-KUUUUUUN!!
WHOOSH
JUMP, OR YOU'RE NEXT!!
UM...
WHOAAAAA!!
EVA-00
BOTH ANKLE-BRACING SYSTEMS ENGAGED! ARMOR ATTACHMENT COMPLETE!
ALL SYSTEMS ONLINE!
IT'S DONE.
YEAH... IT'S A SLIGHTLY UNORTHODOX WAY OF DOING IT, BUT...

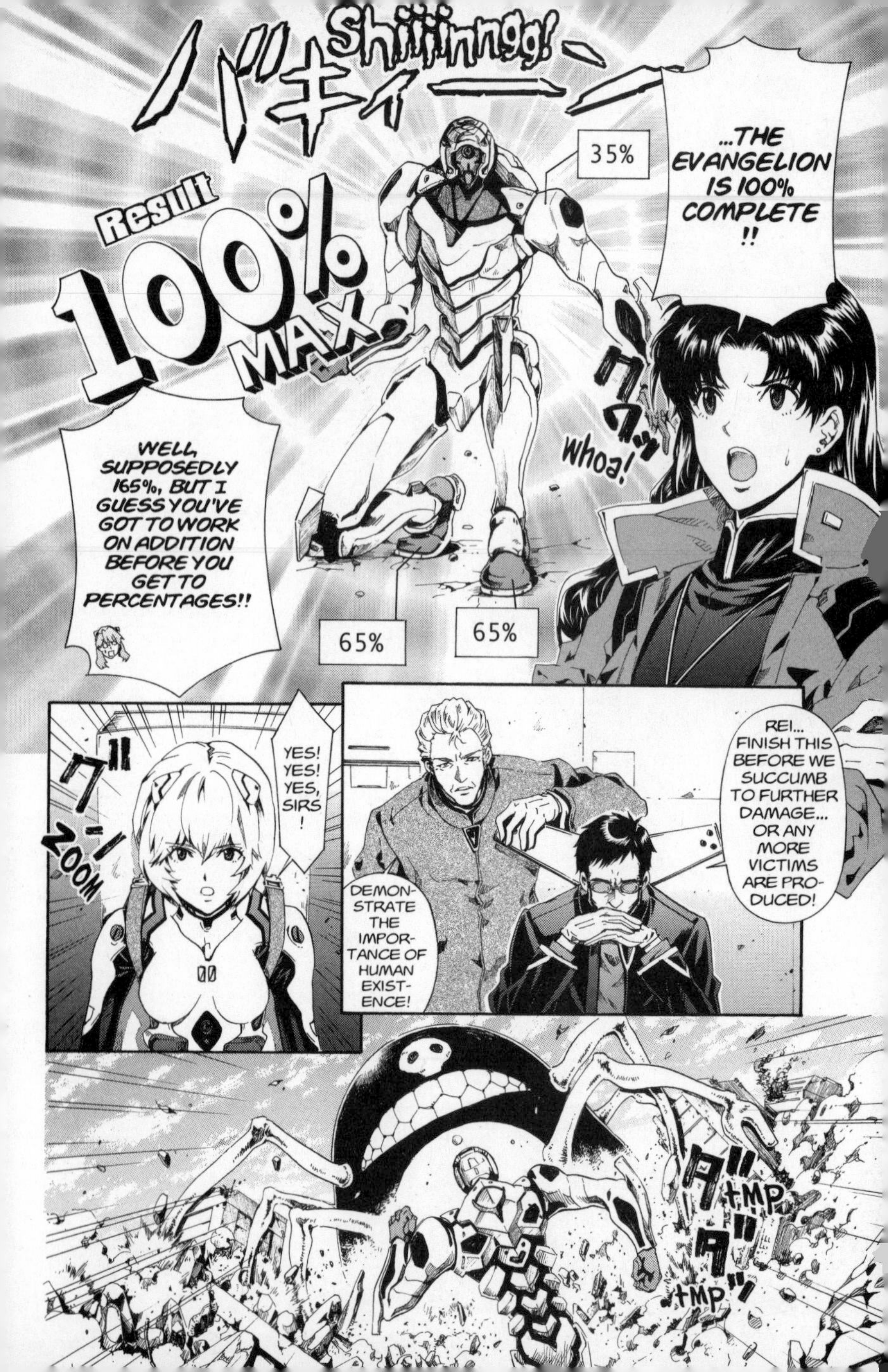
Shiiiinngg!
...THE EVANGELION IS 100% COMPLETE !!
35%
Result
100% MAX
whoa!
65%
65%
WELL, SUPPOSEDLY 165%, BUT I GUESS YOU'VE GOT TO WORK ON ADDITION BEFORE YOU GET TO PERCENTAGES!!
REI... FINISH THIS BEFORE WE SUCCUMB TO FURTHER DAMAGE... OR ANY MORE VICTIMS ARE PRO-DUCED!
DEMON-STRATE THE IMPOR-TANCE OF HUMAN EXIST-ENCE!
YES! YES! YES, SIRS !
ZOOM
tmp
tmp

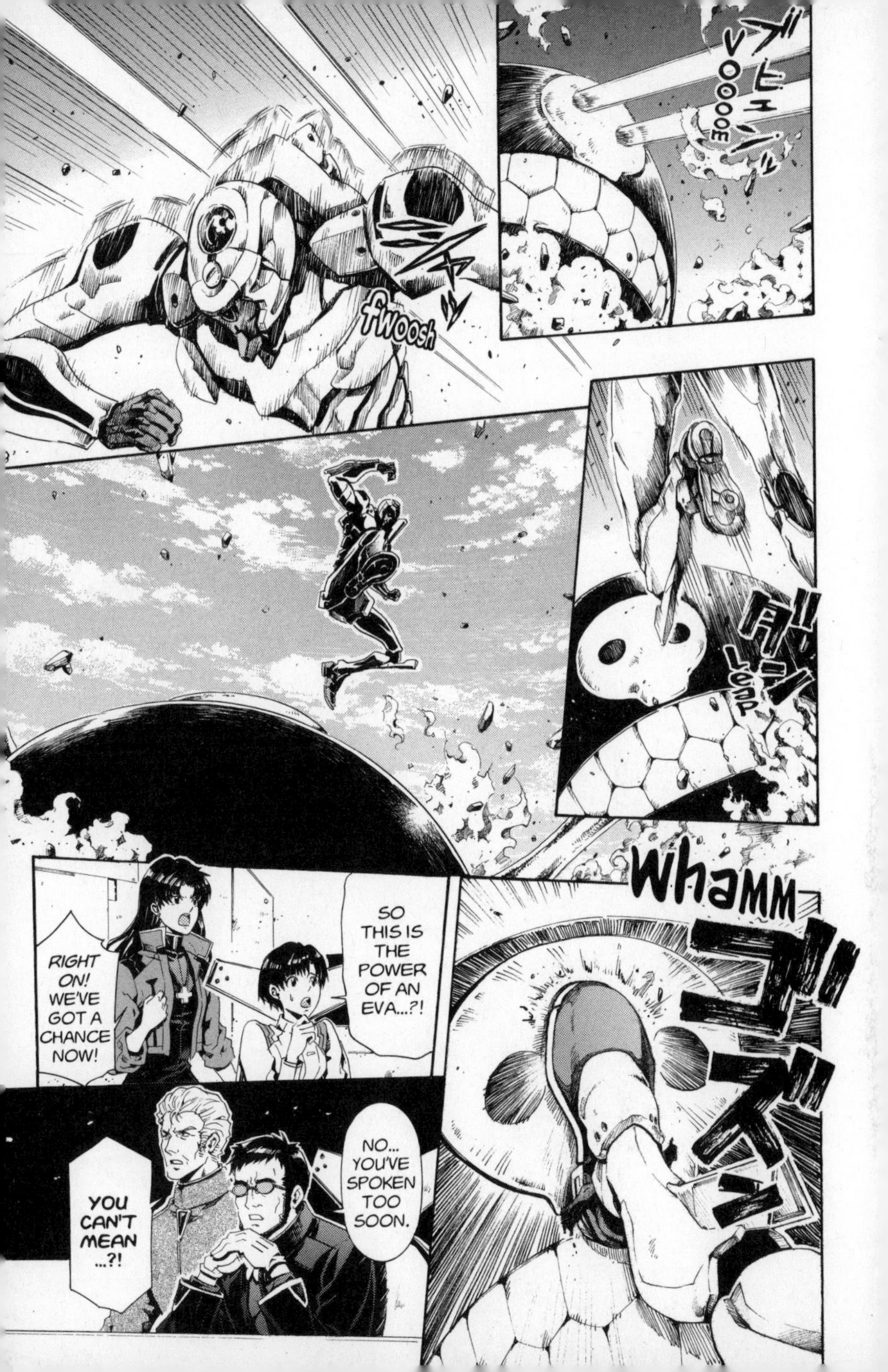
VOOOOM
fwoosh
LEAP
WHAMM
SO THIS IS THE POWER OF AN EVA...?!
RIGHT ON! WE'VE GOT A CHANCE NOW!
NO... YOU'VE SPOKEN TOO SOON.
YOU CAN'T MEAN ...?!

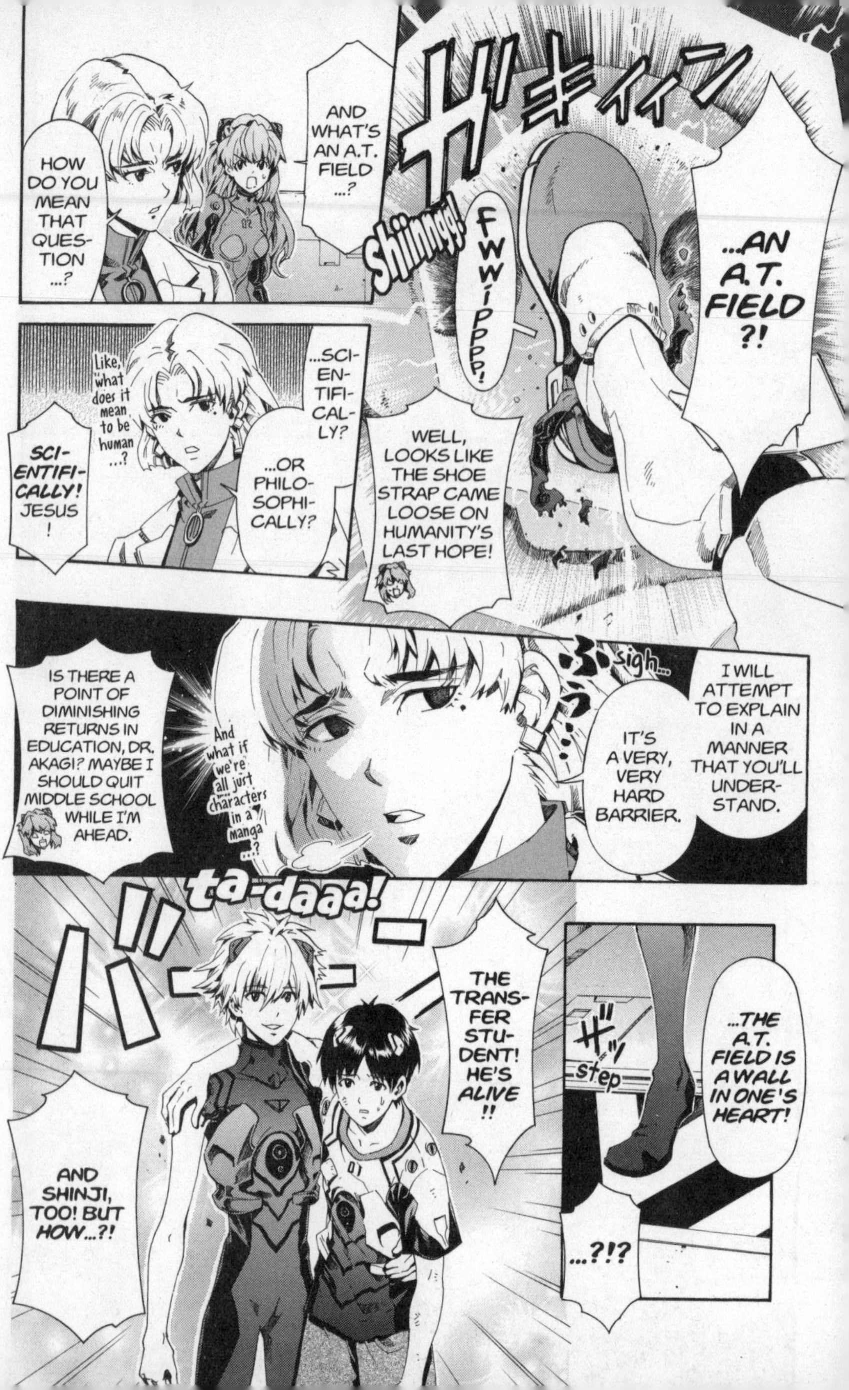
ザキィィン
shiinngg!
FWWIPPPP!
...AN A.T. FIELD ?!
WELL, LOOKS LIKE THE SHOE STRAP CAME LOOSE ON HUMANITY'S LAST HOPE!
AND WHAT'S AN A.T. FIELD ...?
HOW DO YOU MEAN THAT QUESTION ...?
...SCIENTIFICALLY?
...OR PHILOSOPHICALLY?
Like, "what does it mean to be human"...?
SCIENTIFICALLY! JESUS!
ふぅ... sigh...
I WILL ATTEMPT TO EXPLAIN IN A MANNER THAT YOU'LL UNDERSTAND.
IT'S A VERY, VERY HARD BARRIER.
IS THERE A POINT OF DIMINISHING RETURNS IN EDUCATION, DR. AKAGI? MAYBE I SHOULD QUIT MIDDLE SCHOOL WHILE I'M AHEAD.
And what if we're all just characters in a manga ...?
ザッ step
...THE A.T. FIELD IS A WALL IN ONE'S HEART!
...?!?
バーン
ta-daaa!
THE TRANSFER STUDENT! HE'S ALIVE!!
AND SHINJI, TOO! BUT HOW...?!

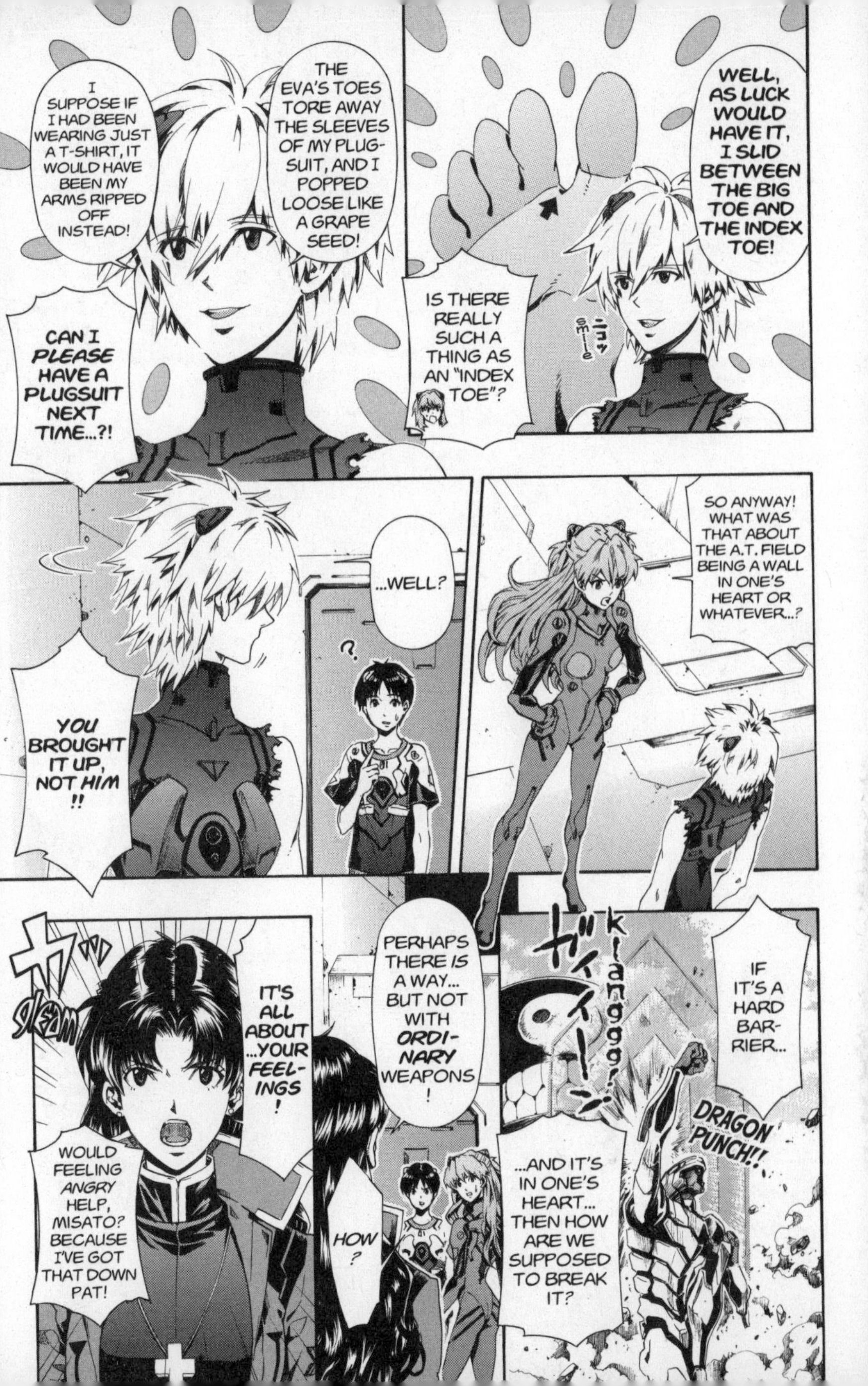
WELL, AS LUCK WOULD HAVE IT, I SLID BETWEEN THE BIG TOE AND THE INDEX TOE!
ニコッ smile
IS THERE REALLY SUCH A THING AS AN "INDEX TOE"?
THE EVA'S TOES TORE AWAY THE SLEEVES OF MY PLUG-SUIT, AND I POPPED LOOSE LIKE A GRAPE SEED!
I SUPPOSE IF I HAD BEEN WEARING JUST A T-SHIRT, IT WOULD HAVE BEEN MY ARMS RIPPED OFF INSTEAD!
CAN I *PLEASE* HAVE A PLUGSUIT NEXT TIME...?!
SO ANYWAY! WHAT WAS THAT ABOUT THE A.T. FIELD BEING A WALL IN ONE'S HEART OR WHATEVER...?
...WELL?
?
YOU BROUGHT IT UP, NOT *HIM*!!
IF IT'S A HARD BARRIER...
klanggg!
DRAGON PUNCH!!
...AND IT'S IN ONE'S HEART... THEN HOW ARE WE SUPPOSED TO BREAK IT?
PERHAPS THERE *IS* A WAY... BUT NOT WITH *ORDINARY* WEAPONS!
HOW?
IT'S ALL ABOUT ...YOUR FEELINGS!
gleam
WOULD FEELING *ANGRY* HELP, MISATO? BECAUSE I'VE GOT THAT DOWN PAT!

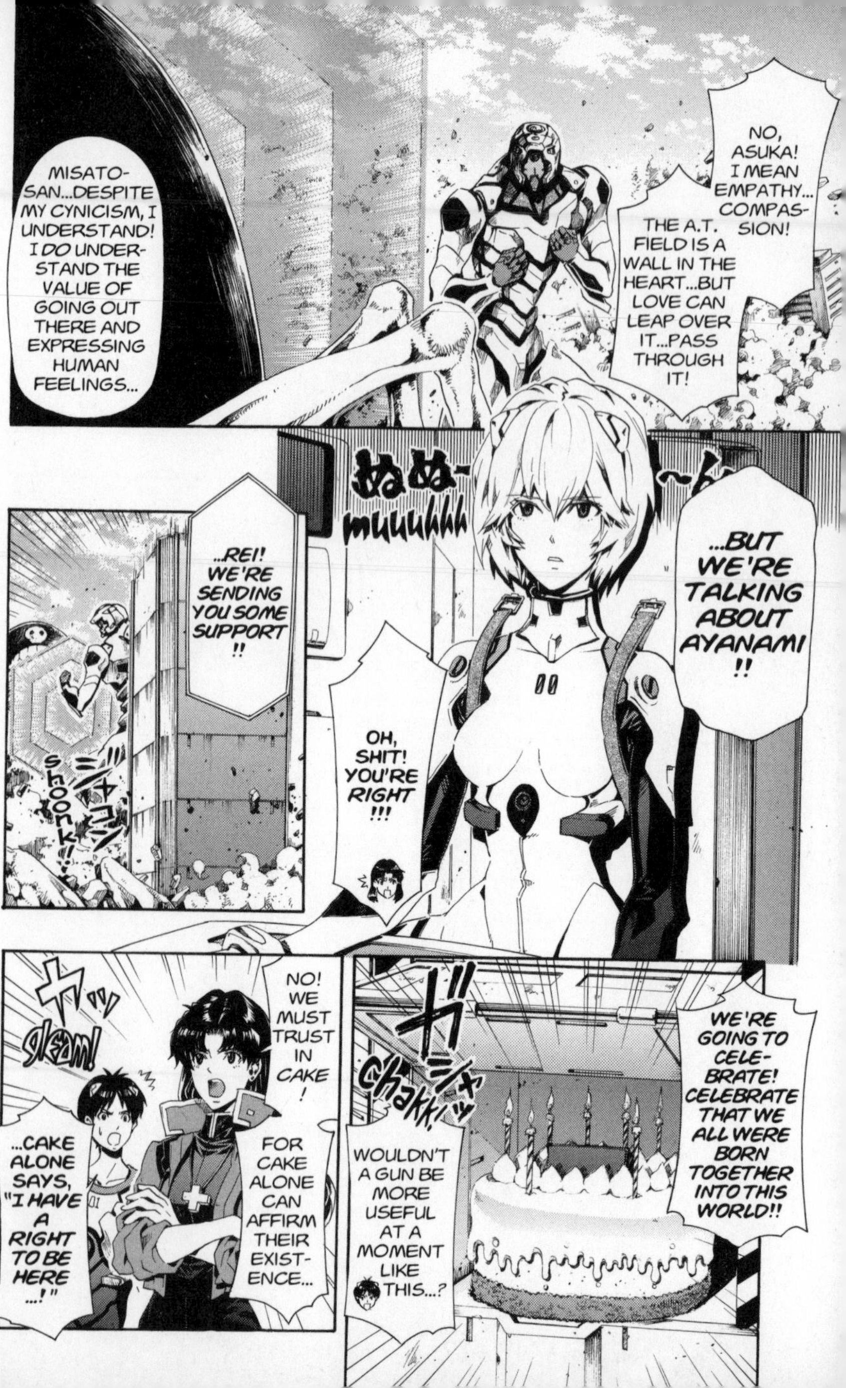
NO, ASUKA! I MEAN EMPATHY... COMPASSION!
THE A.T. FIELD IS A WALL IN THE HEART...BUT LOVE CAN LEAP OVER IT...PASS THROUGH IT!
MISATO-SAN...DESPITE MY CYNICISM, I UNDERSTAND! I DO UNDERSTAND THE VALUE OF GOING OUT THERE AND EXPRESSING HUMAN FEELINGS...
ぬぬー ～ん
muuuhhh
...BUT WE'RE TALKING ABOUT AYANAMI!!
OH, SHIT! YOU'RE RIGHT!!!
...REI! WE'RE SENDING YOU SOME SUPPORT!!
shoonk!!
ガシャッ
chakk!
WE'RE GOING TO CELEBRATE! CELEBRATE THAT WE ALL WERE BORN TOGETHER INTO THIS WORLD!!
WOULDN'T A GUN BE MORE USEFUL AT A MOMENT LIKE THIS...?
キッ
gleam!
NO! WE MUST TRUST IN CAKE!
FOR CAKE ALONE CAN AFFIRM THEIR EXISTENCE...
...CAKE ALONE SAYS, "I HAVE A RIGHT TO BE HERE...!"

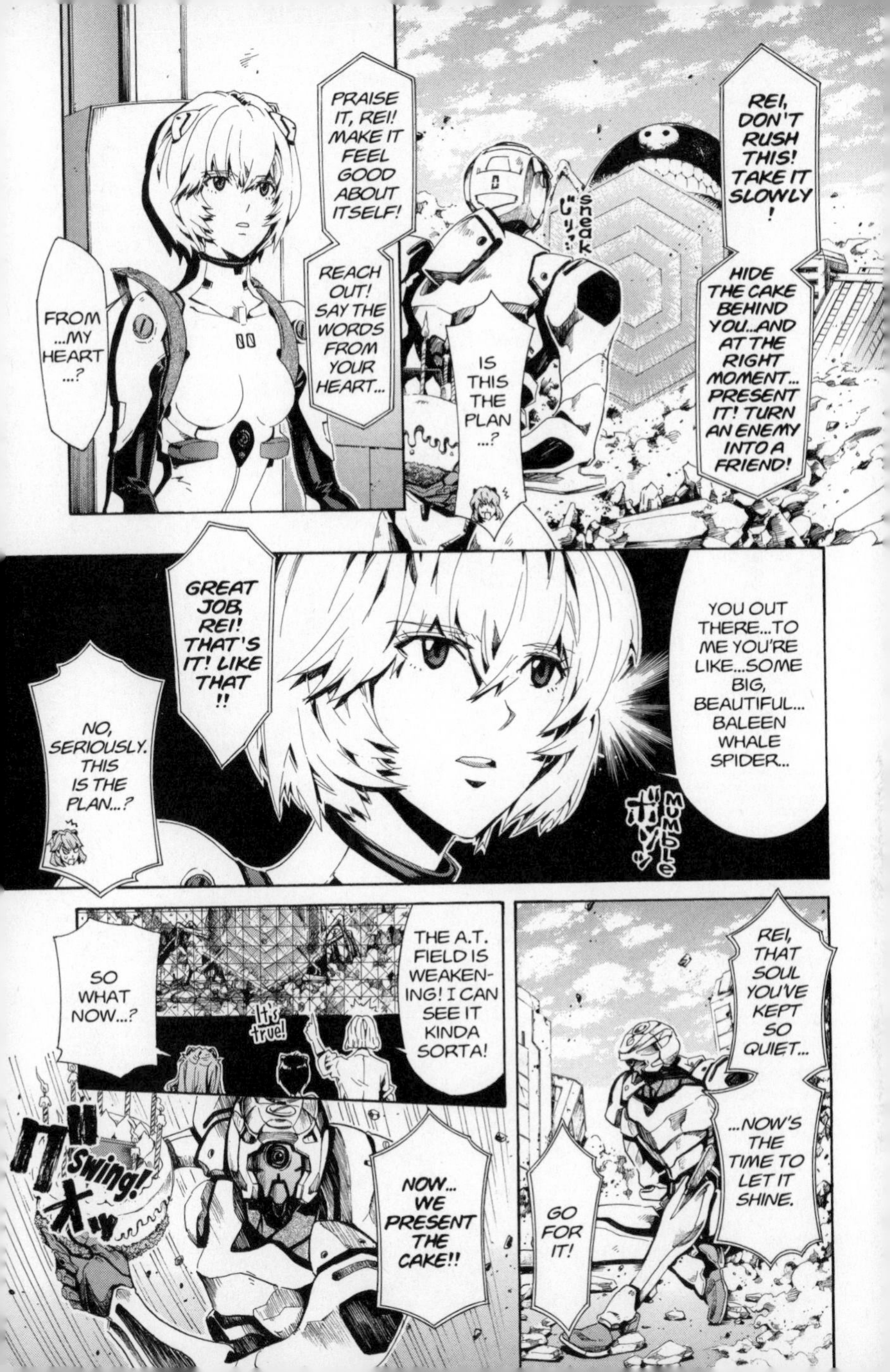
REI, DON'T RUSH THIS! TAKE IT SLOWLY!
HIDE THE CAKE BEHIND YOU...AND AT THE RIGHT MOMENT... PRESENT IT! TURN AN ENEMY INTO A FRIEND!
sneak
IS THIS THE PLAN ...?
PRAISE IT, REI! MAKE IT FEEL GOOD ABOUT ITSELF!
REACH OUT! SAY THE WORDS FROM YOUR HEART...
FROM ...MY HEART ...?
YOU OUT THERE...TO ME YOU'RE LIKE...SOME BIG, BEAUTIFUL... BALEEN WHALE SPIDER...
mumble
GREAT JOB, REI! THAT'S IT! LIKE THAT !!
NO, SERIOUSLY. THIS IS THE PLAN...?
REI, THAT SOUL YOU'VE KEPT SO QUIET...
...NOW'S THE TIME TO LET IT SHINE.
GO FOR IT!
THE A.T. FIELD IS WEAKEN-ING! I CAN SEE IT KINDA SORTA!
It's true!
SO WHAT NOW...?
NOW... WE PRESENT THE CAKE!!
Swing!

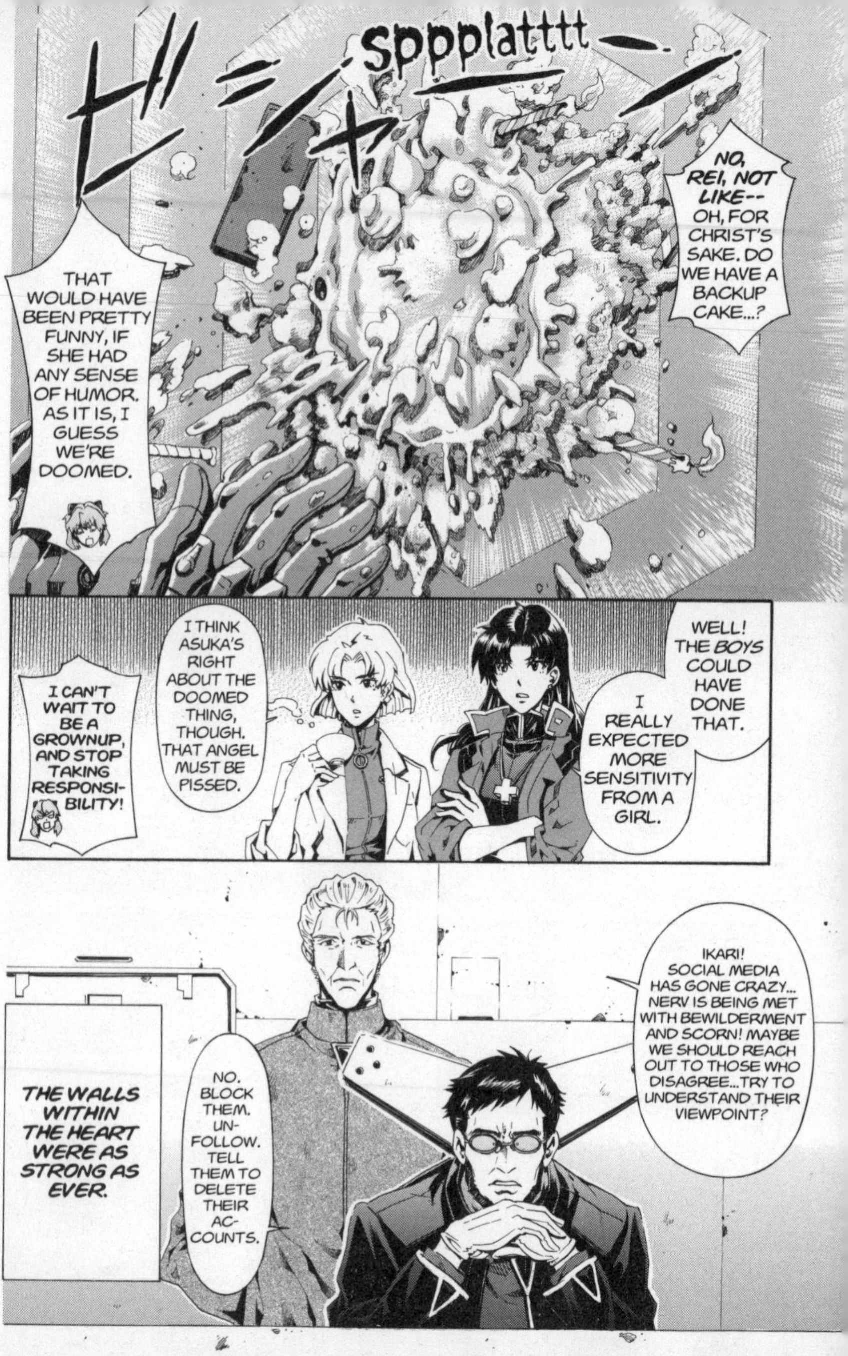
sppplatttt
NO, REI, NOT LIKE-- OH, FOR CHRIST'S SAKE. DO WE HAVE A BACKUP CAKE...?
THAT WOULD HAVE BEEN PRETTY FUNNY, IF SHE HAD ANY SENSE OF HUMOR. AS IT IS, I GUESS WE'RE DOOMED.
WELL! THE BOYS COULD HAVE DONE THAT.
I REALLY EXPECTED MORE SENSITIVITY FROM A GIRL.
I THINK ASUKA'S RIGHT ABOUT THE DOOMED THING, THOUGH. THAT ANGEL MUST BE PISSED.
I CAN'T WAIT TO BE A GROWNUP, AND STOP TAKING RESPONSI-BILITY!
IKARI! SOCIAL MEDIA HAS GONE CRAZY... NERV IS BEING MET WITH BEWILDERMENT AND SCORN! MAYBE WE SHOULD REACH OUT TO THOSE WHO DISAGREE...TRY TO UNDERSTAND THEIR VIEWPOINT?
NO. BLOCK THEM. UN-FOLLOW. TELL THEM TO DELETE THEIR AC-COUNTS.
THE WALLS WITHIN THE HEART WERE AS STRONG AS EVER.

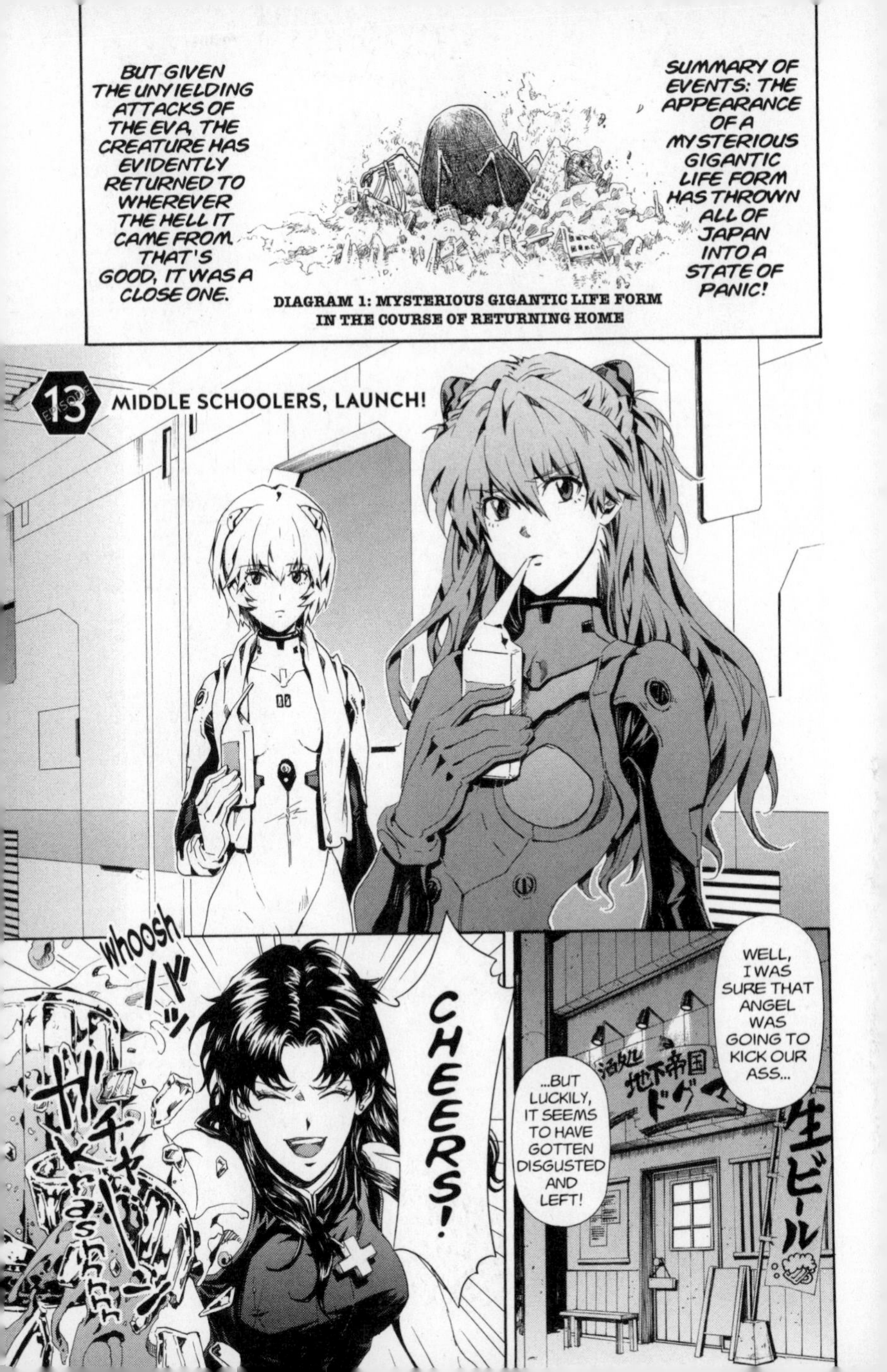
SUMMARY OF EVENTS: THE APPEARANCE OF A MYSTERIOUS GIGANTIC LIFE FORM HAS THROWN ALL OF JAPAN INTO A STATE OF PANIC!
BUT GIVEN THE UNYIELDING ATTACKS OF THE EVA, THE CREATURE HAS EVIDENTLY RETURNED TO WHEREVER THE HELL IT CAME FROM. THAT'S GOOD, IT WAS A CLOSE ONE.
DIAGRAM 1: MYSTERIOUS GIGANTIC LIFE FORM IN THE COURSE OF RETURNING HOME
13 EPISODE
MIDDLE SCHOOLERS, LAUNCH!
WELL, I WAS SURE THAT ANGEL WAS GOING TO KICK OUR ASS...
...BUT LUCKILY, IT SEEMS TO HAVE GOTTEN DISGUSTED AND LEFT!
酒処 地下帝国 ドグマ
生ビール
CHEERS!
whoosh
krash

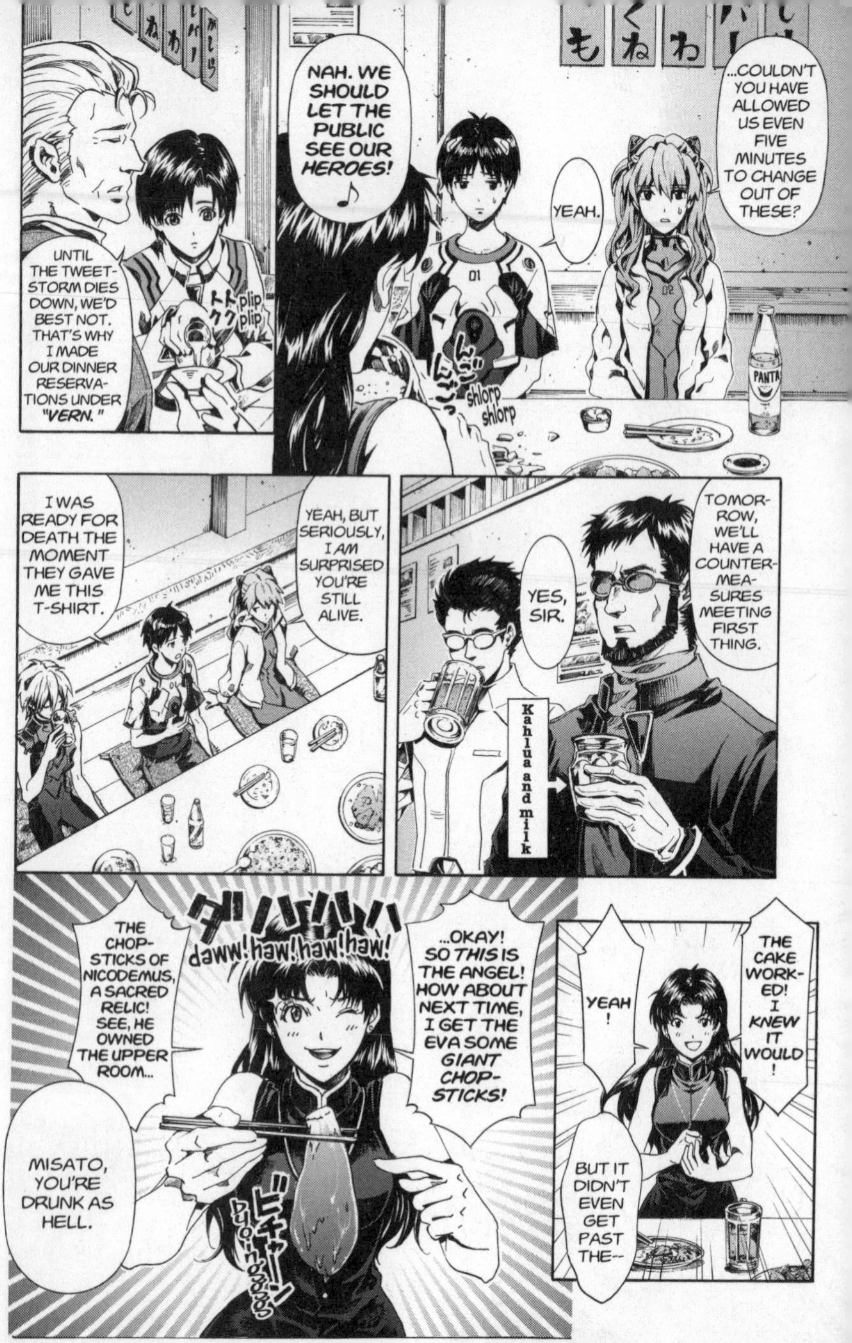

...COULDN'T YOU HAVE ALLOWED US EVEN FIVE MINUTES TO CHANGE OUT OF THESE?
YEAH.
NAH. WE SHOULD LET THE PUBLIC SEE OUR *HEROES!* ♪
shlorp shlorp
UNTIL THE TWEET-STORM DIES DOWN, WE'D BEST NOT. THAT'S WHY I MADE OUR DINNER RESERVATIONS UNDER *"VERN."*
plip plip
TOMORROW, WE'LL HAVE A COUNTERMEASURES MEETING FIRST THING.
YES, SIR.
Kahlua and milk
YEAH, BUT SERIOUSLY, I *AM* SURPRISED YOU'RE STILL ALIVE.
I WAS READY FOR DEATH THE MOMENT THEY GAVE ME THIS T-SHIRT.
THE CAKE WORKED! I *KNEW* IT WOULD!
YEAH!
BUT IT DIDN'T EVEN GET PAST THE--
daww! haw! haw! haw!
...OKAY! SO *THIS* IS THE ANGEL! HOW ABOUT NEXT TIME, I GET THE EVA SOME *GIANT CHOPSTICKS!*
THE CHOPSTICKS OF NICODEMUS, A SACRED RELIC! SEE, HE OWNED THE UPPER ROOM...
MISATO, YOU'RE DRUNK AS HELL.

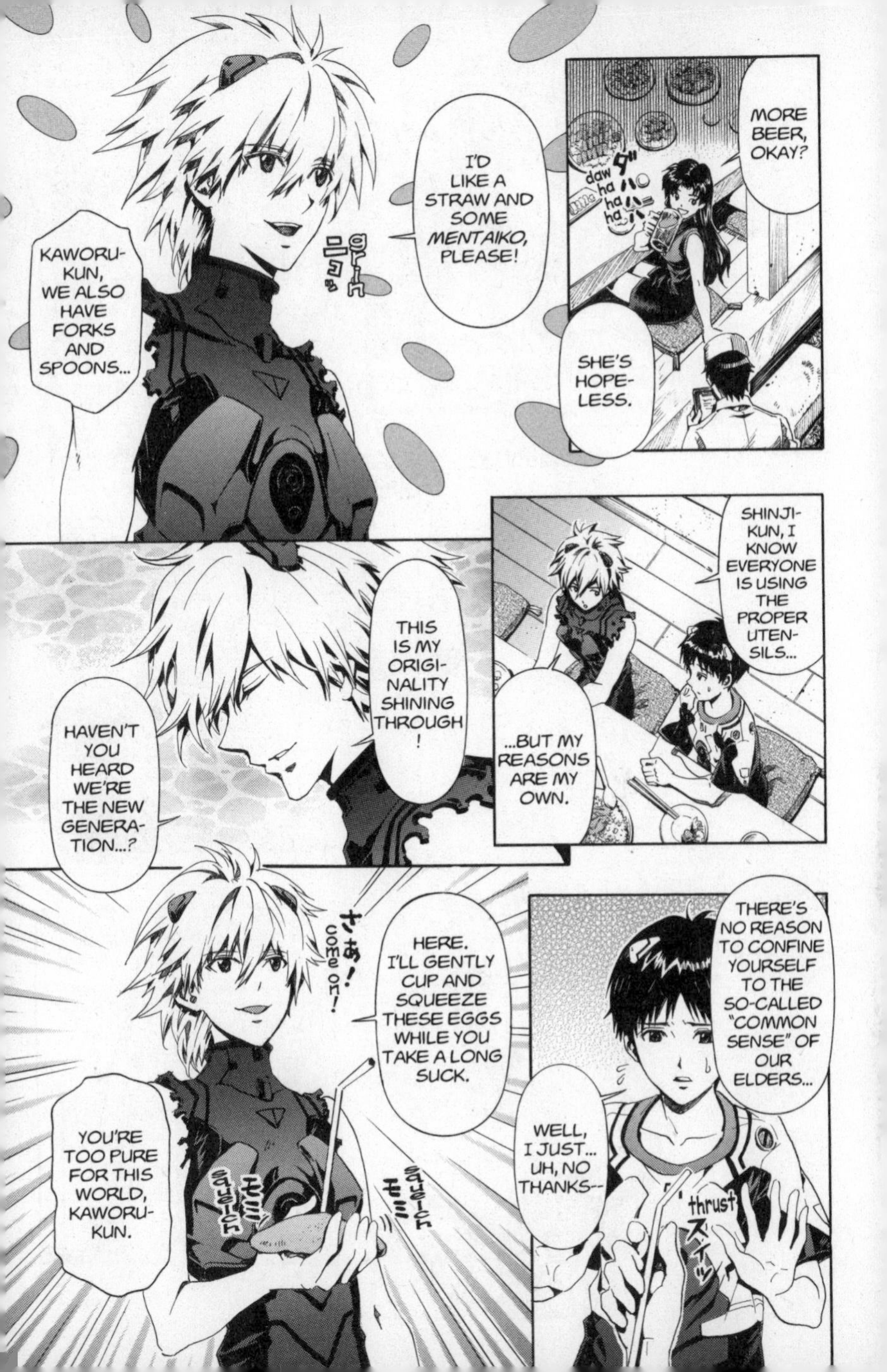
MORE BEER, OKAY?
daw ダ
ha ハ ha ハ ha ハ
SHE'S HOPE-LESS.
I'D LIKE A STRAW AND SOME *MENTAIKO*, PLEASE!
grin ニコッ
KAWORU-KUN, WE ALSO HAVE FORKS AND SPOONS...
SHINJI-KUN, I KNOW EVERYONE IS USING THE PROPER UTEN-SILS...
...BUT MY REASONS ARE MY OWN.
THIS IS MY ORIGI-NALITY SHINING THROUGH!
HAVEN'T YOU HEARD WE'RE THE NEW GENERA-TION...?
THERE'S NO REASON TO CONFINE YOURSELF TO THE SO-CALLED "COMMON SENSE" OF OUR ELDERS...
thrust スイッ
WELL, I JUST... UH, NO THANKS--
come on! さあ!
HERE. I'LL GENTLY CUP AND SQUEEZE THESE EGGS WHILE YOU TAKE A LONG SUCK.
squelch モミ
squelch モミ
YOU'RE TOO PURE FOR THIS WORLD, KAWORU-KUN.

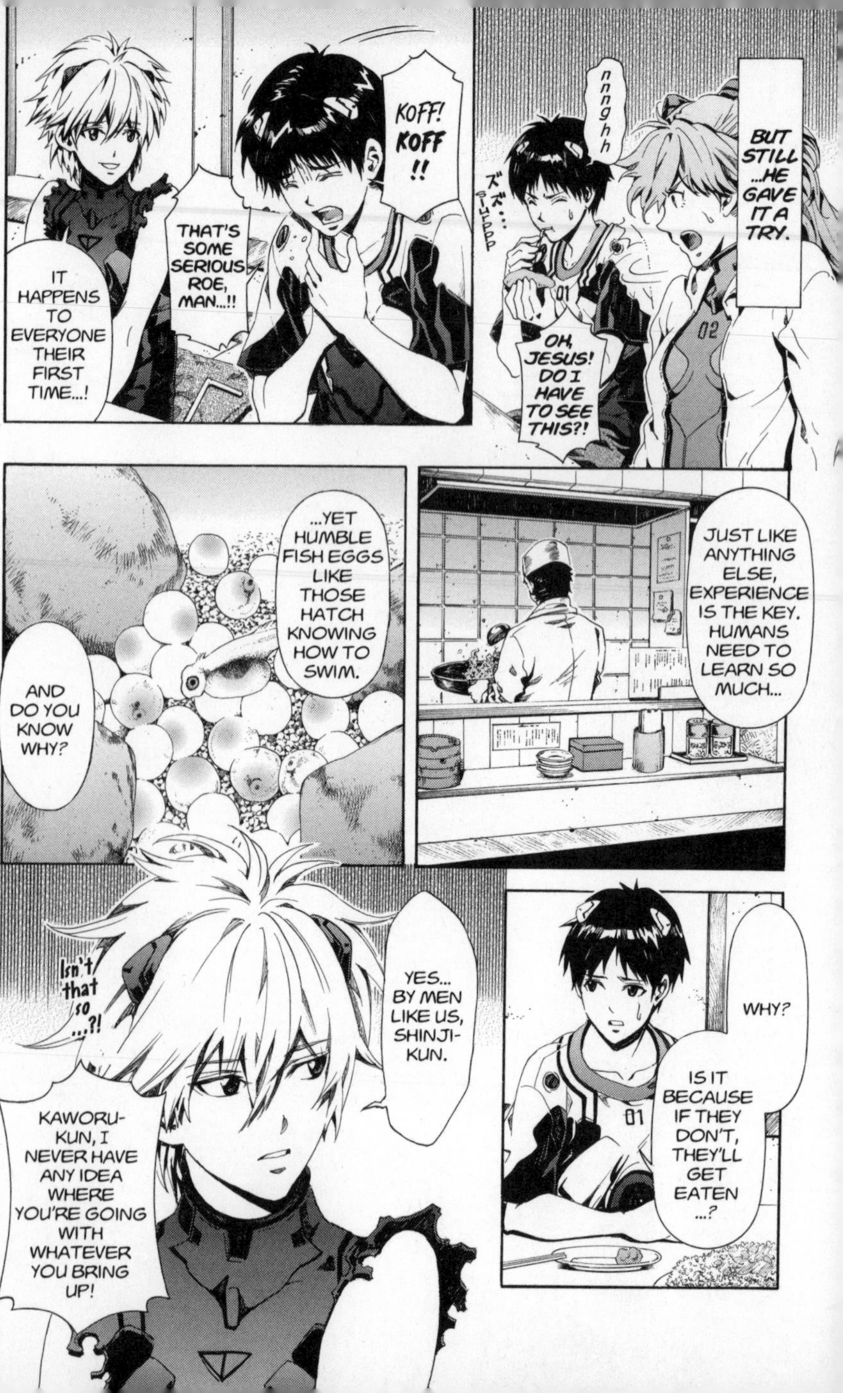
BUT STILL ...HE GAVE IT A TRY.
nnnghh
ズズ...
SHLRPPP
OH, JESUS! DO I HAVE TO SEE THIS?!
KOFF! KOFF!!
THAT'S SOME SERIOUS ROE, MAN...!!
IT HAPPENS TO EVERYONE THEIR FIRST TIME...!
JUST LIKE ANYTHING ELSE, EXPERIENCE IS THE KEY. HUMANS NEED TO LEARN SO MUCH...
...YET HUMBLE FISH EGGS LIKE THOSE HATCH KNOWING HOW TO SWIM.
AND DO YOU KNOW WHY?
WHY?
IS IT BECAUSE IF THEY DON'T, THEY'LL GET EATEN ...?
YES... BY MEN LIKE US, SHINJI-KUN.
Isn't that so ...?!
KAWORU-KUN, I NEVER HAVE ANY IDEA WHERE YOU'RE GOING WITH WHATEVER YOU BRING UP!

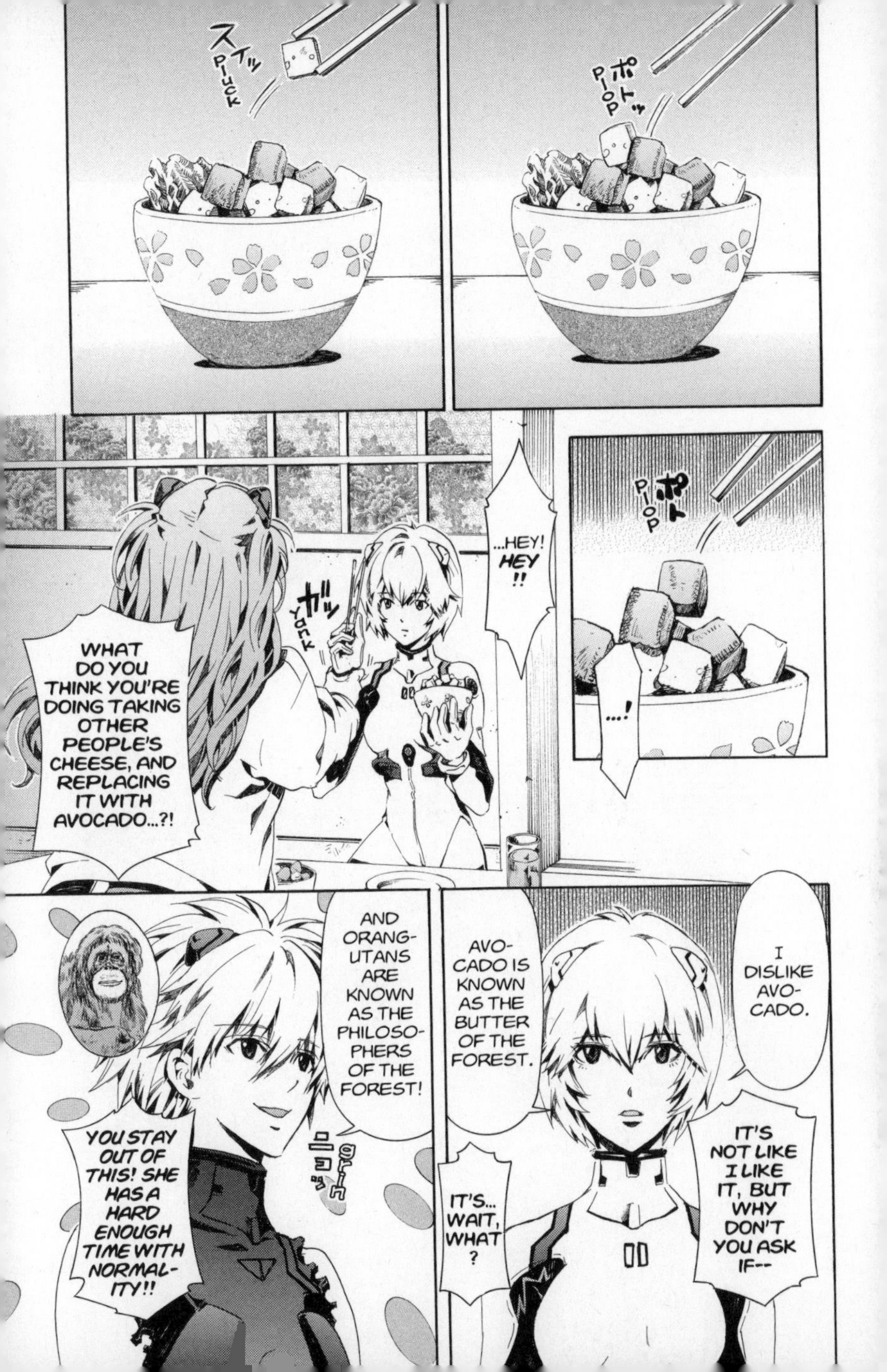
ポトッ
PLOP
スイッ
PLUCK
ポト
PLOP
...HEY! HEY!!
...!
ガッ
YANK
WHAT DO YOU THINK YOU'RE DOING TAKING OTHER PEOPLE'S CHEESE, AND REPLACING IT WITH AVOCADO...?!
I DISLIKE AVO-CADO.
AVO-CADO IS KNOWN AS THE BUTTER OF THE FOREST.
IT'S NOT LIKE I LIKE IT, BUT WHY DON'T YOU ASK IF--
IT'S... WAIT, WHAT?
AND ORANG-UTANS ARE KNOWN AS THE PHILOSO-PHERS OF THE FOREST!
YOU STAY OUT OF THIS! SHE HAS A HARD ENOUGH TIME WITH NORMAL-ITY!!

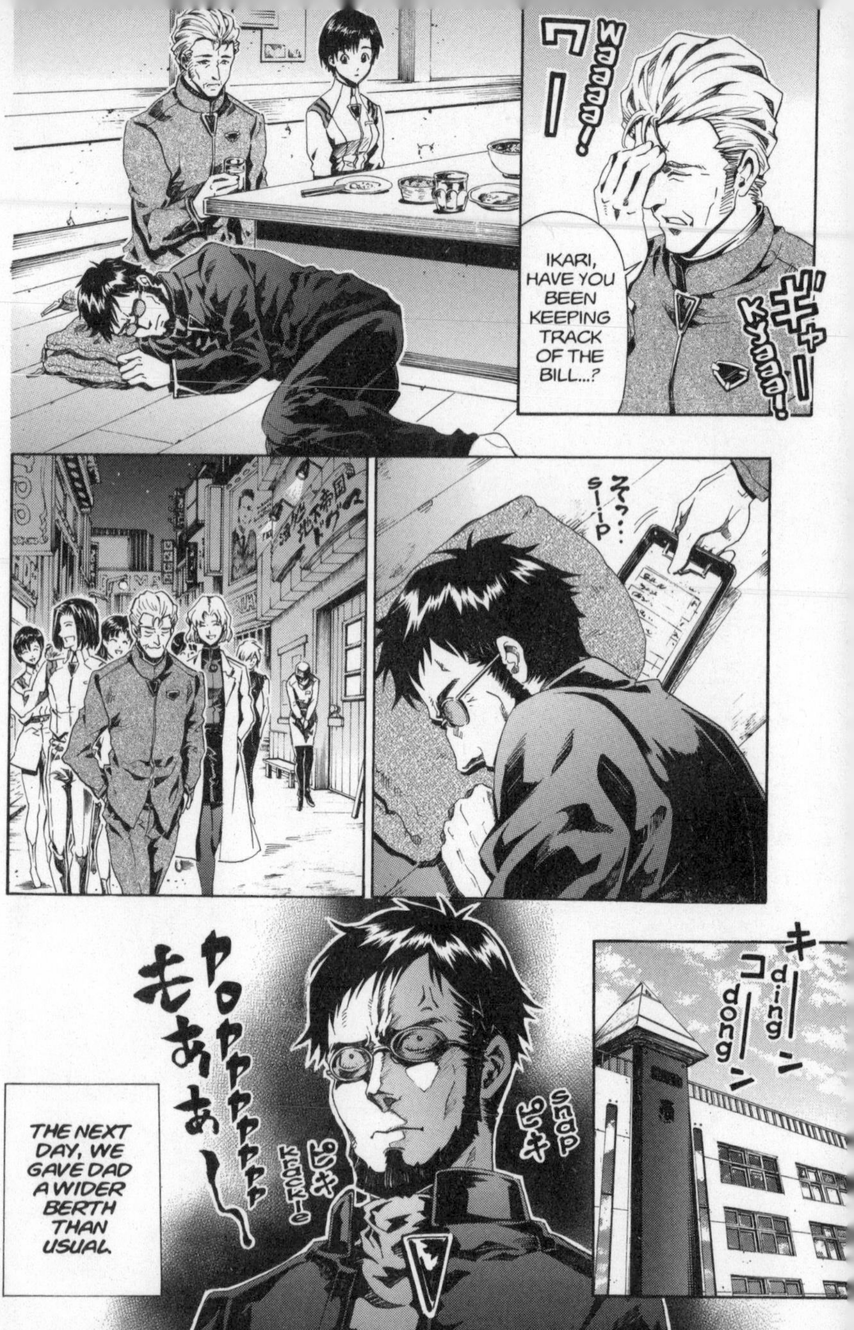
Waaaaa!
IKARI, HAVE YOU BEEN KEEPING TRACK OF THE BILL...?
Kraaaa!
s-l-ip
ding
dong
snap
krackle
THE NEXT DAY, WE GAVE DAD A WIDER BERTH THAN USUAL.

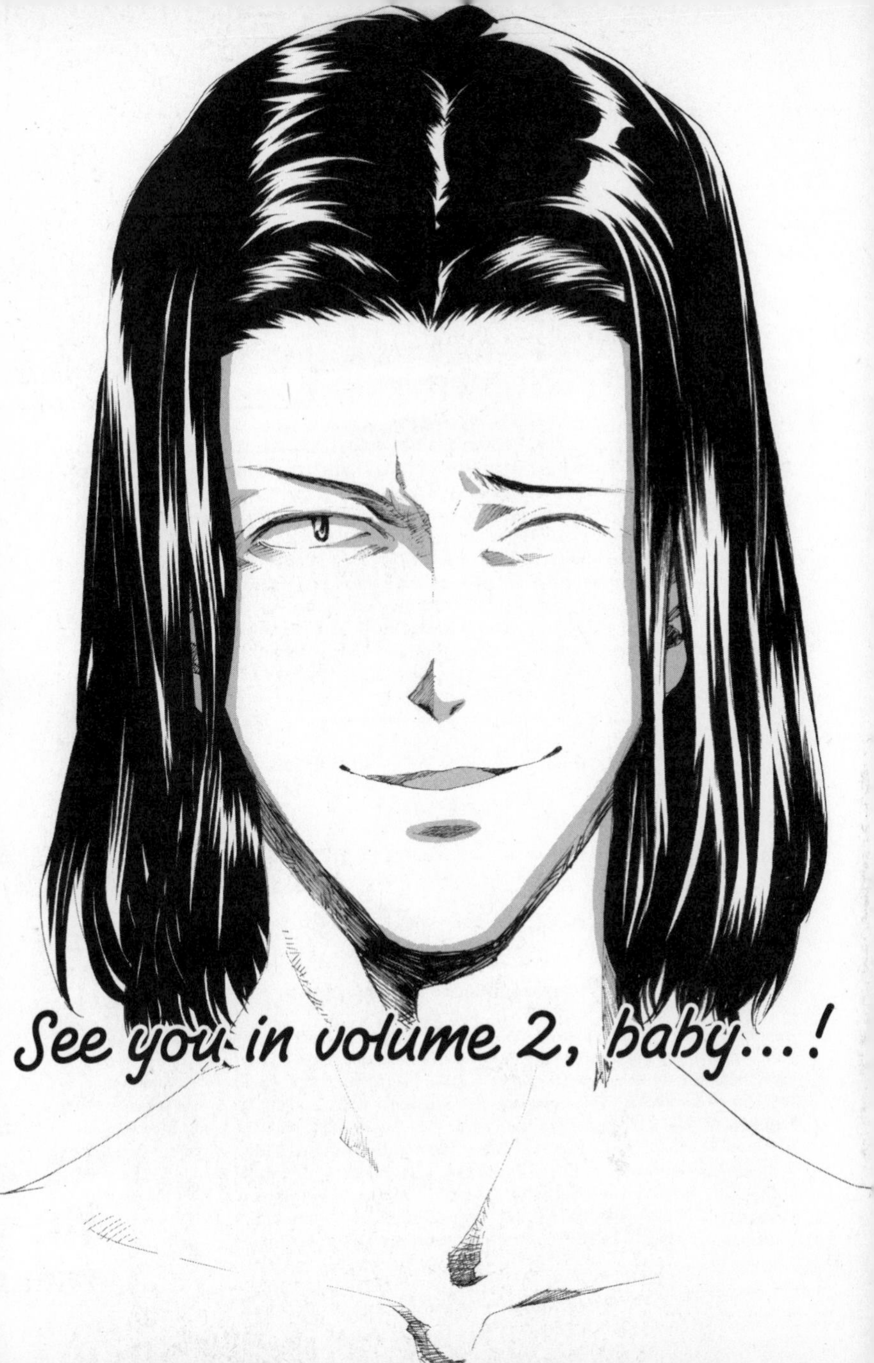
See you in volume 2, baby...!

PRESIDENT AND PUBLISHER
Mike Richardson

DESIGNER
Sarah Terry

DIGITAL ART TECHNICIAN
Christina McKenzie

English-language version produced by
Dark Horse Comics

Neon Genesis Evangelion: Legend of the Piko Piko Middle School Students Volume 1
First published in Japan as NEON GENESIS EVANGELION PIKOPIKO CHUUGAKUSEI DENSETSU Volume 1. Illustration by YUSHI KAWATA and YUKITO. © khara. First published in Japan in 2014 by KADOKAWA CORPORATION, Tokyo. English translation rights arranged with KADOKAWA CORPORATION, Tokyo, through TOHAN CORPORATION, Tokyo. This English-language edition © 2017 by Dark Horse Comics, Inc. All other material © 2017 by Dark Horse Comics, Inc. Dark Horse Manga™ is a trademark of Dark Horse Comics, Inc. All rights reserved. No portion of this publication may be reproduced or transmitted, in any form or by any means, without the express written permission of Dark Horse Comics, Inc. Names, characters, places, and incidents featured in this publication either are the product of the author's imagination or are used fictitiously. Any resemblance to actual persons (living or dead), events, institutions, or locales, without satiric intent, is coincidental.

Published by Dark Horse Manga
A division of Dark Horse Comics, Inc.
10956 SE Main Street | Milwaukie, OR 97222

DarkHorse.com

To find a comics shop in your area, call the Comic Shop Locator Service
toll-free at 1-888-266-4226

First edition: May 2017 | ISBN 978-1-50670-151-6

1 3 5 7 9 10 8 6 4 2
Printed in the United States of America

Greetings from Yukito—perpetually paralyzed with shyness.

Hello, everyone. I'm the person that was tasked with drawing this, Yukito.

You may have read some of the earlier *Eva* stories Kawata-san and I did in *Evangelion Comic Tribute* [also available from Dark Horse—ed.]. Now we've been given this opportunity to do *Legend of the Piko Piko Middle School Students*, a whole new manga series on the "*Eva* meets gaming" theme . . . and you've just read volume 1. What did you think?

People know that when *Evangelion* first hit the airwaves in 1995, it sparked a social phenomenon. However, that was when I was still in grade school. We only got a few channels on our TV at home, and furthermore, there wasn't even a video rental shop in my area! The upshot is that I'm one of those people who didn't actually get to see the anime until the twenty-first century rolled around. Before that, I only knew the series through the Kadokawa film comics of the anime—which I would buy with the money I got for New Year's—and through Yoshiyuki Sadamoto's *Evangelion* manga—which my parents bought for me, and which I would read countless times.

What you see in the front cover art for *Piko Piko* is me trying to channel all the love I got from reading those *Evangelion* books as a teenager. However, the things that make **this** *Evangelion* book wonderful are no credit to me, but rather to my wonderful writer, Kawata-san. We both hope to see you here again for volume 2.

—Grandchild of their grandma, Yukito.

ILLUSTRATOR
YUKITO
Favorite Angel: 5th

SCENARIO
YUSHI KAWATA
Favorite plan: Operation Yashima

MISATO'S FAN SERVICE CENTER

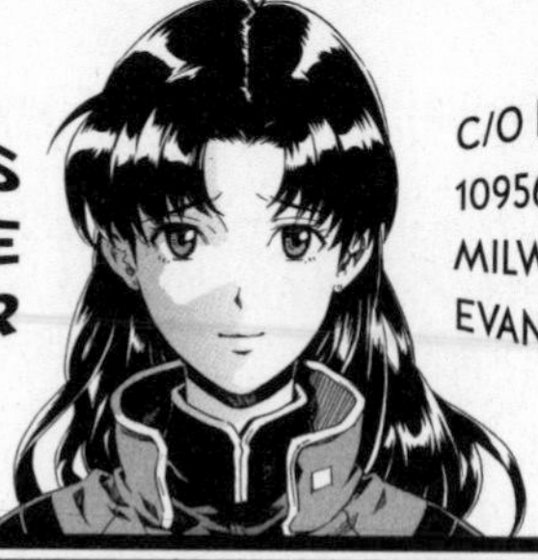

C/O DARK HORSE COMICS
10956 SE MAIN STREET
MILWAUKIE, OR 97222
EVANGELION@DARKHORSE.COM

Welcome to our new *Evangelion* manga series . . . which of course means once again we're reserving a space right here for you, the reader, in Misato's Fan Service Center–this is where we'd like to see your letters, comments, fan art, and cosplay photos, as long as they're *Eva* related! Send in your contributions to the address above, and if they include image files, please try to give us the highest quality version you have (300 dpi and above) so it'll look great in print!

In the meantime, if you're hungry for the latest in *Evangelion* information, I'd like to highly recommend you check out Aaron Clark's Eva Monkey channel on YouTube (whose logo is on the next page). You might be familiar with his *Evangelion* panels at Otakon; he's also the person who produced the *Eva* update video shown at the Dark Horse *Evangelion* panel in 2015.

One of the things that set Eva Monkey apart from other online info sources is that Aaron doesn't just repeat the same old rumors and stories; he puts in the research to get the truth. For example, we all know *Evangelion* was referenced in the film *One Hour Photo*, starring the late Robin Williams, but how and why did it happen? Eva Monkey sought out and interviewed the Grammy Award–winning writer and director of *One Hour Photo*, Mark Romanek, to get the real story!

We hope to see you soon at an anime con in 2017 . . . and as always, we'll look forward to hearing from you in Misato's Fan Service Center!

–CGH

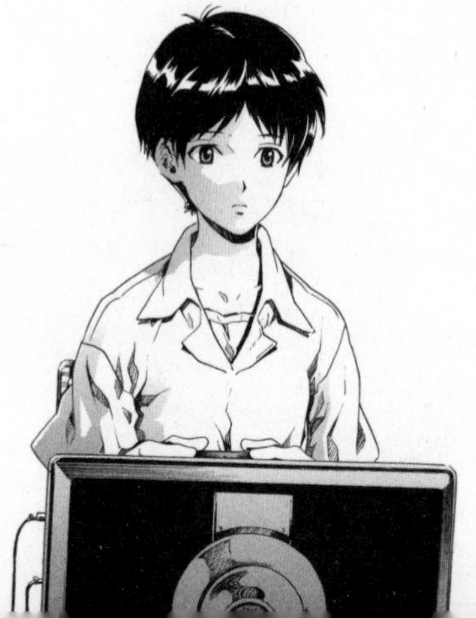

EVAMONKEY

YOUTUBE.COM/EVAMONKEY

I started EvaMonkey.com fifteen years ago, during the earliest years of my *Evangelion* fandom. At the time, there was no tetralogy of films reimagining the original TV series. There was only one manga series, which was midway through its fourteen-volume run. And the films *Death & Rebirth* and *The End of Evangelion* had not yet been released domestically. It's an achievement that after two decades, *Evangelion* has not only remained culturally relevant, but has grown beyond the original series into a tremendous multimedia franchise.

In the fifteen years since I began working on Eva Monkey, we've seen the rise of social media, web video, and crowdfunding. Fan sites are all but a thing of the past, so I'm proud to still be around and to have more or less kept up with the trends.

Before the first episode of *Evangelion* had aired, writer and director Hideaki Anno shared a quote in the afterword of the first volume of Yoshiyuki Sadamoto's *Neon Genesis Evangelion* manga, stating that "to live is to change." For my part, I've changed my focus with Eva Monkey over the past year to producing video content for YouTube. I've been pleasantly surprised at the level of interest in a channel devoted solely to *Evangelion*-related content.

My desire is to explore the many facets of the ever-expanding *Evangelion* franchise and its fandom, including news, reviews, interviews, analysis, visual essays, convention panels, and more. I hope you'll check out what I have to offer, and look forward to what I have planned for the future.

–Aaron Clark, EvaMonkey.com

REPENT, SINNERS!
THEY'RE BACK!

Panty & Stocking with Garterbelt

Miss the anime?
Try the *Panty & Stocking with Garterbelt* manga! Nine ALL-NEW stories of your favorite filthy fallen angels, written and drawn by TAGRO, with a special afterword by *Kill La Kill* director Hiroyuki Imaishi!
978-1-61655-735-5 | $9.99

NEON GENESIS EVANGELION

Dark Horse Manga is proud to present new original series based on the wildly popular *Neon Genesis Evangelion* manga and anime! Continuing the rich story lines and complex characters, these new visions of *Neon Genesis Evangelion* provide extra dimensions for understanding one of the greatest series ever made!

NEON GENESIS EVANGELION Campus Apocalypse

STORY AND ART BY MINGMING

VOLUME 1
ISBN 978-1-59582-530-8 | $10.99

VOLUME 2
ISBN 978-1-59582-661-9 | $10.99

VOLUME 3
ISBN 978-1-59582-680-0 | $10.99

VOLUME 4
ISBN 978-1-59582-689-3 | $10.99

NEON GENESIS EVANGELION COMIC TRIBUTE

STORY AND ART BY VARIOUS CREATORS

ISBN 978-1-61655-114-8 | $10.99

NEON GENESIS EVANGELION THE Shinji Ikari Detective Diary

STORY AND ART BY TAKUMI YOSHIMURA

VOLUME 1
ISBN 978-1-61655-225-1 | $9.99

VOLUME 2
ISBN 978-1-61655-418-7 | $9.99

TONY TAKEZAKI'S NEON GENESIS EVANGELION

STORY AND ART BY TONY TAKEZAKI

ISBN 978-1-61655-736-2 | $12.99

NEON GENESIS EVANGELION THE SHINJI IKARI RAISING PROJECT

STORY AND ART BY OSAMU TAKAHASHI

VOLUME 1
ISBN 978-1-59582-321-2 | $9.99

VOLUME 2
ISBN 978-1-59582-377-9 | $9.99

VOLUME 3
ISBN 978-1-59582-447-9 | $9.99

VOLUME 4
ISBN 978-1-59582-454-7 | $9.99

VOLUME 5
ISBN 978-1-59582-520-9 | $9.99

VOLUME 6
ISBN 978-1-59582-580-3 | $9.99

VOLUME 7
ISBN 978-1-59582-595-7 | $9.99

VOLUME 8
ISBN 978-1-59582-694-7 | $9.99

VOLUME 9
ISBN 978-1-59582-800-2 | $9.99

VOLUME 10
ISBN 978-1-59582-879-8 | $9.99

VOLUME 11
ISBN 978-1-59582-932-0 | $9.99

VOLUME 12
ISBN 978-1-61655-033-2 | $9.99

VOLUME 13
ISBN 978-1-61655-315-9 | $9.99

VOLUME 14
ISBN 978-1-61655-432-3 | $9.99

VOLUME 15
ISBN 978-1-61655-607-5 | $9.99

VOLUME 16
ISBN 978-1-61655-997-7 | $9.99

VOLUME 17
ISBN 978-1-50670-083-0 | $9.99

Each volume of *Neon Genesis Evangelion* features bonus color pages, your *Evangelion* fan art and letters, and special reader giveaways!

DARK HORSE MANGA

DarkHorse.com

AVAILABLE AT YOUR LOCAL COMICS SHOP OR BOOKSTORE
To find a comics shop in your area, call 1-888-266-4226 • For more information or to order direct: • On the web: darkhorse.com
E-mail: mailorder@darkhorse.com • Phone: 1-800-862-0052 Mon.–Fri. 9 AM to 5 PM Pacific Time.

NEON GENESIS EVANGELION IKARI-SHINJI IKUSEI KEIKAKU © OSAMU TAKAHASHI 2011. © GAINAX • khara. First published in Japan in 2006 by KADOKAWA SHOTEN Publishing Co., Ltd., Tokyo. NEON GENESIS EVANGELION GAKUEN DATENROKU © MINGMING 2010 © GAINAX • khara. First published in Japan in 2008 by KADOKAWA SHOTEN Publishing Co., Ltd., Tokyo. NEON GENESIS EVANGELION: COMIC TRIBUTE © khara • GAINAX. NEON GENESIS EVANGELION IKARI-SHINJI TANTEI NIKKI © Takumi YOSHIMURA © GAINAX • khara. TONY TAKEZAKI NO EVANGELION © khara. English translation rights arranged with KADOKAWA SHOTEN Publishing Co., Ltd., Tokyo, through TOHAN CORPORATION, Tokyo. Dark Horse Manga™ is a trademark of Dark Horse Comics, Inc. All rights reserved. (BL 7077)

FLCL

STORY BY GAINAX
ART BY HAJIME UEDA

OMNIBUS

The complete *FLCL* manga adaptation—
now with bonus color illustrations and
remastered story pages!

"This show will change your life."
—Adult Swim

ISBN 978-1-59582-868-2
$19.99

FROM THE STUDIO THAT BROUGHT YOU *EVANGELION!*

DARK
HORSE
MANGA

AVAILABLE AT YOUR LOCAL COMICS SHOP OR BOOKSTORE To find a comics shop in your area, call 1-888-266-4226
For more information or to order direct: • On the web: DarkHorse.com
E-mail: mailorder@darkhorse.com • Phone: 1-800-862-0052 Mon.–Fri. 9 AM to 5 PM Pacific Time.